Crime and Law in England, 1750–1840

How was law made in England in the eighteenth and early nineteenth centuries? Through detailed studies of what the courts actually did, Peter King argues that parliament and the Westminster courts played a less important role in the process of lawmaking than is usually assumed. Justice was often remade from the margins by magistrates, judges and others at the local level. His book also focuses on four specific themes – gender, youth, violent crime and the attack on customary rights. In doing so it highlights a variety of important changes – the relatively lenient treatment meted out to women by the late eighteenth century, the early development of the juvenile reformatory in England before 1825, i.e. before similar changes on the continent or in America, and the growing intolerance of the courts towards everyday violence. This study will prove invaluable to any one interested in British social, political or legal history.

PETER KING is Professor of History at the Open University, Milton Keynes. His previous publications include *Crime, Justice and Discretion: Law and Social Relations in England, 1740–1820* (2000).

D1375873

Past and Present Publications

General Editors: LYNDAL ROPER, *University of Oxford*, and
CHRIS WICKHAM, *University of Birmingham*

Past and Present Publications comprise books similar in character to the articles
in the journal *Past and Present*. Whether the volumes in the series are collections
of essays – some previously published, others new studies – or monographs, they
encompass a wide variety of scholarly and original works primarily concerned with
social, economic and cultural changes, and their causes and consequences. They will
appeal to both specialists and non-specialists and will endeavour to communicate
the results of historical and allied research in the most readable and lively form.

For a list of the titles in Past and Present Publications, see end of book.

Crime and Law in England, 1750–1840

Remaking Justice from the Margins

PETER KING
Open University

CAMBRIDGE
UNIVERSITY PRESS

CAMBRIDGE UNIVERSITY PRESS
Cambridge, New York, Melbourne, Madrid, Cape Town, Singapore,
São Paulo, Delhi, Dubai, Tokyo

Cambridge University Press
The Edinburgh Building, Cambridge CB2 8RU, UK

Published in the United States of America by Cambridge University Press, New York

www.cambridge.org
Information on this title: www.cambridge.org/9780521129541

First published 2006
Reprinted 2008
This digitally printed version 2009

A catalogue record for this publication is available from the British Library

ISBN 978-0-521-78199-2 Hardback
ISBN 978-0-521-12954-1 Paperback

This volume is dedicated to
my parents Gwen and Trevor Holmes

Contents

Part IV The attack on customary rights

Preface

This book is the product of three major periods of writing. The opening chapter draws together threads from all the other work in the volume, old and new, and then presents some major new research findings on the summary courts as part of a broader project designed to provide fresh approaches to the analysis of law and justice in the period from the mid-eighteenth century to the 1840s. The first three major parts of the book – those on juvenile crime, gender, and non-lethal violence – then bring together four new chapters and three past essays, and are designed to explore a number of themes that have emerged from the research on these topics I have undertaken during the last ten years. The final part is the product of a longer project on gleaning and customary right. I am thankful to *Past and Present* for permission to republish chapters 2 and 10 – originally published in number 125 (1989), 116–50 and Number 160 (1998), 116–60; to *The Journal of Interdisciplinary History* for similar permission in relation to Chapter 7 originally published in Volume 27:1 (1996), 43–74; to UCL Press as it then was, for permission in relation to the reproduction of chapter 5 which was originally published in M. Arnot and C. Usborne (eds.), *Gender and Crime in Modern Europe* (London,1999), 44–74; to *Law and History Review* for permission to republish chapter 9, originally published in Volume 10:1 (1992), 1–31. I owe particular thanks to the ESRC for the funding I received as part of its Crime and Social Order Initiative (L210252020), to the AHRB for research-leave funding, to University College Northampton for matching that funding and to the Open University who have given me the time to complete a longer and fuller introduction to the volume. It is not possible to thank all the diverse record repositories I have visited whilst doing this project but I am particularly grateful to the National Archives, the British Library, the Hackney Archives Office, the Essex Record Offices, the Suffolk Record Offices, the Lancashire Record Office, the London Metropolitan Archives, and the Cornwall Record Office.

I would like to offer particular thanks to my old friends – both staff and students – from the History Department at University College Northampton (as it was then) where I spent all but the last year of the time when I was writing the various parts of this volume. I particularly enjoyed working with Elizabeth Hurren and being regularly brought to book and kept in order by Cathy Smith. My thanks also to Julia Bush and Sally Sokoloff for their leadership of the school and the department through the many changes in the sector and in the institution – and of course for their friendship. I especially appreciated the sense of humour and support of all the staff of the Nene Centre for Research over the years and particularly for the laughter, advice and kindness offered by Charlotte Spokes and Maria Isaac. I would also like to thank my new colleagues at the Open University where it has been great to begin working with a group of stimulating historians of crime. My particular thanks go to Clive Emsley. A very wide range of people have very kindly read one or more of the chapters in this book and many are mentioned in individual pieces. I am grateful for the excellent research assistance given to me at various points in the preparation of this material by Cris Gostlow, Joan Noel and Esther Snell. Particular thanks for kindness massively beyond the bounds of duty or reciprocity go to Joanna Innes, Randy McGowen and John Beattie. I have also been very grateful for comments on the opening chapter given by Simon Devereaux, Nic Rogers, Drew Gray, Ruth Paley, Steve Hindle, Clive Emsley, John Carter Wood, Michael Lobban, Tom Nutt, Peter Rushton, Norma Landau, David Lieberman, Bruce Smith, Doug Hay and Steve King. I am thankful also for comments on an earlier version given by various participants in the American Society for Legal History Conference in Austin Texas in October 2004, in the North American Conference on British Studies in Denver 2005 and in the Legal History Seminar at University of Illinois. I would like to thank the Past and Present series for inviting me to do a volume which included older work alongside the new. This opportunity to draw that work together in one place has enabled me to reflect on it and add to it in new ways which I hope have born fruit in the opening chapter in particular. I have chosen not to alter the five chapters that are reproduced here but to leave them as they were originally printed mainly because three of the four parts of this book had new pieces in them which indicated any new work that had come out since the reproduced work was completed.

I cannot thank my wife Lee and my son Josh sufficiently for their love and support while I wrote up this work. It is great to share my life with them and I am sorry for the times that I have not been as present as I would like to have been because I have been working on, or thinking about, this stuff. My thanks also go to my wonderful parents Gwen and Trevor who have always been so kind, generous and interested. I would also like to thank the Greenbelt festival, the community of Christians at St Giles Northampton and particularly the CoT emerging church group for many insights and so many good friendships. Thanks to Mark and Jane Dowson especially and to the late James Linnell. I miss you James. For different kinds of inspiration I have also looked to a number of other sources. For chapters 9 and 10 in particular I owe a huge amount to the late E. P. Thompson; and more generally for the heart to keep going to Henri Nouwen, Richard Rohr, Philip Yancey and Bruce Cockburn. I thank God for all these people, for their writing, and most of all for their commitment to love, mercy and justice.

Peter King,
Pitsford, Northamptonshire

Figures

Tables

1. *Shaping and remaking justice from the margins. The courts, the law and patterns of lawbreaking 1750–1840*

The late eighteenth and early nineteenth centuries witnessed many high profile changes in the criminal justice system of England and Wales. The capital code, which had threatened so many property offenders with the long shadow of the gallows, was repealed. Formal, centrally initiated policing and prison reforms increased in importance and moved from an initial reliance on permissive and enabling legislation towards a greater emphasis on compulsion and centrally organised inspection. The causes of these changes, their impact and the degree to which local reforms had already achieved major changes before formal legislation was introduced have all produced extensive debates among historians of crime. However, in the process other important dimensions of criminal justice history were often marginalised in the early stages of the development the field. Four of the most obvious of these – gender, youth, attitudes to non-lethal violence and the criminalisation of customary rights – are focused on here. None of these areas attracted major attention from parliament or from central government for most of the period from 1750 to 1840, yet in each the courts systematically pursued policies which often had a major role in shaping how justice was actually experienced on the ground. By studying the courts' policies in relation to these issues – and in the case of youth and gender by analysing related changes in patterns of formal prosecution – this volume forms part of a broader recent movement among historians which aims to provide a more holistic picture of the ways the criminal justice system was shaped and remade in this period. In the process it highlights both important changes and substantial, yet often neglected, elements of continuity in attitudes to crime, in prosecution patterns and in court policies towards offenders. The chapters on juvenile delinquency (Part I), for example, highlight a major transformation in attitudes and prosecution patterns, as well as substantial, if more gradual changes in punishment policies towards the young. The chapters on gender (Part II), by contrast, foreground two major continuities: first, in women's levels of involvement in recorded crime which did not decline in the ways recently implied by work on the vanishing female offender; and second, in the ways the courts tended to offer more lenient treatment to female offenders throughout the period. Part III then highlights another major, but neglected discontinuity – the quiet but successful criminalisation of non-lethal violence – while Part IV analyses a somewhat surprising continuity – the failure of a carefully orchestrated set of central-court judgements to criminalise one of the poor's most substantial customary rights.

In focusing on these four dimensions of criminal-justice history, this volume therefore contributes to a number of specific debates. However, it also aims to raise some important and more general issues about the ways justice was sometimes shaped and remade from the margins in this period. In particular, this long initial chapter is designed to open up a new set of agendas by focusing on one highly significant and neglected set of themes that emerge from the studies presented here – the local, decentralised nature of many of the means by which justice was shaped and remade in the period between 1750 and 1840. This initial chapter therefore involves, amongst other things, a re-evaluation of the role of parliamentary legislation, central-government initiatives and the Westminster courts, and the development of alternative perspectives which foreground the roles of various courts, of magistrates and of other local actors in shaping, and sometimes in remaking, key areas of the criminal-justice system. The complex interactions between the centre and the localities that molded eighteenth-century criminal judicial practice provide many challenges to the historian. At the centre, for example, the processes through which legislation was produced have proved very hard to unravel. While the wording of the statutes themselves is easily accessible, it is often very difficult to understand the balance of forces that resulted in their being passed or the intentions of those who initiated them. Each act of parliament has its own history and its own complicated relationship to practice on the ground. However, by focusing a lot of their attention on the major courts, and by sometimes giving legislative activity rather too central a role in their accounts of reform, historians may have underestimated the importance of local rather than central initiatives within the balance of interactions which determined the nature of justice in this period. In the long eighteenth century, it will be argued here, the justice delivered by the courts was shaped and remade as much from below, from within and from the margins as it was from the centre.

This argument will be developed, first by analysing various changes in criminal-justice practice that are highlighted in the studies in this volume (section 1), and secondly by briefly scrutinising existing work on the major courts to extract relevant themes (section 2). Sections 3 to 5 of this introduction will then use a variety of sources to present a more detailed picture of the ways that the practices of the relatively neglected summary courts shaped important aspects of the nature of justice during the eighteenth and early nineteenth centuries. The interconnections of the local and the central, and the institutional and personal overlaps between the two will then be discussed (section 6). Having thus explored the two-way relationship between court practice on the ground and statutory or other initiatives at the centre, it will be argued that a greater emphasis needs to be given to the former if we are to develop a full and balanced model of the reform process (Section 7). The perspectives that can be opened up by a more general exploration of the relationship between the central and the marginal will then be used to address two further questions raised by the essays in this volume (Section 8). First, the relative neglect of gender and age dimensions in formal, statutory law will be contrasted with their decisive influence on the way the courts actually disposed of those accused before them at the local level. Secondly, the extensive regional differences in both criminal justice traditions and in patterns of recorded lawbreaking observed in case studies of particular regions (Chapters 7 and 8) and in the national data available for all counties (Chapter 6), will form the basis for a discussion of the relationship between centre and periphery within the eighteenth- and early nineteenth-century state.

I

When historians have analysed the complex interactions between the centre and the localities which shaped how the criminal law and its administration were reformed in the eighteenth and the first half of the nineteenth centuries, statutes and legislative activity have often played a central role. Much of the very extensive research now available on the history of policing, for example, focuses around the role of key policing acts such as those of 1829, 1839 and 1856, although recent work has also indicated that many important locally initiated changes had already occurred by the 1820s. Equally, the growth of the 'bloody code' and the processes that led to the repeal of the vast majority of it in the 1830s and 1840s has inevitably attracted a large amount of research.[1] This use of statutory change as a foundation for structuring our understanding of (and establishing a clear chronological framework for) criminal justice reform is highly understandable. There were many reforms in the period from the late seventeenth century to the middle of the nineteenth in which parliament played a central role. An extensive rewards system to encourage the apprehension of

---

[1] For textbooks that foreground legislative turning points – D. Taylor, *Crime, Policing and Punishment in England 1750–1914* (London, 1998); P. Rawlings, *Crime and Power. A History of Criminal Justice 1688–1998* (Harlow, 1999), 66–100; a considerable amount of work has recently highlighted changes happening in London before 1829 – A. Harris, *Policing the City. Crime and Legal Authority in London 1780–1840* (Ohio, 2004); E. Reynolds, *Before the Bobbies. The Night Watch and Police Reform in Metropolitan London 1720–1830* (Stanford, 1998); R. Paley, 'An Imperfect, Inadequate and Wretched System? Policing London before Peel', *Criminal Justice History*, 10 (1989), 95–123. L. Radzinowicz, *A History of English Criminal Law and its Administration from 1750, The Movement for Reform*, 5 volumes – fifth with R. Hood (London, 1948–68), i.

major felons was first developed and then dismantled by parliament, for example, and amongst its many other initiatives it also transferred responsibility for a
growing list of offences to the summary courts during this period.[2] However, the
detailed studies of local judicial decision-making (and of how various specific
kinds of offenders were dealt with) which are included in this volume suggest
that in parallel with continued research on the role of parliament and of central
government we need to give serious attention to the ways the courts themselves
shaped the nature of justice as it was actually delivered on the ground. In the
eighteenth and early nineteenth centuries a series of important changes in judicial practice took place within dimensions of the criminal justice system that
are not normally foregrounded in discussions about its reform, and in many of
these cases legislative change seems to have played a less central role than the
informal decisions made by the courts themselves. In looking at all the four
dimensions investigated here, it becomes increasingly clear that some of the
key changes in judicial policies (and sometimes the core assumptions which
structured all judicial decisions) were not determined primarily by parliamentary legislation or by central government. Rather it was the informal practices,
and not infrequently the decisive reforms, adopted by court judges, juries, local
magistrates and other local decision-makers that played the most important role
in the interactions which shaped these areas of criminal justice policy. In all
these subject areas it is possible to identify significant changes in practice which
their creators would have seen as changes from worse to better (i.e. as reforms)
which were not overtly related to any specific legislative initiatives. These are
dealt with in more detail in later chapters but six specific examples are worth
brief discussion here in order to illustrate the more general argument.

One of the most interesting areas involves the fundamental changes that
occurred in quarter-sessions policies towards non-lethal violence (chapters 7
and 8). The work presented here on the contrasting counties of Essex and
Cornwall, along with research recently completed on London and earlier sound-
ings in Surrey, has indicated clearly that assault was increasingly criminalised
in the late-eighteenth century.[3] Indictment for assault was turned from what
had been mainly a civil process, resolved by compensation and/or a fine, into a
criminal trial which usually, although by no means always, ended in imprisonment. In the mid-eighteenth century most people indicted for assault pleaded
guilty and were fined a nominal amount after making an agreement to com-
pensate their victims. By 1820 very few pleaded guilty because most of those

[2] Radzinowicz, *A History*, 2, 57–111.
[3] G. Smith, 'The State and the Culture of Violence in London 1760–1840', PhD thesis University
of Toronto 1999; N. Landau, 'Indictment for Fun and Profit: a Prosecutor's Reward at Eighteenth-
Century Quarter Sessions', *Law and History Review*, 17 (1999), 507–36; J. Beattie, 'Violence
and Society in Early Modern England', in A. Doob and E. Greenspan (eds.), *Perspectives in
Criminal Law*, (Aurora Ontario, 1985), 49–50.

convicted of assault were imprisoned. Those found guilty of assault were now subjected to very similar imprisonment terms to those imposed on petty thieves. Even though the assaults they committed were often minor in character, those accused of non-lethal violence at quarter sessions were subjected to quite severe sanctions by the 1820s – a policy that had been extremely rare in almost every part of England sixty or seventy years earlier.

Two further examples of major shifts in the direction of criminal justice practices that cannot be related directly to legislative changes emerge from the work presented here on juvenile delinquency. The first involves a gradual but important change in the technical legal immunities enjoyed by young offenders. The erosion of the principle of *doli incapax*, which had offered significant protection to offenders aged up to fourteen, and of the less formal notions that had offered some protection to older juveniles aged roughly between fifteen and seventeen, can be clearly traced in the major courts of the early nineteenth century. This important shift, which appears to have been totally unrelated to any formal central policy announcement or legislative change, affected both the pre-trial and public trial experience of juvenile felons. Both petty-sessions magistrates and the major courts seem overall to have moved from policies that favoured diversion (i.e. informal sanctions not involving indictment or imprisonment) to policies that prioritised strategies involving public discipline (Chapters 2 and 3). An increasing proportion of magistrates moved away from the informal resolution of such cases and subjected suspected juvenile felons either to summary imprisonment (primarily as vagrants or 'reputed thieves') or to commitment to gaol to await formal trial. Those that reached formal trial then found that jurors, who in the eighteenth century had brought in a much higher rate of acquittals in cases involving juveniles, had now reversed that policy and were less likely to find younger offenders not guilty.[4] The effect of these policies, and of victims' growing tendency to take juvenile offenders before a magistrate, was a very rapid increase in the number of juvenile offenders being convicted by the courts.

These changes in turn can be linked to another significant informal shift in criminal justice policies. In the early nineteenth century the judges at the Old Bailey, and to a lesser extent elsewhere, were deeply ambivalent about every sentencing option available to them, and particularly about the imprisonment of juveniles (Chapter 3), but no formal legal channel existed whereby they could commit juvenile convicts to a reformatory institution. They did not, however, let this prevent them from doing just that. Mobilising the fiction of the 'respited judgement' and the formal recording of a nominal fine, the Old Bailey began

---

[4] H. Shore, *Artful Dodgers. Youth and Crime in Early Nineteenth-Century London* (1999), 117; M. Wiener, *Reconstructing the Criminal. Culture, Law and Policy in England 1830–1914* (Cambridge, 1990), 51–2.

to send fairly large numbers of juvenile offenders to the London Refuge for the Destitute and to a lesser extent to the Philanthropic Society (Chapter 4). By the early 1820s the former was an important destination for convicted juvenile offenders and many were sent there direct from the courts. Although formal legal advice made it clear that the Refuge could not by law restrain the inmates from leaving, in practice they were only allowed out very occasionally and the average juvenile inmate was subjected to a two-year training programme by this formally enclosed institution. A reformatory sentencing option for juveniles had been invented and by the late 1810s the most easily serviceable philanthropic institution available at that time, the Refuge for the Destitute, was quietly being given a large annual grant by the government in order to ensure that that option remained available. The courts having initiated an informal, and strictly speaking illegal, new criminal justice policy, central government then, somewhat later, backed that initiative with cash (Chapter 4).

Detailed research on gender and justice (Chapters 5 and 7) reveals a fourth area in which a range of sentencing and punishment policies were also altered on the ground without either any legislative change taking place, or any evidence being created that central government had initiated, or even had any prior warning of, these changes. The later eighteenth century and the early decades of the nineteenth witnessed the almost complete abandonment of the public punishment of women but not of men. At both the assizes and the quarter sessions, the public whipping of women who had been convicted of theft was completely abandoned between 1750 and 1800, not only in London and the home counties, but also in some remoter regions such as Cornwall. This change, which affected the lives of large numbers of female offenders, occurred several decades before parliament formally changed the law and made the public whipping of women illegal in 1817.[5] A similar, if slightly more protracted process was occurring in relation to the hanging of women (Chapter 5). By the late eighteenth and early nineteenth centuries it was extremely rare for any female property offender to be hanged but relatively large numbers of males were still going to the gallows.[6] As the circuit judges changed the meaning of the capital code by drastically reducing the proportion of convicts whom they

---

[5] P. King, *Crime, Justice and Discretion in England 1740–1820* (Oxford, 2000), 286; G. Morgan and P. Rushton, *Rogues, Thieves and the Rule of Law. The Problem of Law Enforcement in North-east England 1718–1800* (London, 1998), 134–5 implies a slightly later survival of female public whipping. Parliament banned the whipping of female vagrants, but not of male ones – G. Smith, 'Civilised People Don't Want to See That Kind of Thing: The Decline of Public Physical Punishment in London 1760–1840' in C. Strange, *Qualities of Mercy: Justice, Punishment and Discretion* (Vancouver, 1996), 39.

[6] King, *Crime, Justice*, 281–2; *Parliamentary Papers* (henceforth *P.P.*), 1819, xvii, 228 – If murder is excluded 3 out of 54 females (5.5 per cent), and 139 out of 488 males (28.5 per cent) capitally convicted in Lancashire 1798–1818 were hanged. V. Gatrell, *The Hanging Tree. Execution and the English People 1770–1868* (Oxford, 1994), 7.

left to hang – a process, which effectively repealed the capital parts of some of these statutes well before parliament actually changed the statutory law – female offenders were particularly advantaged. Here, as in the case of public whippings, an informal movement away from public, physical punishments tended to express itself most fully, in its early stages at least, in cases involving female convicts. Even when allowance is made for the differences in the types of offence that men and women tended to be indicted for, a deeply gendered policy about public physical punishments, which in part reflected the generally lighter sentences given to women, was developed by the courts in this period with only minimal input from the centre.[7]

The fifth example highlighted in this volume illustrates the problems experienced by those who tried to use the central courts to create new legal sanctions that would reform the behaviour of the poor. The complex legal initiatives and counter strategies that occurred in this period in relation to the poor's customary right to glean the corn left in the fields after harvest also indicate the power of the local in legal disputes at a number of levels. Chapters 9 and 10, which focus on the origins and impact of the attempts of an association of farmers and others to use judgements handed down in one of the central Westminster courts to take control of the gleaning fields, highlight the fragility of 'law' created at the centre. Apart from the structural problem that the force of local custom could take the place of the general common law as established by the central civil courts, those who wanted to control gleaning also faced several other difficulties. On the few occasions when cases reached the major courts jurors strongly resisted attempts to redefine gleaning as theft. More important, the magistracy in many localities simply refused to back the Court of Common Pleas 1788 decision to make gleaning illegal and sometimes supported the gleaners against farmers who had tried to use force to expel them from the fields. The farmers may have succeeded, at considerable expense and after two attempts, in getting a high-court judgement that made gleaning illegal, but making this stick in the local courts proved almost impossible (Chapter 10). Local decision-makers refused to enforce a ruling that went against their sense of justice, and thus remade the law at the local level in ways which thwarted the overt attempts of the farmers to use the Westminster courts to redefine gleaning as a crime.

The evidence cited briefly in chapter 2, which indicates that magistrates made increasing use of various informal powers to deal summarily with large numbers of juveniles whose actions could have been defined as felonies, also pinpoints

---

[7] D. Palk, 'Private Crime in Public Places. Pickpockets and Shoplifters in London 1780–1830' in T. Hitchcock and H. Shore (eds.), *The Streets of London from the Great Fire to the Great Stink* (London, 2003) rightly points out that in comparing the treatment given to male and female pickpockets, for example, we are not comparing like with like, since female pickpockets operated mainly in enclosed spaces at night whereas male ones operated mainly in open spaces and often in the daytime.

a sixth arena in which 'justice in practice' often failed to coincide with the rulings to be found in the law books and the statutes. In performing their roles as committing magistrates in felony cases, JPs had long exercised considerable discretion, but the period under scrutiny here appears to have witnessed major informal changes in the ways these courts processed many property offenders. The summary courts increasingly, and without any statutory authorisation, took on the business of judging which property offenders should be sent on for trial and which cases should be dismissed, be resolved by the payment of compensation, or end in the summary imprisonment or impressment of the offender.[8] There is some evidence that these practices began well before the eighteenth century – especially in and around London where John Beattie has shown that those accused of grand as well as petty larceny were often summarily imprisoned 'without legal warrant' in the City Bridewell and in the Middlesex houses of correction. However, although research in this area is still at a fairly early stage and there are few sources that shed light on earlier periods, it seems likely that the practice of dealing with theft cases at the summary level without recourse to the jury courts was becoming much more widespread. In the City of London Beattie's research suggests a very significant shift between the 1690s and the 1730s as the magistrates increasingly took on the business of enquiring into the nature and strength of the case presented by both sides. Moreover, there is considerable evidence that these procedures had become even more central by the final years of the century. In the 1730s around half of theft cases were being dealt with informally but Drew Gray's recent work on the City's magistrates' courts in the 1780s and 1790s indicates that by then a very much smaller percentage of such cases were being sent on for jury trial. By the end of the century the norm was for these cases to be dealt with at the summary level so that effectively a felony trial might end at three points – before a magistrate, at the grand jury stage, or at a formal and public petty jury trial.[9] By the late eighteenth century, moreover, there is evidence that three trials was often an

---

[8] King, *Crime, Justice*, 87–94; G. Morgan and P. Rushton, 'The Magistrate, the Community and the Maintenance of an Orderly Society in Eighteenth-Century England', *Historical Research*, 76 (2003), 74.

[9] For a rare seventeenth-century justicing book – from an area of Essex near to London, which shows some use of informal resolutions in felony cases – J. Sharpe (ed.), *"William Holcroft his Booke" Local Office Holding in Late Stuart Essex* (Chelmsford, 1986); J. Beattie, *Policing and Punishment in London 1660–1750* (Oxford, 2001), 24–30, 95–107; D. Gray, 'Summary Proceedings and Social Relations in the City of London 1750–1800' forthcoming thesis, University of Northampton; comparison of such figures is sometimes problematic, however, because it is sometimes very difficult to agree on a definition of what precisely constitutes an accusation of theft. 'No thief in England' the chairman of the Cornwall quarter sessions told the grand jury in 1796 during a revealing overview of the system, 'can be punished till . . . he has had the advantage it may be said of three trials – First before the magistrate commits, Second before the grand jury and Thirdly before another jury.' Cornish Record Office, AD604 Address to the Gentlemen of the Grand Jury Easter 1796.

underestimate. Many thieves were being put through at least four adjudication procedures. As regular weekly petty-sessions meetings began to be established in more and more divisions, magistrates in many areas further increased their discretionary powers in felony cases by developing (on their own initiative) a system in which many felony accusations were first heard by a single magistrate, and then sent on if necessary to the next petty sessions – where further cases might be informally resolved or summarily dealt with before a residue was sent on for jury trial.[10] This system, which involved holding offenders 'for further examination' for considerable periods, was also based on extremely shaky legal foundations and resulted in considerable conflict – an issue that will be returned to later in this introduction.

The gap between the law as laid down in the justicing handbooks and practice on the ground widened in the early nineteenth century. The law books continued to insist that in felony cases preliminary hearings were not to be used as filters, but it was becoming increasingly clear that this was established practice in many areas. By the 1830s this was even being openly admitted by many commentators, although not yet by the justicing handbooks. In 1837, for example, the most widely read justices' handbook was still insisting that 'if there be an express charge of felony, on oath, against the prisoner, though his guilt appear doubtful, the justice cannot wholly discharge him but must bail or commit him.' However, in the same year, a prominent metropolitan JP openly admitted to parliament that magistrates were 'in the practice of applying their summary jurisdiction even beyond the spirit, certainly beyond the words, of the law . . . assuming to themselves the power of adjudicating in cases of actual felony.' Equally the criminal law commission's report on juvenile offenders, which was also published in 1837, was in no doubt that this was normal practice in this context. 'The discretion of absolutely discharging a prisoner is already assumed by many magistrates, though without any direct authority by the law;' they reported, 'and it is now not an unfrequent practice to dismiss charges for trivial offences against children, not withstanding the evidence adduced may have clearly established the commission of a felony.' The commissioners then went on to suggest that, since the informal practices that had been developed by the summary courts were widely felt to be very useful, they needed to be both legalised and standardised. 'If the exercise of such a discretion is desirable, it should', they concluded, 'be expressly sanctioned by law, and defined, and limited, as far as possible, upon some rational and consistent principle.' This recommendation finally began to bear fruit in 1847, when the first of a series of acts (targeted initially only at juvenile offenders) began the formal statutory transfer of minor larceny trials into the summary courts. After half a century or more parliament had finally

---

[10] For a critique of these developing procedures – G. Paul, *Address to His Majesty's Justices of the Peace for the County of Gloucester* (Gloucester, 1809), 106.

acknowledged changes in justicing practice that had long been visible on the ground.[11]

II

The extensive research already completed on the prosecution, trial and punishment of felons in the major courts also makes it clear that in this period the interactions between legislative and non-legislative activity were often complex and were rarely unidirectional. Several different types of interaction between centrally directed initiatives and those that arose from changing practice on the ground can be identified in this work. While many statutes initiated or encouraged important changes in practice that were in sympathy with the intentions of the legislators, others, by contrast, stimulated a widespread counter-reaction on the ground. Equally ground–up initiatives were not infrequently ignored by the legislature (and by formal central government bodies) for such long periods that they effectively became 'law' as a result. Other local, court-based initiatives led fairly directly to legislative activity, which was designed either to legitimise them or to bring them under at least partial control (or both).

In analysing these different forms of interaction, however, historians have been hampered by the fact that the surviving evidence tends to foreground legislation and central government-based initiatives and to downgrade informal, local, court-based changes. For example, the first of the (admittedly over-simplified) scenarios briefly listed above – that in which statutes led to changes that were at least roughly in line with the intentions of those who created them – is the easiest to identify and discuss. Successful parliamentary legislation left by far the clearest records, often produced a printed debate, and usually resulted in the creation of documentation about its implementation because the courts formally recorded their responses to it. The major-court records make it clear, for example, that the legislation on the reimbursement of prosecutors costs introduced from 1752 onwards was broadly successful in its stated aims, although the records also indicate that the courts often went beyond the limitations imposed by statute, giving help to categories of prosecutor that the legislature had excluded.[12] Equally, although recent research has highlighted the similarities between the old police and the new, it is not difficult to establish that the acts of 1829, 1839 and 1856 did change the ways

---

[11] R. Burn, *The Justice of the Peace and Parish Officer* (London, 13th edn, 1776), iv, 318–19; King, *Crime, Justice*, 87–94; J and T. Chitty (eds.), *The Justice of the Peace and Parish Officer by Richard Burn*, 28th edn (London, 1837), ii, 121; B. Smith, 'Did the Presumption of Innocence Exist in Summary Proceedings?', *Law and History Review*, 23 (2005), 191–9; *P.P.*, 1837, xxxi, 8; C. Emsley, *Crime and Society in England 1750–1900* (2nd edn, London, 1996), 204.
[12] King, *Crime, Justice*, 49–52.

policing was organised in ways that were not usually contrary to the legislators intentions[13].

It is also relatively easy to find evidence about the second type of interaction listed above – that in which the delivery of justice on the ground was shaped by strong reactions against specific legislative initiatives. The reward system for example, while encouraging the prosecution of some major felons, was widely believed to have increased acquittal and partial verdict rates. It also stimulated the development of more protective evidentiary rules.[14] More centrally, eighteenth- and early nineteenth-century commentators (and parliamentary enquiries) focused much attention on the ways prosecutors, jurors, judges and those involved in pardoning processes reacted against the rapid expansion of the bloody code. The apparent tension between parliament's continual passing of more and more capital statutes and their decreasing use in practice remains one of the most striking features of criminal justice in the long eighteenth century. Moreover, many of the methods by which the courts mitigated or nullified the harshness of the capital code – such as partial verdicts – have left considerable evidence in the court records. Not surprisingly, therefore, this has formed an important theme in the historiography.[15]

However, when the key form of interaction that produced change was not one that was dominated by the centre, when ground–up initiatives produced no legislative reaction or formal central government response but still had a significant impact on the way justice was practised, it was very rare for the same depth of archives to be created. Change often took place more gradually and open discussion in print was frequently absent. Formal recording was not always deemed necessary. Indeed some changes were deliberately recorded in opaque ways by those who initiated them. The Old Bailey's informal move to reformatory sentencing, for example, can only be fully reconstructed because the internal records of the Refuge for the Destitute happen to have survived (Chapter 4). In analysing these informally initiated aspects of changing patterns of justice it is therefore much more difficult to work out precisely what changes were occurring, when they were introduced, and who was introducing

---

[13] Harris, *Policing the City*; Reynolds, *Before the Bobbies*; Paley, 'An Imperfect'; C. Emsley, *The English Police. A Political and Social History* (Harlow, 1991), 1–42; On rural policing and the reforms – D. Philips and B. Storch, *Policing Provincial England 1829–1856* (Leicester, 1999).

[14] J. Langbein, *The Origins of Adversary Criminal Trial* (Oxford, 2003), 151–8, 293–5.

[15] J. Beattie, *Crime and the Courts in England 1660–1800* (Oxford, 1986); D. Hay, 'Property, Authority and the Criminal Law' in D. Hay *et al.* (eds.) *Albion's Fatal Tree* (London, 1975), 17–63; Radzinowicz, *A History*, i, P. King, 'Decision-makers and Decision-making in the English Criminal Law 1750–1800', *Historical Journal*, 27 (1984), 25–58; J. Langbein, 'Albion's Fatal Flaws', *Past and Present*, 98 (1983), 96–120; P. Linebaugh, '(Marxist) Social History and (Conservative) Legal History: A Reply to Professor Langbein', *New York University Law Review*, 60 (1985), 212–43; King, *Crime, Justice*, 232–7.

them. No one in this period declared *doli incapax* to be void for those aged seven to fourteen, but by a careful analysis of the court records on felony prosecution it is possible to observe it ebbing away. No one in London, Essex or Cornwall announced that henceforward only men would be publicly whipped, but the records make it clear that in one way or another this became the policy of the quarter sessions. Turning points that have dates attached to them because they involved legislation inevitably attract our attention more than slow, geographically diffuse, variegated changes that only gradually solidify into major transitions in the way justice was practised, but this does not make the latter form of change any less significant.

Very often, of course, major transitions were the result of a number of policy changes some of which originated in the courts whilst others came from parliament or from other central bodies. This was certainly the basis of the most important set of changes in penal policy witnessed in this period – the creation of a range of effective secondary punishments for use against various categories of felons. As John Beattie has pointed out, a number of initiatives were introduced in the late seventeenth and early eighteenth centuries 'some originating in the courts and others in parliament'.[16] The main initial push to introduce transportation as a major option seems to have come from the judges. Parliament played only a minor, reactive role at this stage. By 1670, Beattie suggests, 'The courts, and now perhaps parliament, were well on the way toward filling the broad unoccupied middle ground in the penal system.'[17] In the early eighteenth century the balance changed. In 1706 parliament passed an act that resulted in a brief period when a greater use was made of imprisonment. It then facilitated a decisive shift towards the transportation option through the Transportation Act of 1718, but after this the initiative seems to have largely passed back to the localities.

The timing of what was probably the most important penal change of the period under scrutiny here, the rise of imprisonment to become the dominant sentencing option in property-crime cases, had relatively little to do with parliament. In some areas a large number of quarter-sessions accused were affected by the adoption of imprisonment as a major sentencing option for petty larceny long before prison reform itself had begun to be widely discussed in parliament or elsewhere. The assize judges began to make extensive use of imprisonment sentences in major felony cases in 1771–2, but in various provincial areas the initiative had been taken much earlier. Imprisonment had become an important sentencing option at quarter-sessions level in Northumberland and Newcastle before 1750.[18] A similar movement began in Essex during the 1750s – i.e. well before either the transportation crisis of the mid-1770s or Howard's widely

---

[16] Beattie, *Crime*, 470.   [17] *Ibid.*, 471 and 477.
[18] Morgan and Rushton, *Rogues, Thieves*, 73; King, *Crime, Justice*, 261–72.

publicised book on prison conditions focused attention on the subject. Moreover, when it came to implementing the new ideas that Howard, Hanway and others were developing about solitary confinement and the development of reformatory prison regimes, the main impetus came from the localities. The introduction of sentences specifically stipulating 'solitary confinement' in the 1780s and 1790s, for example, can be found in the quarter-sessions records of some counties but not in those of others. More important, the first forty years of major prison reform and in particular the scattered movement to build new penitentiary-style institutions were essentially quarter-sessions, county-level initiatives. Central government's attempts in the second half of the 1770s to create nationwide statute-based reforms in the prison system failed because it was politically impossible to impose legislation that would involve local authorities in any substantial expense. The county authorities simply refused to implement the relatively minor changes to local houses of correction required by the 1776 Hulks Act, for example, and the centrally funded penitentiaries envisaged by the 1779 Penitentiary Act failed to materialise. The first major wave of reformed prisons was therefore built mainly on the initiative of JPs rather than of MPs.

Clearly in the area of penal policy the precise roles played by parliament, by government bodies, by the assize judges, and by the quarter-sessions magistrates, differed across time and between different areas. The statutes of 1706 and 1718 stand out as important landmarks but so do the less formal changes in sentencing practices initiated by the courts in the mid-seventeenth and mid-eighteenth centuries and the county-level prison reforms initiated in the last quarter of that century.[19] It is very difficult to trace either the precise process by which decisions were made or the influence that the different decision-makers may have had on one another, but the main responsibility for taking the initiative in this area seems to have alternated between the courts and parliament, or at the very least to have been shared in different proportions in different subperiods.

The detailed research conducted by John Langbein and others on another important area – the transformation of the criminal trial – provides an excellent case study of a set of related areas of criminal justice practice that were reformed primarily by the courts themselves rather than in response to central initiatives. The sources are highly problematic and much depends on the careful reading of voluminous printed trial reports, but the overall picture is clear. The period from the late seventeenth century to the 1830s witnessed three interrelated changes – the growth of a web of evidentiary rules, the coming of much more adversarial

---

[19] D. Eastwood, *Government and Community in the English Provinces 1700–1870* (London, 1997), 136; M. Ignatieff, *A Just Measure of Pain. The Penitentiary in the Industrial Revolution 1750–1850* (London, 1978), 96–105; S. Devereaux, 'The Making of the Penitentiary Act 1775–9', *Historical Journal*, 42 (1999), 405–33; the 1779 Act did change sentencing structures to some extent – Beattie, *Crime*, 573–5.

forms of trial, and the growing influence of counsel over the trial process. All three changes came in a piecemeal fashion. The key decision – to allow defence counsel into the felony trial – was the result of the rulings of various individual judges. To quote John Langbein, 'The change in practice did not take the form of an authoritative decision or directive, but rather emerged from the judges' exercise of their residual discretion.'[20] The lawyers themselves then gradually demanded and achieved greater freedom of manoeuvre. The lawyerisation of the felony trial was primarily brought about by the judges' discretion and by the lawyers' exploitation of the space that the judges offered to them. In 1836, parliament finally legislated in this area, giving counsel formal permission to sum up the case for the defence, but by then counsel had played a vital role in the process by which the criminal trial had been transformed.[21] The emergence of more elaborate rules of evidence in the criminal trial also began, Langbein concludes, in the exercise of the judges' individual discretion but, 'as the consensus on a particular point grew stronger among the judges, the principle tended to find expression as a norm from which neither judge nor jury ought to depart – a rule of law.' How did this new system of trial develop? Neither parliament nor central government was involved in any formative way and even the circuit judges themselves seem to have acted more often as individuals than as a body. 'The authorities in whose hands the system developed did not design it', Langbein concludes, 'Adversarial criminal trial developed across the eighteenth century without forethought.' Individual judges decisions had gradually solidified and developed a consensus which in turn had facilitated the process 'of turning fact into law.'[22]

III

The informal way in which gradual changes by individual judges became first consensus, then precedent and finally an established 'law of evidence' is a reminder of the two-way nature of the relationship between law and practice in this period. Even in the criminal law, which is usually seen as much more statute based than any other field of law, legal change might come about primarily through court-based decisions. It may be easier to identify occasions when new laws changed the ways justice was done, but the practice of justice on the ground also shaped and remade law in ways that may have been equally fundamental. Very few of the surviving sources offer historians a window onto these types of changes. There are virtually no printed reports of trial proceedings below the assizes level and precious few at that level outside London. The magistrates who shaped court practice at the quarter sessions and in the summary courts very rarely publicly discussed or recorded their informal judicial practices. However,

---

[20] Langbein, *The Origins*, 174–5.   [21] *Ibid.*, 178–344.   [22] *Ibid.*, 216.

in order to understand the two-way interactions between statute and practice, and their differing roles in shaping the nature of justice, it is vital to scrutinise the most heavily used and most foundational area of court practice – that of the summary courts. After all it was in these courts that the vast majority of the population were most likely to come into contact with the criminal justice system, and for many eighteenth-century men and women it would have been their only point of contact. It is fortunate, therefore, that at the end of his volume on the *History of the Poor Laws*, Richard Burn, author of by far the most popular justices' handbook of the period, offered some detailed case studies that shed very considerable light on this shady area.[23] These suggest that it would not have been difficult to find many areas of summary-court practice in which, like the laws of evidence example given above, the nature of the way justice was administered may have been based primarily on customary practices rather than on statute.

In a complex discussion of the question of 'how far justices of the peace have power to compel witnesses to appear and give evidence in matters depending before them', for example, Burn noted a number of interesting developments. 'Proceeding against witnesses, by indictment, or otherwise, for their contempt in not appearing would be expensive, and certainly ineffectual', he observed, 'therefore the justices, as it seemeth, for the sake of convenience, have altered the course of proceeding in this respect which only the law ought to have done.'[24] The 'summary method of proceeding' when apprehending the accused had caused equal problems. Two key authorities, Coke and Hale were at complete odds on this. 'The one speaks of what was the strict law; the other of the practice which has prevailed against it', Burn noted, quoting Hawkins, one of the century's leading criminal lawyers. The solution being

> that the practice of justices of the peace in relation to this matter has now become a law . . . yet in as much as justices of the peace claim this power by connivance rather than any express warrant of law . . . a justice of the peace cannot well be too tender in proceedings of this kind.

In concluding on the law in relation to the summonsing of those accused of misdemeanours Burn came to the same basic conclusion. 'Custom and long practice' he wrote, 'seem to have made the law in this particular, and not the law to have established the custom.' The magistrates' right to discipline victims who failed to turn up and prosecute offenders committed for jury trial may also

[23] P. King, 'The Summary Courts and Social Relations in Eighteenth-century England', *Past and Present*, 183 (2004); P. Griffiths, 'Bodies and Souls in Norwich: Punishing Petty Crime, 1540–1700' in S. Devereaux and P. Griffiths (eds.), *Penal Practice and Culture, 1500–1900; Punishing the English* (Basingstoke, 2004), 86; R. Burn, *The History of the Poor Laws with Observations* (1764), in a chapter which the printer labelled 'Other defects in the justices law', Burn pointed to a considerable number of areas of 'justice of peace' law, which 'seem to want amendment', 242 –270.

[24] *Ibid.*, 257.

have been built on shaky foundations. In January 1821 several London papers reported that 'Mr Duncan Campbell, who is well known at the Police offices for his careful observance of Acts of Parliament', having charged a boy with robbing him on direct and incontrovertible evidence, refused to let the clerk draw up the usual recognizance binding him to appear at the Old Bailey to prosecute. The Lord Mayor then made it clear that since 'the Act of Parliament rendered it imperative upon the person robbed to prosecute . . . in the event of refusal to enter into a recognizance . . . the person robbed must himself go to prison.' However, Campbell insisted that although he must give evidence 'there was . . . no act that compelled a man to prosecute a thief'. The City Solicitor was then sent for and agreed with the Mayor that Campbell must go to prison but when Campbell called his bluff the solicitor found to his dismay that the Act of Philip and Mary which he thought justified his ruling in fact contained 'not one word upon the subject of compelling any person to prosecute.' 'The learned gentleman then admitted an error in the manner of binding persons over to prosecute.' 'Mr Campbell', he admitted, 'was in the right' and the Mayor was left to observe ruefully that 'the legislature must interfere to remove the impediment.'[25]

Burn also suggested that the ways in which the putative fathers of illegitimate children were dealt with, and imprisoned, by the courts often had little basis in statute law:

> It hath been the practice ever since Dalton's time, to bind the reputed father of a bastard child to the good behaviour, and if it is lawful to do that, it is lawful to . . . commit him to gaol if he shall not find sureties. But the legality of that practice may be questioned. . . . The acts giving jurisdiction to the justices of the peace, are for the indemnification of the parish, with regard to the maintenance of the bastard child: on a suit merely civil, between the parish officers on the one hand, and the reputed father on the other: and to bind a man to the peace or good behaviour, on complaint of the parish officers, on a charge only of such an offence, of which afterwards he may be acquitted . . . is a power given by no statute.

The problem did not end there however. Burn also had difficulties in justifying this summary-court procedure at common law. 'Before the acts of parliament, giving cognisance to justices of the peace in cases of bastardy, this was solely an ecclesiastical offence, punishable in the spiritual court,' he pointed

---

[25] *Ibid.*, 258–65, Although he does not fully specify the context, Henry Pye took Burn to task for this approach in H. Pye, *Summary of the Duties of a Justice of the Peace out of Sessions with some Preliminary Observations* (2nd edn, London, 1810), xii. Only in 1848 was formal authority given to magistrates to issue warrants to compel the accused's attendance. B. Smith, 'Circumventing the Jury: Petty Crime and Summary Jurisdiction in London and New York City. 1790–1855', PhD, Yale University, 1996, 188–9; *The Times* 16 Jan. 1821; *London Chronicle* 16 Jan. 1821 and for Campbell causing more trouble later 16 Feb. 1821.

out. 'Therefore the punishment thereof as a crime properly belongs still to the spiritual court'. This was certainly not stopping magistrates in many areas from making large numbers of commitments on precisely this basis. The Chelmsford goal calendar for Christmas 1753, for example, listed three men from three separate parishes committed by three different magistrates for 'begetting' various women 'with child which is likely to be born a bastard and to become chargeable to the parish . . . and refusing to find sureties'. A random survey of the Colchester house of correction calendars between October 1788 and April 1790 reveals that fifteen of the ninety-four prisoners incarcerated there during this period were men 'committed for want of sureties for a bastard child' – i.e. about one fifth of the seventy-five male prisoners. Colchester may have been rather untypical – a broader sample of different Essex gaols across the second half of the eighteenth century suggests slightly over 10 per cent of the men committed to Essex gaols were imprisoned for bastardy offences of this kind. However, this was certainly a significant subgroup amongst the incarcerated – much more important for example than game offenders who in both samples were four times less numerous than those imprisoned for bastardy. If Burn's account is correct, a very significant subgroup of eighteenth-century prisoners seem to have been imprisoned as a result of informal justicing practices that had very little basis in statute, and were reliant in part on the dubious assumption that crimes previously dealt with by the ecclesiastical courts could now be tried summarily by the magistrates.[26]

In describing 'other defects in the justices' law' Burn also quite casually referred to the fact that magistrates regularly failed to meet the requirements of statutes in several other areas.

It frequently happens, that where a thing is to be done by two justices, as (for instance) the making an order of removal of a poor person, great inconvenience arises, both to the parties, and to the justices, where the justices (as is often the case) live at a great distance from each other . . . and this, it is to be feared, causes the justices sometimes, absurdly and ridiculously enough . . . to adjudge the settlement when they are twenty miles asunder, by one of them taking the examination, and certifying to the other, who sets his hand to the order of removal without further ceremony.

[26] Burn, *History*, 290; King, 'The Summary Courts', 159; Essex Record Office, Q/SMg 17; Q/SBb 333–9. In his justices manual Burn is more circumspect, but even here he quietly points out the inconsistency of statute in relation to the binding over of the named putative father: 'it doth not appear very clearly, for what purpose he shall be bound by the justice to appear at the sessions at all: it cannot be by way of punishment; for it may turn out, on hearing the cause, that he shall not be the reputed father – but the words of the act must be pursued and therefore he must be bound', Burn, *The Justice*, 13th edn (1776), i, 176. For an excellent study of the bastardy laws in action – T. Nutt, 'Illegitimacy and the Poor Law in Late-Eighteenth and Early Nineteenth-Century England', PhD thesis, University of Cambridge, 2006.

Burn then went on to recommend that 'in these, and many other such like cases, as in the making of orders of bastardy, levying highway penalties, levying the poor rates – it might be reasonable to give power to one justice to proceed by himself alone'[27]. There is considerable evidence that Burn was not exaggerating in his description of magistrates' frequent disregard for the law in this area. The defence produced by William Garrow during an Old Bailey case thirty-five years later revealed that some London magistrates, who did not even have the excuse of distance, regularly left blank signed forms for each other so that one justice could do the work that legally required two.[28] Henry Pye was almost certainly aware of this practice when he wrote his short guide to justices out of sessions in 1810. Among the key issues he highlighted at the beginning of that volume was the following rather loaded reminder.

> As there are many acts to be done which require the authority of two or more justices, and as this must imply that their joint opinion is required by such direction, it is clear, from common sense, as well as from the determination of the courts above, that the two magistrates ought to be together when they act.

Burn, who put a similar reminder at the front of his manual, was almost certainly simply recommending that statute law should quietly follow and legalise an already widespread and longstanding practice.[29]

The extent to which everyday justicing practice in relation to certain kinds of offenders frequently ignored the formal law also emerged from Burn's highly critical remarks about the administration of the laws against begging and vagrancy. In relation to the 'pernicious practice' of issuing itinerant passes, he observed in 1764 that although 'the law whereof hath been long since abolished', yet

> there are printed forms in almost every corporation . . . fetched out of some old books, which in their day were right and proper. Or they are brought down by tradition, without consulting any books at all, or knowing in any reasonable degree what is the law of the kingdom. I have seen a tinker's licence, solemnly signed and sealed by justices of the peace, founded upon an act of parliament repealed above a hundred and fifty years before

The magistrates' widespread misuse of vagrant passes in ways that were 'directly contrary to law' continued to produce similar complaints. In 1790, a number of practices followed by many magistrates in dealing with vagrants were openly denounced, first by the Proclamation Society and then by the printed resolutions passed by the magistrates from over thirty counties who

---

[27] Burn, *History*, 281.

[28] *Old Bailey Sessions Papers*, 8 May 1799, indictment of Timothy Brian *et al.*

[29] H. Pye, *Summary of the Duties of a Justice of the Peace*, 2nd edn (London, 1810), xii–xiii; Burn, *The Justice*, 10th ed., (1766), i, xxxii; There is evidence that it remained fairly standard practice to hear such cases singly in the early 1840s – Smith, 'Circumventing', 178.

that society had called together in London. The propositions the society cir-
culated before the meeting were extremely critical of the magistracy. These
included

> First, that passing vagrants, without previously inflicting some punishment
> upon the vagrant, according to 17 Geo II, is illegal. Second that passing
> vagrants without previous examination or enquiry into their settlements in
> the presence of a justice of the peace is illegal. Third that justices of the
> peace, by signing blank passes, which are filled up by their clerks, and by
> which vagrants are passed, whom the justices never examine or even see, are
> guilty of a misdemeanor.

In response, the sixty or so magistrates assembled from all over England and
Wales (including Middlesex) made no attempt to deny that these 'illegal' practices were being followed. The Proclamation Society had already collected
extensive evidence that in Surrey, London and Middlesex passes were being
'granted generally and indiscriminately', and it seems to have been widely
believed that

> the justices of the City of London and Middlesex never removed paupers by
> a regular order of removal, but sent them to their respective parishes by a
> vagrant pass, though these paupers had committed no act of vagrancy, and
> were not in any degree, subject to the statute concerning vagrants.

Instead of denying the practices the magistrates therefore contented themselves
with denouncing them. 'The indiscriminate passing of vagrants, without whipping or confinement, according to 17 Geo II is a practice extremely mischievous
and injurious', they announced, before going on to be equally critical of 'the
granting of vagrant passes without a previous examination' and the 'highly
improper', practice of 'signing blank passes by justices of the peace'. The
meeting then went on to resolve that a subcommittee be formed in order to
draft a new statute on the subject. However, although this became law in 1792,
and 'expressly enacted, that no magistrate should ever order a vagrant to be
conveyed by a vagrant pass, till he either had been whipped or imprisoned at
least seven days', its effect seems to have been minimal. If Edward Christian,
who was hired after the meeting to draft the 1792 statute, is any guide, parliament was still completely unable to control the justices' behaviour. 'That
statute is almost entirely disregarded', Christian wrote in the late 1810s. 'The
abuse now is, perhaps, a thousand times as great as it was before the passing of
the act.' The London and Middlesex justices were giving 'walking passes' to
large numbers of vagrants which were 'perfectly illegal' not only in Christian's
opinion but also in that of Lord Chief Justice Ellenborough. The City of London
was still printing 'blank illegal passes . . . with the City arms at the top' and
these practices were by no means confined to the capital. Similar blank passes
were being publicly sold by printers for the use of English county magistrates
and in Scotland 'these kinds of permits to beg' were being 'illegally' issued

by magistrates in Edinburgh, Glasgow and Leith who, when asked 'by what authority they granted such passes . . . returned a polite answer, that they had done it from time immemorial.'[30]

New legislation such as the 1792 act sometimes failed to change the behaviour of the courts because it was poorly drafted. Charles Durnford, the editor of the 1810 edition of Burn's *Justice*, for example, openly pointed out the contradictions sometimes found in the vagrancy acts, as well as taking great pains to show that the King's Bench Judges' attempts to rule on those contradictions were based on a complete misreading of them. However, the magistrates' determination to develop and stick to their own procedures also arose from the over-harsh nature of the vagrancy laws and the problems which this could create. 'The vagrant act . . . defeats its own purposes by the severity of its penalties', John Scott argued in 1773. 'Here is no distinction made between the vilest impostor, and the most inoffensive accidentally distressed traveler: the magistrate, if he acts according to law, is constrained (however widely cases may differ) indiscriminately to punish before he can relieve.' Burn was well aware that this resulted in the magistrates flagrantly ignoring the law. 'An act of parliament says, such a person shall be taken up as a rogue and vagabond. A justice of the peace says, permit him to pass', he observed. 'Kings have been sometimes censured for setting themselves above the law; but justices of the peace have been suffered to pass unnoticed.'[31]

Burn may not, of course, have always been correct in casting such aspersions on the everyday practices of justices out of sessions. However, his assertions are frequently backed up by other sources, and there can have been very few magistrates in eighteenth-century England who understood the law in relation

---

[30] Burn, *History*, 116–17; *Statement and Propositions from the Society for Giving Effect to His Majesty's Proclamation Against Vice and Immorality Delivered to the Magistrates* (London, 1790), 1–17; *Resolutions of the Magistrates Deputed from the Several Counties of England and Wales . . . by the Desire of the Society for Giving Effect to His Majesty's Proclamation Against Vice and Immorality* (London, 1790), 1–14; *Report of the Committee of the Society for Giving Effect to His Majesty's Proclamation Against Vice and Immorality for the Year 1799* (London, 1799), 14; E. Christian, *Charges Delivered to the Grand Juries in the Isle of Ely upon Libels, Criminal Law, Vagrants, Religion, Rebellious Assemblies etc etc for the Use of Magistrates and Students of the Law* (London, 1819), 12–17 and 143–199. In 1800 Christian had made it clear why the 'abuse' of 'removing paupers by a pass who had committed no act of vagrancy, and who ought to have been removed by an order of removal' which had been attacked by 32 Geo. iii. c.45 had developed. 'For', he wrote, 'the effects of an order of removal and a vagrant pass are very different; in the first case, the parish removing, bears all the travelling expenses of the paupers; but the expense of conveying vagrants by a pass, is borne by each county through which they are carried.' Blackstone, *Commentaries*, 13th edn with notes and editions by E. Christian, (1800), iv, 169.

[31] Burn, *The Justice*, 21st edn, (1810), v, 727–9; This edition was edited by Durnford and John King but the latter made it clear in the next edition that this section was not his idea – Burn, *The Justice*, 22nd edn, (1814), v, 596; *Observations on the Present State of the Parochial and Vagrant Poor* (London, 1773) 3–4 (authorship attributed to John Scott); Burn, *History*, 117.

to the activities of the summary courts better than Richard Burn. He published fifteen editions of his manual in his lifetime and on every occasion he systematically revised each heading both by adding new statutes and by 'selecting from the reports such adjudicated cases as seemed best to explain the laws on which the determinations of the courts' were based. However, when he implied that magistrates set themselves 'above the law', Burn may well have been exaggerating in order to make his point. He never argued that rural JPs were abusing their legal authority in order to line their own pockets, and closer scrutiny of his discussion of areas such as the punishment of putative fathers suggests that in these situations justices were not necessarily either making completely new law or entirely ignoring the old. Rather they were pushing the boundaries of justicing practice and procedure beyond what was specifically allowed by existing formal legal authority. In most of the areas he discussed Burn did not argue that justices of the peace were acting completely illegally, but only that there was 'great doubt' about the formal legal foundations of many of their practices and that those practices were especially difficult to trace in statute-based law.

Burn's discussion of the 'defects in the justices law' included a considerable number of other criticisms that cannot be followed up in detail here, and he expressly stated that this was not intended to be a comprehensive list. He offered only a few examples and ended the relevant chapter by pointing out that 'there are many other particulars, no doubt, relating to, or connected with the office of a justice of the peace, that may want regulation; which every man's observation will suggest, that hath acted for any considerable time under the commission of the peace.' The reflections of other JPs on this sensitive subject are much more difficult to uncover, although Edward Christian, who was also a magistrate, made his thoughts on the administration of the vagrancy laws abundantly clear. However, when propertied men were unhappy with the summary courts' processes they sometimes left eloquent testimony about their defects. The justices' administration of the game laws produced a range of criticisms from various groups, for example, and another area that came under heavy criticism was the justices' almost unlimited powers when it came to the licensing of alehouses. Here it was widely argued that magistrates acting 'contrary to the spirit and true content of the several statutes . . . have assumed a power to suppress and refuse such licences at their discretion . . . inconsistent with the principles of the constitution, contrary to law and destructive of the property of individuals.' By the 1820s, the fact that 'the unconstitutional power given to justices' was 'subject to no human control' was attracting immense criticism and reform was soon to follow. Overall, therefore, a close look at Burn's comments, combined with the observations that can sometimes be made of other summary-court practices, suggests that there were very substantial areas of slippage when it came to the application of parliamentary statutes, and that at this level magistrates had very considerable room for manoeuvre.[32]

IV

In attempting a more general evaluation of the extent to which summary-court practice was based on statute, on common law principles, on developing customary practice in the lower courts themselves, or indeed on the whim of the individual magistrate, the historian encounters severe archival problems. The most obvious categories of records – the notebooks of individual JPs and the examination and minute books of the petty sessions – very rarely if ever record the legal/statutory basis for the magistrates' actions. Nor, in many cases, is that basis clear from the brief records left about the content of the proceedings. This is not necessarily surprising. Often what is being noted down in the summary-court records is as much the production of a remedy – the creation of a solution to a problem – as it is a reaction to a formal accusation/prosecution. The summary courts operated in a number of modes, from the purely criminal to the purely civil, and a great number of cases fell into ambivalent areas between these two, as Burn's discussion of bastardy commitments makes clear. Pending more detailed work on the summary-court archives, on magistrates correspondence, on pamphlets and on other relevant material, conclusions must remain extremely speculative. However, from our current state of knowledge it would appear that four factors worked together, at least until the 1820s and 1830s, to strengthen the capacity of the summary courts to shape, and sometimes to remake, justice as it was practised on the ground – the multiplicity of law and the confused state of statute law; the mixture of civil and criminal modes in which these courts operated; the wide powers magistrates had grown accustomed to exercise when dealing with the disorderly labouring poor; and the relative lack of effective supervision exercised over these courts.

The profound disquiet which most legal commentators felt about the statute law before consolidation began in the late 1820s almost certainly had an impact, at various levels, on the attitudes of magistrates. As David Lieberman has recently pointed out, 'An overwhelming body of eighteenth century legal opinion held that most of the uncertainty of English law was in fact due to the confusions produced by the poorly expressed, misconceived and enormously verbose statute law.' The huge upsurge in parliamentary legislative activity that

---

[32] Burn, *History*, 242, 290–5; R. Burn, *The Justice*, 16th edn, (1788), i, xvi–xviii which includes a discussion of his practices by his son who took over his mantle after his death in 1785; P. Munsche, *Gentlemen and Poachers. The English Game Laws 1671–1831* (Cambridge, 1981); J. Adolphus, *Observations on the Vagrancy Act and on Some Other Statutes and on the Powers and Duties of Justices of the Peace* (London, 1824); S. Anderson, 'Discretion and the Rule of Law: The Licensing of Drink in England 1817–40', *Legal History*, 23 (2002), 48.

can be observed after 1688 has been the subject of considerable research in recent years, and older notions that criminal legislation was largely passed on the nod with little critical review have rightly been modified. There was often considerable parliamentary debate and in the process many measures failed to pass.[33] Extensive debate in parliament did not, however, necessarily produce better legislation. Indeed some contemporaries believed it had a very negative effect:

> From the various modifications and alterations to which the original draft is subject in its passage through the houses, in compliance with the suggestions of various members, and to meet the interests of various classes, any perspicuity, and brevity, and simplicity which may happen originally to belong to it, are too often obscured and overlaid by the patchwork additions that it receives

a writer in the *Quarterly Review* argued in 1828. These 'hodge podge acts' caused 'the most absurd confusion in the statute book, and the greatest difficulty in referring to and ascertaining the law upon any particular subject.' Whether or not debate and amendment slightly improved the quality of the statutes or further undermined it, our growing awareness of the effort that was often put into the passing of individual acts of parliament should not blind us to the fact that, as an overall body of law, the statute book that resulted was deeply flawed and was subjected to extremely heavy criticism. This clearly was evident in the first half of the eighteenth century. 'The statute laws are now becoming so voluminous and intricate, and by making and mending new quibbles and blunders which daily arise like Hydra's heads, are in such a way of increasing, that . . . I fear they will become the grievance of the subject, and the shame of the nation,' one commentator wrote in 1742. By the later eighteenth century, however, these criticisms had become even more wide-ranging. The newspapers were often very critical. 'We are sorry to observe the great increase of laws and the careless manner in which many Acts of Parliament are drawn up', *The Times* remarked. 'If the framers of them were subject to a penalty for leaving so many loop-holes . . . the public would have them drawn up in a more simple style, so as to be understood without amendments.' The writers of legal books were even more scathing. From Blackstone to Bentham, from Burn to Barrington a chorus of voices expressed frustration, indignation and sometimes downright condemnation of the statute law. Blackstone was

---

[33] J. Innes and J. Styles, 'The Crime Wave: Recent Work on Crime and Criminal Justice in Eighteenth-Century England' in A. Wilson (ed.), *Rethinking Social History. English Society 1570–1920 and its Interpretation* (Manchester, 1993), 247; J. Hoppit, 'Patterns of Parliamentary Legislation 1660–1800', *Historical Journal*, 39 (1996) 109–131; P. Langford, *Public Life and Propertied Englishmen 1689–1798* (Oxford, 1991), 139–48; J. Hoppit, *Failed Legislation 1660–1800, Extracted from the Commons and Lords Journals* (London, 1997); D. Lieberman, *The Province of Legislation Determined. Legal Theory in Eighteenth-Century Britain* (Cambridge, 1989), 237.

deeply critical of the 'specious embellishments and fantastic novelties' of the legislators, and focused on 'the mischiefs that have arisen to the public from inconsiderate alterations in our laws'.[34] Bentham talked of the unfathomable nonsense 'to be met with in our statute book'. The eighteenth-century historian of the statutory law, Daines Barrington, described in some detail the chaotic nature of the statute book, while also pointing out that it contained obsolete and mistranslated material that should never have been there at all. Burn, concluded his influential justice's manual, by observing that 'The statutes at large . . . have in the process of time become very cumbersome and very intricate.' He then mapped out his proposed solution to the 'acknowledged disorder and confusion' of the statute book. This, like similar suggestions made by other widely read commentators such as William Eden and Samuel Romilly, involved not only composing consistent statutes but also repealing all those which 'are virtually repealed by subsequent contradictory statutes . . . are obsolete . . . are rendered useless by subsequent statutes enacting the same things over again with alterations and amendments . . . are frivolous, that is, which cannot possibly, or probably never will be executed.'[35]

The inaccuracies, inconsistencies, inadequate wording and innate contradictions of the statute book were amongst the most commonly criticised features. Its 'disorder and confusion' arose not only from the failure to repeal old statutes or from the inadequate wording of new ones. The statutes lacked consistent principles and were rarely based on general propositions.[36] Quality was not the only problem however. The extreme particularity of much of the legislation and its failure to cover important areas meant that the statute law was at best a patchwork. Paradoxically, however, the huge volume of statutes created even greater difficulties. This 'great bog of uncoordinated lawmaking' (to quote Paul Langford), ever expanding but always unplanned and lacking any clear or rational principles, was highly problematic. The statutes' verbosity and above all their sheer volume made them, to many observers, such a dark labyrinth that they were beyond the mastery of all but a few. This was a problem for all the population. The 'abundance of penal laws', Burn wrote, 'though not put into execution, yet hang over the subject as a snare, and may be put in execution

[34] *Quarterly Review*, 37 (1828), 152; *The Times*, 31 Jan. 1800; Anon, *Observations on the Vagrant Laws* (London, 1742), 13; W. Blackstone, *Commentaries on the Laws of England*, 4 vols. 1765–9, (Oxford, 1765), i, 10. Durnford suggested that the inclusion of a highly contradictory and confusing clause in a much used vagrancy act was caused by the fact that 'it was proposed by some member of parliament after the bill had gone through some of its stages without his being aware of the provisions made in the preceding parts of the act.' Burn, *The Justice*, 21st ed., (1810), v, 727.

[35] Lieberman, *The Province*, 18 and 187–9; Burn, *The Justice*, 13th edn (1776), iv, 435–6. 'Obsolete and useless statutes should be repealed; for they debilitate the authority of such as still exist.' Eden wrote, indeed they 'left the living to perish in the arms of the dead.' W. Eden, *Principles of Penal Law* (London, 1771), 19.

[36] Lieberman, *The Province*, 16.

at any time; insomuch that every man, almost every day of his life, incurs the penalty of one or other of them'. However, it was even more of a problem to individual magistrates. If, as one Lord Chancellor suggested as early as 1756, the statute books were now so swollen 'that no lawyer, not even one of the longest and most extensive practice, can pretend to be master of all the statutes', what chance did the average JP have? Not much, if many contemporary observers are to be believed. 'The statutes of the realm have thus become a sealed book' one noted. 'A country gentleman . . . could no more dream of opening the statutes and ascertaining for himself the punishment affixed to a given offence . . . than he could hope with accuracy to interpret a Runic inscription.'[37]

While in some areas, including the specific statutes that permitted magistrates to try particular minor forms of appropriation such as vegetable and wood theft, the law was reasonably clear, in many, if not most, it left considerable room for interpretation. Some parts of the statutory patchwork were very threadbare indeed. In others there was too much statutory law and simpler ways through the labyrinth needed to be established. Burn himself had to begin the first volume of his justices' manual by laying out forty-three rules he had decided to use in 'the construction of statutes'. These rules themselves were based on his selective use of legal treatises, on the patchy privately collected printed case law then available, and on his observations of court practice. The rules were far from simple on occasions. Rule 12, for example, attempted to deal with one of the problems the judges often wrestled with – that the preamble to an act was very often inconsistent with its content – by suggesting, amongst other things that, 'the preamble shall not restrain the operation of the enacting part.' Rule 40 highlighted the capacity of the courts to effectively ignore the law. 'No damages can be given to the party grieved, upon an indictment, or any other criminal prosecution', Burn noted, 'but it is everyday practice in the courts of King's Bench, to induce defendants to make satisfaction to prosecutors, for the costs of the prosecution, and also for the damages sustained, by intimating an inclination on that account to mitigate the fine due to the King'.[38]

Statutes were only one component of the common law-based legal frameworks of the eighteenth century. Other forms of law were also important. In the eighteenth century the map of the law contained many colours. While some very substantial areas were of a statutory hue, others exhibited varying mixtures – a blending of the colours of largely unwritten common law traditions, of patchily recorded judge's law and of the processes that had emerged from the customary practices of the courts themselves at various levels. Throughout the eighteenth century the substantive criminal law was often regarded as complex,

[37] Langford, *Public*, 156; Burn, *History*, 244–5; Lieberman, *The Province*, 14–15; *Quarterly Review*, 37 (1828), 156. This was not a new problem – S.Hindle, *The State and Social Change in Early Modern England 1550–1640* (Basingstoke, 2002), 10–11.
[38] Burn, *The Justice* 10th edn (1766), I, xxiv–xxxii.

capricious, crammed with obscure distinctions, prone to self-contradiction, and without obvious sense or rationale. For example, statutory and non-statutory areas overlapped in problematic ways. Burn's rules for the construction of statutes observed that 'a statute made in the affirmative, without any negative implied or expressed, does not take away the common law', and the overlaps between the common law and statute law therefore offered considerable opportunities for the courts to undermine the activities of the legislature. For example, prosecutions against those who attempted to undermine traditional food-marketing practices by forestalling, regrating and engrossing continued to be brought under the common law in various courts and sometimes with the encouragement of the high-court judges, nearly thirty years after parliament had made its views plain by repealing all statutory regulation of these practices in 1772.[39]

This multiplicity of law presented both problems and opportunities to the unpaid, amateur magistrates of eighteenth-century England. Most of them wanted, above all, to establish convenient and workable practices. Some had at least a smattering of legal training and others had access to limited legal advice from their clerks, but most almost certainly drew what little law they needed mainly from discussions with fellow JPs and from occasional forays into the growing body of legal literature published for their benefit – justices' manuals, abridgements of statutes, law dictionaries and more specialist legal treatises. However, even the most popular and most lucid of these volumes – Burn's *Justice of the Peace and Parish Officer* was not without its problems. Producing this multi-volume work was a huge labour in itself. In the introduction to the last edition of his manual printed before his death in 1785, Richard Burn pointed out that over 400 relevant acts had been passed or repealed since the first edition in 1754 and that 'so many new matters are in every sessions of parliament brought under the jurisdiction of these justices . . . that every new edition, in order to keep pace with the law, is in effect a new book.' As subsequent editions of Burn's manual rapidly expanded under new editors, reaching six very large volumes and over 6500 pages by the 1830s, many justices found it far too cumbersome. 'The fatigue of learning it (the law) through the medium of such voluminous instructions' was so 'discouraging', that shortened editions were not infrequently, although not necessarily successfully, attempted. Young magistrates in particular, one JP noted in 1813, could not be expected, as unpaid amateurs, to put in the work necessary to master these huge volumes. 'The unpaid magistracy of the country' one observer noted a few years later,

---

[39] *Ibid.*, xxiv; K. Smith, *Lawyers, Legislators and Theorists. Developments in English Criminal Jurisprudence 1800–1957* (Oxford, 1998), 2; D. Hay, 'Moral Economy, Political Economy and Law', in A. Randall, and A. Charlesworth (eds.), *Moral Economy and Popular Protest. Crowds, Conflict and Authority* (London, 2000), 93–122; D. Hay, 'The State and the Market in 1800: Lord Kenyon and Mr Waddington', *Past and Present*, 162 (1999), 101–162.

were not regularly schooled in legal principles, neither were they 'particularly addicted to legal investigation'. They might purchase a set of Burn's volumes or have them supplied to them by a quarter-sessions bench eager to encourage their county magistrates to relate their practices more closely to the formal law, but they could hardly be expected to wade through these huge manuals at regular intervals.[40] Nor when they did so, did magistrates necessarily feel constrained by what they read in them, as their very loose readings of the law in relation to felony accusations and the various 'defects' pinpointed by Burn's writings clearly indicate. The law as laid out in Burn or in other volumes of popular legal literature was a vital and very convenient starting point for the magistrates. However, the much publicised deficiencies of the statutory law and the sheer multiplicity of different types of legal inputs that could contribute to 'the law' left room for pragmatic interpretations and, on occasions, for the development of magisterial practices which owed more to convenience or to instrumental considerations than they did to any established foundations in written law.

The fact that the summary courts worked in a mixture of both civil and criminal modes formed a second important aspect of the context within which the nature of justice was shaped at this level. Even setting aside their roles in settlement, bastardy and tax evasion cases the majority of the hearings that came before the magistrates were more civil than criminal in nature.[41] The two often elided into one another, of course, but given that property-appropriation cases rarely formed more than a fifth of such hearings, an arbitrational, semi-civil mode of proceeding often dominated the caseloads of these courts. Many master–servant disputes, for example, were civil in nature. The most common form of summary-court hearings, those that related to an alleged assault, have yet to be fully researched by historians but these were clearly as much civil as criminal proceedings. Very few were sent on for formal indictment or resulted in the defendant being bound over to keep the peace. The most common solution was an agreement that often involved compensation as well as the payment of costs. Typical conclusions to assault proceedings before the Durham magistrate Reverend Tew, for example, were 'They paid £1. 1s and charges', 'agreed at 8s 6d', 'agreed at £1. 15s'. In 1770 the Surrey JP Richard Wyatt made a similar entry. 'John Gunner paid 8s to Elizabeth Eldridge, the assault being proved'. However, the legal basis for this awarding of damages by the summary courts

---

[40] Burn, *The Justice* (16th ed. which reprints the introduction to the 15th edn, 1788), i, xvi; Various writers took on the task of editing after Burn's death. The 28th edition was J. and T. Chitty (eds.), *The Justice of the Peace and Parish officer by Richard Burn*, (London, 1837) which ran to 6521 pages. W. Dickinson, *A Practical Exposition of the Law Relative to the Duties of a Justice of the Peace* (London, 1813, 2 vols.), i, vi; Adolphus, *Observations*, 43; Pye, *Summary of the Duties*; Smith, 'Circumventing', 445. On the legal literature – W. Holdsworth, *A History of English Law* (London, 1966) xii, 101–178.

[41] King, 'The Summary', 137.

remained extremely sketchy until 1828, when the Offences against the Person Act both gave them the formal right to levy a fine and reduced their capacity to arbitrate by insisting that the fines be paid into parish funds. Before that date Burn's justices' manuals highlighted the crossover between the civil and the criminal but made no mention of the possibility of resolution at the summary level. 'The wrong doer', he noted, 'is subject both to an action at the suit of the party, wherein he shall render damages and also an indictment at the suit of the King, whereby he shall be fined.' The former would have been via an action brought ultimately to the *nisi prius* side at the assizes, the latter by indictment, usually at the quarter sessions.[42]

The fact that the vast majority of assault cases were resolved informally in the summary courts and that a considerable number of property-appropriation cases also ended in similar agreements, alerts us to the degree to which civil law-based traditions of judicial practice could easily slide over into areas of business which in formal law might be thought of as criminal in nature. The relative freedom many magistrates enjoyed to move from civil to criminal modes and back again, as they felt necessary, is well illustrated by Samuel Whitbread's reaction to the following complaint recorded in his justicing notebook in 1811. 'Thomas Barton to complain that Edward Smith will not give him a barrel back which he lent him. Wrote a note to say that if he did not return it I should issue a warrant against him for a theft.' When no satisfaction was given by the next day a warrant was duly issued and Smith was brought before the court. The result was the production of what was essentially a civil remedy created by the threat of a criminal prosecution, albeit one that might not have stood up in court. 'Heard the complaint', Whitbread recorded, 'ordered Smith to pay 5s for the barrel, 2s for the wedges and all expenses.' He followed a similar policy in another case brought three years later, offering to grant a warrant if a man who had appropriated five dozen hurdles did not 'satisfy' the owner by the following morning. Whitbread's core aim in such cases and in many others seems to have been to produce what he thought would be a useful, flexible and roughly just solution to the case brought before him. He also called before him local residents whose creditors complained that they had refused to pay their debts and many other cases in which damages were being sought. When John Field's hogs did a great deal of damage by running into his neighbour's

---

[42] Morgan and Rushton, 'The Magistrate', 68–70; D. Gray, 'The Regulation of Violence in the Metropolis. Assault and its Consequences in the City of London in the Late Eighteenth Century.' *London Journal* (forthcoming); G. Morgan and P. Rushton (eds.), *The Justicing Notebook of Edmund Tew, Rector of Boldon* (Woodbridge, Surtees Society, vol. ccv, 2000), 128–134: For similar examples A. Cirket (ed.), *Samuel Whitbread's Notebooks, 1810–11, 1813–14*, 49, 'Settled 12s. 6d. to Eyres. 7s 6d to Bozzard, 2s 6d to constable, 2s to room'; King, 'The Summary Courts'; Anon, 'Lord Lansdowne's Act', *The Law Magazine*, 1 (1828), 139–140; Burn, *The Justice*, 10th edn (1766), i, 102; Blackstone, *Commentaries*, iii, 120–1; iv, 213. The action would have been of *trespass vi et armis*.

wheat, Whitbread summoned him to appear and ordered him to pay 12 shillings.[43]

In these and in other cases involving disputed payments, unreturned property, assaults and minor disputed frauds or appropriations, Whitbread, like Tew and most other magistrates whose justicing books have survived, aimed mainly to produce a remedy that would solve the problem presented to them and keep the peace in the broadest sense. Thus in a considerable number of the cases that came before them, the summary courts followed practices which seem to have tuned in extensively with what some historians have portrayed as the core features of the 'common law frame of mind'. In substantial subgroups of cases the magistrates provided a system of remedies that could be flexible and adaptive. Their aim, within the constraints provided by their relatively broad interpretations of the relevant legal frameworks, was to provide useful solutions to problems based on notions of policy, of justice and of the need to keep the peace in the communities whose members brought cases to them. When, as they not infrequently did, the summary courts operated less from a clear body of rules and more from a strong sense of the need to find appropriate remedies, and when the notions of justice that the magistrates of a given locality shared arose to some extent out of common practice and a sense of the pragmatic and acceptable solutions available, the summary courts were surely reflecting the broader common law traditions that still shaped much of the legal process in this period. Common law reasoning was pragmatic, contextual, unsystematic and multi-layered. At an informal level it therefore shared many characteristics with the ways magistrates approached those summary hearings in which they were not presented with a clear criminal accusation, and with some of the ways they dealt with those in which there was such an accusation.[44]

It would be wrong, of course to assume that magistrates operated in these informal ways in all types of cases. What emerges from the few sufficiently detailed summary-court records available is a spectrum of reactions to different types of case. At one end, serious felonies such as highway robbery or burglary and certain types of summarily triable thefts, such as poaching, were most likely to produce a formal response, a committal for trial or a summary conviction. At the other end, common complaints such as unpaid debts, employees seeking the payment of wages, friendly society members seeking the assistance that

---

[43] On the difficulties of dividing civil and criminal, private and public see D. Lieberman, 'Mapping Criminal Law: Blackstone and Categories of English Jurisprudence', in N. Landau, *Law, Crime and English Society 1660–1830* (Cambridge, 2002), 139–61; Cirket (ed.), *Samuel Whitbread's Notebooks*, 40, 47–8, 59 and 129; E. Silverthorne (ed.), *Deposition book of Richard Wyatt, JP, 1767–1776* (Surrey Record Society 30, 1978), 16; R. Shoemaker, *Prosecution and Punishment. Petty Crime and the Law in London and Rural Middlesex 1660–1725* (Cambridge, 1991), 81–94.

[44] M. Lobban, *The Common Law and English Jurisprudence 1760–1850* (Oxford, 1991), 9–15; G. Postema, 'The Philosophy of the Common Law' in J. Coleman and S. Shapiro (eds.), *The Oxford Handbook of Jurisprudence and Philosophy of Law* (Oxford, 2002), 589–603.

they felt entitled to or paupers seeking relief would receive a civil-style trial or a benefit tribunal type of hearing. In between, a great range of cases were dealt with in the flexible way discussed above. Assault cases in particular, unless an official was the victim, usually ended with what was effectively a civil remedy, although occasionally resort was made to formal binding over or prosecution. The range of summary-court response modes was, of course, broader than this simple spectrum would suggest. Minor infractions of the laws relating to alehouses, false weights and measures, wagons, turnpikes, etc. were fairly routinely tried and fixed fines were often imposed. Practice varied immensely from case to case, and might also depend on the social status of the accused. When dealing with middling men the magistrates were usually more careful to follow established procedures and to use, if possible, the forms laid out for them in the printed justices' handbooks. At the other end of the social scale, however, the opposite was often the case. The justices assumed wide and often ill-defined powers to punish the idle and mobile poor and this formed the third important aspect of the context within which justice was shaped at this level.

The summary courts of the eighteenth and early nineteenth centuries imprisoned very large numbers of labouring men and women for being 'idle and disorderly', for 'vagrancy', and for a huge variety of other very poorly defined offences. In counties like Devon and Cornwall in the early 1820s, for example, the numbers summarily imprisoned for 'acts of vagrancy' alone considerably outnumbered those committed for trial as felons.[45] The legal basis on which many of these commitments were made was extremely sketchy. Most, as Joanna Innes has pointed out, were made 'under generally framed – and loosely interpreted – Elizabethan and Jacobean laws.' Despite a growing number of specific statutes that identified particular offences and procedures, well into the nineteenth century the summary-court regulation of the disorderly poor continued to be based mainly on long-established practices that had only the thinnest of statutory foundations. Virtually any unhelpful practice indulged in by the poor could be used to label them as idle and disorderly and therefore suitable for temporary incarceration in the local house of correction. Most eighteenth-century gaol calendars do not describe the precise infraction involved. James Finch, for example, was simply charged with 'being a very loose and disorderly fellow and behaving very insolent before the justice', but when details are included they can be very illuminating. Mary Tabor was imprisoned in 1768 'for threatening to inoculate her children with the smallpox in order to spread the distemper in the parish'.[46]

---

[45] *P.P.*, 1826–7, xix, 185; and *P.P.*, 1824, xix, 223–6.
[46] J. Innes, 'Prisons for the Poor: English Bridewells 1555–1800' in F. Snyder and D. Hay (eds.), *Labour, Law and Crime. An Historical Perspective* (London, 1987), 86–7; Griffiths, 'Bodies and Souls', 103; ERO Q/SBb 194, 252–3.

Reading these prison calendars suggests strongly that when it came to disciplining the poor, many eighteenth-century magistrates, following the long-established practice of the lower courts, often simply imprisoned those whom they thought needed disciplining and left any contemporaries who had legal scruples to scratch around in the obscure clauses of centuries-old statutes to find some justification for their actions. Some of the categories of behaviour for which the poor were punished that can be found in the calendars can be matched up fairly easily with specific statutes, and particularly with the categories used by the 1744 Vagrant Act, but many others cannot. Prostitutes, for example, continued to be imprisoned on a considerable scale throughout this period, despite the fact that there were no statutes that specifically labelled their activities as illegal. Given the confusion that resulted, the agents of the law, as Henderson has recently pointed out, had to rely on tradition and custom. The very vagueness of the various legal formulas under which prostitutes were arrested could be useful however, as it enabled relatively large numbers of women to be taken up.[47] Similarly, by using their very general powers in relation to the idle and disorderly to imprison 'pilferers' and others who might otherwise have been accused of minor larcenies, magistrates greatly increased their potential authority – a process that was further extended by a series of acts passed from the later eighteenth century onwards, which gradually granted to urban and then rural justices the right to arrest 'reputed thieves' and 'suspected persons'. In disciplining the poor many summary courts developed customary ways of operating which gave them very considerable freedom to act in ways that best fitted the pragmatic needs of those who held authority at the local level. Justice in this context was more about policy than about the following of strict legal procedures, in part perhaps because the poor found it very difficult to appeal against the decisions of the magistracy.[48]

Although in some types of case, such as those involving a vagrant pass issued by a single magistrate, there was no possibility of appeal, various limited forms of appeal were possible, in theory at least, following most categories of summary-court hearings. However, during the long eighteenth century legal practice in this area developed into a complex mixture of contradictory precedents and dubious statutory initiatives. As parliament devolved increasing powers to the summary courts and the Star Chamber ceased to function, the judges of the King's Bench reacted by developing new supervisory roles for themselves

---

[47] T. Henderson, *Disorderly Women in Eighteenth-Century London. Prostitution and Control in the Metropolis 1730–1830* (London, 1999), 76–98. F. Dabhoiwala, 'Sex, Social Relations and the Law in Seventeenth and Eighteenth-Century London' in M. Braddick and J. Walter (eds.), *Negotiating Power in Early Modern Society* (Cambridge, 2001), 94.

[48] B. Smith, 'Circumventing', 114; T. Sweeney, 'The Extension and Practice of Summary Justice in England 1790–1860', PhD thesis, Cambridge, 1985, 93–108; Shoemaker, *Prosecution and Punishment*, 37–9, 182.

through the use of writs of *certiorari* (they already had a limited capacity to act against incorrect warrants by writ of *habeas corpus*). Parliament, in turn, then began to pass various clauses forbidding removal to King's Bench in certain types of case and introducing the possibility of using the quarter sessions instead. The latter route, described by one contemporary as 'the miserable and inadequate resource of an appeal to the session', was not very widely used. It was expensive and appeals were only heard by fellow justices and not by a jury. 'Few of the activities of petty sessions or the single justice', Landau concluded, 'were scrutinised by the supreme court of the county'.[49] In 1836 only one appeal against a summary conviction was made to the Essex quarter sessions although well over a thousand offenders a year were being committed to prison for summary offences and many more were being fined. The Cornish quarter sessions also heard only one such appeal. Inter-parish disputes over settlement matters not infrequently resulted in appeals to the major courts but summary convictions very rarely led to this outcome.[50]

In most types of case the potential for appeal by writ of *certiorari* was at least technically maintained by the King's Bench throughout this period, despite parliament's attempts to limit it. However, the processes involved remained highly problematic from the point of view of the appealing party, and it was virtually impossible for those without access to considerable funds to initiate an appeal. Parliament had insisted in 1740 that those who obtained a *certiorari* had to enter into a £50 recognisance and be liable if unsuccessful for the defendant's (usually very considerable) costs.[51] Moreover, the King's Bench generally restricted the grounds of an appeal to a review of the written record and to ensuring that the justices had acted within their jurisdictions. A review of the justices' decisions on the actual facts was not therefore usually allowed. Moreover the capacity of the King's Bench to undertake any significant review of the written record was further constrained by parliament's introduction of new forms which required only a minimal record to be made of summary convictions and which 'grew daily more lax' and less informative in the level of detail they demanded. Research on the ways the appeal process actually worked in practice is still at an early stage. The voluminous and technically complex records of the King's Bench have been one of the last archival bastions to be breached by historians of crime. Early work in this field suggests, however, that very few cases were brought and that even fewer were successful. Occasional appeals to King's Bench may have

---

[49] On the fact that parishes could not appeal against vagrant passes – T. Caldecott, *Reports of Cases Relative to the Duty and Office of a Justice of the Peace* (London, 3 vols. 1786–1800), i,18; E. Newton, *The Whole Duty of Parish Officers* (London, 1792), 112; Adolphus, *Observations*, 49; N. Landau, *The Justices of the Peace, 1679–1760* (Berkeley, 1984), 260, 343–56.

[50] *P.P.*, 1837–8, xliv, 299; *P.P.*, 1831, xv, 117–120; Landau, *The Justices*, 260 and 352. The London area, where attorneys were more often present at summary hearings had a somewhat larger number of appeals – Smith, 'Circumventing the Jury', 214.

[51] Dickinson, *A Practical Exposition*, i, 366; Landau, *The Justices*, 351.

gradually begun the process of creating a body of case law that might eventually constrain the justices' actions, and some London police magistrates may have begun to take the prospect of review by the King's Bench more seriously by the early nineteenth century. However, the degree to which the decisions of the King's Bench were recorded, communicated and (most important), acted upon outside London remains very difficult to calculate. Until the nineteenth century it would be unwise to assume that most magistrates either knew about, or felt constrained by, most of the case law that was gradually accumulating through the decisions laid down by the Westminster courts.[52]

Other ways of disciplining errant magistrates seem to have proved even more difficult to use. Hay's research on Staffordshire suggests that the King's Bench, afraid of frightening off the amateur, unpaid magistracy, were incredibly reluctant to allow them to be prosecuted for any misdemeanours they may have committed in office – even when their decisions were not only ignorant and mistaken but also ill-willed. The rural magistracy, he concludes, were effectively insulated from legal retribution – a conclusion that is confirmed by the fact that only just over two criminal informations a year were brought against the entire magistracy of England and Wales in the 1820s and 1830s. Many more of the less wealthy people who appeared before the summary courts may well have wanted to complain, but may simply have found the magistrate too powerful to gainsay. The only person who threatened the clerical magistrate Edmund Tew with the King's Bench between 1750 and 1765 ended up in gaol and was forced to apologise to Tew before the whole parish.[53] We know very little about civil suits against magistrates. However, most were only possible once the King's Bench had quashed the original judgement and since this rarely happened, the number of such suits that were successful must have been relatively small. The various safeguards created by parliament to prevent justices being liable for significant sums, appear to have been so successful that by the early nineteenth century even those who acknowledged that it was proper to protect the unpaid magistracy were having doubts. 'I am far from thinking that captious actions against justices ought to be encouraged' a barrister observed in 1824. However, in his anger at the much wider powers given to magistrates by the recent vagrant act, he was also very critical of parliament's stance. 'Ample provision has been made by different statutes for the protection of justices who act illegally in the execution of their extensive duties', he wrote. 'It seems rather extraordinary

---

[52] B. Smith, 'Circumventing', 212; Landau, *The Justices*, 346–54; Adolphus, *Observations*, 104; D. Hay, 'Dread of the Crown Office: the English Magistracy and the King's Bench, 1740–1800' in Landau (ed.), *Law, Crime*, 25; D. Hay, 'England 1562–1875: The Law and its Uses' in D. Hay and P. Craven (eds.), *Masters, Servants and Magistrates in Britain and the Empire 1562–1955* (Chapel Hill, 2004), 91.

[53] Hay, 'Dread of the Crown Office', 43; *P.P.*, 1831, xv, 87; *P.P.*, 1834, xlviii, 249. In the 14 years for which information is available (1820–33) 33 cases were heard. Morgan and Rushton, 'The Magistrate', 75.

that they who undertake to execute the laws should be so absolutely protected in the perversion and violation of them.' The effect, he argued was to encourage some magistrates, including the Middlesex police justices paid by the state, to take little notice of the law. 'In many instances', he wrote, 'the certainty of immunity produces an obstinate wrongheadedness and a determined contempt for the law. I have heard from the mouths of some such declarations as this "Well, I shall do as I please; if I am wrong, I am indemnified."'[54] Much more research needs to be done in this area but at this stage it appears that the various legal provisions which might have facilitated appeal against the decisions of the summary courts looked more useful in the law books than they were in reality. Unlike the modern English legal system where systematic review and appeal is usually possible and the lower courts therefore view themselves as inextricably bound by the decisions of the superior courts, the eighteenth-century summary courts were much less constrained by a systematic judicial hierarchy. At times they were hardly constrained at all. Nor did they operate at a time when government bureaucracy was sufficiently large to enable the magistrates' activities to be effectively monitored from above. The Earl of Minto's observation that 'magistrates . . . are responsible to no one' may have been an exaggeration by the time he made it in the 1830s, but in many situations it came close to describing the eighteenth-century reality. By various processes, Landau concluded, 'both judges and parliament shielded the nation's amateur rulers . . . The justices' rule was praiseworthy, even when strictly speaking it happened to be illegal.' The central authorities knew that they needed the confidence of the justices and they acted accordingly. 'Frequent mistakes are committed in the interpretation of the law' one commentator noted in 1829. 'It cannot be expected that gentlemen, not professionally educated, and who have their private affairs to manage, can always be *au fait* to the matters brought before them; and while their services continue gratuitous it hardly appears reasonable to subject them to severer discipline.' In the eighteenth century, as Hay has recently concluded, 'the high law of King's Bench effectively protected the low law of most provincial justices from being questioned, curbed or controlled.'[55] In the process the legal system,

---

[54] Landau, *The Justices*, 353–4; Pye, *Summary of the Duties*, xv–xvi; Adolphus, *Observations*, 99–101; Magistrates who dared to arrest lawyers who were acting improperly during summary proceedings were occasionally taken by those lawyers to the Westminster courts for assault or false imprisonment – J. Oldham, *The Mansfield Manuscripts and the Growth of English Law in the Eighteenth Century* (Chapel Hill, 1992), ii, 1023–6, 1042–4. On one of those two occasions the plaintiff actually won the case and obtained one shilling in damages and costs. However, this victory may not be unrelated to the fact that the lawyer who was manhandled on this occasion was 'an attorney of the King's Bench' – surely revealing a major tactical error by the Bow Street magistrate who ordered his forcible removal.

[55] D. Philips, 'A Weak State? The English State, the Magistracy and the Reform of Policing in the 1830s', *English Historical Review*, 119 (2004), 879; Landau, *The Justices*, 252–5; Hay, 'Dread of the Crown Office', 45.

if system we can call it, created a very large space within which the magistrates could shape and sometimes remake justicing practice in the summary courts.

V

By the second quarter of the nineteenth century things were beginning to change. The space available to magistrates may have been gradually contracting by the end of the eighteenth century – especially in London where the summary courts were open and lawyers were almost certainly much more in evidence. However, despite some attempts to lay down more specific procedural rules in certain sorts of cases, great leeway continued to be available in most areas of summary-court practice well into the nineteenth century. Moreover, in some ways statutory activity could be seen as briefly increasing their discretionary powers. Certainly the passing of a number of acts in the early 1820s – such as the Vagrancy Acts and the 1820 Malicious Trespass Act – brought a barrage of criticism about the criminalisation of behaviour which some observers felt had not previously been systematically subjected to summary prosecution.[56]

In the second quarter of the nineteenth century the balance changed decisively. Parliament and central government seized the initiative with a series of legislative changes, and the notion that only parliament had the authority to introduce legal change began to take an increasing hold. Government ministers for the first time played a major and growing role in initiating and pushing through legislation on crime and justice issues, while, by contrast, the judges of the central courts became much more timid about their potential law-making role.[57] The larceny acts were consolidated in 1827. In 1828 the summary court role in assault cases was regularised and their powers much more clearly defined. Between 1847 and 1855, after thirty years of debate, a series of acts finally provided a solid statutory basis for the ways many magistrates had long dealt with certain types of felony cases. Most important of all perhaps, various small-scale attempts to regularise magistrates' practices culminated in 1848–9 in a series of acts that established a standard set of procedures for the English summary courts.[58]

---

[56] M. Roberts, 'Public and Private in Early Nineteenth-Century London: The Vagrant Act of 1822 and its Enforcement', *Social History*, 13 (1988), 273–94; Adolphus, *Observations*; S. Magarey, 'The Invention of Juvenile Delinquency in Early Nineteenth-Century England', *Labour History* (Canberra), 34 (1978), 11–27.

[57] J. Innes and A. Burns, 'Introduction', to their edited volume, *Rethinking the Age of Reform. Britain 1780–1850* (Cambridge, 2004), 51; J. Baker, *An Introduction to English Legal History*, 4th edn (London, 2002), 217.

[58] Smith, 'Circumventing', 405–66 on the formalisation of summary jurisdiction 1825–55. On the 1828 act as a decisive step see J. Carter Wood, *Violence and Crime in Nineteenth-Century England. The Shadow of our Refinement* (London, 2004), 29; D. Bentley, *English Criminal Justice in the Nineteenth Century* (London, 1998), 22–5.

In important respects therefore, the period from the mid-1820s onwards witnessed central initiatives that on the one hand confirmed by statute the ways that the summary courts had already shaped and sometimes remade justicing practice, while at the same time making it much more difficult for those courts to be so innovative in the future. The pattern of lawmaking in general was changing by the mid-nineteenth century. The relationship between the courts and parliament was also altering significantly. Parliament was becoming more dominant in the lawmaking process, while at the same time government was gradually drawing the business of legislation into its own hands. Other government reforms, such as the introduction of the New Poor Law in 1834 and of a new statutory framework for the regulation of alehouses, not to mention the coming of the new police, were also seriously eroding certain important areas in which magistrates had enjoyed extensive decision-making powers. By mid-century the trade unions were demanding changes in another important area of summary business – master–servant law – and new mechanisms of appeal against magistrate's decisions were beginning to be introduced. The summary courts were moving into an almost completely criminal mode and the number of areas in which magistrates enjoyed extensive freedom was gradually declining.[59]

At this stage of research historians still know relatively little about the mind set, the discursive frameworks and ways of seeing their roles, that shaped the actions of those who ran the summary courts from the late seventeenth to the early nineteenth century. Attitudes and practices would have varied to some extent according to context, geography and individual personality. When acting as a group at petty sessions, magistrates sometimes approached matters rather more formally than when sitting alone. London magistrates, who often operated in open courts and increasingly frequently in the presence of lawyers, would not necessarily have had the same attitudes as rural JPs acting alone in their own parlours. Social background could also influence attitudes. Clerical magistrates, marginal gentry and parvenus trying to work their way into county society may have approached the role in a more distanced manner than the few long-established gentry who were still active magistrates in the areas were they had large landholdings.[60] In London, trading justices would have brought a more entrepreneurial perspective in some types of case, and the stipendiary magistrates, who became increasingly significant after 1792, may sometimes have been more attuned to government agendas. Magisterial attitudes would

[59] P. Atiyah, *The Rise and Fall of Freedom of Contract* (Oxford, 1979), 254–5, 383–6; Lobban, *The Common Law*, 186–7; S. Anderson, 'Discretion and the Rule of Law: The Licensing of Drink in England 1817–40', *Legal History*, 23 (2002) 45–59; Bentley, *English Criminal Justice*, 24–5. The Webbs labelled this period perhaps rather over-dramatically as the years of 'The Stripping of the Oligarchy' – S. and B. Webb, *English Local Government from the Revolution to the Municipal Corporations Act: The Parish and the County* (London, 1906), 602–5.
[60] King, 'The Summary Courts'; Landau, *The Justices*, 333–66 for a sophisticated analysis of changing models of justicing. King, *Crime, Justice*, 110–25.

also have changed over time. Towards the end of the period, as procedures in the summary courts became a matter of increasing concern, more attention may have been paid to formal legal frameworks. However, many of the core practices, such as the filtering of felony cases, and the semi-civil adjudication of assaults and of many other offences, can be observed in a very wide variety of summary courts from the rotation offices and post-1792 police courts of the metropolis to the rural justicing rooms of Tew, Whitbread and Hunt.[61] There was diversity but there was also a huge amount of common ground.

The magistrates of England rarely, if ever, challenged the statutory law directly, but they could still, on occasions, render it largely superfluous. Many took a very pragmatic approach, working their way around it when they thought it necessary to do so. The law might say that two magistrates had to sit together to hear certain types of cases, but when this was simply too inconvenient the justices not infrequently developed means of circumventing the statutes. The law might require that summary conviction certificates be systematically sent for filing to the quarter sessions but the records of the latter make it clear that most magistrates honoured this regulation only in the breach. The same flexible approach also characterised the justices' methods of handling their statutory obligation to funnel all felony accusations on to the major courts. It often seemed unjust or impolitic to send felons against whom the evidence was not especially strong on for jury trial and it also involved a lot more expense, time and paperwork than dealing with them summarily. Magistrates therefore found ways round the law when they thought it appropriate to do so. There are interesting parallels here with civil law developments. Just as, to quote Lieberman, 'eighteenth-century lawyers were well aware that prominent portions of their law had developed through judicial evasion of acts of parliament', so many justices of the peace must have been equally aware, as Burn certainly was, that at least some of their practices were also quiet evasions of statute law. They could not openly go against statute but they did not always have to go with it, and for this reason some aspects of summary-court practice appear to have owed less to statute law than to the gradual solidification of the magistrates own procedures and also perhaps to the much vaguer set of notions inherited from the broad traditions of the common law.[62]

---

[61] N. Landau, 'The Trading Justice's Trade' in Landau, *Law, Crime*, 46–70; J. Innes, 'Statute Law and Summary Justice in Early Modern England' (unpublished paper 1986).

[62] Lieberman, *The Province*, 53. Holdsworth, *A History*, xii, 107 comments on the 'power of the common law to impose its own conceptions on other systems of law'. Introducing the concept of the common law in this context is inevitably highly problematic. Definitions differ and it is often assumed that common law equals judge-made law. In reality however, common law is not just judicial law, case law or judge-made law but also includes customary law and unwritten law – A. Simpson, 'The Common Law and Legal Theory' in his edited volume, *Oxford Essays in Jurisprudence*, 2nd series (Oxford, 1973), 77. Here I have followed Postema by defining it in a way more appropriate to the period before the nineteenth century when the concept of *stare*

As Burn's critique, and our observations of various aspects of court procedure have shown, justice's law and the practice of justice were not always
easily reduced to precise and positive rules. We therefore need (to borrow terms
from another debate) to be less positivistic in our approach to the ways justice
and even 'law' were made in the long eighteenth century. Legal positivism
which, crudely defined, views the law as a formal logical system of laid down
rules and tends to base its view of all law on the model of statute law, has had a
major influence on the philosophy of law since the nineteenth century. However,
its usefulness in approaching the legal history of the eighteenth century, with
its weaker legislative frameworks and lack of a solid hierarchy of court jurisdictions, is not always apparent. Although rulings made by the higher courts
on the contradictions found in the statutes sometimes added some consistency,
the law in the eighteenth century was not a discrete and logically consistent
code of rules. Nor was there a complete and systematic hierarchy of courts that
could fully ensure consistency, particularly in relation to the summary courts.
For example, the lack of any specific legally laid down spatial divisions at summary level, which gave complainants the ability to choose which local justice
they went to, added a market-led element to an already disjointed jurisdictional
picture. The law and the structure of the courts were more chaotic and muddled,
less cut and dried, than a positivistic perspective would imply. Statutes were
sometimes worked round as much as they were worked through, whilst at the
same time some of the justices' practices gradually solidified into law, or were
made law by parliament in a post hoc fashion.

For the student of justice before the nineteenth century it may therefore
be more fruitful to borrow from the ideas of those legal theorists who focus
primarily on the law in action rather than the law in books. To them the idea
that legal rules are certain and that their application to specific cases by the
courts is simply a rational, mechanical and largely bureaucratic process is often
a myth, albeit a very potent one. Their perspective is more 'bottom up' and
starts, as we have here, with the everyday workings and customary practices
of the courts. To fully understand the lower courts and the ways they helped to
shape the nature of justice, it is important to define law not simply as black-letter
law but also as a group of real practices played out in the courts in response
to the situations presented to them. We will get closer to understanding what
justice meant to those who had contact with the courts in the eighteenth century
by defining law in a non-doctrinal way as what the courts in a particular place
will do in the next case brought before them, rather than as what the courts

---

decisis was fully established. Common law in the eighteenth century would not necessarily have
been seen as 'a structured set of authoritatively posited, explicit norms' but rather as 'a body of
practices and patterns of practical thinking', as common custom and 'common reason tried by
time'– Postema, 'Philosophy of the Common Law', 588–91.The issue of how these concepts can
be made relevant to an analysis of the civil, the criminal and the mixed civil/criminal hearings
of the summary courts is too large to be pursued here but is worthy of further study.

should do if they followed statute law, or what the courts say they are doing, or what contemporary jurists who wanted to justify their actions said they were doing.[63] Justice, and law in this broader sense, were shaped by many forces in the eighteenth century and, in the summary courts at least, it is as useful to start with the customary practices of the courts as it is to search the statute books, the justices' law manuals or the unsystematically and privately recorded case law that found its way into print. Neither practice nor print is sufficient in itself, for justice was shaped by the complex interactions between law in action and the law in books. However, by prioritising the latter, we may have underestimated the extent to which justice was shaped and sometimes remade from below within the English legal system.

VI

Eighteenth-century England was, it appears, home to a multi-layered system of criminal justice administration, each layer of which was able to shape some areas of justice in practice – to shape the way justice was done. The lowest level, the summary courts, probably had the most room for manoeuvre. They were less open and less lawyer-penetrated, and their decisions were very difficult to take to appeal. At the same time their geographical diffusion and their ad hoc administrative arrangements made them the most diverse and least connected of the court structures. Change was therefore easier to achieve but at the same time it tended to be more piecemeal, less debated and less fully co-ordinated. At the quarter-sessions level criminal business was held in open court and formal law had more of a hold on trial procedure and post-trial disposal, but these courts also exercised considerable autonomy. Since, as Eastwood has recently argued, most quarter sessions developed an independent capacity for policy-making during the Hanoverian period, it is hardly surprising that in substantial areas of criminal justice practice, such as the use of imprisonment in assault cases, the ending of the public whipping of women or the introduction of solitary confinement stipulations into sentencing policies, they made substantial innovations. 'The principle responsibility for policy in key areas such as poor relief, police, penal policy and social policy lay with magistrates as an agency and quarter sessions as an institution,' Eastwood has pointed out, and since the magistracy and the quarter sessions were 'accountable to no-one', it is hardly surprising to find both the summary courts and the sessions remaking certain aspects of justicing policy. Finally, although the assizes and the Old

---

[63] Simpson, 'The Common Law', 80–88; on the different strands of legal realist thought and its connection to later legal theory see, for example, M. Freeman, *Lloyd's Introduction to Jurisprudence*, 7th edn (London, 2001), 684–91, 799–813, 1040–56; R. Cotterell, *The Politics of Jurisprudence. A Critical Introduction to Legal Philosophy* (London, 1989), 188–215; S. Anleu, *Law and Social Change* (London, 2000), 6–9. D. Seipp, 'The Laws many Bodies, and the Manuscript Tradition in English Legal History', *Journal of Legal History*, 25 (2004).

Bailey were under the heaviest scrutiny because their proceedings were not only public but were also (in the latter case at least) regularly reported in print, change was also generated at this level too. The judicial policies of the assize courts may have been more in tune with the centre because the assize judges spent most of their year running the higher courts at Westminster, or because they had closer links with government (for whom some had already served in such positions as attorney general or solicitor general). However, by evolving new practices on the ground the assizes were also able to change important aspects of justice such as the strictness of evidentiary rules and the development of new sentencing options.[64]

Our understanding of the multiple interactions that shaped the nature of justice as it was experienced in these courts remains very limited because many key areas have yet to be researched. For example, one of the central issues – the extent to which the judgements handed down by the various Westminster courts actually influenced local practice – needs to be meticulously researched on a case by case basis, as the analysis of the 1788 gleaning judgement in chapters 9 and 10 makes clear. The limited case studies so far available indicate that both the degree to which case law was created by the major courts, and the impact that that case law had on the ground, depended very much on which facet of the law was involved. Where propertied interests were at stake and lawyers were frequently employed, case law might accumulate quite rapidly. The settlement laws, for example, and in particular the hearings at various levels of the court system that might end in the removal of a pauper, soon became surrounded by a huge body of case law. These matters affected ratepayers' pockets very directly and individual vestries were willing to pay for lengthy litigation in order to avoid responsibility for potentially expensive paupers. Case law therefore proliferated very rapidly. By the 1830s over 650 pages of Burn's manual were dedicated to summarising settlement and removal law, making it a legal minefield in its own right. Yet, even here it is extremely difficult to establish to what degree, and at what point, the case law that had been created by the central courts began to have a significant impact on actual magisterial practice. As one eighteenth-century observer noted in relation to appeals against removal orders,

> it may seem strange, that any doubt should remain on this subject, after so many cases have been resolved in the Kings Bench; but let anyone consider, how little those resolutions are known to the generality of country gentlemen; and when known how little they are regarded.[65]

---

[64] Eastwood, *Government*, 109; The Webbs even wrote about 'An extra-legal county hierarchy'- *Parish and the County*, 550–1; Smith, *Lawyers, Legislators*, 52.

[65] Chitty, *The Justice*, iv, 269–927; for the detailed archival work on the lawyers' role – C. Vialls, 'The Laws of Settlement: Their Impact on the Poor Inhabitants of the Daventry Area of Northamptonshire 1750–1834', PhD thesis Leicester University 1998; Anon, *Remarks on the Laws relating to the Poor with Proposals for their Better Relief and Employment by a Member of Parliament* (London, 1735), 12.

In other areas of the law the impact of the central courts is more easily assessed because they were so infrequently involved in adjudicating relevant cases. For example, case law relating to the key questions often raised by the poor themselves, such as when the semi-destitute should be paid poor relief, or by what legal mechanisms could employers be brought to book for not paying wages, was often very thin on the ground. Lacking the stimulus provided by groups of rich litigants willing to employ counsel to pursue every debatable legal issue, these areas of case law tended to develop very slowly, if at all. Equally the wide powers claimed by magistrates on the basis of a few dubiously interpreted clauses in early modern statutes, which enabled them to incarcerate any poor person whom they deemed to be idle and disorderly, remained largely unaffected by the development of complex case law structures until relatively late in the period being studied here.

When one of the few effective eighteenth-century departments of state became involved, the situation might be rather different, particularly if Britain's national security was at stake. In the controversial area of impressment law, for example, the admiralty invested considerable legal resources in attempting to protect the activities of its press gangs. In particular it tried to ensure that favourable judgements handed down by both the provincial assizes courts and by the Westminster courts were consolidated and brought to bear, if possible, on future magisterial decisions.[66] However, even this relatively well-resourced arm of government was not always successful in influencing the decisions made by the summary courts. Magistrates sometimes expressly refused to back press warrants, especially when impressment occurred before war was officially declared. In many towns and cities the magistrates frequently used both legal and illegal means to frustrate recruitment. Liverpool's magistracy, partly in response to popular pressure, threatened to throw any impressment officer who tried to operate in their jurisdiction into gaol and in the later eighteenth century the City of London was equally uncooperative.

The law in this area was difficult to unravel. The activities of the press gangs were very heavily criticised and often lacked any formal statutory backing. As Nicholas Rogers has recently pointed out, 'naval impressment was a very contentious issue in the eighteenth century, involving a good deal of give-and-take among the interested parties about what was legal.'[67] However, the City of London authorities exhibited precious little of the required flexibility. Although only the most radical of those involved in the government of the City continued to challenge the overall legality of impressment, the city authorities insisted that their magistrates should be in control of the process. Their resulting refusal to back press warrants in the City caused considerable problems both

[66] N. Rogers, 'Impressment and the Law in Eighteenth-Century Britain' in Landau (ed.), *Law, Crime*, 71–94.

[67] *Ibid.*, 72–5; N. Rogers, *Crowds, Culture and Politics in Georgian Britain* (Oxford, 1998), 100–6; N. Rodger, *The Wooden World. An Anatomy of the Georgian Navy* (London, 1986), 168–9.

during the temporary mobilisation of 1770 and at the beginning of the American War a few years later. Moreover, when a fresh mobilisation occurred in 1787 a direct confrontation was widely reported. 'The Lord Mayor has declared his resolution not to back any press warrants', *The Times* observed in late September. He also insisted that anyone taken up with a view to impressment 'be carried before him, or some other City magistrate, before they are sent on board the tender.' Although legal opinion was divided about whether the local magistrates' consent was strictly necessary in this situation, the London justices backed this edict up with force. 'Orders are given', several newspapers reported in early October 'to the City patrol, that if they see any press gang drag any person out of the city without taking them before a magistrate, to . . . apprehend the officer and gang that they may be punished.'[68] A few days later this resulted in a direct confrontation between the City's chief magistrate, the Lord Mayor, and the leading figures in the government. When the Prime Minister, the first Lord of the Admiralty and the Lord Chancellor called a meeting and demanded that he 'back the press warrants for the City', the Lord Mayor 'doubted their legality.' The Lord Chancellor then haughtily responded that 'his Lordship might be a very good tradesman, but he was not a politician' and that as to the warrants 'he (as Lord Chancellor) pronounced them to be legal.' However, the Lord Mayor refused to agree and, if the newspaper reports are correct, neither side gave way. 'Mr Pitt said that press-warrants were legal. The Lord Mayor however still doubted and withdrew.' Since the latter gave strict orders to the city marshalls the same day 'to see that no persons are attempted to be pressed in the City, but what are previously brought before him or some of the aldermen for examination,' the Lord Chancellor's definition of the law had not prevailed over that of the magistrates. The city authorities were, however, divided over the issue and after considerable debate this led to various compromise gestures including the offering of a bounty, but not, it seems, to a change in the City's policies towards press warrants.[69]

The role played by the Admiralty and other central government bodies, not to mention the intractability of many urban magistrates on this subject, meant that impressment law was a very exceptional area. There was much at stake and the resulting conflicts were often well publicised. High-court judges and even the Lord Chancellor were prepared to explicitly clarify their view of the law, albeit

---

[68] Rogers, *Crowds, Culture*, 104–19; J. Woods, 'The City of London and Impressment 1776–7', *Proceedings of the Leeds Philosophical Society*, 8 (1956), 111–27; *The Times*, 29 Sept. 1787; *The World*, 9 Oct. 1787; *London Chronicle*, 6–9 Oct. 1787; Rodger, *The Wooden World*, 168; For the background to the conflict and the use the London courts themselves made of impressment as a means of dealing with accused felons – P. King, 'War as a Judicial Resource. Press Gangs and Prosecution Rates 1740–1830', in Landau, *Law, Crime*, 97–116. The City patrol had only been formed a few years earlier – A. Harris, 'Policing and Public Order in the City of London, 1784–1815', *London Journal*, 28, (2003) 1–20.

[69] *London Chronicle*, 9–11 and 11–13 Oct. 1787.

with indifferent results. However, in fields of law where national security was not an issue, neither central government nor the Westminster courts tended to get so involved, especially if the substantial material interests of the propertied, or politically sensitive issues such as impressment, were not at stake. In most areas, therefore, case law developed much less systematically and took much longer to take hold on the ground. For a considerable part of the eighteenth century the reporting of case law in most types of criminal cases remained extremely patchy, rudimentary and of only limited use. Even the gradual growth of legal treatises and textbooks did not necessarily solve the problem. The textbooks themselves differed in style according to the motives and attitudes of the compiler and some of them contained many dubious judgements. Their dissemination was patchy, their authority was questioned and their authors were sometimes heavily criticised by other lawyers. Many were 'hasty indigested things', one mid-eighteenth-century authority argued, 'mere fragments of learning, the rummage of dead men's papers, or the first essays of young authors . . . They always bewilder the reader, and frequently mislead him.' In some areas, such as the laws governing press gangs, case law might develop considerable purchase. However, in many more everyday areas of criminal justice administration, decisions often failed to be included in case reports and even if they were their impact may have been minimal. As Martin Wiener has recently pointed out in his work on the nineteenth century, case law rarely spoke with one voice. Moreover the existence of three technically equal Westminster courts at the centre, all of which might pass judgements relevant to a specific area of legal practice such as game offences, caused further confusion. For these reasons and for more pragmatic ones, the lower courts might simply ignore the decisions of the Westminster courts as they often did in the case of the 1788 gleaning judgement discussed in chapters 9 and 10. Moreover, the 1788 judgement was not the only well-publicised case in which Lord Loughborough, who was chief justice of the Court of Common Pleas between 1780 and 1793 and then Lord Chancellor, failed to change the practices of the summary courts. He was equally unsuccessful three years earlier when, despite a very public pronouncement that one of the examination procedures in widespread use in these courts had no legal foundations, he singularly failed to alter practice on the ground.[70]

---

[70] The first regular and quickly available published series of reports brought out for King's Bench started in 1785 – J. Baker, *An Introduction to Legal History*, 4th edn (London, 2002), 184; Holdsworth, *A History*, xii, 138–9; *P.P.*, 1834, xxvi, 52 quoting Foster's *Crown Law* published in 1762. J. Oldham, 'Law-Making at *Nisi Prius* in the Early 1800s', *Journal of Legal History*, 25, (2004) 224–5. M. Wiener, *Men of Blood: Violence, Manliness, and Criminal Justice in Victorian England* (Cambridge, 2004), 14; the tripartite division of responsibility was sometimes further complicated by the different political/ideological stances of the men who sat in each court – J.Getzler, 'Judges and Hunters: Law and Economic Conflict in the English Countryside, 1800–60' in C. Brooks and M. Lobban (eds.), *Communities and Courts in Britain 1150–1900* (London, 1997), 227.

By the second half of the eighteenth century the summary courts in many areas were imprisoning a very considerable number of prisoners for short periods of time 'for further examination.' However, the legal foundations for this practice were far from clear. Apart from the vague powers they exercised 'over persons of ill fame', the magistrates' use of the further examination procedure was based mainly on a statute passed in 1752. This allowed them to incarcerate suspects for a maximum of six days on three conditions – that the case be examined before two magistrates, that an examination of the offender be transmitted to the next sessions to be filed, and that during that six days the overseers of the poor 'advertise in some public paper, a description of the offender and anything that shall be found on him'. However, neither provincial nor London magistrates let this prevent them (often after hearing cases alone) from holding offenders for various periods of time – sometimes without taking an examination and usually without sending in the relevant documentation to the sessions or bothering to advertise the details of the accused in the papers. The latter condition was in any case very difficult to fulfil outside London, because the weekly nature of most provincial newspapers meant that it would often have been impossible to place an advert within the period fixed by statute. Even in London, where it would have been possible, such advertisements do not appear to have been placed in most cases. The courts had clearly developed their own practices with very little reference to formal legal structures.[71]

These developing summary-court practices came under serious central-court scrutiny, however, in the mid-1780s when the Bow Street magistrate William Addington, made the mistake of imprisoning a 'respectable publican' for nearly a week for further examination without even taking an examination from the accused. When the publican then brought an action against Addington at the Court of Common Pleas, Lord Loughborough immediately censured the practice and was 'highly offended' when a Bow Street clerk appearing for the defence claimed that, owing to the weight of business, 'it was usual practice to imprison for further examination.'

Lord Loughborough announced the law would not endure such practice. It was an abominable practice when men were taken up only on *suspicion*, to

---

[71] King, *Crime, Justice*, 93–5; Burn, *The Justice* (1776), iv, 318–19. It was also stipulated that 'the accused should have been arrested upon a general privy search or by special warrant' and for this reason Burn placed the relevant reference under the heading of 'vagrants'. Early eighteenth-century legal writers had generally recognised the magistrates' right to hold prisoners for no longer than three days in this context; G. Jacob, *An Appendix to the Modern Justice* (London, 1718), 33; S. Blackerby, *Cases in Law Wherein Justices of Peace have a Jurisdiction* (London, 1717), 76 and 109; see also M. Bacon, *A New Abridgement of the Law by a Gentleman of the Middle Temple* (5 vols., London, 1736–66) v, 166. However more flexible phrases such as 'a reasonable time' can be found in nineteenth-century texts – Burn, *The Justice*, 24th edn (1825), i, 1008–9; In addition those found in possession of horses suspected to be stolen could be detained for 6 days under 26 Geo III. c. 71 – see Burn, *The Justice*, 21st edn (1810), ii, 743.

commit them to gaol and load them with irons – and this before any evidence
was given against them . . . It was a mode of proceeding pregnant with all
the evils of an *ex post facto* law; the constitution abhorred it, and from him
it should ever meet with reprobation.

After Loughborough made it clear that committing for further examination
threatened the liberty of the subject and that 'he would not allow such a defence
to be set up before him as a legal one' the verdict was in little doubt. *The Times*
reported that 'the jury gave the plaintiff £300 damages with full costs of suit.'[72]

The following day *The Times* expressed admiration at Lord Loughborough's
zeal and his reprobation of those 'magisterial tyrants the justices'. The judgement would, it hoped, 'operate in terrorem, and restrain not only the individual
but all his brethren from the exercise of repression in future.' It soon became
clear, however, that this well-publicised high-court judgement had had virtually
no impact at all. *The Whitehall Evening Post*, which had also reported the original judgement went on noting commitments for further examination without
making any reference to the fact that it had just been so heavily criticised and
The Times specifically commented on its lack of impact. 'Notwithstanding the
damages given against Mr Justice Addington for postponing the examination
of accused parties,' it reported a few days later, 'the practice is continued by
the justices of the rotation offices.' After quoting the case of John Strickland,
who had just been kept in prison for six days 'without any proof against him'
and then re-examined and released 'the felony with which he stood charged
not being proved', the paper expressed its disgust that the justices continued to
follow the practice despite Lord Loughborough's pronouncement in the Court
of Common Pleas that 'it was contrary to the law and the constitution.'[73]

Lord Loughborough's attempt to lay down the law on this issue may have
briefly influenced the relevant entry in Burn's justicing manual. In the 1770s
Burn completely ignored the problems provincial magistrates would have had
in placing adverts within six days, but in the first new edition to come out after
1785 the manual's editor did finally acknowledge that 'by the shortness of the
time limited for advertising this (the 1752 Act) seems chiefly calculated for
places within the bills of mortality.' However, it is clear from the summary-
court records that, despite the lack of any statutory backing, the widely publicised strictures of a high-court judge and the tactful reminder offered by Burn's
manual, magistrates both in London and in the provinces continued to make

[72] *The Times*, 5 Dec. 1785. This incident was part of a longer history of conflict. The London
magistrates' use of further examination strategies had also come under heavy fire in the previous
decade. For an exploration of this see J. Beattie, 'John Fielding and the Bow Street Magistrates
Court' (forthcoming).
[73] *The Times*, 6 and 10 Dec. 1785; *Whitehall Evening Post*, 3–6 and 10–13 Dec. 1785; Other papers
reported Strickland's imprisonment for re-examination without referring to the Common Pleas
case at all – *Morning Post and Daily Advertiser*, 3 and 9 Dec. 1785.

very wide use of this strategy. By the later 1790s, the new caveat found in the 1788 edition had been removed from subsequent editions of Burn's justice's manual. Given that customary practice in the summary courts had ignored all these warnings and blithely continued to act 'contrary to law and the constitution' the additional clause had presumably become an embarrassment. By the first two decades of the nineteenth century witnesses before various parliamentary committees, and many other contemporary observers, made it clear that Loughborough's pronouncement that imprisonment for further examination was against the law was being almost completely ignored. In 1816–17 an average of 500 prisoners a year were being committed to the Cold Bath Fields House of Correction 'for re-examination' and the period of imprisonment involved was usually between ten days and a fortnight. Nor was the practice confined to the metropolis. In 1809 the chairman of the Gloucestershire quarter sessions was highly critical of his fellow magistrates who, for reasons 'of convenience or of local utility' were subjecting large numbers of accused felons to long periods of imprisonment for further examination without any authority that could be 'proved to be lawful'. In Bristol alone, for example, he found that out of a sample of 1871 commitments 596 were 'suspected felons detained for further examination', and that the average period of their detention was 'more than 14 days.' A decade and a half later it emerged that the Monmouthshire justices were following similar practices when a man accused of horse theft was held for over two months without being either further examined or committed for trial.[74] The 1785 case therefore seems to offer further support for Hay's suggestion that it would be 'misleading to assume that the lay magistrates of the eighteenth century were always aware of the doctrine in the high courts, or greatly constrained by it.' Even if they were aware of Lord Loughborough's pronouncements they clearly worked round them so effectively as to virtually nullify their effect.[75]

Research on the impact of high-court decisions is still at a very early stage and needs to be done on a detailed case-by-case basis. However, given that both systematic reporting of criminal law cases and a formalised notion of precedent were only just beginning to become established at the end of the eighteenth century, it is not surprising that many of the judgements in relation to criminal law matters handed down by the Westminster courts failed to gain purchase on

---

[74] Burn, *The Justice*, 16th ed. (1788), iv, 366–7; 18th ed. (1797), iv, 267–8; King, *Crime, Justice*, 93–5. *P.P.*, 1818, viii, 67 and 82. Paul, *Address*, 102; The full complexity of common law traditions and case law in this situation has yet to be fully researched. Burn, *The Justice*, 24th edn (1825), i, 1008–10. By the 1840s this source was openly recording the extended uses of further examination, pointing out that in 'the best-regulated police offices there are many instances of prisoners being detained much more than 20 days, between their first being brought up before a justice and their commitment for trial, and being brought up for examination several different days during the interval'. Burn, *The Justice*, 29th edn (1845), i, 471.

[75] Hay and Craven, *Masters, Servants*, 91.

the ground. This may have begun to change in the early nineteenth century, but there were still complex problems to be overcome. The first report of the Royal Commission on the Criminal Law, produced in 1834, highlighted the confusing multiplicity of sources within which the relevant cases might sometimes be discovered. It also stressed the private and 'inexpedient' nature of the individual reports, their frequent failure to even record the result of the case, and their many ambiguities, inconsistencies and mistakes. Moreover, not all case law was of equal value. For example, when the judges in a particular case had disagreed, or when the reporter involved was not held in high esteem, less weight could be given to the decision.[76] Legal treatises came under equally heavy criticism from the commission. These texts and their authors needed to be approached with 'great caution', they suggested. Considerable discrepancies were to be met with even in the best, and many relied on older authorities the greater part of whose works 'from changes that have occurred in the law, have become obsolete.' The relative lack of case law in some areas of the criminal law was also a problem. 'The difficulty experienced in digesting the criminal law from isolated decisions' could lead, they suggested, to different rules being deduced on the same subject. The criminal law commissioners had their own agendas, of course, and they were not well disposed towards the common law, but it appears that a considerable number of contemporaries shared many of their views. Thus, although a growing body of legal handbooks attempting to summarise both case law and the statute law were gradually becoming available between 1800 and 1825, and a few areas such as settlement law were deliberately tackled by the Westminster courts, well into the nineteenth century the judgements of the high courts may have had only a very limited ability to dictate the framework within which the lower courts operated in criminal law cases.[77]

The development of case law and its communication through various means including printed reports and legal treatises was, of course, only one of many ways in which courts at different levels interacted during the long eighteenth century. The twelve judges of the Westminster courts also acted as assizes judges on both the crown and the civil sides. Assizes decisions on matters of law were therefore much more connected to the centre than those taken lower down the court structure. Stronger links were also forged by the fact that individual assizes judges could, if they wished, defer judgement in cases involving difficult matters of law and then take them back to London for final adjudication by the twelve judges. This system was not always consistent and could be very

---

[76] *P.P.*, 1834, xxvi, 122; Smith, *Lawyers, Legislators*, 3 and 14. On the reports and on the gradual establishment of the modern theory of decided cases – Holdsworth, *A History*, xii, 102–17, 127, 146–60.

[77] *Ibid.*, 122–6; Lobban, *The Common Law*, 202–4; J. Innes, 'Governing Diverse Societies' in P. Langford (ed.), *The Eighteenth Century* (Oxford, 2002), 121. Smith, *Lawyers, Legislators*, 3 and 66–72.

opaque. Individual judges did not have to follow this practice and neither the accused nor the prosecutor could insist on such a deferral. Nor did the twelve judges either meet in open court or feel obliged on every occasion to explain, or record in detail, their decisions.[78] However, it did provide a consistency notably lacking at quarter-sessions or summary-court level. The law commissioners were particularly concerned about the defective superintendence of the latter, and about individual magistrate's inability to cope with the complicated and technical nature of the common law in relation to certain crimes. They also remarked on the lack of formal case law development at the quarter-sessions level. 'It is a singular circumstance', they noted, that although the quarter-sessions courts played a very important role in the criminal justice system, 'it is not usual to adduce their authority upon points of law, even in arguments addressed to the same species of tribunal.' This defect was particularly important because, as the commission also noted with concern, there was no mechanism at quarter sessions equivalent to the assizes process of referral to the twelve judges and difficult points of law could not therefore be easily resolved. Indeed, apart from applying to the king for a pardon, there was usually no appeal process of any kind.

> The courts of inferior jurisdiction, as the court of Quarter sessions, for instance, possess no such resources; and thus it happens that whilst in a mere question as to a pauper's settlement, the opinion of Your Majesties Court of King's Bench may be obtained whenever any case of doubt or difficulty arises, yet in cases far more important which concern the commission of offences of great magnitude, and are visited by almost every penal consequence short of capital punishment, no mode is usually left open even for the correction of the most manifest errors . . . The courts of inferior jurisdiction, [they concluded] are very defective in the means by which their proceedings may be superintended.[79]

This did not of course mean that the quarter sessions and the summary courts were unconnected either with each other or with the higher courts. The twelve judges would have made regular contact with the magistrates of each county on their allocated assizes circuits, both through informal meetings and through formal mechanisms such as the charges they read to the grand jury at the beginning of each assizes. Equally, of course, many magistrates active at the summary level also sat on the quarter-sessions bench. Both the formal and informal networks of county society, and the richer gentry magistrates' connections to London and to various national networks meant that even justices living in relatively isolated areas sometimes had extensive contacts outside their neighbourhoods and petty sessions divisions. Although a formal chain of command rarely existed

[78] Baker, *An Introduction*, 522–3; Smith, *Lawyers, Legislators*, 51 and 364.
[79] *P.P.*, 1834, xxvi, 122, 146.

between the Westminster courts, the assizes, the quarter sessions and the summary courts, and although in felony cases formal appeal was often impossible, there were many informal mechanisms through which information could be disseminated and various forms of pressure brought to bear.

Given the institutional and informal, personnel-based, interconnections between the various levels of the criminal justice system, it is important not to overemphasise the differences between local and central initiatives. There were complex and sometimes deep interactions between the two and these were not confined to connections between different courts or court officials. The links between those who made key decisions at county level and both parliament and central government were many and varied. Some magistrates were MPs and a few, such as Whitbread, even had ministerial experience. The connections between those who ran the lower courts and various central institutions are difficult to uncover in the surviving sources, partly because so much of eighteenth-century government was conducted informally, but that does not mean that these connections were unimportant. The growing role that parliament played in domestic government during the long eighteenth century makes it particularly important to assess its relationship to the justicing initiatives being taken on the ground. This relationship was not a simple one and can rarely be reduced to a straightforward central/local dichotomy. Although many magistrates may have tended to bypass certain statutes in practice, this should not be taken to imply that the relationship between parliament and local magistracies was necessarily antagonistic or oppositional. Magistrates influenced parliamentary decisions in a wide range of ways, as well as being, in some cases, MPs themselves. Parliament responded to the demands of a considerable spectrum of local interest groups during the eighteenth century, acting as an adjudicator between groups and localities and facilitating various legislative enterprises. It was an arena in which those involved in government at various levels both developed their own initiatives and influenced, or were influenced by, the ideas of others.[80] However, the number of active magistrates or influential figures at the quarter-sessions level who actually got involved in parliamentary processes to any significant extent remains unclear, and may have been relatively small. The direct overlap between those landowners who became MPs and those who were active magistrates on the ground can easily be exaggerated.

Many substantial gentry were JPs in the eighteenth century but very few of them *did* justice on a regular or even an irregular basis. In almost every county in England and Wales a very small group of highly active JPs shouldered the

[80] Langford, *Public Life*, 166–86; J. Innes, 'The Domestic Face of the Fiscal Military State. Government and Society in Eighteenth-Century England' in L. Stone (ed.), *An Imperial State at War. Britain from 1689 to 1815* (London, 1994), 96–127; J. Innes, 'Parliament and the Shaping of Eighteenth-Century English Social Policy', *Transactions of the Royal Historical Society*, 40 (1990), 63–92.

burden of everyday judicial work and of quarter-sessions attendance, and the
vast majority of these highly active magistrates were prelates, parvenus, poorer
parish gentry or propertied men from professional or trading backgrounds. This
was changing by the early nineteenth century as the more substantial gentry and
aristocracy began to take more interest in these matters. However, between 1750
and 1820 everyday justice was very rarely dispensed by Knights of the Shire or
members of the counties' great gentry families. Nor were the quarter sessions
of most counties dominated or even attended by the bigger landowners. Some
counties did establish regular chairmen for their quarter-sessions meetings and
some of those chairmen were substantial gentry. Others, such as Essex did not.
The role of chairman continued to be rotated and minor gentry and even clergy
might take the position. The relationships between the active magisterial core
and their more substantial land-owning neighbours are difficult to unravel, but
we cannot assume that they had the same views of justice or of the need for
its reform.[81] Nor can we assume that one group was in a clientage relationship
to the other. For this brief period from the mid-eighteenth century to the early
nineteenth, justice was very rarely in the hands of those who were central to
local parliamentary politics or who usually had seats in Parliament. Moreover,
although their interests and viewpoints clearly overlapped, there may well have
been significant differences and disagreements between the land-owning elite
and the active magistracy, as well as between subgroups within each of those
bodies.

The interactions between the various government departments and those
who shaped justicing practices at the local level are also difficult to reconstruct.
Central government, to quote Joanna Innes, became increasingly polyarchic
in the eighteenth century.[82] Power was distributed amongst a range of institutions and departments, and co-ordination was usually, at best, informal. As the
Privy Council's clearing-house role sharply declined, and central government
departments focused increasingly on obtaining the resources required to pursue international rivalries, war and empire, the initiative for shaping domestic
policy – and the responsibility for its everyday administration – increasingly
devolved to the localities. Until 1782, when one secretary of state was allocated responsibility for all home matters (while at the same time being given
responsibility for colonial affairs), it was not always clear which government
department, if any, was responsible for certain categories of business. Moreover, even though the Home Office did develop new functions, such as the
overseeing of the London stipendiary magistrates appointed in 1792, its staff
remained very small in number. From the mid-1770s onwards the government

[81] Langford, *Public Life*, 367–436; King, *Crime, Justice*, 117–120; Innes, 'Governing', 105. On
patterns of chairmen Webbs, *Parish and the County*, 433–7.
[82] Innes, 'The Domestic Face', 98.

did devote some resources to solving the transportation crisis, but unless the maintenance of order was threatened or a major plank of penal policy suddenly collapsed, the secretary of state often remained almost entirely reactive rather than proactive until the 1820s.[83]

Voluntary societies sometimes played an important role in the development of new initiatives as well as in strengthening the interconnections between parliament, government and provincial court practice. The Proclamation Society, for example, not only pressurised parliament to assist in a new reformation of manners initiative, but also briefly acted as a major co-ordinating network for many of those involved at county-quarter-sessions level and below. The reactive nature of the eighteenth-century central state's approach to domestic policy development meant that philanthropic bodies could play a number of roles, as the following examples from the field of juvenile delinquency policies indicate.[84] When the Committee for Investigating Juvenile Delinquency wanted to get a juvenile penitentiary built, it was they who took responsibility for hiring a prison architect and for getting detailed plans drawn up. They then took them to the secretary of state, Lord Sidmouth, who might well have acted on them if he had not been immediately distracted by a major threat to public order (Chapter 3). Equally, it was only after the major courts had begun to make extensive use of another voluntary institution – the Refuge for the Destitute – that government backing finally emerged following the extensive lobbying of Lord Sidmouth and of parliament by the men who ran this voluntary reformatory initiative (Chapter 4). Those who wanted to introduce new policies to deal with 'the alarming increase of juvenile delinquency' also helped to initiate – and then to shape much of the evidence offered to – various parliamentary committees during the 1810s.[85]

In this field the interactions between the Home Office, parliamentary bodies, voluntary societies and changing practice in the courts were complex, but it was clear where the main momentum for change was still coming from at

---

[83] C. Emsley, 'Repression, "Terror" and the Rule of Law in England during the Decade of the French Revolution', *English Historical Review*, 100 (1985), 820. S. Devereaux, 'The Criminal Branch of the Home Office 1782–1830' in G. Smith, A. May and S. Devereaux (eds.), *Criminal Justice in the Old World and the New* (Toronto, 1998), 270–308; Even in priority areas such as the prosecution of seditious libel the Home Office was constrained by lack of staff and was often dependant on magisterial initiative – P. Harling, 'The Law of Libel and the Limits of Repression, 1790–1832', *Historical Journal*, 44 (2001), 107–34.

[84] J. Innes, 'Politics and Morals; The Reformation of Manners Movement in Later Eighteenth-Century England' in E. Hellmuth (ed.), *The Transformation of Political Culture: Late Eighteenth-Century England and Germany* (Oxford, 1990); *Report of the Committee. . . Proclamation . . . 1799* (London, 1799). For a discussion of the reactive nature of the English state – L. Davison, T. Hitchcock, T. Keirn and R. Shoemaker (eds.), *Stilling the Grumbling Hive. The Response to Social and Economic Problems in England 1689–1750* (Stroud, 1992), xv.

[85] *P.P.*, 1817, vii, 428–41, 524–45. Various groups who were working for the repeal of the bloody code, many of whose members were also involved in the juvenile delinquency committee, made similar use of the parliamentary investigation process *P.P.*, 1819, viii.

the beginning of the nineteenth century. The central authorities almost always reacted to changes introduced by the courts and/or suggested by philanthropic bodies, rather than initiating them. By the beginning of the 1820s government ministers, such as Robert Peel at the Home Office, were becoming much more proactive and the initiative was moving towards the centre. However, during the eighteenth century, despite the existence of some significant counter-currents, it seems clear that English central government was gradually disengaging from a number of areas in the administration of domestic government. In the eighteenth century those involved in manning, and shaping the decisions of, the quarter sessions and summary courts rarely experienced the same level of central government surveillance as their nineteenth-century counterparts. Centre and locality were interconnected in a number of ways in the long eighteenth century. However, the decentralised, pluralistic and voluntary-minded nature of the state meant that this was a particularly fruitful period for the development of a range of initiatives from below.[86]

VII

This analysis raises a number of interesting questions about our models of the reform process in late eighteenth and early nineteenth century England. Given the relative freedom sometimes enjoyed by the courts in reshaping justicing practices from within, our models of how change was brought about in the criminal justice system may need to be considerably rethought. Provincial magistrates, in alliance with other local elites and voluntary associations, sometimes used legislative change to achieve their aims, and in some fields of activity parliament not infrequently proved responsive to local needs and interests. Equally, paid metropolitan magistrates such as the Fieldings and Colquhoun were not slow to lobby parliament for legislative changes which might legitimate their activities, extend their fields of operation and increase their chances of obtaining convictions (whilst at the same time advancing their own career prospects). If they were reasonably well connected and were not proposing policies which key government ministers would be likely to object to, magisterial groups might sometimes have been able to choose between either pursuing their reforming project through parliament or simply changing their practice on the ground – the latter being the most likely choice if existing legal structures appeared to allow them sufficient leeway (as the law of misdemeanour did in the case of imprisonment for assault).[87] However, this view of local – central initiatives

---

[86] Innes, 'The Domestic Face', 96–108. P. Langford, *A Polite and Commercial People. England 1727–83* (Oxford, 1989), 693; J. Innes, 'Central Government "Interference": Changing Conceptions, Practices and Concerns, c. 1700–1850' in J. Harris (ed.), *Civil Society in British History: Ideas, Identities, Institutions* (Oxford, 2003), 49.

[87] J. Innes, 'Parliament', 63–8; Radzinowicz, *A History*, ii, 385–90 and iii, 212–13.

as merely different sides of the same coin of magisterial action, as different avenues through which local magisterial elites sought to change things from worse to better in various fields of jucticing policy, fails to give sufficient weight to the amount of local change that was achieved by the courts themselves. Nor does another often-utilised model of relations between the local and central state which assumes that social policy innovations were initiated by the adventurous experiments of local elites/magistrates and then turned into national policies by parliamentary legislation (often initially permissive in nature but decreasingly so as reform progressed).[88] While this may fit the history of some types of reform, it works much less well for the kinds of changes outlined here since one of the major, and most surprising, features of these changes was their wide geographical diffusion. The criminalisation of assault, the growth of petty sessions as a major filter in felony cases, the development of further examination as a widespread practice, the abandonment of whipping for females, etc., were all widely adopted in a range of localities from London to Cornwall long before any legislation had been enacted on these issues. Local magistrates in a wide range of areas systematically (if often gradually) abandoned judicial practices that seemed unsuitable and adopted others that they deemed more appropriate. Moreover, although every areas' chronology of change was slightly different (and research is still at a very early stage), these changes were often broadly national in scope.

Why did magistrates and courts across most of England and Wales develop common approaches and introduce similar types of changes in these areas of judicial policy? The growth of a broader civil society in the long eighteenth century undoubtedly played a role, intersecting as it did with the more limited interactions between local and central government which we explored in the previous section. At the county level, for example, magistrates from different divisions had many opportunities to exchange views not only at assizes and quarter-sessions time but also at the regular dinner clubs, prosecution associations, charity dinners and other voluntary association meetings which mushroomed as increasing numbers of gentry contributed to what has been termed 'the golden age of the county town.' Overlapping with these networks at regional and national level were a huge variety of other arenas of social interaction, such as those which developed in the burgeoning leisure towns, in the growing manufacturing and commercial centres and in London itself. The metropolis with its vast array of voluntary societies, charities, clubs and leisure facilities was particularly important since many members of the different county elites spent a significant part of the year in the metropolis. From the houses of parliament to the coffee houses, from the specialist dining clubs of the stipendiary magistrates to the debating clubs and more informal discussion groups frequented by most

---

[88] Langford, *Public Life*, 157–8.

propertied males, opportunities abounded for the exchange of ideas.[89] Equally important, during the second half of the eighteenth century more specifics links between various London bodies and the provincial magistrates began to develop. For example, London-based philanthropic and moral reform movements such as the Proclamation Society and the Society for Bettering the Condition of the Poor made direct contact with county leaders. Moreover when the magistrates of some counties received information from these bodies on particular projects, such as the reform of the vagrancy laws, they responded by calling specific meetings to discuss the relevant proposal, and on at least one occasion by attending a gathering of provincial magistrates in the capital.[90]

The significance of these links for the types of reform highlighted here can easily be overestimated, however. Neither the publications of these societies nor the rapidly growing body of books, pamphlets and newspapers produced during this period offer much concrete evidence that most of the locally initiated changes in judicial policy discussed here were co-ordinated through these channels. Indeed at this stage of research what seems most remarkable about these sources is the relative lack of any substantial public printed debate about many of the judicial changes discussed here – particularly those that were introduced at quarter sessions. Occasional throwaway observations and tangential discussions are all that seem to have come down to us in relation to the criminalisation of assault at the quarter sessions, for example. Even less was said in print about changing attitudes to the public punishment of women. Many policies took shape on the ground with very little sign of a significant public discourse about them, or if one did appear it did not usually do so until they were well entrenched in court practice. That does not mean that no debate occurred. Surely most county quarter-sessions benches would not have made major changes in court policies without some discussion among themselves. However it does still leave open the question of why such changes can be identified in so many different counties or regions.

[89] P. Borsay, *The English Urban Renaissance, Culture and Society in the Provincial Town 1660–1760* (Oxford, 1989), 29; M. Roberts, *Making English Morals. Voluntary Association and Moral Reform in England 1787–1886* (Cambridge, 2004), 7–16; J. Innes, 'Central Government'; P. Clark, *British Clubs and Societies 1580–1800. The Origins of an Associational World* (Oxford, 2000), espec. 94–148; P. King, 'Prosecution Associations and their Impact in Eighteenth-Century Essex' in D. Hay and F. Snyder (eds.), *Policing and Prosecution in Britain 1750–1850* (Oxford, 1989), 204–5; On London as 'a remarkable cultural gateway' P. Borsay, 'London, 1660–1800: A Distinctive Culture?' in P. Clark and R. Gillespie (eds.), *Two Capitals: London and Dublin 1500–1840* (Oxford, 2001), 167–84; It was 'not only from the number and weight of its members', that the Proclamation Society felt it was 'able to extend its benefits throughout the whole kingdom', but also 'from its comprehending persons from all parts of England, residing during the winter in the capital' – *Report of . . . Society . . . Proclamation . . . 1799*, 13.

[90] Roberts, *Making English Morals*, 33–8; Innes, 'Politics and Morals'; *Statement . . . Proclamation . . . to the Magistrates*, 1–17; *Resolutions of the Magistrates . . . Proclamation*, 1–14; *Report of . . . Society . . . Proclamation . . . 1799*.

Perhaps the explanation lies less in the outcomes of specific printed exchanges or of actual meetings of magistrates and provincial elites, and more in shared cultural assumptions and practical experiences. Those who manned the courts faced much the same pragmatic problems – providing accessible justice without too much personal inconvenience, finding remedies for a whole range of disputes, balancing the needs of the propertied (and of social order) with at least some acknowledgement that the poor were also entitled to justice. Moreover they not only shared the same concerns, they also had to make choices from the same fairly limited range of solutions whatever part of the country they lived in. It is not therefore surprising that they evolved similar policies in most cases, and in particular in relation to the reform of their own court procedures – an area in which legal tribunals were traditionally allowed considerable leeway. More centrally perhaps, despite their differences and internal disputes, most of the magistrates of eighteenth-century England may well have shared a common culture, a common set of habits, conventions and taken for granted assumptions that arose in part from the relatively confident and self-assured mental world of the ruling elite within which they formed a small but highly active minority. The discursive frameworks they brought with them when they performed their various roles in the courts reflected, to some extent at least, a broader cultural consensus among the gentry elite about the kinds of law and justicing practice each social group should expect to receive. The provincial magistrates may not have had access to any meaningful equivalent of the shared oral culture enjoyed by the London-based judges and barristers. Nor did they have any regular rhythm of meetings to rival the periodic discussions that the twelve judges were involved in when they adjudicated on matters of law referred to them from the assize circuits. But this did not mean that those who ran the local courts lacked common ground. Moreover, they also faced very similar pressures from broader forms of social and cultural change. For example, the rise of new sensibilities about violence amongst the more comfortable ranks of society was essentially a national phenomenon, although the precise timing of its impact may have differed between areas. It is hardly surprising therefore that the courts of various regions began thinking about changing their policies towards assault, public whipping, etc., at roughly the same time.[91]

The magistrates who ran the summary courts of eighteenth- and early nineteenth-century England certainly shared one very important characteristic – a very flexible attitude to what might be broadly called the rule of law. While most would have clearly recognised its importance as rhetoric, and would have stoutly defended in theory the freeborn Englishmen's right to jury trial, to

---

[91] E. P. Thompson, *Customs in Common* (1991), 42–7; Langford, *Public Life*, 405; D. Lemmings, *Professors of the Law. Barristers and English Legal Culture in the Eighteenth Century* (Oxford, 2000), 107–48, 295–304; Beattie, *Crime and the Courts*, 427: Langbein, *The Origins*, 212–13.

protection from imprisonment without trial, to be assumed innocent until proved guilty and to equality before the law, in practice many of the judicial practices that we have seen developing here show very little concern for such niceties. Public jury trial was the experience of only a small minority of those who came before the courts in late eighteenth-century England. Even those facing an accusation of felony were increasingly unlikely to face a jury. Attempts to prevent magistrates from holding suspects for long periods without trial for 'further examination' were not generally successful. The large numbers of men and women imprisoned as 'idle and disorderly', as 'reputed thieves' or for the unexplained possession of wood, lead or various kinds of industrial materials would certainly not have been under any illusion that the magistrates who tried them started from the assumption that they were innocent. Equality before the law must also have seemed a very technical notion to servants involved in disputes with their masters, since most employees were well aware that while they were likely to be imprisoned if found guilty, their errant employers would not be. For these reasons the changes outlined here almost certainly did not alter the poor's essentially pragmatic attitude to the law and the courts, nor their generally unconvinced and non-deferential approach to much-trumpeted notions about the legal rights of all free-born Englishmen.[92] However, this did not mean that the poor always lost out as a result of the various ways in which justice was remade by the courts in this period. The impact of the changes highlighted here was not unidirectional and was frequently paradoxical. When accused of theft, for example, it was often in the interests of the poor to be dealt with summarily rather than to be held in gaol for a considerable period awaiting trial. Equally, the informal practice of granting vagrant passes without punishing the recipient could be very helpful to the mobile poor when they wanted to return home. The fact that the magistrates sometimes ignored the law in relation to matters such as the detention of suspects for further examination did not, of course, mean that the vast majority of Englishmen were suddenly in danger of imprisonment without trial. The justices' notebooks have much more to say about arbitrational strategies than about the use of arbitrary power.[93] Indeed, in times of dearth the justices sometimes acted to protect the poor from the potentially crushing power of the farmer-dominated vestries, as it could be argued they did in the 1790s when in various areas JPs laid down new rules to be followed by local vestries

---

[92] King, 'Summary Courts'; Hay, 'England', 67; Smith, 'The Presumption of Guilt and the English Law of Theft, 1750–1850' but see also N. Landau, 'Summary Conviction and the Development of Penal Law', and Smith's response – all in *Law and History Review*, 23, (2005), 133–71; 173–89; 191–9. Labourers who swore at magistrates would be punished, but when a labourer threatened to prosecute a magistrate who had sworn at him that labourer was likely to suffer the consequences, as Joseph Mayett discovered to his cost – P. King, 'Social Inequality, Identity and the Labouring Poor in Eighteenth-Century England' in H. French and J. Barry (eds.), *Identity and Agency in England 1500–1800* (London, 2004), 79.

[93] The sources are, however, inevitably distorted by the fact that magistrates would rarely have openly recorded their arbitrary acts in a way that could be identified by historians.

in relating poor relief to the price of food. When the courts remade justice from the margins they did not necessarily side wholeheartedly with either the middling sort or the poor. Rather their actions are probably best understood in most situations as either pragmatic attempts to solve particular practical problems or as part of a variegated response by criminal justice administrators across the nation to broader cultural shifts such as the decrease in tolerance towards public displays of violence.[94]

The reform process followed many models and it is clear that a wide range of different processes led to changes in justicing practice in the eighteenth century. Some changes were direct responses to parliamentary initiatives. Some were reactions against statutory change. Others were the result of changes made by the courts themselves. However, when magistrates introduced changes in their summary-court practices parliament was often pushed into a deeply reactive role, passing statutes long after changes had been made on the ground, and in the process seeking to formalise and/or legitimise what the courts were already doing. In this context the relationship between parliament and the localities can perhaps best be characterised as one of creative tension. The relationship worked itself out in a number of ways, but in the later eighteenth and early nineteenth centuries it is clear that parliament frequently found itself reacting to, rather than initiating, change. This situation was not always welcomed by those who sat in parliament. In a number of areas of justicing policy there is considerable evidence that magistrates practices on the ground were far from gaining the approval of many MPs. Working magistrates very often wanted to increase their discretionary powers but many parliamentarians were less than enthusiastic, fearing amongst other things that this might threaten the right of jury trial. This can be seen, for example, in the unyielding opposition to change exhibited by the majority of MPs during the thirty-year debate over the projected transfer of felony trials involving juveniles into the summary courts.

There were also, of course, divisions within parliament and the existence of significant subgroups of MPs, such as those of a more radical inclination, who looked unfavourably on the magistrates' very loose interpretations of the law when they threatened the liberty of the subject, produced some illuminating public conflicts. In early January 1795, for example, the pro-reform MP, Thomas Thompson, broke with the normal protocol, which involved tacitly ignoring the summary-court evasions of the statutory law, and publicly challenged their procedures. One of the Bow Street magistrates – following a practice that became increasingly common in the eighteenth century despite the absence of any statutory basis for it – had insisted on impressing a bricklayer's apprentice accused

---

[94] P. Dunkley, 'Paternalism, the Magistracy and Poor Relief in England 1795–1834', *International Review of Social History*, 24 (1979) 380; M. Neuman, *The Speenhamland County. Poverty and the Poor Laws in Berkshire 1782–1834* (London, 1982). P. King, 'Edward Thompson's Contribution to Eighteenth-Century Studies. The Patrician–Plebeian Model Re-examined', *Social History*, 21 (1996).

of stealing, despite the prisoner's refusal to enter either the army or the navy voluntarily. As he was giving sentence one of the spectators in the courtroom stood up and challenged his decision telling him that 'he was acting improperly'. 'Who are you?' the magistrate responded. 'I am Mr Thompson, a member of the House of Commons, and I tell you that you act illegally' was the reply. 'Do you tell me, sitting here as a magistrate that I act illegally?' the magistrate responded. 'I do; for if the boy has committed a crime, he is not to be punished arbitrarily by you, or any other justice; it is to the laws of the land, and to them alone that he is amenable; and I say it is a violation of the liberty of the subject.' The magistrate replied by pointing out that 'the King wanted men' and that 'Mr Thompson might investigate it in the House of Commons, but whether he did or not, he should act as he thought proper.' He then 'sent for Major Leeson and had him enlisted.'[95]

A brief flurry of protest then ensued in one or two of the radical papers. Political life was highly polarised in the mid-1790s. The popular movement for parliamentary reform was at its height, Britain was at war with France, and the recent suspension of the Habeas Corpus Acts combined with several unsuccessful trials of English radical leaders for treason had highlighted the importance of the right to jury trial. When parliament debated the suspension of Habeas Corpus three days after the Bow Street confrontation, Thompson alluded to the case, as he had promised he would do in court, and in the following week the leading pro-radical newspaper, the *Morning Chronicle* published two letters supporting Thompson's stand. However, although the Bow Street court eventually released the apprentice after a period in gaol for further examination, there is very little evidence that the magistrates changed their general practices in response to this challenge. Although this form of impressment had been denounced on the floor of the House as 'scandalous and illegal', and although various passages from venerable law books had been quoted in the newspapers to indicate that their actions lacked any basis in law, they continued to use recruitment into the armed forces as an alternative to formal prosecution and jury trial.[96] We rarely have records of such direct confrontations between the men who were in charge of the summary courts and MPs, government officials

[95] *The Sun*, 3 Jan. 1975; *The Star*, 5 Jan. 1795; *The Morning Chronicle*, 5 Jan. 1795; Smith, 'The State and the Culture of Violence', 75; King, 'War as a Judicial Resource'; C. Emsley, 'The Social Impact of the French Wars' in H. Dickinson (ed.), *Britain and the French Revolution 1789–1815* (Basingstoke, 1989), 216.

[96] *Morning Chronicle*, 6, 9, and 12 Jan. 1795; *The Star*, 6 and 9 Jan. 1795; *The Sun*, 6 and 7 Jan. 1795. Thompson, who was MP for Evesham was one of only forty-one members who voted to end the suspension of Habeas Corpus – R. Thorne (ed.), *The History of Parliament: The House of Commons, 1790–1820* (London, 1986), 367–8; G. Cranfield, *The Press and Society from Caxton to Northcliffe* (London, 1978), 79; E. P. Thompson, *The Making of the English Working Class* (Harmondsworth, 1968), 144–5; F. O'Gorman, *The Long Eighteenth Century. British Political and Social History 1688–1832* (London, 1997), 246; C. Emsley, 'An Aspect of Pitt's Terror: Prosecutions for Sedition during the 1790s', *Social History*, 6 (1981), 157.

or the judges of the Westminster courts. However, the problems experienced by Pitt and the Lord Chancellor in their attempts to control the courts' policies on press warrants, not to mention Lord Loughborough's failure to control further examination practices that were clearly against the statutes, suggest that there were very considerable areas of disagreement, negotiation and compromise.

The relative autonomy not infrequently exercised by the summary courts and the freedom to make significant policy changes sometimes seen in the quarter-sessions and assizes contexts raise interesting questions about the reform process. Were the fundamental changes local magistrates made in their policies towards assault, towards petty-sessions felony trials, etc., in fact successful attempts to quietly circumvent the deep distrust of local judicial autonomy often expressed by central bodies? For example, parliament went on debating the transfer of felony trial to the magistrates' courts for most of the nineteenth century and made only relatively minor changes before 1850. However, there is evidence that from the late eighteenth century onwards petty-sessions practice increasingly evolved into a form of preliminary felony trial. This sometimes caused major problems for those called as witnesses before parliamentary committees. When magistrates and their clerks were asked to describe their current practices in relation to the processing of property offenders their answers were often opaque. They were reluctant to openly admit to various discretionary practices but could hardly deny them either. Equally when the contentious issue of the detention of accused felons for 'further examination' was raised, witnesses tried desperately to convey a sense of current court practice without actually admitting that the procedures followed may not have been legal. When asked by a parliamentary committee in 1818 'Have you known many young persons who have been imprisoned and after different re-examinations discharged?' the prison official involved could only reply weakly that 'it is possible I may have known many.' When asked 'have you ever seen anyone committed there for re-examination upon trifling charges?' he replied even less convincingly that 'I never charged my memory.'[97] In these contexts much-heralded parliamentary reforms, such as the acts of 1847 and 1850 making summary felony trial legal for under-sixteen year olds, look more like admissions of defeat by parliament, more like post hoc legitimations of autonomy already taken, than the major milestones of reform that they are sometimes portrayed as being.

How often were debates about judicial reform in fact covert debates about existing practice and the need to legalise it, control it, generalise it or at the very least admit its existence? For example, the Offences Against the Person Act of 1828, which formally empowered magistrates to fine (or imprison if defaulting) those summarily convicted of common assault, looks very much like a post hoc attempt to bring a range of magisterial practices within a properly established

---

[97] *P.P.*, 1818, viii, 43; and 82 for more open discussion.

criminal justice framework. These observations raise the question of whether or not many 'reforms' in the early to mid-nineteenth century were in fact attempts to take back the initiative from local magistrates. There are certainly some readings of the 1834 Poor Law Reform Act that might fit with such a view. Although the role of magistrates courts as benefits appeals tribunals and as innovators in relief policy was complex, and cannot be discussed in detail here, there can be little doubt that one of the major agendas of the act was to take the power of appeal away from magistrates who, it was thought, were too willing to take the side of paupers in their battles against the parsimonious practices of many parish officers.[98]

The reform of criminal justice administration and, more specifically of the practice of justice, can be thought about within a number of chronological frameworks. For our purposes here, however, it may be most appropriate to think in terms of two main periods. By the second quarter of the nineteenth century parliament was clearly taking the initiative, not only in areas such as prison and policing reform or the repealing of the bloody code which have attracted the most attention from historians, but also in relation to a range of issues – from the standardisation of petty-sessions procedure to the opening up of magistrates courts to public scrutiny – which have been largely ignored, but which had a major impact on everyday justicing practice. The century before this, however, was not a period when the way justice was delivered on the ground was directed primarily from the centre. This period was characterised by localism, discretion and magisterial initiative. The assizes and quarter-sessions courts maintained a capacity for independent decision-making in significant areas, and at petty-sessions level magistrates carved out many new procedures and policies. The ability of the local courts to quietly reform policies towards the punishment of violence, towards the preliminary trial of felons and towards a range of other important judicial matters without direct reference to either parliament or central government raises important questions about the kinds of changes that get called 'reforms'. In many significant fields the operation of justice was remade as much from the bottom up as from the centre down. If we concentrate only on those issues which, because they were debated in parliament or were initiated by central government, generated an extensive public discourse, our understanding of the chronology, origins and nature of reform will be at best partial and could well be seriously distorted.[99]

There are, of course, many dangers in overemphasising the independence of the magistrates and of the locally based courts. The fact that at various levels those courts made major changes without reference to the main legislative body

---

[98] S. and E. Checkland (eds.), *The Poor Law Report of 1834* (Harmondsworth, 1974), 203–41; King, 'Summary Courts'.

[99] As arguably they are in the largest work on the subject – Radzinowicz, *A History*, i–iv.

clearly prompts questions about recent characterisations of the eighteenth century as a period dominated by 'local government at parliament's command'. Yet to replace this by a model of 'local government without reference to parliament' (which the Webbs came close to doing in their early twentieth-century writings) would be equally incorrect and would set up too great a dichotomy between the local and the central.[100] Justice as it was delivered on the ground was shaped and remade by a complex multiplicity of forces. However, only by understanding how much the summary courts, and to a lesser extent the quarter sessions and assizes, were able to reshape significant areas of justicing practice with relatively little reference to parliamentary statute, central government or the decisions of the Westminster courts, can a more balanced picture of the interactions between the centre and the localities that shaped the reform process be created.

VIII

Several dimensions of law and of the practice of justice can be explored by contrasting the central and the marginal and by analysing the relationship between them. Having used a number of themes drawn from the essays presented here to argue that within the court system itself justice was often shaped and remade from the margins – in the lower, more locally based and least centrally supervised courts – I now want to explore two other related applications of the centre–margins model that are relevant to the detailed studies found in this volume. The first emerges from the relative neglect in formal law, but not in justicing practice, of certain key dimensions of the criminal law adjudication process. In a broad sense, each of the four sections of this volume explores one of these dimensions, but the sections on gender and juvenile delinquency provide the most obvious examples. Statute law, case law and common law traditions did not, of course, entirely ignore either of these aspects. *Doli incapax* protected the very young and might extend its umbrella as far as the early teenage years. Moreover one or two specific statutes relating to thefts by servants and apprentices offered protection from prosecution to small subgroups of offenders who were in their mid- to late teens.[101] But overall until the early nineteenth century, and often until 1850 or beyond, formal law did not usually contain any allowances for the age of the offender. Older offenders were not accorded any significant forms of special treatment in law and even juvenile offenders were given the same range of sentences, tried before the same courts, subjected to the same trial procedures and placed in the same penal regimes as adults (Chapters 2

---

[100] D. Eastwood, *Government and Community in the English Provinces 1700–1870* (London, 1997), 19; Webb(s), *The Parish and the County*.

[101] Servants 'within 18 years of age' and apprentices embezzling their masters goods were protected – Burn, *The Justice*, 10th edn (1766), iii, 55; Dickinson, *A Practical Exposition*, ii, 12.

and 3). However, while the formal law paid very little attention to the age of the accused, the opposite was true in the courts themselves. The sentencing and pardoning policies in operation in the later eighteenth century were highly age conscious. The very young and those in middle age were both likely to receive favourable treatment, although the lenient treatment offered to juveniles began to become less obvious in the early nineteenth century (Chapter 3). Equally, those aged in their late teens and early twenties were generally treated more harshly. Age may have been marginal to the concerns of eighteenth-century legislators and may be largely invisible in the justices' manuals, but it was one of the central issues that decided what sentences would be handed out by the courts.[102]

The same was true of gender. This dimension was not completely ignored by the formal law. By the early eighteenth century parliament had insured that benefit of clergy was equally available to both sexes, although until 1790 wives who murdered their husbands were treated more harshly than husbands who murdered their wives. Pregnant women could not be executed until after they had given birth and as a result they were often not hanged at all. Moreover, the doctrine of *feme covert* offered some protection to a rather different sub-group – married women committing offences with or under the influence of their husbands.[103] In general, however, there were no formal legislative distinctions in the eighteenth century between the treatment meted out to women and that to be given to men. The law decreed that they were to be tried and punished in the same way, and specialist penal establishments for women were not deemed necessary by law. Once again, however, detailed work on the court records (Chapter 5) indicates that gender was often an important factor in the treatment received by the accused in the major courts, and it appears from the limited information so far available that this may also have been the case in the summary courts.

In the eighteenth century law in its most directly relevant sense, i.e. as what the courts are most likely to do in the next case brought before them, was greatly affected by issues of age and gender. Magistrates, judges and jurors were deeply influenced by these issues, as were the victims and witnesses who could be so influential in both summary and major-court proceedings. From the point of view of anyone indicted before an eighteenth-century court, their age and gender were vital considerations that might well decide the outcome of the trial. Yet if we take a more traditional definition of law as what the courts are instructed to do by statute and case law etc., in the vast majority of cases, although not in all, gender and sex would appear to be irrelevant. The fact that they were not, and that, for example, male young adults accused of capital crimes were many times more likely to be hanged than middle-aged women or

---

[102] King, *Crime, Justice*, 169–96.   [103] Blackstone, *Commentaries*, iv, 28–9.

young girls, indicates clearly how dimensions of the criminal justice process that appear marginal in the black-letter law created by the centre were anything but marginal in practice. In this sense it could be said that here also the courts were reshaping justice from the margins. It should be noted, however, that while many of these age- and gender-related practices were in one sense a reaction against statutory changes, they do not necessarily imply that central government, parliament or the Westminster courts were unhappy about the policies being pursued on the ground. The favourable treatment given to women and to certain age groups from initial verdicts through to pardoning decisions (Chapters 3 and 5) was designed in part to ensure that, despite the rapid accumulation of capital statutes in the eighteenth century, those deemed as 'deserving' – including other groups such as the mentally ill – would not be subjected to the full harshness of the law.[104] As such it may well have suited the broader purposes of parliament and central government, enabling them to threaten large numbers of offenders with the gallows whilst at the same time ensuring that the legitimacy of the capital code was not undermined by the execution of significant numbers of offenders who would attract too great a degree of sympathy from the public at large. Since there were sometimes clashes between judges and jurors over partial verdicts and jury nullification, compromises were necessary on occasions. Overall, however, the fact that gender- and age-related patterns of judicial practice played a significant role in the eighteenth century, despite the almost complete absence of these dimensions in the formal law, should not be taken to imply that those who made the key decisions in the courtroom were necessarily doing so against the wishes of the central authorities. Indeed, since the assize-court judges were much more closely tied to central concerns than those who ran the lower courts, they would often have been effective vectors in this context for the marrying up of local and central priorities. There were certainly fewer clashes between the centre and the localities over this issue than there were over other aspects of the justicing practices developed by the summary courts.

This gap between the absence of formal law foregrounding gender and age, and the obvious importance of these dimensions in practice began to close in the first half of the nineteenth century. On gender issues the changes were relatively minor and short term – the main area being the early statutory prohibition against the whipping of women – but centrally orchestrated policies towards juvenile offenders began to undergo much more important changes. In the first two thirds of the nineteenth century separate hulks and prisons were opened for juveniles, many juvenile trials were moved into the summary courts, and informal practices such as the covert use of juvenile reformatory sentences (Chapter 4) were finally enshrined in statute as a range of reformatories and

---

[104] On these and other criteria see King, *Crime, Justice*, 221–96.

industrial schools began to develop.[105] Age had come of age within the formal statutory law. In the eighteenth and early nineteenth centuries those who wanted to acknowledge and respond to the needs of juvenile offenders had to work from the margins, but by the mid-nineteenth century the central state was becoming the key player.

The same pattern was followed to some extent in relation to policies towards violence. This can be seen most obviously in the decline in the use of violent public punishments. Here the initiative, once again, came mainly from the courts. Public corporal punishment was gradually marginalised, first for women, then for men and finally for juveniles (Chapters 5 and 8). Equally, by the early nineteenth century the assize judges were reducing the number of capital convicts they were prepared to hang to such a small percentage that women and juveniles were almost completely excluded (Chapters 3 and 5), and only a very small proportion of male adults reached the gallows. Within thirty years the legislature had followed their lead and most of the bloody code had been swept away. The early nineteenth century also witnessed a gradual increase in legislative activity in relation to accusations of non-lethal violence. The informal criminalisation of assault introduced by quarter-sessions courts in various areas in the late eighteenth and early nineteenth centuries was clearly in the vanguard of a broader set of changes that attempted to clamp down on various forms of violent behaviour and particularly on male-on-female violence.[106] Systematic research on the attitudes of the summary courts to different types of violence and in particular to domestic violence is still at an early stage. However, at the quarter sessions at least, it is already clear that magistrates attitudes were beginning to change by the late eighteenth century (Chapters 7 and 8). Once again, therefore, changes begun at the margins without any significant central stimulus were followed by consolidation and more centrally orchestrated legislative activity during the nineteenth century.

The fact that assault was criminalised considerably earlier by the quarter-sessions benches of counties nearer the centre than it was in Cornwall (Chapters 7 and 8) highlights the potential usefulness of the most obvious type

---

[105] L. Radzinowicz and R. Hood, *A History of English Criminal Law and its Administration from 1750. The Emergence of Penal Policy* (London, 1986), v, 133–230.

[106] M. May, 'Violence in the Family: an Historical Perspective' in J.Martin (ed.), *Violence and the Family* (Chichester, 1978), 135–67; A. Clark, 'Humanity or Justice? Wifebeating and the Law in the Eighteenth and Nineteenth Centuries' in C. Smart (ed.), *Regulating Womanhood: Historical Essays on Marriage, Motherhood and Sexuality* (London, 1992), 187–206; J. Hurl-Eamon, 'Domestic Violence Prosecuted: Women Binding over their Husbands for Assault at Westminster Quarter Sessions, 1685–1720', *Journal of Family History*, 26 (2004), 454–5; Wiener, *Men of Blood*, follows the story of changing attitudes to male on female violence in interesting ways which also indicate the differences that continued to occur between central government attitudes and those displayed by the courts on the ground.

of comparison between the central and the marginal that can be made in this context – one that focuses on spatial variations. How much did justicing policies vary between regions? And to what extent did the administration of criminal justice more generally differ in its nature and impact between the centre and what might broadly be termed the periphery of the English state in the long eighteenth century? Variations in quarter-sessions policies between counties need particularly careful scrutiny. Quarter-sessions benches enjoyed considerable autonomy in this period. This can be seen particularly clearly in the way they exercised some of their administrative roles. They not infrequently used methods of taxation that had not been fully authorised by parliament, for example. The eighteenth and very early nineteenth centuries were in many senses the high-water mark of magisterial authority and discretion, as can be seen in the very active role that they played in the realignment of poor law policies in the 1790s.[107] This important and sometimes pivotal role was gradually curtailed and then undermined as the nineteenth century wore on – by poor law changes, by the establishment of a central prison inspectorate, by central government's increasing demands that they reform their policing systems on certain lines, etc. However, in the eighteenth century these changes were only just beginning to be discussed and county-level decision-makers still had much autonomy. Moreover, this clearly affected their decisions on criminal justice policy, even though this was an area in which they were sometimes more constrained by statute than they were in their more administrative capacities.

A number of other areas will have to be researched across a range of topics before regional variations in criminal justice policies can be analysed in detail. However, as Morgan and Rushton have pointed out in their study of the Northeast, it was perfectly possible for county benches to promote styles of punishment entirely distinct from those of their neighbours. The Durham bench, for example, made much more use of whipping throughout the eighteenth century than their counterparts in Newcastle and Northumberland – a pattern that can also be observed in Essex where the boroughs had a strong preference for corporal punishment not shared by the county bench. Equally the Newcastle and Northumberland sessions were exceptional in using imprisonment against more than half of those they convicted of theft in the 1750s and 1760s – a policy rarely pursued to this depth elsewhere at this point.[108]

The limited amount of research so far completed also highlights interesting differences between centre and periphery. The revival of public whipping in the

---

[107] Langford, *Public Life*, 161. Eastwood, *Government*, 107.
[108] Innes and Styles, 'The Crime Wave', 239 called for more regional studies but there are still many regions that are virtually unresearched. Morgan and Rushton, *Rogues, Thieves*, 73–5, and 134: King, *Crime, Justice*, 272–6. P. Griffiths, 'Introduction: Punishing the English' in Devereaux and Griffiths, *Penal Practice*, 20–1.

late eighteenth century, for example, seems to have been much more visible in the North-east and in Cornwall than it was in London.[109] Equally the authorities in counties nearer to the centre seem to have moved to control public hanging rituals much earlier than those on the periphery. Both in London and in Essex the site of the public gallows was moved to the outside of the main gaol in the early 1780s but this was not usually done in counties further away from the centre until several decades later. In Cornwall, for example, executions continued to be held on the edge of Bodmin Moor until the early nineteenth century when they were moved to a position just outside the walls of Bodmin Gaol.[110] The proportion of capitally convicted offenders who were hanged in the eighteenth century may also have been much lower on the periphery than near the centre. As David Jones has pointed out, capital punishment was used more sparingly in Wales than in England, and the same was also true in Cornwall. In the 1770s, for example, 41 per cent of London capital convicts and nearly a third of those found guilty on the Home Circuit were hanged, but if the parliamentary statistics are correct in Cornwall the figure was 13 per cent. Property offenders accused of a capital crime were very rarely hanged in Cornwall. Only 5 per cent went to the gallows in the 1770s compared to nearly two fifths in London.[111] The precise reasons why the London-based assize judges who made most of these decisions were systematically more lenient in Wales and in Cornwall than elsewhere remain difficult to unravel. They may have been responding to strong local traditions and pressures, to the signals put out by the local jurors' extensive use of partial verdicts, or to the relatively low recorded crime levels they found in these areas. There can be no doubt, however, that in some regions on the margins of the eighteenth-century state hanging was a very much less common experience than it was near the centre. Only five Cornish assizes out of twenty ended in a hanging in the 1770s – an era when this would have been treated as a highly unusual event in Essex. Only two property offenders were hanged in Cornwall 1770–9, compared to forty-five in Essex and this was not primarily due to different population sizes since in 1780 the Essex population was only about 22 per cent higher than that of Cornwall.[112]

The relative reluctance of assize judges to hang Cornish convicts was not the only reason why counties like Essex saw more than twenty times more property offenders being hanged in the 1770s. Like those of many other counties on the periphery, the major courts in Cornwall heard very much smaller numbers of cases than their equivalents nearer the centre. When statistics first became

---

[109] R. Shoemaker, *The London Mob. Violence and Disorder in Eighteenth-century England* (London, 2004), 89. Morgan and Rushton, *Rogues, Thieves*, 134.

[110] S. Pocock, *Behind Bars. A Chronicle of Bodmin Gaol* (Truro, 1998), 55.

[111] D. Jones, *Crime in Nineteenth-Century Wales* (Cardiff, 1992), 202; King, *Crime, Law*, 274–5; *P.P.*, 1819, viii, 155–77.

[112] P. Deane and W. Cole, *British Economic Growth 1688–1959* (Cambridge, 1969), 103.

systematically available in 1805 the Cornish indictment rate was 23 per 100,000 compared to a rate of 148 in London and Middlesex. In that year the five counties with the lowest indictment levels in England were Cornwall, Cumberland, Durham, Northumberland and Westmoreland. Overall these five counties managed only 12 per cent of the London rate and 32 per cent of the national rate. Throughout the first half of the nineteenth century these five counties, which by any definition must come close to being considered the most geographically peripheral areas of England, still had the five lowest scores, but the gap between them and London was beginning to close. By 1820–2 their average indictment rate had risen to 36 which represented 15 per cent of the London figure. By 1845–6 their average was 76 (Cornwall was 75) which was 27 per cent of the London figure and about 48 per cent of the national one.[113]

Comparisons between indictment rates in various counties are fraught with difficulties. During the second quarter of the nineteenth century a miasma of county-based statistical analyses were produced by members of the Statistical Society and by a number of writers involved in the convoluted debate about the links between crime and education. Since these often highly elaborate statistical structures were virtually all based on the assumption that indictment rates, and/or levels of change within them, were a guide to real levels of crime, their value is extremely limited.[114] In the context of the understandings that modern historians of crime have developed about the highly variable nature of pre-trial filters and summary court practices in the eighteenth and early nineteenth centuries, such assumptions are clearly untenable. No doubt there were real differences in the levels of appropriation experienced by the inhabitants of different regions, but these are largely unknowable. However, the vast differences between recorded crime rates on the periphery and those at the centre observable in 1805 do raise important questions about the relative penetration achieved by the formal criminal justice system of the late eighteenth-century state in different areas. In exploring the low recorded crime rates found in early nineteenth-century Wales, David Jones emphasised the presence of particularly strong informal mechanisms of punishment and control – of revenge attacks, communal shaming, chapel-based arbitration systems, and other informal compromise-creating and sanctioning mechanisms. It is possible that in areas far from the centre taking an offender to a magistrate, or beyond that to the point of formal indictment, was only resorted to when a whole panoply of other communal measures had failed. 'A species of clanship', one observer noted in 1842, 'renders the Welsh people averse to give evidence against a

---

[113] T. Plint, *Crime in England. Its Relation, Character and Extent as Developed from 1801 to 1848* (London, 1851), 10.

[114] Plint, *Crime*; R. Rawson, 'An Enquiry into the Condition of Criminal Offenders', *Journal of the Royal Statistical Society*, 3 (1840), 331–52; J. Fletcher, *Summary of the Moral Statistics of England and Wales* (Undated but pre-Plint)

neighbour.'[115] The incredibly low indictment rates found in Cornwall and in the far North of England in 1805 suggest that here also stronger customs about the very high priority to be given to informal sanctioning systems may well have survived longer than elsewhere, but it is very difficult to think of a way in which this assumption can be tested.

At the very least these differences alert us to the possibility that the role of the formal criminal justice system may have been much smaller on the periphery of England and Wales. Not only were punishment policies sometimes very different away from the centre, but conceptions about what proportion of, and what types of, offenders were deemed appropriate for formal prosecution may also have been very different. Such conceptions may have lain behind the fact that in the first quarter of the nineteenth century the number of juveniles prosecuted in many parts of rural England did not show the rapid increases found elsewhere (Chapter 2). Equally they may help, to some extent at least, to explain the wide variations in gender ratios amongst recorded offenders discussed in chapter 6. The fact that in the mid- and later eighteenth-century Cornwall, like most areas of the North-east studied by Morgan and Rushton, had considerably higher proportions of females amongst its accused than some regions of rural south-eastern England is not easy to explain. Throughout the eighteenth century London had a much higher proportion of females amongst its indicted offenders, and the 1805 figures confirm this pattern. London had a third more females than the national average in that year. However, the four northern counties of Cumberland, Westmorland, Northumberland and Durham had an even higher percentage of women than London. Why did these four counties, where crime rates were the lowest in England, have almost the highest proportion of females (Chapter 7)? Given the tiny absolute numbers involved, real differences in levels of male and female crime are highly unlikely to be the root cause. Rather it seems likely that those who decided which offenders were to be prosecuted were less willing to filter out women than they were in other areas. The precise role played by magistrates in this process remains very difficult to uncover. However, given that in many areas they filtered a very high proportion of felony accusations, and could also do so on gendered lines if they chose to, differences in summary-court practices between counties (and even between areas within counties) may well have been important. Here, as in the other dimensions of the relations between the central and the marginal analysed in this introduction, it is often very difficult to come to a balanced assessment because appropriate sources are extremely sparse and what archives there are

---

[115] Jones, *Crime*, 6–7. Such customs were almost certainly reinforced in remote areas by the long distances and difficult journeys that were involved in taking a case to one of the major courts.

remain seriously under researched. Many of the detailed studies presented here are attempts to open up specific aspects of these issues. In the process the aim has been to show that by studying the less commented on and less formal law-based aspects of justicing practice in the long eighteenth century, a more nuanced picture can be developed of how justice was shaped and remade by a wide range of courts and other local actors, across a number of dimensions and in a range of spatial contexts.

Part I

Juveniles

2. The rise of juvenile delinquency in England 1780–1840: changing patterns of perception and prosecution

This article focuses on a neglected but historically important transition, the rise to prominence of 'the problem of juvenile delinquency' between the 1780s and the 1830s. In the eighteenth century juveniles were rarely indicted in the courts and contemporaries did not usually regard them as a separate or particularly threatening problem. By the mid-nineteenth century juvenile delinquency was established as a major focus of anxiety among the propertied, and separate penal policies and trial procedures for young offenders were being introduced for the first time.[1] Although major works have been written on juvenile delinquency in the later nineteenth and early twentieth centuries,[2] and on the problematic relationship between youth and authority in the sixteenth and seventeenth centuries,[3] historians have been slow to analyse the major transformations

Acknowledgement: The work for this article was funded by the ESRC as part of its Crime and Social Order Initiative (Award Number L210252020). Thanks are also due to Cris Gostlow, research assistant, for her work on inputting and processing, and to all those who have commented on the conference papers given from the project.

[1] J. Beattie, *Crime and the Courts in England, 1660–1800* (Oxford, 1987), 246–7; P. Parsloe, *Juvenile Justice in Britain and the United States: The Balance of Needs and Rights* (London, 1978); W. Sanders, *Juvenile Offenders for a Thousand Years: Selective Readings from Anglo-Saxon Times to 1900* (Chapel Hill, 1970), 7–175.

[2] B. Weinberger, 'Policing Juveniles: Delinquency in Late Nineteenth and Early Twentieth-Century Manchester', *Criminal Justice History*, 14 (1993); V. Bailey, *Delinquency and Citizenship: Reclaiming the Young Offender, 1914–1948* (Oxford, 1987); J. Gillis, 'The Evolution of Juvenile Delinquency in England, 1890–1914', *Past and Present*, 67 (1975); J. Springhall, *Coming of Age: Adolescence in Britain, 1860–1960* (Dublin, 1986); also his *Youth, Empire and Society: British Youth Movements, 1883–1940* (London, 1977); D. Smith, 'Juvenile Delinquency in Britain in the First World War', *Criminal Justice History*, 11 (1990); S. Humphries, *Hooligans or Rebels? An Oral History of Working Class Childhood and Youth, 1889–1939* (Oxford, 1981); H. Hendrick, *Images of Youth: Age, Class and the Male Youth Problem, 1880–1920* (Oxford, 1990).

[3] A. Beier, *Masterless Men: The Vagrancy Problem in England, 1560–1640* (London, 1988), 54–6; P. Griffiths, *Youth and Authority: Formative Experience in England, 1560–1640* (Oxford, 1996); Sanders, *Juvenile Offenders for a Thousand Years*, 8–37; S. Smith, 'The London Apprentices as Seventeenth-Century Adolescents', *Past and Present*, 61 (1973); N. Davis, 'The Reasons of Misrule: Youth Groups and Charivaris in Sixteenth-Century France', *Past and Present*, 50 (1971); A. Yarborough, 'Apprentices as Adolescents in Sixteenth-Century Bristol', *Journal of Social History*, 13 (1979).

that occurred in the intervening period. Overviews of changing penal policies towards the young have been written, and recurring cycles of fear about youthful hooligans have been traced back to the early nineteenth century.[4] However, the relationship between the rise of juvenile crime and other contemporary changes, such as the onset of industrialisation and rapid urbanisation, the reform of many aspects of the criminal justice system or the broader rise of a more disciplinary social agenda, has not been subjected to detailed scrutiny. The period before the 1830s has been particularly neglected. Margaret May's formative article argued that it was the flood of unofficial enquiries in the 1830s and 1840s that 'elaborated the first clear concept of juvenile delinquency', while Leon Radzinowicz and Roger Hood recently concluded that 'the concept of the young offender' was 'a Victorian creation'. Even Susan Magarey's important article on 'the invention of juvenile delinquency', which suggested that by reforming the police and by criminalising forms of juvenile behaviour previously ignored by the courts parliament legislated juvenile delinquency into existence, focused almost entirely on the late 1820s, 1830s and 1840s.[5]

Because no systematic statistics on juvenile offenders were published before the mid-1830s, the few historians who have attempted to construct theories about when, where and why juvenile delinquency came to be perceived as a major social problem have had to do so without any understanding of what was actually happening in the courts. Building on the preliminary work done by Peter King and Joan Noel on London,[6] which indicated that the prosecution of juveniles increased very rapidly well before the period focused on by May, Magarey and Radzinowicz, this article begins by constructing a much fuller picture of juvenile prosecution patterns using data gathered from the court records of a variety of English regions. It then moves on to discuss changing discourses about, and changing prosecution policies towards, young offenders, as part of a more general exploration of the relationship between the growth of juvenile prosecutions and broader economic, social, judicial and ideological changes.

[4] L. Radzinowicz and R. Hood, *A History of English Criminal Law and its Administration from 1750*, 5 vols. (London, 1948–86), v, 133–230; I. Pinchbeck and M. Hewitt, *Children in English Society*, 2 vols. (London, 1969–73), i, 91–125; ii, 414–95; G. Pearson, *Hooligans: A History of Respectable Fears* (London, 1983).

[5] M. May, 'Innocence and Experience: The Evolution of the Concept of Juvenile Delinquency in the Mid-Nineteenth Century', *Victorian Studies*, 17 (1973), 117; Radzinowicz and Hood, *History of English Criminal Law*, v, 133; S. Magarey, 'The Invention of Juvenile Delinquency in Early Nineteenth-Century England', *Labour History*, 34 (1978). For other insights into this period, see also P. Rush, 'The Government of a Generation: The Subject of Juvenile Delinquency', *Liverpool Law Review*, 14 (1992); M. May, 'A Child's Punishment for a Child's Crime: The Reformatory and Industrial Schools Movement in Britain, 1780–1860' (PhD thesis, University of London, 1981); J. Muncie, *The Trouble with Kids Today: Youth and Crime in Post-War Britain* (London, 1984), 30–6.

[6] P. King and J. Noel, 'The Origins of "The Problem of Juvenile Delinquency": The Growth of Juvenile Prosecutions in London in the Late Eighteenth and Early Nineteenth Centuries', *Criminal Justice History*, 14 (1993).

The resulting analysis of the origins of juvenile delinquency as a specifically defined social problem raises a number of interrelated questions. Can the rise of juvenile prosecutions be simply linked, as some general histories have suggested,[7] to a real increase in crime caused by the rapid migration, social dislocation and family breakdown that sometimes accompanied urbanisation and industrialisation in this period? Were there other demographic, economic and social changes – such as the decline of apprenticeship and living-in service – which produced a real rise in juvenile crime? Alternatively, given the highly discretionary nature of the criminal justice system in the final half-century before the coming of the new police, was it the changing attitudes of victims and committing magistrates, combined with various alterations in the administration of criminal justice, that mainly determined juvenile prosecution rates? Finally, and perhaps most importantly, did a new set of discourses about juvenile delinquency emerge which increased the proportion of victims and magistrates willing to prosecute young offenders, and what was the relationship between those discourses[8] and broader changes in attitudes towards childhood and towards the disciplining of the poor?

I

Any study of patterns of juvenile crime faces three initial problems – defining 'juvenile', defining 'crime', and finding sources systematic enough for robust analysis. The latter is not easy for the period before 1834, when statistics about the ages of offenders first became available on a national basis. The officials of most quarter sessions and assizes courts did not regularly record the age of the accused until well into the nineteenth century. Summary-court clerks virtually never did so. Fortunately, however, gaol calendars or other records containing fairly systematic age information have survived from the late eighteenth century in a minority of counties, eleven of which have been chosen for study here.[9]

---

[7] For example, J. Tobias, *Crime and Industrial Society in the Nineteenth Century* (Harmondsworth, 1972), 42–7; S. McConville, *A History of English Prison Administration*, 1, *1750–1877* (London, 1981), 218–19.

[8] The rather clumsy notion of a 'set of discourses' has been used here instead of the singular 'discourse' because the new discursive formations that arose in relation to juvenile delinquency in the early nineteenth century were not unitary. Although they overlapped and contained many common themes, they also included several alternative ways of seeing, conceptualising and explaining 'the alarming increase of juvenile delinquency'. Indeed, there were even a few observers who were unsure whether it was increasing at all. 'Debates' would be too weak a word, however, for these mushrooming discursive formations were not merely sets of words and arguments. They contained operative notions (and closures) which defined to a greater or lesser degree what could or could not, should or should not, be said and done in relation to juvenile offenders in certain situations.

[9] The following records were sampled: Lancashire Record Office, Preston, QSB/1, QJC, Lancashire Assizes Gaol Calendars and Quarterly Prison Calendars in the Recognizance Rolls, 1801–5,

Even in these areas some problems remain. Only the Old Bailey records, which began in 1791, provide almost complete coverage. Elsewhere, administrative practices were not always consistent. The recording of ages was sometimes dropped after a few years (as it was in the Home Circuit Agenda Books in 1787). The only sources available in many areas, the gaol calendars, survive only intermittently and have often been damaged. In most counties and in most years, calendars are not available for all six quarter sessions and assizes hearings. In some areas very patchy survival produces rather small samples, particularly for the pre-1793 period. Given this sporadic survival it is rarely possible to create data on the absolute numbers of juveniles indicted in any particular county.[10] However, the sources do allow the proportion of offenders who were juveniles to be compared across time and among regions.

In order to ensure compatibility, the types of evidence put into the data sets has to be strictly defined. While the Home Circuit Agenda Books and the Old Bailey Registers present no problems, because they only listed those about to be tried, the gaol calendars were rather different. They often included both prisoners awaiting trial and those already sentenced to imprisonment or transportation post-trial. Only the former were entered in the data sets because jury verdicts and sentencing policies varied between age groups, which meant that post-conviction prisoners were not a typical sample of those originally indicted. The analysis was also confined to those accused of felony. Those indicted or summarily tried for misdemeanours, such as assault, false balances, and offences against the poor laws, were not usually held in gaol before trial and relatively rarely appeared in the gaol calendars. When contemporaries spoke about crime they seldom included misdemeanours.[11] Their sense of the current level of crime was based on the number of felons tried before the major courts. There are, therefore, good theoretical as well as practical reasons for focusing on felony. The Gloucestershire, Berkshire, Shropshire, Bristol and Lancashire gaol

1820–2; Shropshire Record Office, Shrewsbury, Shropshire Gaol Calendars, vols. i–ii, 1786–92, 1819–22, 1826–8; Gloucestershire Record Office, Gloucester (hereafter GRO), QSG/2, Gloucestershire Gaol Calendars, 1789–93, 1806–11, 1820–2, 1825–7; City of Bristol Record Office, Bristol, Sessions Bundles Gaol Calendars, 1786–92, 1794–1805, 1820–2 (Bristol, it should be noted, was not in the county of Gloucestershire but had a separate, county-level jurisdiction for both quarter sessions and assizes); Berkshire Record Office, Reading, Q/SR 207, 210–35, Q/SR 340–51, Q/SR 370–9, Gaol Calendars on the Sessions Rolls, 1786–92, 1819–21, 1826–8 (if rolls did not survive, the parallel series B/Epb was used); Public Record Office, Kew (hereafter PRO), HO 26/1–2, HO 26/26–8, London and Middlesex Criminal Registers, 1791–3, 1820–2. The HO 26 series lists all offenders confined in Newgate. These included both those from the county of Middlesex and those from the City of London. Offenders awaiting trial from these two jurisdictions form the basis of the data presented here. For the five Home Circuit counties (Surrey, Kent, Essex, Hertfordshire, Sussex), see PRO, Assi 31/13–15, 18–19, 23–4, 25, Assizes Agenda Books, 1782–7, 1799–1801, 1820–1, 1827.

[10] The calendars are also patchy in their coverage of those awaiting trial at borough sessions.

[11] Although the felony–misdemeanour division did not completely follow the division between those crimes that contemporaries labelled as serious and those they did not, it was close.

calendars all included both quarter-sessions and assizes data in every period. The five Home Circuit counties (Essex, Hertfordshire, Kent, Surrey and Sussex) and the Old Bailey data which covered both Middlesex and the City of London related to assize indictments only throughout the period and therefore excluded some non-capital cases. However, non-aggravated larceny dominated the data sets of all eleven counties and, although it must be kept in mind that minor thefts are slightly less well represented around London, all the data sets are therefore broadly comparable.[12]

The precise age groups to be examined were decided by reference to contemporary definitions. The term 'juvenile' was preferred to 'youth' as the keystone of this study because 'juvenile' was clearly the central word around which a new discourse was developing in the early nineteenth century.[13] Throughout the early modern period, 'youth' was perceived and experienced as a very gradual learning process, a long journey to adulthood, usually lasting until the mid-twenties or beyond (i.e. until the achievement of domestic independence at marriage). The links between crime and this period of extended youth or young adulthood were well understood by early modern commentators and previous work on the age structure of offenders has confirmed that eighteenth-century men and women were most vulnerable to prosecution between their late teens and their mid-to-late twenties.[14] Although eighteenth-century dictionaries overlapped the terms, often defining 'juvenile' as simply 'youthful' or 'young',[15] the growing debates about 'the alarming increase of juvenile delinquency' in the early nineteenth century focused on an earlier part of the lifespan. Those who spoke about juveniles did not all agree about the precise age group to which they were referring. For a few, 'juvenile' coincided with what others called 'childhood' (i.e. the years up to about age fourteen, the age at which offenders ceased to enjoy the partial legal immunities provided by *doli incapax*). At the other extreme, those wishing to stress the vast extent of juvenile depravity stretched their definitions to include anyone under twenty-one. However, the vast majority of those who were asked by parliamentary committees to define

---

[12] Non-aggravated larceny, being a form of property theft, was not deemed a capital offence. For a discussion of comparability and intercourt transfers, see King and Noel, 'Origins of "the Problem of Juvenile Delinquency" ', 20.

[13] The most obvious example is the seminal *Report of the Committee for Investigating the Causes of the Alarming Increase of Juvenile Delinquency in the Metropolis* (London, 1816), but in the subsequent investigations by parliamentary committees 'juvenile' remained the keyword.

[14] I. Ben-Amos, 'Service and the Coming of Age of Young Men in Seventeenth-Century England', *Continuity and Change*, 3 (1988); also her *Adolescence and Youth in Early Modern England* (London, 1994); P. King, 'Decision-Makers and Decision-Making in the English Criminal Law, 1750–1800', *Historical Journal*, 27 (1984).

[15] Juvenile was defined as 'youthful, sprightly, brisk' in N. Bailey, *An Universal Etymological English Dictionary*, 24th edn (London, 1782); as 'Young, youthful' in T. Sheridan, *A Complete Dictionary of the English Language*, 2nd edn (London, 1789); also in S. Johnson, *A Dictionary of the English Language*, 8th edn (London, 1792).

Table 2.1 *Proportion of property offenders aged 0–17*

		1782–93	1794–1811	*c.*1820–2	Later 1820s
1.	Shropshire (all)	10	–	9	10
1a.	Industrial Shropshire	10	–	11	11
1b.	Shrewsbury	14	–	9	14
1c.	Rural Shropshire	10	–	8	9
2.	Berkshire	11	–	4	16
3.	Bedfordshire	–	8	7	7
4.	Gloucestershire	15	12	14	17
5.	Bristol	28	10	28	–
6.	Lancashire (all)	–	13	26	–
6a.	Lancashire (excluding Liverpool and Manchester)	–	9	18	–
6b.	Liverpool	–	–	22	–
6c.	Manchester	–	17	34	–
7.	Salford Hundred	–	12	30	23
8.	London and Middlesex	10	–	23	–
9.	Surrey	8	–	17	15
10.	Kent	8	–	10	16
11.	Essex	10	–	8	10
12.	Hertfordshire	8	–	19	11
13.	Sussex	5	–	12	11
14.	All five home counties	8	7	13	13

Source: notes. 9, 17.

what they meant by juvenile did not go beyond the age of seventeen (0–17 being the age range recommended for the juvenile reformatory proposed in 1817) or, at the very broadest, nineteen.[16] These two age groups are therefore used as the basis for Tables 2.1 and 2.2.[17]

Contemporary debates also shaped the decision to focus primarily on property crime. Many forms of juvenile behaviour from gambling to sabbath-breaking worried contemporaries, but it was 'juvenile depredators', juveniles who stole property, that formed the primary target of their concerns. The other potential focus, violent crime, was notably absent from contemporary discussions about

[16] The 1828 Select Committee on Criminal Commitments and Convictions, for example, included evidence using the following groupings, 0–14, 0–17 and even 0–20: *P.P.*, 1828, vi, 470, 480, 486. Plint used 0–19 for his calculations: T. Plint, *Crime in England* (London, 1851), 92. D. Philips, *Crime and Authority in Victorian England* (London, 1977), 161. For evidence presented to the 1817 Committee on the State of the Police of the Metropolis advocating a juvenile penitentiary for 0–17 year olds, see *P.P.*, 1817, vii, 431.

[17] Tables 2.1 and 2.2 are based on the data collected on individual offenders from the counties and cities listed in n. 9 above, and on limited statistics kept by contemporaries for three other areas. For Bedfordshire manuscript tables of criminal statistics, 1801–78, see Bedfordshire Record Office, Bedford (hereafter BRO), QSS/4. For Warwickshire, see *P.P.*, 1828, vi, 444; *P.P.*, 1831–2, xxxiii, 2. For Manchester and the Salford Hundred as represented by those imprisoned in the New Bailey Prison, Salford, see *P.P.*, 1828, vi, 520–3.

Table 2.2 *Proportion of property offenders aged 0–19*

		1782–93	1794–1811	*c.*1820–2	Later 1820s
1.	Shropshire (all)	17	–	22	22
1a.	Industrial Shropshire	23	–	28	21
1b.	Shrewsbury	20	–	26	30
1c.	Rural Shropshire	17	–	19	21
2.	Berkshire	22	–	13	30
3.	Bedfordshire	–	–	–	–
4.	Gloucestershire	22	22	26	35
5.	Bristol	39	19	47	–
6.	Lancashire (all)	–	21	40	–
6a.	Lancashire (excluding Liverpool and Manchester)	–	17	29	–
6b.	Liverpool	–	–	37	–
6c.	Manchester	–	26	48	–
7.	Salford Hundred	–	–	–	–
8.	London and Middlesex	21	–	38	–
9.	Surrey	21	–	35	29
10.	Kent	20	–	20	34
11.	Essex	16	–	21	27
12.	Hertfordshire	17	–	17	22
13.	Sussex	17	–	20	25
14.	All five home counties	19	14	25	29
15.	Warwickshire	–	–	–	43

Sources: notes 9, 17.

juvenile lawbreaking and the data collected on felonies not involving property appropriation indicates why. Not only do non-property crimes, such as murder and rape, form a very small proportion of felony indictments (usually 5–10 per cent) but also juveniles were much less well represented among these types of offence. In London in 1791–3, for example, less than 1 per cent of non-property offenders were under eighteen.[18] Tables 2.1 and 2.2 therefore focus on property crimes alone, although given the small numbers of non-property felonies indicted, the percentages would not have been very different if these had been included, as they were in some of the sources used for Figure 2.1.[19]

This data on the proportions of offenders who fell within various definitions of the word juvenile cannot be summarised briefly without considerable

[18] Based on sample years and sources listed in n. 9 above. In London, Bristol and Shropshire, for example, juveniles were always under-represented among non-property crime felony indictments.
[19] Sources for Figure 2.1 were BRO, QSS/4; *P.P.*, 1828, vi, 523; Gloucestershire Gaol Calendars (n. 9 above); also Heather Shore's count of London offenders from the Criminal Registers: PRO, HO 26. I would like to thank her for letting me use data here collected for her PhD thesis, 'The Social History of Juvenile Crime in Middlesex, 1790–1850' (University of London, Royal Holloway College, 1996).

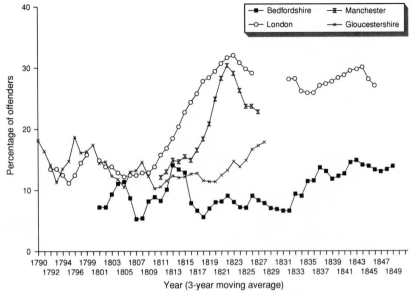

Figure 2.1   Percentage of offenders aged 0–17 years, Bedfordshire, Gloucestershire and Manchester, and 0–18 in London 1790–1850.
Note: Based on 3-year moving averages.
Sources: See note 19.

simplification. Indeed, most of the twenty subregions in Tables 2.1 and 2.2 could be given separate detailed treatment if space allowed.[20] Still, despite the lack of pre-1793 data for some areas, and of wartime or later 1820s data for others, several clear changes emerge. First, the wartime period (1794–1811) was not a period when juveniles made an increasing impact on indictment levels. In fact, in some areas, such as Bristol and the Home Counties, a considerable decline occurred.

---

[20] The subregions in Tables 2.1 and 2.2 and Figure 2.1 were defined as follows. Shropshire was divided into three subregions: Shrewsbury borough; the industrial and mining area (Astley Abbotts, Barrow, Benthall, Broseley, Dawley, Eyton upon the Weald, Lilleshall, Priors Lee, Wellington, Little Wenlock, Madeley, Willey, Wrockwardine, Preston upon the Weald Moors and Stircheley); and rural Shropshire, which was defined as the rest of Shropshire. The industrial–mining subregion was decided upon using mainly B. Trinder, *The Industrial Revolution in Shropshire* (London, 1973). Unfortunately, several of these parishes were in the obscure jurisdiction of the borough of Much Wenlock, where clerks did not record the ages of the accused, which reduces sample sizes especially in the early period. Lancashire was divided more simply into Liverpool, Manchester and Salford Town, and the rest of Lancashire, the first two areas being defined as listed in *VCH Lancaster*, 2, 343–9.

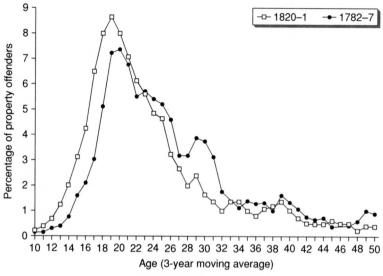

Figure 2.2   Age structure of all property offenders: Surrey 1782–7 and 1820–1.
Note: Based on 3-year moving averages.
Source: Public Record Office, London, Assi/31/13–15, Home Circuit, Assize Agenda Books, 1782–7; Assi/31/23–4, 1820–1.

In wartime many young males were either recruited before they committed crimes or diverted into the armed forces after they had done so without being indicted.[21] Lacking systematic information on recruitment practices and pre-trial hearings, the exact impact of war on juvenile prosecutions cannot be gauged. Long-term trends are therefore best evaluated by comparing the two peacetime periods, 1782–93 and 1815 onwards.

These two periods both began with rapid demobilisation and overcrowded labour markets. Both also witnessed rising indictment rates and heightened anxieties about crime. However, the impact that these broad changes had on juvenile prosecution levels seems to have been very different in the two periods. In London and Surrey (a county whose indictments came largely from its metropolitan area) the proportion of offenders under eighteen more than

---

[21] On changes between wartime and peacetime, and wartime recruitment, see D. Hay, 'War, Dearth and Theft in the Eighteenth Century: The Record of the English Courts', *Past and Present*, 95 (1982); P. King, 'War, Judicial Discretion and the Problems of Young Adulthood', *Social History Society Newsletter*, 9 (Spring 1984); P. King, 'War as a Judicial Resource. Press Gangs and Prosecution Rates 1740–1830' in N. Landau (ed.), *Law, Crime and English Society, 1660–1840* (Cambridge, 2002). The impact of war was particularly great in ports such as Bristol where press gangs were very active, which may explain the large falls in Tables 2.1 and 2.2 during wartime.

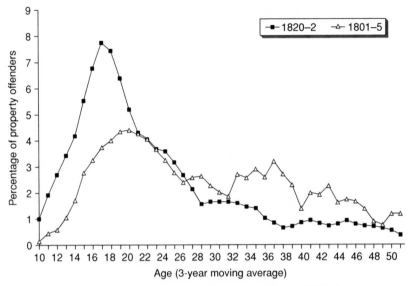

Figure 2.3   Age structure of property offenders: Manchester 1801–5 and 1820–2.
Note: Based on 3-year moving averages.
Source: Lancashire Record Office, Preston, QSB/1, QJC Lancashire Assizes Gaol Calendars and
Quarterly Prison Recognizance Rolls, 1801–5, 1820–2.

doubled between 1785–93 and 1820–2 (Table 2.1, Figures 2.1 and 2.2).[22] The
proportion under twenty increased by about three quarters to 38 and 35 per cent
respectively (Table 2.2).

By 1820–2 this age group had grown to dominate the age structure of indicted
property offenders not only in the metropolis but also in Liverpool, Bristol,
Warwickshire (where 90 per cent of indictments came from Birmingham)[23]
and Manchester (Table 2.2, Figure 2.3). However, while the 1820–2 data sets
for regions mainly centred on large cities showed very high proportions of
0–19 year olds among the indicted at between 35 and 48 per cent, Berkshire,
rural Shropshire and the other four still predominantly rural Home Counties
achieved only about half that level, at between 13 and 24 per cent. The rural
and declining proto-industrial county of Gloucestershire, the mining and iron-
producing region of Shropshire, the small provincial centre and minor textile
factory town of Shrewsbury, and Lancashire (excluding Manchester, Salford

[22] The pattern of change in the age structures of the accused 1791–3 to 1820–1 in London was
very similar to that found in Surrey: see King and Noel, 'Origins of "the Problem of Juvenile
Delinquency" ', 21.
[23] *P.P.*, 1828, vi, 445.

and Liverpool), formed an intermediate group at between 26 and 29 per cent.[24] The data for 0–17 year olds shows an even more polarised pattern for 1820–2. While in predominantly agricultural regions such as Bedfordshire, Berkshire and rural Shropshire this group averaged only 4–8 per cent of indicted property offenders, in the major cities and the catchment area of the Salford Gaol (i.e. Manchester, Salford, and the Salford Hundred, which included rapidly growing industrial towns such as Bolton and Oldham) they averaged four times these amounts at 22–34 per cent. Those areas with some form of manufacturing or proto-industrial base – industrial Shropshire, Shrewsbury, Gloucestershire – again achieved a slightly higher level than the agricultural areas, but were a long way behind the big cities at 9–14 per cent (Table 2.1, Figure 2.1).

Figure 2.1 (which includes London data for 0–18 year olds 1791–1850 kindly made available by Heather Shore) makes the urban–rural contrast particularly clear. While in London and Manchester the percentages rose very dramatically in the later 1810s to a peak in the early 1820s, Bedfordshire shows no long-term increase at all until the mid-1830s. By 1821 Manchester's percentages were three times higher than Bedfordshire's. A huge urban/rural gap had emerged. That gap was not present in the early 1800s when Bedfordshire had much the same proportion of juvenile offenders as Gloucestershire, London and the Salford Gaol/Manchester area. The same pattern of rough equality can be seen in the pre-1793 data (Tables 2.1–2.2). Despite the small sample sizes available in some subregions for this early period, every area except Bristol produced figures between 16 and 23 per cent. Since Gloucestershire and Berkshire each had very slightly higher proportions of juveniles than London and Surrey, the clear urban-to-rural hierarchy observable in 1820–2 is simply not in evidence thirty years earlier. Although the lack of pre-1793 data for Lancashire and Manchester[25] may make the 1815–22 period appear slightly more exceptional than it really was, all the information available suggests that the late 1810s and early 1820s were a unique period in the history of indictable juvenile crime. Not only were consistent and large urban–rural contrasts firmly established by

---

[24] Of the four other Home Counties, Sussex and Hertfordshire remained largely rural. Kent and, to a lesser extent, Essex contained gradually increasing neo-metropolitan areas where they bordered with London. By 1827, Kent, which had the fastest-growing London suburbs, was experiencing juvenile indictment percentages as high as Surrey, while rural Hertfordshire and Sussex were not. Shrewsbury is interesting because it was one of the thirty largest towns in England in 1801 and, more importantly, between 1786–92 and 1820–1 its manufacturing industry expanded vigorously with the opening of several textile mills. The Shropshire coalfield experienced its most rapid expansion and time of greatest prosperity in the late eighteenth century. B. Trinder, 'The Textile Industry in Shrewsbury in the Late Eighteenth Century' and 'The Shropshire Coalfield', in P. Clark and P. Corfield (eds.), *Industry in Eighteenth-Century England* (Leicester, 1994). Gloucestershire was a predominantly rural county. South Gloucestershire's once-thriving textile industry went into severe decline after 1815. J. Mann, *The Cloth Industry in the West of England from 1640 to 1880* (Oxford, 1971).

[25] The Lancashire sources do not start to record ages until 1801.

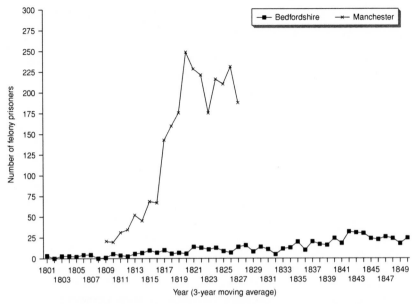

Figure 2.4   Number of felony prisoners under 18: Bedfordshire and Manchester area 1801–50.
Note: Based on 3-year moving averages.
Source: Bedfordshire Record Office, Bedford, QSS/4, Parliamentary Papers, 1828, vi, 523.

1820–2, but also by that time certain urban areas had experienced a veritable deluge of recorded juvenile crime.

Because they are based on percentages, Tables 2.1 and 2.2 and Figure 2.1 understate the extent of that deluge and of the contrasts between the experiences of urban and rural magistrates. Felony indictment levels tripled nationwide between 1805–7 and 1820–2 and, since the urban areas, where juveniles' percentages were rising most rapidly, also had much higher than average indictment rates and faster-growing populations, they experienced a phenomenal increase in the actual number of juveniles being indicted, as the comparison of the Bedfordshire and Manchester data in Figure 2.4 makes clear.[26]

The second quarter of the nineteenth century witnessed a very different pattern of indictable crime rates as many agricultural areas began to catch up with the higher rates exhibited in metropolitan regions between 1805 and 1820.[27] The data from the later 1820s in Tables 2.1 and 2.2 and Figure 2.1 suggests that

[26] On the tripling of indictment rates, see C. Emsley, *Crime and Society in England, 1750–1900*, 2nd edn (London, 1996), 35; on higher indictment rates 1801–21 in urban areas, see Plint, *Crime in England*, 10; on higher population growth rates, see P. Deane and W. Cole, *British Economic Growth, 1688–1959* (Cambridge, 1969), 103.

[27] Plint, *Crime in England*, 10.

the urban–rural contrasts in the proportions of offenders who were juveniles were also becoming less polarised. In London, Surrey and, to a much greater extent, in the Manchester area, the percentage had fallen by the later 1820s, while in some rural areas, such as Berkshire and Sussex, although not in all, considerable increases had begun to become evident.

The nationwide county-based statistics on crimes committed by all age groups which became available for the first time in 1834, albeit only for 0–16 year olds,[28] confirm the continued leadership of counties with large urban areas. At 20 per cent, Bristol's remained the highest in England. Surrey and London/Middlesex held second and third places with 15 per cent. Lancashire and Warwickshire were both in the top six at 13 per cent. However rural counties like Sussex and Gloucestershire (where the cloth industry was now in terminal decline) were no longer far behind at 11 per cent, as were several other rural counties such as Devon and Norfolk.[29] This tendency towards urban–rural convergence continued into the 1840s when the criminal statistics were reorganised to give data on 0–19 year olds. For 1844–6, Thomas Plint calculated that this age group formed 28 per cent of indicted offenders in his sample of 22 agricultural counties (which included Berkshire, Essex, Hertfordshire and Sussex), 30 per cent in his six manufacturing counties (which included Lancashire and Warwickshire) and 34 and 36 per cent in Surrey and Middlesex.[30]

More interestingly perhaps, although exact comparisons are difficult, there appears to have been no increase in the overall proportion of indicted offenders aged 0–19 between 1820–2 and the mid-1840s. Between 1842 and 1847 the national data indicates that 29 per cent of indicted offenders were in that age group. Given that in 1820–2 London and Lancashire, which accounted for over a third of all indicted offenders, had percentages of 38 and 40 per cent for 0–19 year olds, that Bristol, Surrey and Warwickshire had similar percentages, and that the remaining counties about which information is available averaged 21 per cent, the proportion of indicted offenders aged 0–19 was almost certainly very similar to that found in 1842–7.[31] The period up to the early 1820s therefore contrasts markedly with the two decades that followed. The first twenty years or so of the nineteenth century witnessed a decisive shift in the proportions and numbers of juveniles being indicted for property theft, and it was rapidly expanding industrial and commercial cities like Manchester and established metropolitan centres like London and Bristol that brought about that change.

---

[28] The criminal statistics were reorganised in 1833. The 1834 tabulations included age data for the first time for ages 0–12, 13–16 and 17–21. The last group cannot be broken down, however, and cannot be regarded as juvenile. See V. Gatrell and T. Hadden, 'Criminal Statistics and their Interpretation', in E. A. Wrigley (ed.), *Nineteenth-Century Society: Essays in the Use of Quantitative Methods for the Study of Social Data* (Cambridge, 1972), 341–2.

[29] Based on the data for 1834–6: *P.P*, 1835, xlv; 1836, xli; 1837, xlvi.

[30] Plint, *Crime in England*, 98, 163–4.

[31] 1842–7. National data from May, 'Child's Punishment for a Child's Crime', 624.

However, in the next two decades the urban–rural polarities of 1820–2, seen in both general indictment rates and in the proportion of offenders who were juveniles, began to diminish. At the same time, the impact that juveniles made on indictments ceased to increase and may even have declined very slightly.

What caused this change after 1820–2? While the very gradual long-term growth in the proportion of rural indictments that involved juveniles was important, the main momentum for change almost certainly came, once again, from urban areas such as London, Manchester and Liverpool. Figure 2.1 suggests that the juvenile percentages found in the Manchester area declined fairly rapidly after 1822, but it considerably understates that decline because it is based on a three-year moving average. In 1821, 32 per cent of the indictable offenders held in the Salford Gaol were aged 0–17. By 1827, the figure was 21 per cent. Figure 2.1 suggests a similar if less spectacular decline in London and this pattern can be confirmed by comparing our 1820–2 data on 0–16 year olds with that found in the 1834–6 criminal returns. In London percentages declined from 17 to 15 per cent, in Lancashire from 20 to 13 per cent.[32] The mid- to late 1820s clearly witnessed a major change. On first sight this seems difficult to explain since neither area experienced economic or social changes that drastically improved the lives of juveniles between the early and late 1820s. However, the shadowy world of summary jurisdiction may well provide the answer.

Very few summary courts kept any systematic records before the 1830s and it was extremely rare for the age of the accused to be recorded. However, their activities clearly had an important influence on the pattern of juvenile indictments. Eighteenth-century magistrates heard a wide range of cases, both civil and criminal. In law, their role in property crime cases was heavily circumscribed. All those accused of felonies were to be sent for trial at the quarter sessions or assizes. Parliament had given magistrates the right to deal summarily with a small subgroup of minor thefts, such as wood and vegetable stealing, poaching or the false-reeling of yarn. These were primarily rural forms of appropriation and their urban equivalents remained largely outside legislatively sanctioned summary jurisdiction. In reality, many urban magistrates and some rural ones had long found ways of using their other summary powers, such as those relating to vagrants, in order to punish at least a small minority of potentially indictable offenders. Such practices were rarely recorded. In wartime, forced enlistment into the armed forces was frequently used as an alternative to trial for felony. In peacetime, eighteenth-century magistrates in a number of areas may have quietly and fairly consistently used various other summary options.[33] It was only after the end of the eighteenth century that various changes in both

---

[32] *P.P.*, 1828, vi, 520–3; data for 1820–2 based on sources in n. 9; for 1834–6, see n. 29.

[33] For a discussion of the informal ways in which eighteenth-century magistrates dealt with some cases using summary powers or the power to commit the accused 'for further examination', see P. King, *Crime, Justice and Discretion in England, 1740–1820* (Oxford, 2000), chapter 4. On

law and practice began to increase the impact of summary jurisdiction on this type of offender.

Initially the changes were largely confined to London. The acts in 1792 and 1800 which set up the Middlesex Stipendiary Magistracy and the Thames Police Office gave London JPs increasing powers to convict various types of property offenders for unlawful possession or as suspected or reputed thieves. Despite the lack of evidence it is clear that by the mid-1810s these changes were having some impact. Between 1813 and 1817, 10 per cent of property offenders in the Middlesex House of Correction at Coldbath Fields had been summarily convicted as reputed thieves. However, it was only after the 1822 and 1824 Vagrancy Acts, which extended magistrates' powers in relation to reputed thieves and suspects, that summary proceedings began to be extensively substituted for jury trial. Between 1813–17 and 1827–8 the average annual number of reputed thieves held at Coldbath Fields rose from 53 to over 500. The establishment of the Metropolitan Police force in 1829 brought a further acceleration. By 1831–3 an average of 2,500 people were being convicted by London magistrates as either reputed thieves or suspicious characters. The majority of London's property crime cases were now being dealt with summarily. By 1840–2 when statistics first became available the same was also true in Manchester, Liverpool and, to a lesser extent, Birmingham.[34]

In Manchester the key change almost certainly came in the early 1820s. In 1822, a local police act regulating the fairly recently appointed Manchester and Salford stipendiaries enabled arrests to be made for unlawful possession. In the same year the Vagrancy Act extended the summary powers to convict property offenders as reputed thieves or suspected persons already available in London to all of England.[35] In Manchester the result seems to have been the rapid development of a system similar to that found in London, whereby summary convictions were imposed on an increasingly large proportion of potentially indictable offenders. This in turn may well explain the rapid decline in the proportion of Manchester's indicted offenders who were juveniles in the five years immediately after the 1822 Vagrancy Act (Figure 2.1), because these new summary powers were mainly used to deal with juvenile offenders. Contemporaries often remarked on this and although statistical evidence is fragmentary the pattern is clear. The Coldbath Fields data for 1816–17 indicates that 71 per cent of reputed thieves were under 20, whereas only 32 per cent of

---

wartime use of recruitment, see King,'War'; See also T. Sweeney, 'The Extension and Practice of Summary Jurisdiction in England, c. 1790–1860' (PhD thesis University of Cambridge, 1985).

[34] Sweeney, 'Extension and Practice of Summary Jurisdiction', 183–216, 401–25; *P.P.*, 1816, v, 384; *P.P.*, 1818, viii, 288–9.

[35] R. Burn, *The Justice of the Peace and Parish Officer*, 28th edn, 6 vols. (London, 1837), vi, 121–2. This change was consolidated in the 1824 Vagrancy Act – Sweeney 'Extension and Practice of Summary Jurisdiction', 108.

felons committed for trial were in that age group. Returns for the late 1830s confirm that the majority of those convicted of unlawful possession or of being suspicious characters or reputed thieves were juveniles.[36]

Thus, by quietly dealing with an increasing proportion of property offenders summarily, the magistrates of London and Manchester put an end to the rapid rises in the proportions of indicted offenders who were juveniles seen in the 1810s and early 1820s (Figure 2.1). In these key cities of London, Manchester, Liverpool and Birmingham, which contributed about a third of all English indictments, the informal rise of summary jurisdiction had a major impact on the age structure of indictable offenders after 1822. The stagnation or decline in the proportion of indictable offenders who were juveniles in urban areas between 1820–2 and the early 1840s did not reflect a levelling off in the number or percentage of juveniles being prosecuted, but rather their transfer between jurisdictions. Magarey was right in stressing the importance of the summary legislation and policing changes of the 1820s and 1830s but wrong to conclude that juvenile delinquency was 'invented' or 'legislated into existence' in this period.[37] Recorded juvenile delinquency was not invented in the 1820s and 1830s; it was transferred and given a further boost by the strategic use that urban magistrates made of the increasingly wide discretionary powers these summary acts gave them. Although the long and heated debate about the sanctity of jury trial meant that parliament did not formally grant magistrates the power to try larceny cases involving juveniles until 1847–50,[38] the magistrates of the largest urban areas simply developed their own system of summary trial for the majority of property offenders and then used it most extensively to deal with juveniles.

By contrast no such major transformation occurred in rural areas. The Malicious Trespass Acts of 1820 and 1827 did result in an increasing number of property offenders being summarily convicted, and a number of these would have been juveniles caught raiding orchards, gardens and woods, but these acts were not used primarily against juveniles. In 1840–1 only 17 per cent of those convicted under these acts were under 17, whereas 32 per cent of reputed thieves were in that age group.[39] The Vagrancy acts of 1822–4 also seem to have been used relatively rarely against rural property offenders if the Gloucestershire House of Correction data is any guide.[40] Historians have

---

[36] *P.P.*, 1817, vii, 552; *P.P.*, 1818, viii, 288–9; Sweeney 'Extension and Practice Summary Jurisdiction', 223.

[37] Magarey, 'Invention of Juvenile Delinquency', 24–5.

[38] May, 'Innocence and Experience', 14.

[39] J. Fletcher, 'Progress of Crime in the United Kingdom: Abstracted from the Criminal Returns for 1842 and the Prison Returns for the Year ended Michaelmas 1841', *Journal of the Statistical Society*, 6 (1843), 230.

[40] I am thankful to Peter Bullock for making available data collected from the GRO Prison Registers confirming this: GRO, Q/Gri 16/1–3, GBR – G3/.

largely neglected the rural summary courts and firmer conclusions cannot be reached until a detailed study has been conducted. However, it seems likely that while in London, Liverpool and Manchester summary conviction had become the usual experience for property thieves by the 1830s and 1840s, in rural areas this did not occur until after parliament formally transferred certain types of offence to summary jurisdiction in 1847, 1850 and 1855.[41]

Thus, just as the large urban areas spearheaded the rapid rise in the proportion of indicted offenders who were juveniles in the period before 1822, so in the years that followed it was the magistrates of the big cities who took the lead in transferring juvenile property offenders into the murky world of informal summary jurisdiction. By doing so they further increased the numbers and proportions of juveniles who were imprisoned or processed by the criminal justice system. This in turn explains, in part at least, why anxieties about juvenile offenders and their treatment continued to rise in the later 1820s, 1830s and 1840s, despite the fact that the proportion of juveniles among indicted offenders showed no significant overall increase after the early 1820s. Underlying changes were also occurring in rural areas. The proportion of rural indicted offenders who were juveniles rose slowly between 1820 and the 1840s, and growing use of the Malicious Trespass Acts, combined with a growing intolerance of wood and vegetable thieves, may have gradually brought increasing numbers of rural juvenile offenders into the summary courts.[42] However, both before and after 1820, it was the large urban areas that experienced the most rapid changes. Those who had to spend their formative years in the great expanding cities of early nineteenth-century England were uniquely vulnerable. Urban juveniles found themselves at the cutting edge of both the rapid increase in indictment rates between 1805 and 1822 and the swift expansion of urban summary jurisdiction in property crime cases from 1822 onwards.

It was mainly boys rather than girls who were at risk. The proportion of indicted offenders who were women fell considerably in almost every part of England in the first third of the nineteenth century, and in urban areas like Manchester the proportion of young offenders who were female fell rapidly in the 1810s, at precisely the time when juvenile prosecution rates were rising most precipitously.[43] The growing discourse about juvenile delinquency was highly gendered. The deviant careers of young males and young females

---

[41] This, at least, is the broad conclusion of Sweeney, 'Extension and Practice of Summary Jurisdiction'.

[42] Young offenders were particularly prevalent among those accused of wood stealing and hedge breaking: 16 per cent of the prisoners in the Northleach House of Correction in Gloucestershire were aged 0–17; also 25 per cent of wood thieves and a similar percentage of vegetable and fruit thieves were 0–17. See GRO, Q/Gn4.

[43] This was also the case in London: see King and Noel, 'Origins of "the Problem of Juvenile Delinquency" ', 21–2. For the Manchester-area data, see *P.P.*, 1828, vi, 523.

were stereotyped in very different ways. 'The boys mostly become thieves and the girls prostitutes', was the assumption upon which the 1817 parliamentary committee based some of its questions, while the Committee for Investigating the Alarming Increase of Juvenile Delinquency in the Metropolis confined its investigations in 1815 entirely to boys.[44] Any explanation of the rapid increase of juvenile indictments in the early nineteenth century must therefore focus mainly on boys.

II

While the stagnation or decline after 1822 in the proportion of indicted urban offenders who were juveniles can be clearly linked to the rise of summary jurisdiction, the rapid growth of juvenile indictments before 1822 and the sudden appearance of a large gap between urban and rural experiences of juvenile recorded crime between 1783–93 and 1820–2 cannot. London was probably the only region where significant transfers of juveniles into the summary courts began before 1820. Even there it was only after the legislative and policing changes of 1822–4 and 1829 that this transfer began to affect a large proportion of juvenile offenders, as the rapid growth of juvenile percentages among London's indicted offenders before 1822 makes plain (Tables 2.1–2.2, Figure 2.1). During the period on which this article primarily focuses, the period between the 1780s and the early 1820s, when juveniles first made a major impact on indictable crime, transfers to the summary courts therefore played only a minor role. The significance of changes occurring elsewhere in the criminal justice system should not be underestimated. The potential impact of alterations in the attitudes and practices of those who were responsible for bringing juveniles to the courts was immense and will need to be carefully scrutinised. However, many historians have started from the opposite assumption – that the rises in recorded juvenile crime in this period were due to actual increases in juvenile lawbreaking which can be linked to various economic and social changes – and it is this assumption that will therefore be tested first.

In discussing the period after 1815, James Walvin, for example, first highlights the 'growing bands of children cast adrift on the streets and finding themselves unable to survive by legal means'. He then concludes: 'In essence this juvenile crime was but another manifestation of the growing pains of a new urban society'. Here he draws heavily on J. J. Tobias, who suggested in *Crime and Industrial Society in the Nineteenth Century* that

[44] *P.P.*, 1817, vii, 351; *Report of the Committee for Investigating the Causes of the Alarming Increase of Juvenile Delinquency in the Metropolis.*

the towns were growing rapidly . . . their population, ever increasing, was predominantly a young one, and the young town-dwellers were faced with a host of unfamiliar problems . . . Receiving no assistance from their families or employers . . . they . . . found solutions by adopting the techniques, the habits and the attitudes of the criminals. There was thus, in London and the other larger towns in the latter part of the eighteenth century and the earlier part of the nineteenth century, an upsurge of crime which was the fruit of a society in rapid transition.[45]

While the data in Tables 2.1 and 2.2 and Figures 2.1–2.4 may appear at first glance to support generalised assumptions such as these, on close inspection the links between the 'rapid transitions' of this period and real increases in juvenile lawbreaking prove less easy to establish. What, for example, was the precise relationship between the growth of juvenile crime and the changing age structure of the population? Since the proportion of 0–14 year olds in the national population reached its peak in the 1820s at 39 per cent compared to 29 per cent in 1670, this relationship cannot be easily dismissed.[46] The fact that juvenile crime came to be perceived as an alarming and new problem at exactly the point when dependency ratios were at an all-time high and when the child-labour market was flooded is almost certainly no coincidence. Since legal immunities meant that only a handful of those under 10 years of age were ever indicted for property crime,[47] the vital age group was the 10–19 year olds. Here the picture was rather different. Although the proportion of the London population aged 0–9 continued to rise between 1789 and 1829, the proportion aged 10–19 fell slightly.[48] Elsewhere in England there may have been a small increase in 10–19 year olds between 1786 and 1821, but this certainly cannot explain the doubling of juvenile crime percentages in some areas over the same period. Indeed, as the 1821 census data in Table 2.3 shows, there was no consistent relationship between the proportion of 10–19 year olds in a region's population and its level of juvenile prosecutions. London and Surrey had the smallest proportions of 10–19 year olds but some of the highest juvenile crime rates. Bristol and Shropshire had the same proportions of 10–19 year olds, but Bristol's indictable offenders contained twice as many juveniles as Shropshire's. Only in Manchester, which had the highest proportions in both

[45] J. Walvin, *A Child's World: A Social History of English Childhood, 1800–1914* (Harmondsworth, 1982), 57; Tobias, *Crime and Industrial Society*, 42.

[46] E. A. Wrigley and R. Schofield, *The Population History of England, 1541–1871: A Reconstruction* (Cambridge, 1981), 216–17, 528–9.

[47] The doctrine of *doli incapax* made it legally impossible to indict any offender under the age of seven and meant that culpability remained extremely contestable until the age of fourteen: W. Blackstone, *Commentaries on the Laws of England*, 4 vols. (London, 1765–9), iv, 22–4.

[48] J. Landers, *Death and the Metropolis: Studies in the Demographic History of London, 1670–1830* (Cambridge, 1993), 180.

Table 2.3 *Proportion of property offenders aged 0–19 compared to proportion of general population aged 10–19*

	A Percentage of offenders 0–19 1820–2	B Percentage of population 10–19 1821	C Relationship B to A (%)
Shropshire (all)	22.3	22.0	+1
Industrial Shropshire	27.7	22.2	+25
Shrewsbury	25.9	21.9	+18
Rural Shropshire	19.1	22.0	−13
Berkshire	13.4	21.0	−36
Gloucestershire	25.6	21.1	+21
Bristol	46.7	22.1	+111
Lancashire (all)	39.7	22.5	+76
Lancashire (excluding Liverpool and Manchester)	28.8	22.6	+27
Liverpool	36.8	20.5	+80
Manchester	47.5	23.3	+104
London and Middlesex	37.6	18.1	+108
Surrey	35.4	19.8	+79
Kent	20.3	20.8	−2
Essex	20.8	20.8	0
Hertfordshire	23.9	21.8	+10
Sussex	19.6	21.5	−9
All five home counties	25.3	20.8	+22

Sources: notes 9, 17, 49. Very few offenders were under 10, effectively making column A directly comparable with B. Column C calculated as A–B divided by B times 100.

indices, can a small part of the increase in juvenile prosecutions be ascribed to the predominance of 10–19 year olds in its general population.[49]

Some historians have also stressed the impact of migration. Sean McConville not only linked the growth of juvenile crime to the fact that 'the swollen towns had a predominance of young people', but stressed that 'internal migration and immigration from abroad swamped the towns both physically and administratively'. Tobias was more explicit:

The rapid growth of the towns in the earlier part of the nineteenth century was a major factor causing or maintaining a high level of crime, and in particular juvenile crime. A flood of migrants, and especially young migrants, entered

[49] On the small national increase in 10–19 year olds, see King and Noel, 'Origins of "the Problem of Juvenile Delinquency" ', 22. The 1821 census data (*P.P.*, 1822, xv) was calculated by taking the total of 0–19 year olds and dividing it by the total population for each county or subregion, excluding those whose ages were unknown. Column C in Table 2.3 was calculated by subtracting the percentage in column B from the percentage in column A, dividing the resulting figure by the figure in column B and then multiplying by 100. This produces a rough index of differentials.

the towns . . . A new way of life was called for, and many must have given up the struggle to adapt . . . and turned instead to . . . crime.[50]

However, the role of migration is called into question by the unique information on the place of birth of all indicted offenders available for London for 1791–3 only. This indicates that while three quarters of adult offenders were migrants only a third of 0–17 year-old offenders were born outside London. Given the fact that throughout this period most migrants came to London in their late teens or early to mid-twenties (in the case of Irish migrants slightly later), this is not especially surprising. Still, for London and Surrey at least, Figure 2.5[51] casts grave doubt on the links Tobias and others have made between migration, social dislocation and the rise of juvenile crime. These links were probably stronger in Manchester. The higher proportion of 0–19 year olds in the population (Table 2.3) may well reflect the fact that the rapidly growing demand for young workers in the expanding factory sector brought many young and vulnerable migrants to the area. This raises a further question: was there any relationship between juvenile indictment rates and differences in employment levels among the young across the various regions studied?

As Hugh Cunningham's recent work has shown, in most towns and agricultural areas underemployment and unemployment were the norm for children in the late eighteenth and early nineteenth centuries. It was only in some proto-industrial regions and in the new manufacturing and factory areas that demand for juvenile labour was high. Although reports produced in the late 1810s on the causes of juvenile delinquency stressed 'the want of suitable employment for children in early life; whence arise habits of idleness and dissipation',[52] the data on juvenile indictment rates suggests no consistent relationship between these two variables. Agricultural areas such as Sussex, Berkshire and rural Shropshire had low juvenile indictment rates and acute youth unemployment problems, while London and Surrey had high juvenile indictment rates and acute youth unemployment problems. The factory and handloom-weaving area around Manchester had some of the fastest growing and highest juvenile prosecution rates in England, but also offered the most rapidly expanding employment opportunities for the young; the Birmingham area experienced a fairly similar combination.[53]

---

[50] McConville, *History of English Prison Administration*, i, 218–19; Tobias, *Crime and Industrial Society*, 201.

[51] PRO, HO 26/1–2 is the source for Figure 2.5. For the age profiles of migrants and non-migrants, see P. King, 'Female Offenders, Work and Lifecycle Change in Late Eighteenth-Century London' *Continuity and Change*, 11 (1996), 61–90.

[52] H. Cunningham, 'The Employment and Unemployment of Children in England, c. 1680–1851', *Past and Present*, 126 (1990); *Report of the Committee of the Society for the Improvement of Prison Discipline and for the Reformation of Juvenile Offenders* (London, 1818), 13.

[53] M. Fielding and M. Winstanley, 'Lancashire Children in the Nineteenth Century', in M. Winstanley (ed.), *Working Children in Nineteenth-century Lancashire* (Preston, 1995), 9, talks of

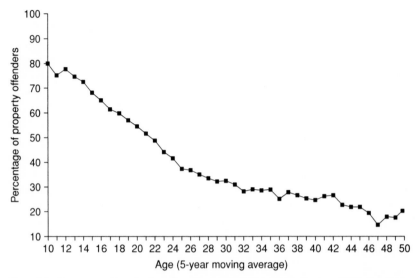

Figure 2.5   Percentage of London-born in each age group of property offenders: Old Bailey 1791–3.
Source: Public Record Office, London, HO26/1-2, London and Middlesex Criminal Registers, 1791–3.

The level of juvenile employment alone is, of course, a very inadequate indicator. The quality and nature of the work involved, the level of control exercised by employers, the degree of job security, the hours worked and a number of other dimensions of the work experience that are difficult to analyse were also important. One vital aspect of the changing relationships between juveniles and their employers that can be assessed, because contemporaries worried about it and historians have extensively researched it, is the decline of apprenticeship and living-in service.

'near full employment for older children and teenagers'; M. Cruickshank, *Children and Industry: Child Health and Welfare in North-West Textile Towns during the Nineteenth Century* (Manchester, 1981), 6–15, describes employers 'scouring the countryside to recruit children' during the period of transition from domestic to factory labour between the late eighteenth century and the 1830s. In 1833, 41 per cent of Lancashire and Cheshire workpeople (according to the Factories Inquiry) were aged 0–17: F. Collier, *The Family Economy of the Working Class in the Cotton Industry, 1784–1833* (Manchester, 1965), 68. A high proportion of handloom weavers were also children: D. Bythell, *The Handloom Weavers* (Cambridge, 1969), 61. By the later 1820s this sector began to experience severe problems, but, like London, the Lancashire industrial towns were at a high-water mark in terms of family income in the early 1820s: J. Walton, *Lancashire: A Social History* (Manchester, 1987), 110. On Birmingham and high child employment, see P. Hudson, *The Industrial Revolution* (London, 1992), 124; M. Rowlands, 'Continuity and Change in an Industrialising Society: The Case of the West Midlands Industries', in P. Hudson (ed.), *Regions and Industries* (Cambridge, 1989), 128–9.

Apprenticeship was undoubtedly changing between the 1780s and the early 1820s. In south-east England the mean age at which apprenticeship ended fell from twenty to seventeen and outdoor apprenticeship was replacing the old system under which the apprentice lived in the master's house. By the 1820s apprenticeship had become a more contractual and purely economic relationship, Keith Snell recently concluded, 'rather than one of subsumption and familial control'.[54] The timing and extent of these changes varied widely, and in rapidly expanding trades such as cotton handloom weaving (which reached peak numbers just before the 1826 slump) the apprenticeship system never fully took hold, but in urban areas, where a substantial proportion of the population still went through an apprenticeship, the potential impact of these changes remained considerable.[55] In both London and Birmingham the growth of outdoor apprenticeship was blamed by some early nineteenth-century commentators for the decline of discipline and the rise of crime among the young. The impact of this change can be exaggerated, however. There is abundant evidence from Daniel Defoe, Francis Place and many others that indoor apprentices were as unruly and as prone to thieving as outdoor ones. Despite its deregulation by parliament in 1814, apprenticeship remained a very widespread, if changing, institution in many urban areas in the early 1820s.[56]

Service in husbandry, by contrast, was very rapidly disappearing in several areas. The decline of rural living-in service accelerated from the 1780s onwards and it was almost extinguished in most of southern and eastern England in the years immediately after 1815. Thus, by the 1820s, most labouring parents could no longer look to local farmers to house and feed their children from their early to mid-teens onwards, but had themselves to take total responsibility for maintaining and controlling them. Contemporaries were not slow to point out the dire consequences of this change. In 1828 a Sussex magistrate linked the increase of crime to the fact that 'servant lads are not taken into the farmhouses and kept in subjection as they used to be, but live more at home with their own parents and are their own masters; in consequence they go where they please, instead of being kept in orderly habits'.[57] Although Bedfordshire, Berkshire, Essex, Hertfordshire and Sussex were all among the prime areas affected by

---

[54] K. Snell, *Annals of the Labouring Poor: Social Change and Agrarian England, 1660–1900* (Cambridge, 1985), 228–69, esp. 236, 253.

[55] Bythell, *Handloom Weavers*, 52–3; Snell, *Annals of the Labouring Poor*, 228–69; P. Linebaugh, *The London Hanged: Crime and Civil Society in the Eighteenth Century* (London, 1991), 62, concludes that two fifths of the London hanged had started an apprenticeship.

[56] *P.P.*, 1816, v, 222; *P.P.*, 1828, vi, 446; M. George, *London Life in the Eighteenth Century* (London, 1966), 268–9. For fuller discussion of London, see King and Noel, 'Origins of "the Problem of Juvenile Delinquency" ', 24–5. J. Lane, *Apprenticeship in England, 1600–1914* (London, 1996), 7, suggests the 1814 act did not affect the numbers being apprenticed.

[57] A. Kussmaul, *Servants in Husbandry in Early Modern England* (Cambridge, 1981), 114–29; *P.P.*, 1828, vi, 453; Snell, *Annals of the Labouring Poor*, 67–103.

this decline between the 1780s and 1820s, the proportion of juveniles found among their accused showed no overall change. Moreover, they continued to have much the same rates of juvenile recorded crime as rural Shropshire, where service in husbandry remained an important social institution well beyond the 1820s.[58] Both the rural juveniles of southern and eastern England and the urban apprentices of areas like London and Birmingham therefore became increasingly vulnerable to labour market fluctuations in this period and more likely to live out their teenage years in their parents' houses rather than outside them. However, while the percentage of prosecuted offenders who were juveniles rose drastically in London and Surrey, they hardly changed at all in these rural areas, despite the fact that the continued survival of apprenticeship probably meant that the institutions regularly employing and controlling teenagers collapsed more quickly in most rural areas than in urban ones. Once again it has proved impossible to link a specific set of economic and social transitions affecting the young to changes in juvenile indictment percentages.

Some contemporaries saw the factory itself as a generator of crime. A parliamentary committee asked a Mancheter magistrate in 1828 'Do many of the juvenile delinquents come from the factories?'

'A great many', he replied, 'and I am sorry to say there is a source of crime from their being congregated together in large manufactories, that circumstance leads naturally to demoralise the people who are confined there, especially the children'.[59] Since the area around Manchester had very high juvenile indictment rates such comments appear highly pertinent, but those rates were equally high in Bristol and in London (once the age structure of the general population is allowed for), and these areas contained virtually no factories. Was there any overall relationship between the rise of juvenile crime and the process of industrialisation?

Comparative criminologists such as Marshall Clinard and Daniel Abbott have not been shy about asserting that a strong relationship exists between the rise of juvenile crime and 'urban development, industrialisation and commercialisation'. In *Crime and Modernisation*, Louise Shelley argued that historically juvenile delinquency only becomes a problem with 'the advent of urbanisation and industrialisation'.[60] However, industrialisation is a very problematic term. At the broadest level the years of juvenile delinquency's first emergence in the late eighteenth and early nineteenth centuries were clearly a significant, if

---

[58] Kussmaul, *Servants in Husbandry*, 20–1, on the survival of service in husbandry as an important institution in Shropshire as late as 1851, when it had all but disappeared in the South and East.

[59] *P.P.*, 1828, vi, 499. For similar arguments in the late 1810s, see M. Ignatieff, *A Just Measure of Pain: The Penitentiary in the Industrial Revolution, 1750–1850* (London, 1978), 156.

[60] M. Clinard and D. Abbott, *Crime in Developing Countries: A Comparative Perspective* (New York, 1973), 83; L. Shelley, *Crime and Modernisation: The Impact of Industrialisation and Urbanisation on Crime* (Carbondale and Edwardsville, 1981), 52.

small, subperiod within the very much longer process of transformation historians have chosen to call industrialisation. Yet this tells us virtually nothing about
the precise vectors through which industrialisation influenced either the level
of juvenile prosecutions or the changing ways in which juvenile delinquency
was conceptualised. In particular, by indiscriminately linking industrialisation
and urbanisation such statements may well confuse rather than clarify the position. It is not easy to find evidence through which the separate relationship
between industrialisation and the rise of juvenile prosecutions can be explored.
Significant industrial developments that were not accompanied by the growth
of large cities rarely occurred in counties where age data on offenders has
survived. When they did, the subregions concerned were often too small to produce a sufficient number of indictments for meaningful analysis. However, as
already noted, the presence of proto-industry in Gloucestershire, or of growing
cotton manufacturing communities in Lancashire outside the Manchester and
Liverpool areas, did produce slightly higher proportions of juvenile offenders
than the rural areas. Moreover, in Shropshire, where despite small indictment
numbers subregions affected by factory growth (such as Shrewsbury) and by
mining or iron production (such as that around Colebrookdale) can be isolated
within a mainly rural area, the age structure of offenders in these three areas
does show at least minor differences consistent with the theory that non-city-
based manufacturing areas produced 20 to 25 per cent higher proportions of
teenage offenders than purely rural regions (Figure 2.6). However, since the
overall comparison of rural juvenile percentages with those of the large urban
areas (Tables 2.2–2.3) produces four-times-greater differentials (80–100 per
cent), the impact of manufacturing is perhaps best evaluated by comparing the
major urban areas.

The recent movement among economic historians away from nationally
based indicators and towards the study of regional transformations has helped
to reassert the extent to which the industrial revolution increased the differences
between regions in this period. It has also focused attention on the relatively
small number of dynamic industrial areas which were creating the internal critical mass of economic, financial and social changes necessary to transform the
economic life of a region.[61] Of the six urban areas in which large increases
in the proportions of juveniles among the indicted can be seen in Tables 2.1,
2.2 and Figure 2.1, three were involved in various ways in such regional transformations. In Manchester the population nearly quadrupled between 1780
and 1820, turning it into the second-largest city in England. By 1820, Manchester had been transformed by its immensely rapid growth as a manufacturing
and commercial centre; similarly, in the area around it some communities had
grown six- or sevenfold as cotton factories and handloom-weaving employment

---

[61] Hudson, *Industrial Revolution*, 101–32.

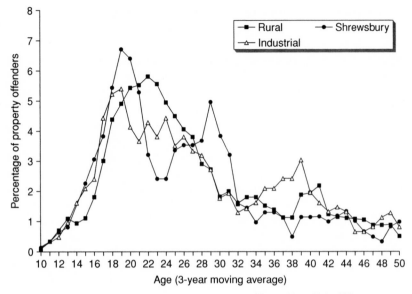

Figure 2.6   Age structure of property offenders sub-areas of Shropshire 1786–1828.
Note: Based on 3-year moving averages.
Source: Shropshire Record Office, Shrewsbury, Shropshire Gaol Calendars, i–ii, 1786–92, 1819–22, 1826–8.

mushroomed. It was, in the words of Asa Briggs, 'the shock city of the age'. Linked in part to this transformation was the very rapid emergence of the international trade and commercial life of Liverpool, which was England's second-largest port by 1820. Its population tripled between 1780 and 1821, making it England's third-largest city. In the same period Birmingham was also part of a regional transformation no less profound for being based on the multiplication of small workshops rather than factories and benefiting immensely from what Hudson has called 'economies of agglomeration'. This transformation was slightly less rapid in Birmingham, where the population more than doubled between 1780 and 1820, but it was equally as pervasive as that witnessed in Lancashire.[62]

The other three urban areas where large increases in, or very high levels of, juvenile prosecutions can be observed were not involved in rapidly transforming regional economies between 1780 and 1820. Bristol's population rose by less than half in this period. Its port was in relative decline and although its economy

[62] Population estimates are based on P. Corfield, *The Impact of English Towns, 1700–1800* (Oxford, 1982), 183; E. Evans, *The Forging of the Modern State: Early Industrial Britain, 1783–1870* (London, 1983), 407–9; A. Briggs, *Victorian Cities* (Harmondsworth, 1968), 96; Hudson, *Industrial Revolution*, 123.

was diversifying to some extent, its lack of either a strong industrial base or an economically vibrant hinterland meant that it was slipping down the urban and shipping tonnage leagues almost as fast as Manchester and Liverpool were shooting up them. London and the metropolitan area of Surrey grew at an intermediate pace; their populations less than doubled between 1780 and 1820. London adapted itself to changes taking place elsewhere and profited from those changes, but while London's economy was never static and the position of skilled labour was being eroded in some trades in the nineteenth century, the capital witnessed no fundamental changes. Its service sector remained large and its manufacturing sector was notable for the absence of major restructuring and for its gradual and relative decline.[63]

In contrast to their very different economic experiences, however, all six of these urban areas had very high proportions of juveniles among their indicted offenders in the early 1820s. Bristol and Manchester's percentages were almost identical, as were London and Liverpool's. It is therefore very difficult not to agree with the contemporary observation that it was 'not manufacturing Manchester but Multitudinous Manchester'[64] that was the key. Why, then, was the level of urbanisation so important?

Many late eighteenth- and early nineteenth-century sources suggest that England's greatest cities contained large numbers of unemployed or semi-destitute juveniles living, and sometimes sleeping, on the streets. These problems were not new. Complaints about idle and impoverished children can be found in London, Bristol, Liverpool and elsewhere in the seventeenth and early eighteenth centuries.[65] However, as population began to grow throughout England and increased particularly rapidly in many urban areas in the late eighteenth and early nineteenth centuries, these complaints grew more numerous.[66] Urban areas may not have had higher proportions of juveniles than their rural neighbours in 1821, but they did contain much larger and more rapidly increasing absolute numbers of young people. Moreover, by the later eighteenth century, poorer parishes in many urban areas were making much less adequate poor-relief provision for children and teenagers than their rural counterparts.

[63] K. Morgan, 'The Economic Development of Bristol, 1700–1850', in M. Dresser and P. Ollerenshaw (eds.), *The Making of Modern Bristol* (Tiverton, 1996); Evans, *Forging of the Modern State*, 407–9; E. Pawson, *The Early Industrial Revolution* (London, 1979), 199–201; R. Lawton and C. Pooley, *Britain, 1740–1950: An Historical Geography* (London, 1992), 92; L. Schwarz, *London in the Age of Industrialisation* (Cambridge, 1992), 3–4; Landers, *Death and the Metropolis*, 63.
[64] Plint, *Crime in England*, 124, quoting John Clay, a Lancashire prison chaplain who published widely on this subject in the second quarter of the nineteenth century.
[65] Pinchbeck and Hewitt, *Children in English Society*, 1, 104–7; H. Cunningham, *Children of the Poor: Representations of Childhood since the Seventeenth Century* (Oxford, 1991), 21–3.
[66] Cunningham, *Children of the Poor*, 23–30; Ignatieff, *Just Measure of Pain*, 183. Many early nineteenth-century commentators were aware of the need 'to prevent every youth from idling about': see *P.P.*, 1816, v, 127, for an example.

Compulsory pauper apprenticeship was more common in urban areas and more often involved either a degrading trade or a term in a northern factory. In most rural parishes, children were still eligible for outrelief in their mid-teens, a tradition reinforced by the growth of the Speenhamland system, which increased the vulnerability of young unmarried independent males to unemployment, but also increased the assistance given to teenagers who were still at home. In London's poorer parishes, by contrast, outrelief was rarely an option and even the less favourable alternatives of indoor relief in a crowded workhouse or compulsory parish apprenticeship were not automatically offered to the teenage poor.[67] Nor were the capital's many charities able to bridge the gap. At the Old Bailey in 1821, Philip Meades, a 'wretched looking young lad', was discharged after pleading in his defence that 'he had not tasted food for several days; that he had applied to the parish officers of Ealing for relief repeatedly . . . and that they refused to assist him telling him there was plenty of work'. Analysing the relationship between juvenile crime and 'starvation' in London in 1818, the report of the Society for the Improvement of Prison Discipline indicated that Meades's experience was commonplace. 'It is in vain to exclaim', they wrote, 'that by the Laws of England no such extremity is permitted, that the parishes or workhouses afford a retreat, it may be so in theory, the truth is otherwise in practice'.[68]

However, most of these urban–rural differences were well in place by 1783–93 and cannot therefore explain why the percentage of juveniles among the accused was very similar in that period and in the first decade of the nineteenth century, but then suddenly diverged in the 1810s (Figure 2.1). Nor do they explain the rapid increase in the proportion of juveniles found among the London and Surrey accused between the 1780s and the 1820s. The children of the London labouring poor were as ill provided for and as vulnerable to destitution in the peacetime post-demobilisation years of 1783–93 as they were in the years following the peace of 1815. While it is possible that continued population growth may have increased the proportion of children vulnerable to destitution between these two periods, considerable evidence points in the opposite direction. In the 1780s and 1790s real wages were

---

[67] Pinchbeck and Hewitt, *Children in English Society*, i, 194–7; 2, 496–9; George, *London Life in the Eighteenth Century*, 223–39. In 1816 an act that prevented the shipping of parish apprentices over long distances limited the options available to parish authorities: Cunningham, *Children of the Poor*, 30–2. The treatment of children during the last half-century of the Old Poor Law remains to be adequately researched.

[68] *London Chronicle*, 16 Jan. 1821; *Report of the Committee of the Society for the Improvement of Prison Discipline* (London, 1818), 13. For another case of a boy who begged to be allowed relief or to be taken into the workhouse but was refused on a technicality, see *London Chronicle*, 21 Nov. 1821. Many charitable relief organisations existed in eighteenth-century London, but they were clearly inadequate: see D. Andrew, *Philanthropy and Police: London Charity in the Eighteenth Century* (Princeton, 1989).

falling. Between 1810 and 1820 they rose fairly rapidly. Overall, it appears unlikely that living standards fell between the 1780s and the early 1820s.[69] The rapid rise of juvenile percentages among the indicted thieves of both London and Surrey in this period cannot therefore be explained simply by reference to the vulnerability, poverty and inadequate poor relief provision experienced by the urban young. To understand Tables 2.1 and 2.2 it is also necessary to look at the changes occurring within the criminal justice system and at the changing ways in which perceptions of juvenile offenders were being constructed.

III

As many contemporaries were aware, the threefold increase in general indictment levels seen in the first two decades of the nineteenth century did not necessarily reflect a substantial increase in lawbreaking activity. Only a tiny fraction of property offenders were actually indicted in this period. A very small increase in the proportion of victims who chose to prosecute rather than to use informal alternatives could therefore produce large increases in recorded crime. In the late eighteenth and early nineteenth centuries a number of changes in the administration of criminal justice may have encouraged more victims to indict offenders. A series of acts made it easier and less expensive to prosecute in the major courts. The growing proportion of capital convicts who were given conditional pardons rather than hanged may also have reduced victims' reluctance to prosecute. The building of new reformatory-style prisons in many counties from the later eighteenth century onwards may, temporarily at least, have reinforced the belief that minor offenders might be reformed by indictment and imprisonment. The establishment of stipendiary magistrates in London, Manchester, Salford and elsewhere, and the development of semi-entrepreneurial policing networks around them, may have made it easier for victims to detect offenders. In the absence of any systematic evidence about the choices victims, police and magistrates made, however, the impact of these changes on the proportion of indicted offenders who were juveniles can only be guessed.[70]

---

[69] Although real wages are a problematic source, most London real wages indices are higher in 1820–1 than in 1791–3: L. Schwarz, 'The Standard of Living in the Long Run: London, 1700–1860', *Economic History Review*, 2nd series, 38 (1985). More recently the same author concluded 'poverty in eighteenth-century London was, if anything, greater than in the nineteenth century': Schwarz, *London in the Age of Industrialisation*, 182.

[70] D. Philips, 'A New Engine of Power and Authority: The Institutionalisation of Law-Enforcement in England, 1780–1830', in V. Gatrell, B. Lenham and G. Parker (eds.), *Crime and the Law: The Social History of Crime in Western Europe since 1500* (London, 1980); Emsley, *Crime and Society in England*, 186–7; P. King, 'Crime, Law and Society in Essex, 1740–1820' (PhD thesis University of Cambridge, 1984), 354–7, on declining hanging rates; Ignatieff, *Just Measure of*

There are few indications that the increased expenses given to prosecutors operated in any age-specific way on the mix of offenders brought to the courts.[71] The Legislation in 1818 which ended the practice of giving an automatic £40 reward to those who obtained certain types of capital convictions, may have meant that professional thief-takers were less inclined to wait until juveniles graduated to major offences before they arrested them. However, Bennet's Act of 1826 was probably the key change in this area.[72] Did the decline in the proportion of those sentenced to death who were actually hanged (dropping from 48 per cent in London in 1784–90 to less than 10 per cent 1816–18) affect attitudes to juveniles?[73] If the Society for the Improvement of Prison Discipline was right in reporting that 'there is scarcely anyone of common humanity who would not shudder at taking away the life of a child under sixteen or seventeen',[74] the even more rapidly declining incidence of juvenile executions may have reassured an increasing proportion of prosecutors and thus undermined previous taboos about prosecuting juveniles. This in turn would have increased the relative impact of juveniles on indictments. The rapid increase in the proportion of prosecuted pickpockets who were juveniles after that offence ceased to be a capital crime in 1808 supports this view to some extent,[75] but the general effect may have been small until after the key period of 1820–2. The rest of the capital code was still largely in place at this point and, despite the declining proportion of juveniles being executed, rapid rises in capital indictment rates meant that the absolute numbers going to the gallows rose by 50 per cent between 1805 and 1818.[76] As V. A. C. Gatrell has recently pointed out, as many people were hanged in London in the 1820s as in the 1790s. Moreover, although none of those executed was under 15, at least 2 per cent

Pain; R. Paley, 'An Imperfect, Inadequate and Wretched System? Policing London before Peel', *Criminal Justice History*, 10 (1989).

[71] If the increased compensation for prosecution costs being given to felony victims by the early nineteenth century led to disproportionate increases in the number of minor felony prosecutions, as suggested in M. DeLacy, *Prison Reform in Lancashire, 1700–1850* (Stanford, 1986), 46, this could have increased very slightly the overall proportion of indicted offenders who were juveniles, if juveniles were over-represented among minor felons (as tentatively suggested in King and Noel, 'Origins of "the Problem of Juvenile Delinquency" ', 33). However, juveniles were not usually over-represented among minor felonies in most of the areas covered in Tables 2.1 and 2.2, and the possible impact of this change is therefore unclear.

[72] Radzinowicz, *History of English Criminal Law*, ii, 79–82; V. Gatrell, *The Hanging Tree: Execution and the English People, 1770–1868* (Oxford, 1994), 574. The acts were 58 Geo. III, c. 70 and 7 Geo. IV, c. 64.

[73] London figures are based on *P.P.*, 1819, viii, 138–9. National figures available from 1805 onwards show a fall from 18 per cent for 1805–7 to 9 per cent in 1816–18: *ibid.*, 126–7.

[74] *Report of the Committee of the Society for the Improvement of Prison Discipline*, 16.

[75] King and Noel, 'Origins of "the Problem of Juvenile Delinquency" ', 32–3.

[76] *P.P.*, 1819, viii, 127. Between 1805–7 and 1816–18 the percentage of capitally convicted offenders that were hanged was halved, but the average annual numbers executed rose from 63 to 103 because of the large rise in the absolute number of offenders sentenced to death: Gatrell, *Hanging Tree*, 19.

of the London hanged were aged 15–17 between 1801 and 1825. It was not until around 1830 therefore that most victims would have been absolutely sure that a teenager they had prosecuted for a major offence would not end up on the gallows.[77] Moreover, since the decline in the percentage of capitally convicted offenders who were hanged was a nationwide phenomenon, it should have undermined taboos about prosecuting juveniles in both urban and rural areas. The fact that juvenile indictments only increased proportionately in urban areas therefore calls into question the potential impact of changing attitudes to hanging. As Gatrell has demonstrated, although reformers talked endlessly of prosecutors' squeamishness about bringing people to court under capital law, there is little evidence of this before the late 1820s.[78]

The impact of penal reform on juvenile indictments rates is difficult to unravel. Did a belief in the reforming power of the new prisons of itself persuade a significant number of victims to push more juvenile offenders into the criminal justice system? On balance this seems unlikely. The zeal of the prison reformers waxed and waned between the 1780s and the 1820s. It also varied widely between counties. Some of the areas that came early and enthusiastically to prison reform, such as Sussex and Berkshire, had very low juvenile indictment rates in 1820; others, such as the Manchester area, had very high ones. Although at least one observer in the late 1820s believed that 'the improved discipline of gaols induces many magistrates to commit, where formerly they would not have done it', fears about the potentially contaminating effect of imprisonment on young offenders remained widespread and influential up to and beyond the Gaols Act of 1823.[79] However, while its direct impact may have been small, the widespread concern about prison reform and prison conditions that resurfaced in the 1810s contributed in various ways to another key development of that

---

[77] Gatrell, *Hanging Tree*, 7; B. Knell, 'Capital Punishment: Its Administration in Relation to Juvenile Offenders in the Nineteenth Century and its Possible Administration in the Eighteenth', *British Journal of Criminology*, 5 (1965), 199–200, indicates that no one under 15 was executed in London between 1801 and 1836. However, his unpublished typescript deposited with the Radzinowicz Library, Institute of Criminology, Cambridge University (QPPea3), confirmed that the period 1800–25 did see the execution of some 15–17 year olds: B. Knell, 'The Bloody Code: The History of its Administration and Abolition: The Capital Punishment Debate from the Seventeenth Century to the Year 1868', chapter 5.

[78] Gatrell, *Hanging Tree*, 19. The work on areas outside London has therefore cast doubt on the tentative conclusion in King and Noel, 'Origins of "the Problem of Juvenile Delinquency" ', 32–6. However, it remains possible that the reformers were right about the impact of the capital code in cases involving juveniles. For an example, see Samuel Hoare: 'The great severity of our penal code, by which prosecutors are constantly deterred from proceeding against a culprit . . . operates strongly on their minds, particularly when they consider that the victim may be a mere child': *P.P.*, 1817, vii, 529.

[79] Ignatieff, *Just Measure of Pain*, 102; R. Evans, *The Fabrication of Virtue: English Prison Architecture, 1750–1840* (Cambridge, 1982); DeLacy, *Prison Reform in Lancashire*; P. Southerton, *Reading Gaol by Reading Town* (Stroud, 1993), 12; *P.P.*, 1826–7, vi, 12.

period – the growth of a new set of discourses about the 'alarming increase of juvenile delinquency'.

The roots of this multifaceted change in attitudes towards juvenile offenders were complex. Many of the key elements of the discourse were by no means new. Most of the policy initiatives and social attitudes that shaped early nineteenth-century discussions can already be seen in the 1780s and early 1790s, albeit in a shallower and more experimental form. The building of reformatory-style prisons in some counties, the beginnings of a debate about urban policing and about the repeal of the capital code, growing concern about idle children, a movement towards the provision of basic education facilities for the poor in the shape of Sunday schools, industrial schools and so on, can all be identified in the 1780s – a decade which also witnessed the setting up of the Philanthropic Society which established the first residential institution 'for the reform of criminal poor children'.[80] What was new about the next post-war period, the late 1810s and early 1820s, was both the intensity of the debates about these issues and the growing focus upon juvenile crime. Later eighteenth-century commentators, such as John Howard, Jonas Hanway and Patrick Colquhoun, were aware of the activities of young thieves and of the difficulties in preventing them from being further corrupted by imprisonment, but they showed few signs of intense interest in, or alarm about, juvenile offenders.[81] By the mid-1810s the tone of public discussions was very different. As recorded crime rates rose rapidly with the coming of peace, the conviction that juveniles were responsible for a great deal of crime intensified. The report of the Committee for Investigating the Alarming Increase of Juvenile Delinquency in the Metropolis, set up in 1815 by a group of London philanthropists and penal reformers, concluded that 'some thousands of boys in the metropolis were daily engaged in the commission of crime' and that this 'alarming depravity' was 'hourly extending its influence over the youth of the poor'. These themes recurred regularly in the various parliamentary investigations into policing, crime and criminal justice

---

[80] Ignatieff, *Just Measure of Pain*, 80–113; J. Whiting, *Prison Reform in Gloucestershire, 1776–1820* (London, 1975); Radzinowicz, *History of English Criminal Law*, i, 301–496; 3, 1–140; T. Laqueur, *Religion and Respectability: Sunday Schools and Working Class Culture, 1780–1850* (New Haven, 1976); Cunningham, *The Children of the Poor*, 37; *An Account of the Nature and Present State of the Philanthropic Society Instituted in 1788 for the Prevention of Crimes . . . and for the Reform of Criminal Poor Children* (London, 1804); Andrew, *Philanthropy and Police*, 182–7.

[81] Pinchbeck and Hewitt, *Children in English Society*, i, 104–25; J. Hanway, *The Defects of the Police* (London, 1775), 31, 53, 59–61, 241; also his *A New Year's Gift to the People of Great Britain* (London, 1784), 43–4; J. Howard, *The State of the Prisons*, 2nd edn (Warrington, 1780), 10–13, 44–5, 55. P. Colquhoun, *A Treatise on the Police of the Metropolis*, 5th edn (London, 1797), vii–xi, 13, 34–7, 58, 89, 113–4, 119, 125, 439, for example, refers in passing to boys, apprentices and other young people as offenders, yet he never singles out young or juvenile offenders as a particular problem.

set up from 1816 onwards.[82] Juvenile delinquency had arrived as a separately identified social problem and as a source of intense concern.

This sudden increase in anxiety about juvenile crime may initially have been partly due to the publicity skills of a highly active body of London-based Quakers, evangelicals and other philanthropists whose involvement in the related campaigns for the repeal of the capital code and for prison reform had made them increasingly aware of the problem of juvenile delinquency and had inspired the formation of the committee in 1815.[83] However, the committee's activities represented only a small part of a much wider explosion in public debate which occurred around 1815. Debates on penal and policing issues, and on the reasons for the post-war increase in recorded crime, helped in turn to generate the first hesitant (and methodologically naive) attempts to investigate the roots of criminal behaviour, the ages and backgrounds of offenders and the effects of various judicial policies upon them. Although these debates and investigations covered all age groups, juvenile offenders came to play an important part within them. Those involved in the growing movement against capital punishment found cases involving juveniles particularly moving; indeed, the execution of one young offender in 1815 was a formative moment in the creation of the committee that year. When that committee began to focus more on imprisonment in 1818 the link with juvenile delinquency remained strong, as the title chosen for the new organisation – the Society for the Improvement of Prison Discipline and for the Reformation of Juvenile Offenders – indicates.

---

[82] Beattie, *Crime and the Courts in England*, 246–7; *Report of the Committee for Investigating the Causes of the Alarming Increase of Juvenile Delinquency in the Metropolis*; Sanders, *Juvenile Offenders for a Thousand Years*, 102–34. See also *P.P.*, 1816, v; *P.P.*, 1817, vii; *P.P.*, 1818, viii: all are Select Committee Reports on the Police of the Metropolis which contain much on juvenile delinquency, especially the 1817 report which included the full report of the 'Alarming Increase' committee and interviewed some of its prominent members. *P.P.*, 1819, vii, a report on the state of the gaols, included a specific section headed 'Juvenile Offenders', 149–72. The momentum continued during the 1820s: *P.P.*, 1826–7, vi; *P.P.*, 1828, vi. Among the pamphlets that referred to juvenile offenders and their treatment, see, for example, H. Bennet, *A Letter to the Common Council . . . on the Abuses in Newgate* (London, 1818); T. F. Buxton, *An Inquiry whether Crime and Misery are Produced or Prevented by our Present System of Prison Discipline*, 2nd edn (London, 1818); G. Chandler, *Two Sermons on the Prevention and Correction of Crime* (London, 1823); J. Eardley-Wilmot, *A Letter to the Magistrates of Warwickshire on the Increase of Crime* (London, 1820); also his *A Second Letter to the Magistrates of Warwickshire* (London, 1820).

[83] For a more detailed analysis, see Chapter 3. A detailed study of the individuals involved in the influential 1815 Committee for Investigating the Causes of the Alarming Increase of Juvenile Delinquency in the Metropolis, and its successor, 'The Society for the Improvement of Prison Discipline and for the Reformation of Juvenile Offenders' (SIPD), indicates clearly that the genesis of this new discourse overlapped with, and was deeply influenced by, a number of other contemporary movements. The resurgence of prison reform, the growing campaign against capital statutes, the ongoing reformation of manners movement and the widespread rise of concern about urban policing were perhaps the most important, but the anti-slavery and child-labour campaigns, and the various philanthropic initiatives offering aid to the 'deserving' poor, also had a role to play. See also May, 'Child's Punishment for a Child's Crime', 73–175.

Those who stressed the reforming potential of properly regulated prisons naturally focused heavily on the most malleable group of offenders – the young – while at the same time their investigations into the current state of the prisons led them to highlight the large numbers of juveniles who were held in inadequately segregated prisons and who were therefore being corrupted by older, more 'hardened' offenders.[84]

However, the gradual growth of knowledge about juvenile delinquency which emerged, both as a by-product of the investigations of penal reformers and as a result of the hundreds of interviews with juvenile offenders conducted by members of the 1815 Committee, by no means fully explains why the rapid growth of recorded crime rates and anxieties about crime between 1782 and 1793 produced no significant increase in alarm about juvenile delinquency, while the same circumstances in the later 1810s did. As Gatrell has pointed out, the elite's relative tolerance of the criminal and riotous poor began to decline after the 1780s. By 1820, the political and cultural climate had been transformed and crime had become the repository for broader fears about social change and about the stability of the social hierarchy. As anxieties about the social consequences of urbanisation and industrialisation, and about the growth of popular radicalism and disorder increased (and peaked around 1820), those concerns were frequently linked to a constellation of fears about crime – fears which were reinforced by the publication of national indictment statistics from 1805 onwards that showed that recorded crime was increasing rapidly.[85]

Juvenile offenders, as powerful representatives of the shape of the future and as potential mirrors of the broader state of social order, were especially likely to be seized upon as particularly dangerous manifestations of these broader social problems, as symbols of the nascent insubordination, idleness and family degeneration of many sections of the burgeoning urban working class. While all types of crime could become a convenient, if not necessarily appropriate, vehicle for the expression of more general fears about social change, juvenile crime had a particularly magnetic quality in this regard.[86] This may have been partly linked either to the fact that the proportion of children in the population was at an historic high or to the rapid growth of debates about child labour

---

[84] On the parallel debates, see R. McGowen, 'The Image of Justice and Reform of the Criminal Law in Early Nineteenth-Century England', *Buffalo Law Review*, 32 (1983); Ignatieff, *Just Measure of Pain*, 143–89. On the hiatus in these debates for two decades after 1789, see Gatrell, *Hanging Tree*, 327. See W. Tallack, *Peter Bedford: The Spitalfields Philanthropist* (London, 1865), 16–17, 36–9, for the impetus for the 1815 committee. A major theme of that committee's report and of other parliamentary reports and contemporary pamphlets (see n. 82) was the contaminating effect of imprisonment on young offenders: for example, *P.P.*, 1817, vii, 439, 495, 529.

[85] V. Gatrell, 'Crime, Authority and the Policeman State', in F. M. L. Thompson, (ed.) *The Cambridge Social History of Britain, 1750–1950* iii, *Social Agencies and Institutions* (Cambridge, 1990), 244–50.

[86] Ignatieff, *Just Measure of Pain*, 156; Rush, 'Government of a Generation'; Gatrell, 'Crime, Authority and the Policeman State', 251.

in factories that occurred after 1815.[87] However, broader shifts in attitudes both towards childhood and towards social discipline almost certainly played a very significant part in fuelling increasingly widespread alarm about juvenile delinquency in the early nineteenth century.

The complex and often class-specific ways in which attitudes towards childhood were changing in this period makes it difficult to generalise, but the early nineteenth century may well have been both a pivotal point and a time of significant disjunction. While there remained many continuities in the nature of the affectionate bonds between parents and children,[88] there can be little doubt that the way childhood was conceptualised was changing by the later eighteenth and early nineteenth centuries. Despite various differences (between evangelical and romantic views, for example), the properties classes had almost all embraced a more child-centred approach by 1820. Childhood was marked off as a special and separate time within which it was felt necessary to protect the young, to fence them off from painful experiences, to give them 'a childhood'. However, these attitudes were not generally extended to the children of the labouring sort until after 1830. In the meantime, the children of the urban poor – underemployed and with little educational or welfare provision – were often perceived as idle, and their idleness in turn was seen as promoting vice and crime. As May has pointed out, the marginal street-based lifestyle of scavenging, odd-jobbing and sometimes petty thieving, which economic, social and demographic realities forced upon many children and juveniles in the early nineteenth century, clashed increasingly with middle-class ideals about a protected, home-centred, constantly nurtured childhood. Moreover, the street children's apparent freedom challenged the ordered, hierarchical notions within which middle-class childhood was constructed. At a time when the properties saw children both as dependants and as repositories of virtue, the children of the poor seemed to them to be increasingly independent and full of vices.[89]

This clash almost certainly formed an important background to the growing concern about juvenile delinquency in the early nineteenth century. It may also have helped to ensure that another feature of that period, the burgeoning movement to regularise and deepen society's disciplinary regimes – to reform simultaneously both the structure of penalty and the manners of the poor – focused significantly on the young as well as the adult population. As increasing energy was invested in a variety of projects designed to discipline and moralise the poor, from the prohibition of street gambling to the provision of better education facilities, knowledge and concern about the children of the poor

[87] Cunningham, *Children of the Poor*, 50–71.

[88] Continuities have recently been stressed by L. Pollock, *Forgotten Children: Parent–Child Relations from 1500 to 1900* (Cambridge, 1983).

[89] H. Cunningham, *Children and Childhood in Western Society since 1500* (London, 1995), 61–78; Cunningham, *Children of the Poor*, 92; May, 'Child's Punishment for a Child's Crime', 63.

rapidly increased.[90] Humanitarian motives had a part to play in these processes. The juvenile poor evoked sympathy as well as fear, particularly if they were orphans or had been abandoned or exploited by their parents. For a brief period in the 1810s even the parents of young offenders received some sympathy. 'The supply of labour in the metropolis has been greater than the demand', noted the report of the 1815 Committee, 'the distress to which the poor have been exposed from this circumstance has in great measure produced that laxity of morals which has rendered a considerable number of parents regardless of the welfare of their children'.[91] At heart, however, most of the social policy initiatives of this period expressed a growing sense that it was imperative not only to reform the inner lives, habits and self-discipline of the poor, but also to focus particular effort on the young, as the group most likely to respond to this emerging 'discourse of character', as Martin Weiner has termed it.[92]

For those who were young and poor in the early nineteenth century this produced a paradoxical situation. While their special qualities, needs and problems were the focus of increasing attention and concern, the result was not more material assistance but rather more intrusion into their everyday lives: more intense scrutiny and an increasing likelihood that they would be on the receiving end of formal legal sanctions. In the mid-eighteenth century, many aspects of plebeian culture had been largely ignored by the elite and by the courts. Between 1780 and 1820, a growing urge to control the poor (which could be seen as part of the broader movement 'to insert the power to punish more deeply into the social body', about which Michel Foucault has written so powerfully) brought important changes.[93] From a policy of ignoring, or dealing informally with, the minor infractions of the poor (a policy which modern criminologists broadly call diversion), the early nineteenth century witnessed a transition to a situation in which an increasing proportion of such offenders were being formally disciplined by prosecution in the courts. This movement from diversion to discipline was particularly pronounced in relation to the young. It affected both verdicts and sentencing policies, but its most important impact was on prosecution levels. As one magistrate remarked in 1828, 'I remember in former days persons were taken and pumped upon, or something of that

[90] Gatrell, 'Crime, Authority and the Policeman State', 250, on the growth of 'disciplinary responses to the poor' in the half-century after 1780; M. Roberts, 'Public and Private in Early Nineteenth-Century London: The Vagrant Act of 1822 and its Enforcement', *Social History*, 13 (1988); Radzinowicz, *History of English Criminal Law*, iii, 141–207; 4, 1–104; M. Roberts, 'The Society for the Suppression of Vice and its Early Critics, 1802–12', *Historical Journal*, 26 (1983); M. Wiener, *Reconstructing the Criminal: Culture, Law and Policy in England, 1830–1914* (Cambridge, 1990), 1–91.

[91] Cunningham, *Children of the Poor*, 4; *P.P.*, 1817, vii, 434.

[92] Wiener, *Reconstructing the Criminal*, 39–45.

[93] M. Foucault, *Discipline and Punish: The Birth of the Prison*, trans. Alan Sheridan (Harmondsworth, 1977), 80–2.

sort, but now they are handed over to the police and tried on it, and that tends very much to the increase of crime; because many of them are juvenile offenders'.[94] Immediate physical punishments by the local community, such as being 'pumped upon', which had been thought particularly appropriate for juveniles, were increasingly frowned upon in the early nineteenth century as tolerance of interpersonal violence began to decline.

One 1820s observer wrote, The practice formerly was that if a boy of twelve or fourteen years of age committed any petty offence . . . he was corrected on the spot; but now it is impossible to do so, an information would immediately be laid against the person so inflicting summary punishment and he would be indicted for an assault.[95]

The informal punishment of juvenile thieves by parents and schoolteachers may also have been in decline. By 1820, the London newspapers frequently carried reports of summary hearings during which parents asked the court to formally punish their own children because they were stealing either from neighbours or from their own homes. In 1828, a Leeds barrister spoke of 'many offences being tried as felonies, and the parties taken up now who used to be either punished by the parents or schoolmaster'.[96] In the early 1820s, diversionary tactics were still employed on occasions by many JPs who feared imprisonment would simply corrupt young offenders even further, but the vital prime movers – the victims – were beginning to move decisively towards direct judicial discipline and away from informal sanctions in cases involving juveniles.[97] Given that victims rarely recorded their decisions, the extent of this change is difficult to measure. However, there can be little doubt that the growth of a new set of discourses about juvenile delinquency and its 'alarming increase' in the 1810s, which was rooted in the interactions between broader social anxieties, penal reform, changing attitudes to childhood and the growing urge to discipline the poor, had a vital impact on the number of juveniles indicted for felony.[98] As these changing attitudes encouraged a growing proportion of victims to prosecute young offenders, juvenile prosecution levels began to rise, thus further increasing anxieties about juvenile crime and reinforcing the movement among victims towards a greater use of formal prosecutions in such cases. The

---

[94] *P.P.*, 1828, vi, 490.

[95] *Ibid.*, 440. On changing attitudes to interpersonal violence, see chapter 7.

[96] *P.P.*, 1828, vi, 484; *P.P.*, 1819, vii, 166; *London Chronicle*, 3 Oct., 26 Jan. 1821.

[97] Weiner, *Reconstructing the Criminal*, 51. Imprisonment of juveniles for their first offence was not infrequently cited as a cause of the growth of crime: W. Forsythe, *The Reform of Prisoners, 1830–1900* (London, 1987), 23; *P.P.*, 1816, v, 57, 262; *P.P.*, 1817, vii, 494–5.

[98] Given the frequent recurrence of observations about the decline of informal ways of dealing with young offenders over the last two hundred years (most recently as the 'in the old days the policemen gave them a clip round the ear' story), the decline of diversion at any particular period cannot be assumed from a few such observations, but the evidence in the early nineteenth century does appear overwhelming: Magarey, 'Invention of Juvenile Delinquency'.

incredibly rapid rises in the proportion of indicted offenders who were juveniles that occurred in London and Manchester in the later 1810s (Figure 2.1) suggest strongly that in urban areas, where large pools of young unprosecuted offenders had long existed, this spiralling effect may have had a major impact. It remains an open question whether, as John Muncie has suggested, the post-1815 period witnessed a specific moral panic about juvenile gangs and juvenile crime alone.[99] The London newspapers of the mid-to-late 1810s reported many cases involving young offenders. Occasionally they even ran small headlines such as 'juvenile depredations' or 'youthful delinquency' and made comments about 'the great increase of crime, especially among the juvenile part of the community'.[100] However, juvenile crime was only one theme, albeit an important one, within the broader constellations of anxieties and crime-related panics that preoccupied the newspapers of the post-1815 period.

What is clear, despite the difficulties of studying the geographical diffusion of such attitudes, is that this new awareness of an 'alarming increase of juvenile delinquency' and the accompanying debates about how it was to be dealt with, made very little impact on most parts of rural England until the end of the 1820s. Asked in 1828 whether there had been a 'more than proportionate increase of crime among the younger part of the community', a Suffolk gentleman replied, 'I do not think that there is'.[101] London was the main focal point of anxiety about juvenile crime in the mid-1810s, but the big provincial cities were not far behind. The first provincial asylum for juvenile offenders was set up near Birmingham in 1818, and by the end of the decade the Birmingham magistrate Eardley-Wilmot was already writing extensively on the 'increasing evil' of juvenile delinquency. At its foundation in 1818, the Society for the Improvement of Prison Discipline and for the Reformation of Juvenile Offenders had nearly thirty Manchester subscribers. Its first report recorded:

Juvenile delinquency is indeed at its height in the metropolis; but unfortunately it is not confined by any local limits – Manchester has a large share of youthful criminals, and other populous towns more or less according to circumstances. An Institution on the same principles as the Society in London would be very desirable at Manchester; perhaps also at Bristol, Leeds and other great manufacturing towns.[102]

By the end of the 1820s, the quarter-sessions benches of some rural counties, such as Devon, were also beginning to take note of juvenile crime, but in the

[99] Muncie, *Trouble with Kids Today*, 24–6, 34.
[100] *London Chronicle*, 20 June 1821, for 'great increase'. Other headlines included 'Training Children for Thieves', *London Chronicle*, 24 Oct. 1821; see also, for example, *London Chronicle*, 25 Apr., 25 Oct. 1821.
[101] *P.P.*, 1828, vi, 456.
[102] H. Powell, *A Memoir of the Warwick County Asylum Instituted in the Year 1818* (Warwick, 1827); Eardley-Wilmot, *Second Letter to the Magistrates of Warwickshire*, 4; *Report of the Committee of the Society for the Improvement of Prison Discipline*, 21, and members list.

parliamentary committees of 1826–8 it was still the magistrates of growing urban areas – of Birmingham, Bath, Bristol, Leeds, Sheffield and Manchester – who were emphasising the growth of juvenile offenders, while most rural magistrates remained preoccupied with a broader age range: young unmarried men.[103] 'Do you observe that there are a great number of juvenile offenders committed?', the 1826 Committee asked a gaoler from rural Suffolk. 'We have some', he replied, 'but not so many perhaps as in the manufacturing districts'.[104] A growing awareness of juvenile delinquency among rural victims and magistrates may have been one of the reasons why the proportion of indicted offenders who were juveniles began to increase slowly in some rural counties by the end of the 1820s (Tables 2.1–2.2). However, during the key period of the 1810s and early 1820s the new set of discourses about the alarming increase of juvenile delinquency seems to have gained a substantial foothold primarily in the large urban areas. It was only in these areas that the movement from diversion to discipline was well in train by 1820. Before the Vagrancy Acts of 1822–4 that movement mainly affected juvenile indictments. After 1822–4 those who wanted to discipline the children of the urban poor made increasing use of summary proceedings as the disciplinary agenda deepened.[105]

IV

A broad study such as this, covering a wide variety of regions over half a century and surveying the impact of a number of variables at the most general level, inevitably raises as many questions as it answers. Were there areas or time periods when relative decreases in the number of offenders in older age groups created the misleading impression that juvenile prosecutions were increasing? Would the urban–rural differences in juvenile prosecution percentages seen in the early 1820s appear as great if age information on those tried summarily for predominantly rural offences such as wood stealing was available? At the level of individual localities, why was Bristol so exceptional before 1793 when juveniles formed nearly twice as high a proportion of indictments as in any other urban or rural area (Tables 2.1–2.2). The pre-1793 Bristol sample is small and the city was exceptional administratively, being the only large provincial centre where the borough court had both capital and non-capital jurisdiction,[106]

[103] May, 'Child's Punishment for a Child's Crime', 81; *P.P.*, 1826–7, vi, 32, 34, 37–8, 54, on rural worries about young unmarried men; *P.P.*, 1828, vi, 444–5, 457, 490, on urban juveniles.

[104] *P.P.*, 1826–7, vi, 44.

[105] Magarey 'Invention of Juvenile Delinquency'; Roberts, 'Public and Private in Early Nineteenth-Century London'.

[106] The small elite that ran Bristol therefore had tremendous discretionary range being committing magistrates, quarter-sessions bench, and also performing the assize judge's role: M. Harrison, *Crowds and History: Mass Phenomena in English Towns, 1790–1835* (Cambridge, 1988), 57–69.

but without detailed research the Bristol data remains enigmatic. Equally, only a detailed local study, and the discovery of age information for the Manchester-area offenders before 1801, would enable a full evaluation to be made of George Fisher's recent contention that it was the desire to reform the large number of juveniles coming into their courts which lay behind the extensive prison reforms introduced by the magistrates of the Salford Hundred around 1790.[107] Comparative work on juvenile prosecution levels in other countries, which is only just beginning for this early period, will no doubt raise further questions.[108] However, despite the immensely wide variety of factors that could have affected English juvenile prosecution levels between the 1780s and the 1820s, certain tentative conclusions can be drawn.

The rapid early nineteenth-century growth in the proportion of indicted offenders who were juveniles, and the concentration of that growth in the big cities, was linked to a particular conjunction of material, judicial and discursive changes. Many urban juveniles were employed in the least-desirable, lowest-paid and most precarious jobs. They were surrounded by bulging open shop fronts servicing the ever-growing material needs of the prosperous middle classes;[109] yet many of these young people were penniless, unable to find work or shelter. They were therefore tempted to resort to forms of scavenging which were, at best, on the borderlines of petty theft. The existence of a growing number of vulnerable, ill-provided-for urban juveniles, and of a general increase in post-war anxieties about rising crime rates, provided the preconditions for a major increase in juvenile prosecutions. However, these preconditions along with various experiments in relation to policing and prison reform were also present in the 1780s and early 1790s, when the proportion of prosecutions involving juveniles showed no sudden increases and when no systematic urban–rural differences can be identified. What was novel in the 1810s was the way that broader sociopolitical anxieties, reforming agendas, philanthropic energies and changing attitudes to childhood focused on, and helped to create, a new set of discourses about the 'alarming increase' of juvenile offenders in urban areas. The demographic realities caused by an exceptionally youthful age structure, the economic realities that forced increasing numbers of children onto the streets

[107] G. Fisher, 'The Birth of the Prison Retold', *Yale Law Journal*, 104 (1995).
[108] Although considerable work has been done on penal institutions designed to deal with juvenile offenders in various European countries, the only equivalent research on levels of juvenile offending and on changing attitudes to the prosecution of juveniles is J. Christiaens, 'The Alarming Increase of Juvenile Criminality: The Perception and Character of a Nineteenth-Century Problem in Belgium' (paper given to the European Social Science History Conference, Amsterdam, May, 1996).
[109] May, 'Child's Punishment for a Child's Crime', 37. The growing availability of easy targets for petty theft in open shop fronts should not be underestimated as a possible influence on levels of lawbreaking. On London street children, see J. Wade, *A Treatise on the Police and Crimes of the Metropolis* (London, 1829), 159–61.

in London and in other non-factory cities, and the lack of established informal traditions of dealing with juvenile offenders in the newer cities like Manchester where child employment was available, may all have contributed to the growth of urban juvenile indictment rates. Equally, a number of changes in criminal justice administration, such as the declining proportion of capital convicts who were actually hanged or the brief resurgence of the belief that imprisonment could reform as well as deter, may also have undermined previous diversionary traditions in relation to juveniles. But at the core of the very rapid and specifically urban growth in juvenile indictment rates seen in Tables 2.1 and 2.2 and Figure 2.1 was a new desire to discipline rather than ignore juvenile offenders. Ambivalent though they were about the possible effects of imprisonment on the young, increasing numbers of urban victims and magistrates moved first towards indicting young offenders and then towards having them tried summarily. In doing so they were both reacting to, and fuelling, a new set of discourses about the rapid growth of juvenile delinquency which lay at the heart of these changes in juvenile prosecution levels. The children of the urban poor may well have been driven to adopt new and more extensive appropriation strategies in the early nineteenth century. Without systematic self-report studies we may never know. What is clear, however, is that victims and criminal justice administrators were beginning to think very differently about how to react to juvenile crime in the big cities of early nineteenth-century England, and their changing attitudes were almost certainly the prime movers behind the rapid growth of urban juvenile indictment rates. The cities were the key locations, but it was the minds of the victims as much as the actions of the juvenile poor that generated the unprecedented rise of juvenile delinquency between the 1780s and the 1820s.

3. The punishment of juvenile offenders in the English courts 1780–1830. Changing attitudes and policies

Much has been written about the extensive debates on the treatment of juvenile offenders that characterised the 1830s, 1840s and early 1850s – debates that had an important influence on the major mid-century legislative changes which both established reformatories as the central plank in punishment policies, and transferred juvenile larceny trials into the summary courts. However, the earlier development of attitudes towards the punishment of juvenile delinquents has been relatively neglected and has usually been regarded by historians mainly as a prelude to the broader investigations that took place in the 1830s and 1840s. This is somewhat surprising since the previous period, and in particular the 1810s and 1820s, witnessed not only the emergence of juvenile delinquency as a major focus of social anxiety, but also a huge rise in the number of juvenile offenders being dealt with by the courts.[1] Although the extensive debates of the 1810s and 1820s did not immediately lead to significant legislative change, they undoubtedly affected penal policies on the ground.

[1] J. Carlebach, *Caring for Children in Trouble* (London, 1970); M. May, 'Innocence and Experience: the Evolution of the Concept of Juvenile Delinquency in the Mid-Nineteenth Century', *Victorian Studies*, 17 (1973), 7–29; I. Pinchbeck and M. Hewitt, *Children in English Society. Vol. II; From the Eighteenth Century to the Children Act 1948* (London, 1973); L. Radzinowicz and R. Hood, *A History of English Criminal Law and its Administration from 1750. Vol. v; The Emergence of Penal Policy* (London, 1986), 133–70; M. May, 'A Child's Punishment for a Child's Crime: The Reformatory and Industrial School Movement in Britain c. 1780–1880.' (PhD thesis, London, 1981); J. Briggs *et al.* (eds.), *Crime and Punishment in England. An Introductory History* (London, 1996), 172–80; P. Rush, 'The Government of a Generation: The Subject of Juvenile Delinquency', in J. Muncie, G. Hughes and E. McLaughlin (eds.), *Youth Justice. Critical Readings* (London, 2002) 138–58; H. Shore, *Artful Dodgers. Youth and Crime in Early Nineteenth-Century London* (Woodbridge, 1999) discusses the role of the early nineteenth century more fully; P. King and J. Noel, 'The Origins of "the Problem of Juvenile Delinquency": The Growth of Juvenile Prosecutions in London in the Late Eighteenth and Early Nineteenth Centuries', *Criminal Justice History*, 14 (1993), 17–42 and chapter 2. For recent surveys that are broader spatially and temporally – H. Shore and P. Cox 'Re-inventing the Juvenile Delinquent in Britain and Europe 1650–1950' and P. Griffiths, 'Juvenile Delinquency in Time' both in P. Cox and H. Shore (eds.), *Becoming Delinquent: British and European Youth 1650–1950* (Aldershot, 2002) 1–22 and 23–40.

There was considerable room for non-legislative innovation and penal change within the criminal justice system of the early nineteenth century. Judges, jurors and those involved in the pardoning process could choose between a wide range of potential outcomes in their dealings with juvenile offenders.[2] They could also set up, or adapt for penal purposes, various voluntary-sector penal institutions (as the next chapter will indicate). This chapter explores the different ways in which those discretionary powers were actually used, and the extent to which penal polices towards juveniles changed before 1830. In the process it also analyses the growing debates which emerged in the 1810s and early 1820s about each of the punishment options available for juveniles. The chapter therefore has two interrelated aims – to analyse the debates themselves and to assess how those debates related to changes in judicial practice via a study of the actual policies pursued by judges and juries.

Sentencing and punishment policies towards juveniles are almost impossible to analyse quantitatively until the late eighteenth century, because the ages of offenders were not systematically recorded by the courts before that time. However, during the last peacetime period of the eighteenth century (1783–93) this began to change. The statistical part of this study therefore focuses on the two major courts for which the most information on both age and sentencing policies is available – the Old Bailey and the Home Circuit assizes. The inclusion of comparative material for the five Home Circuit counties – Essex, Kent, Surrey, Sussex and Herts – enables an assessment to be made of the role of the metropolis in developing sentencing innovations in relation to juveniles.[3] This material suggests that it may have been primarily in London that new approaches were first developed in the 1810s. By using London material from the peacetime years of 1791–3 (the first two years for which information is available) change over time can also be reviewed in a broader way than previous historians have attempted. Since war severely distorted prosecution and sentencing patterns, because the courts diverted a large proportion of juveniles and young adults into the armed forces before trial, it is only by analysing change between peacetime periods – i.e. the pre-1793 and post-1815 years – that shifting approaches in the late eighteenth and early nineteenth centuries can be identified. In particular this approach enables us to analyse the extent to which juvenile offenders were treated differently in a period of acute anxiety about juvenile delinquency – the later 1810s and early 1820s – than they had been in the previous peacetime period when no equivalent large-scale panic about juvenile offenders was visible – i.e. the 1780s and early 1790s.[4]

---

[2] P. King, *Crime, Justice and Discretion in England 1740–1820* (Oxford, 2000).

[3] This chapter therefore builds on the London-based analysis in Shore, *Artful Dodgers*.

[4] P. King, 'War as a Judicial Resource. Press Gangs and Prosecution Rates, 1740–1830' in N. Landau (ed.), *Law, Crime and English Society 1660–1830* (Cambridge, 2002), 97–116; Shore, *Artful Dodgers*, 162–73 began detailed data collection in 1797 four years after war was declared.

This chapter will argue that the 1810s and early to mid-1820s were a unique period in the development of attitudes to the punishment of juvenile delinquency. The first half of the nineteenth century witnessed three fairly distinct, if overlapping, phases in the development of attitudes towards the punishment of juveniles but historians have tended to focus almost exclusively on the final two (i.e. the period from the late 1820s to the later 1840s, when attitudes hardened as exemplified by the harsh regimes imposed in the new juvenile prison at Parkhurst, and the final stage, the late 1840s and early 1850s, when the special needs of juvenile offenders were increasingly recognised and a more sympathetic national juvenile reformatory system was set up). During the first phase, however, which coincided roughly with the first quarter of the nineteenth century, those who both wrote about juvenile delinquency and made decisions about juveniles in the courts were far less concerned than their counterparts between the mid-1820s and mid-1840s about less eligibility and about insuring that the penalties used were sufficiently punitive. In the 1810s and early 1820s the need to find punishment options that would prevent the further corruption and degradation of juvenile offenders, as well as having at least a reasonable chance of reforming them, was the primary focus. Although from the late 1820s onwards juvenile delinquency came to be linked more specifically to criminal subcultures, and attention focused more and more on persistent offenders,[5] in the 1810s and for much of the 1820s attitudes remained more open. In these years debates about the roots of juvenile delinquency put much less emphasis on persistent offenders and still focused considerable attention on the many possible economic and social explanations for juvenile offending.

Equally, those who were discussing the many penal dilemmas posed by juvenile offenders were still exploring possible treatments and punishments in a fairly open way. The more punitive frameworks of debate which developed in the 1830s and 1840s were only just beginning to take hold. The many questions that were asked about juvenile delinquents and their treatment in the courts, by the Committee for Investigating the Alarming Increase in Juvenile Delinquency, by the Prison Discipline Society, and by the parliamentary committees of the 1810s and 1820s were still to some extent open ended and exploratory.[6]

For an interesting but not entirely successful attempt to locate the key site of change in Manchester – G. Fisher, 'The Birth of the Prison Retold', *Yale Law Review*, 104 (1995), 1235–1324.

[5] Shore, *Artful Dodgers*, 19, argues strongly that 'during the 1820s and 1830s juvenile crime was linked to a much narrower explanation, which was characterised by reference to criminal subcultures and the existence of a criminal class'; Radzinowicz and Hood, *A History*, v, 133–78; F. Driver, 'Discipline Without Frontiers? Representations of the Mettray Reformatory Colony in Britain 1840–80', *Journal of Historical Sociology*, 3 (1990), 272–93.

[6] W. Sanders, *Juvenile Offenders for a Thousand Years* (Chapel Hill, 1970); *Report of the Committee for Investigating the Causes of the Alarming Increase of Juvenile Delinquency in the Metropolis* (London, 1816), *Report of the Committee of the Society for the Improvement of Prison Discipline and for the Reformation of Juvenile Offenders* (London, 1818); *P.P.*, 1813–4, xii; 1818, viii;

Policy was forming slowly. Voluntary experiments had begun as early as 1788 with the foundation of the Philanthropic Society and this and other reformatory endeavours, such as the Refuge for the Destitute opened in 1806, were being discussed as possible models. So was the idea of a separate juvenile penitentiary, detailed plans for which were presented to the Home Secretary in 1817.[7] Equally, the existing penal options were being examined in increasing detail, although, as will become clear, there was deep ambivalence in the minds of many contemporaries about almost every potential punishment available for juveniles. In some areas the debates of the 1810s and early 1820s seem to have been accompanied by very little change in the actual sentencing policies pursued by the courts. In other areas major changes were clearly taking place by the 1820s. This period is worthy of separate study because attitudes remained much more open than they became in the early Victorian period. These years were the crucible in which policies were sifted, discussed and to some extent changed.

I

The most obvious change involved the decisions made not by the judges at the assizes or the Old Bailey but by the jurors of those courts. In part these focused on the youngest subgroup of juvenile offenders, those aged between seven and fourteen. Those accused of felony between these ages might, under certain conditions, benefit from the doctrine of *doli incapax*. Blackstone noted,

> By the law, as it now stands the capacity of doing ill, or contracting guilt, is not so much measured by years and days, as by the strength of the delinquent's understanding and judgement. For one lad of eleven years old may have as much cunning as another of 14 . . . Under seven years of age indeed an infant cannot by guilty of felony; for then a felonious discretion is almost an impossibility in nature: but at 8 years old he may be guilty of felony. Also, under 14, though an infant shall be *prima facie* adjudged to be *doli incapax*; yet if it appear to the court and jury, that he was *doli capax*, and could discern between good and evil, he may be convicted and suffer death.[8]

This doctrine left tremendous discretionary power in the hands of the jurors. Before any offender between seven and fourteen could be found guilty the jury had to believe that the act was committed, to quote one early nineteenth-century

1819, vii; 1828, vi. On the PDS – M. Roberts, *Making English Morals. Voluntary Association and Moral Reform in England 1787–1886* (Cambridge, 2003), 103–41 and its move in the mid-1820s towards harsher policies, 140.
[7] *P.P.*, 1817, vii, 524–30.
[8] W. Blackstone, *Commentaries on the Laws of England*, 4 vols. (Oxford, 1765–9) iv, 23. For European equivalents of *doli incapax* – H. Shore, 'Inventing the Juvenile Delinquent in Nineteenth-Century Europe' in B. Godfrey, C. Emsley and G. Dunstall (eds.), *Comparative Histories of Crime* (Cullompton, 2003), 112–13.

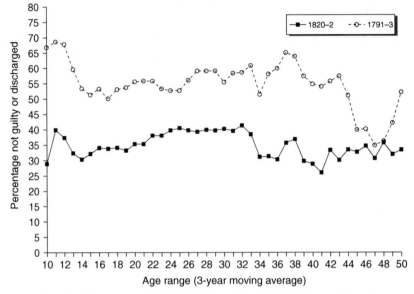

Figure 3.1   Old Bailey: percentage of accused not guilty or discharged by proclamation by age 1791–3 and 1820–2.
Note: Based on 3-year moving averages.

judge, with 'malicious intent'. In other words 'a guilty knowledge that he was doing wrong must be proved by the evidence'.[9]

Did jurors change the way they interpreted this doctrine during the late eighteenth and early nineteenth centuries? It appears that they did. At the Old Bailey 1791–3, for example, all the three property offenders aged between seven and ten were either discharged by proclamation because their indictments had been 'not found' by the grand jury, or were acquitted by the petty jury. Overall two thirds of ten-to-thirteen year olds obtained the same outcome whereas the average rate for all property offenders in these years was just over 50 per cent (Figure 3.1). Thirty years later, between 1820 and 1822, this picture had completely changed. Of the eight seven to nine year olds accused of felony, seven had been found guilty. Moreover, ten- to thirteen-year-olds received almost identical treatment to the accused in general. If anything, the very young were now slightly more likely than those in their twenties and thirties to be found guilty, a trend which Heather Shore has argued continued into the 1830s.[10]

Jurors outside London moved in the same direction. The Home Circuit data shows a very similar pattern (Figure 3.2). There is no evidence in the Home

---

[9] P. Parsloe, *Juvenile Justice in Britain and the United States. The Balance of Needs and Rights* (London, 1978), 111.

[10] All the figures in this chapter are based on three-year moving averages. The London data comes from Public Record Office (henceforth PRO) Criminal Registers HO 26/1–2 and 26–8. It is

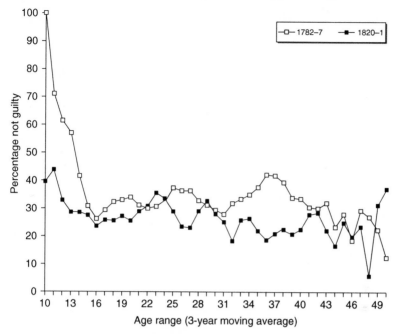

Figure 3.2 Home Circuit: percentage of accused not guilty by age 1782–7 and 1820–1.
Note: Based on 3-year moving averages.

Circuit assize agenda books about 'not found' verdicts but the changing pattern of acquittals by the petty jury is extremely clear. Between 1782 and 1787 all the three Home Circuit offenders aged eleven or under were acquitted, and acquittal rates for those aged under fourteen were 60 per cent, compared with an overall acquittal rate of one third. By 1820–1 the picture had changed dramatically. Only two of the six offenders aged eleven or less were found not guilty and although those aged under thirteen were slightly more likely to be acquitted than average, the difference was minimal. Moreover, a smaller sample for 1827 alone showed a similar, if slightly more irregular, pattern.[11] Although the numbers are very small, at both the Old Bailey and on the Home Circuit any presumption that a child under fourteen was *doli incapax* had effectively disappeared by the 1820s. The attitudinal changes that lay behind the lapse of *doli incapax* into 'desuetued', as the Recorder of Birmingham described it in 1852, were complex,

based on property offenders only. For further discussion see King and Noel 'The Origins'; For Shore's figures see *Artful Dodgers*, 168.
[11] PRO Assi 31/13–15, 23–5 is the source for the Home Circuit graphs. The 1827 sample is relatively small. Only one out of the six offenders under twelve was acquitted, and although four out of six of the thirteen year olds achieved this positive outcome apart from that one peak young offenders received no better treatment than the accused as a whole.

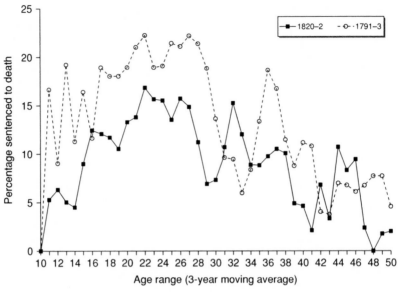

Figure 3.3 Old Bailey: percentage sentenced to death 1791–3 and 1820–2.
Note: Based on 3-year moving averages.

many sided and difficult to unravel. However there can be no doubt that in these courts jurors effectively abandoned it as a working principle between the 1790s and the 1820s.[12]

II

Ironically a residual effect of the *doli incapax* doctrine may have survived, and even grown in importance, in one vital area – capital punishment. A high percentage of the offenders that came before these two courts were liable to be sentenced to death if found guilty as charged. A significant proportion escaped this fate via a partial verdict, which downgraded the charge to a non-capital one.[13] However on the Home Circuit about three fifths of all offenders, and at the Old Bailey about two fifths, were accused of capital crimes and many were convicted in full. Some of these were aged fourteen or under (Figures 3.3 and 3.4). However, none of the property offenders under fourteen convicted in these two courts during the years sampled here were hanged (Figures 3.5 and 3.6), thus confirming Knell's finding that none of the 103 seven-to-fourteen year olds

[12] S. Magarey, 'The Invention of Juvenile Delinquency in Early Nineteenth-Century England', *Labour History*, 34 (1978), 19.

[13] King, *Crime*, 232 – over 12 per cent of assize cases involved partial verdicts 1782–7. A third of aggravated-larceny and housebreaking cases resulted in such verdicts.

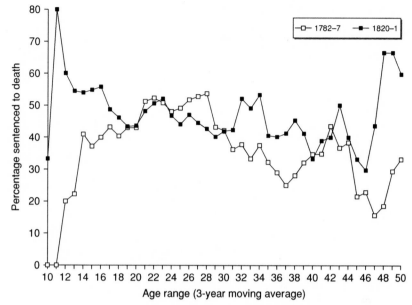

Figure 3.4   Home Circuit: percentage of convicted sentenced to death 1782–7 and 1820–1.
Note: Based on 3-year moving averages.

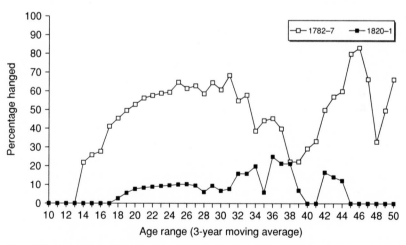

Figure 3.5   Home Circuit: percentage of sentenced to death actually hanged 1782–7 and 1820–1.
Note: Based on 3-year moving averages.

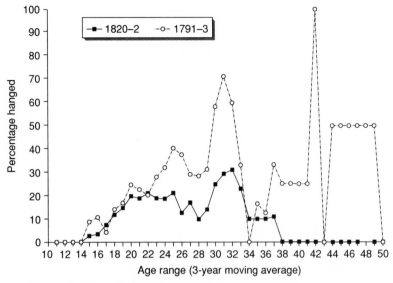

Figure 3.6 Old Bailey: percentage of sentenced to death actually hanged 1791–3 and 1820–2.
Note: Based on 3-year moving averages.

who were sentenced to death in London between 1800 and 1836 were actually executed.[14]

Some important changes did occur in attitudes towards the execution of those in their mid- or later teens between the 1780s and 1820s. Offenders of this age were still not totally immune from the threat of the gallows, but few sixteen or seventeen year olds were actually being hanged. Only two were executed in London 1820–2, although seven eighteen and nineteen year olds met this fate. On the Home Circuit, where those in their mid-teens had been more vulnerable to execution pre-1793 than those at the Old Bailey, a very clear pattern of growing mercy towards all juveniles can been seen by the 1820s (Figure 3.5). In 1782–7, a period of growing anxiety about crime and of extensive debate about the need to cut down on the pardoning of capital offenders, 45 per cent of seventeen-to-nineteen year olds who had been sentenced to death were actually hanged, and over a quarter of fifteen and sixteen year olds met the same fate. By 1820–1 no offender under nineteen and only two nineteen year olds were actually hanged.[15] By 1827 no offender under twenty went to the gallows. As

---

[14] B. Knell, 'Capital Punishment: Its Administration in Relation to Juvenile offenders in the Nineteenth Century and its Possible Administration in the Eighteenth', *British Journal of Criminology*, 5 (1965), 199.

[15] By the 1820s a much smaller percentage of very young offenders were being sentenced to death, partly because pickpocketing and shoplifting of all but the most expensive articles had ceased to be capital offences – L. Radzinowicz, *A History of English Criminal Law and its Administration from 1750*, i, 498–9 and 554.

opinion moved away from capital punishment as a suitable response to property crime in the nineteenth century, juveniles clearly benefited disproportionally from the resulting reluctance to send people to the gallows.

There was virtually no public discussion of the reasons for this change, but growing segments of respectable society seemed to have become convinced that young offenders sentenced to death should be given their support. When a young offender was unfortunate enough to be left to hang these groups frequently mobilised in depth. For example, out of eight London burglars sentenced to hang in 1822 the only two who escaped the gallows were the two youngest, both of whom were seventeen. With support from many local tradesmen, from the foreman of the trial jury, from a former master and from one of the victims, they finally obtained a conditional pardon, despite Home Secretary Peel's opposition. The King himself could not bear the thought of their hanging and Peel, after trying various delaying tactics, had to give way.[16] Many young offenders continued to be sentenced to death on the Home Circuit as well as at the Old Bailey. Indeed, in 1820–1, perhaps because they knew the offenders would not actually be executed, the Home Circuit judges sentenced a very high number of offenders to death. However, by then these were effectively sentences of transportation or imprisonment (depending on the conditions of their pardons) for all those aged under seventeen or eighteen. This was a source of concern to contemporaries because very young offenders were well aware of this policy and had become rather nonchalant in their attitude to the solemn passing of the death sentence, sometimes even gaining status amongst their peers because they had been sentenced to death rather than merely transportation. In 1819 a correspondent of the reformer Sir James Mackintosh complained that of the four thirteen or fourteen year olds sentenced to death in March 1819 'only one seemed affected, and the boys absolutely laughed'.[17] The death sentence was not yet a completely dead letter for juvenile offenders but it appears that public opinion, and even that of the monarch himself, was pushing it inexorably in that direction.

III

Imprisonment's growth from a rarely used post-trial punishment in the 1770s to the most important sanction for convicted property offenders by the late 1780s inevitably put it in the forefront of debates about sentencing policies towards juveniles.[18] By the early nineteenth century large numbers of juveniles were

---

[16] V. Gatrell, *The Hanging Tree. Execution and the English People 1770–1868* (Oxford, 1994), 556–8.

[17] Shore, *Artful Dodgers*, 119; W. Lisle Bowles, *Thoughts on the Increase of Crimes, the Education of the Poor and the National Schools in a Letter to Sir James Mackintosh* (London, 1819), 56.

[18] J. Beattie, *Crime and the Courts in England 1660–1800* (Oxford, 1986), 520–618; King, *Crime*, 261–78.

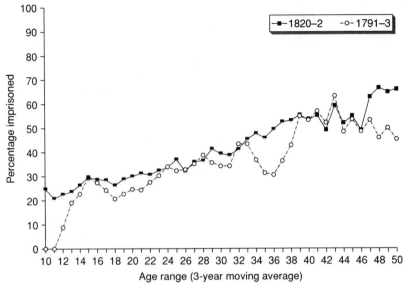

Figure 3.7   Old Bailey: percentage imprisoned 1791–3 and 1820–2.
Note: Based on 3-year moving averages.

being summarily imprisoned under various statutes, committed to gaol awaiting jury trial, or sentenced to incarceration by the judges after conviction. Once a juvenile had been found guilty of a non-capital offence the judges then had to decide whether or not imprisonment was a suitable punishment. On the whole the Old Bailey was much less inclined to imprison juveniles than it was those of older years (Figure 3.7). This was particularly true in the 1790s in relation to those under fourteen but remained clearly observable in the 1820s when less than a quarter of up to thirteen year olds and less than 30 per cent of fourteen to nineteen year olds were imprisoned, compared to a figure of 50 per cent for those in their late thirties and forties.

Outside London there seems to have been less sensitivity to the dangers of imprisoning juveniles. On the Home Circuit there was little difference between the proportion of juveniles given gaol sentences and the proportion of adults who received such punishments, although by 1821 the very young were more likely to escape imprisonment (Figure 3.8). The policy in London was clear, however. Prison sentences were obviously an option that the court tried to avoid in the great majority of cases involving juveniles, while still using it against about half of mature adults. Moreover, when imprisonment was used, those under sixteen were more likely to be given sentences lasting under a month and around twice as likely to avoid sentences of over a year (Table 3.1). This desire to minimise the young's experience of prison is not surprising if the debates

Table 3.1 *Length of imprisonment by age, Old Bailey, 1791–3 and 1820–2*

Age group	Under 1 month	1 to 5.9 months	6 to 11.9 months	12 months or more	Total percentage
1791–3					
0 to 16	9.5	28.6	57.1	4.8	100
17 or over	8.8	36.5	42.8	11.9	100
Sample	27	110	134	35	306
1820–2					
0 to 16	5.6	51.4	30.8	12.2	100
17 or over	2.8	43.1	31.4	22.7	100
Sample	25	351	249	169	794

Sources: PRO HO 26/1–2, 26–8.

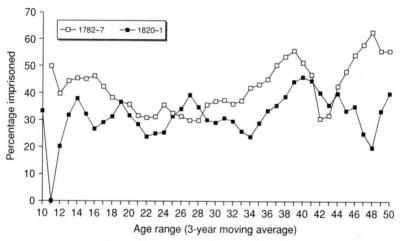

Figure 3.8   Home Circuit: percentage imprisoned 1782–7 and 1820–1.
Note: Based on 3-year moving averages.

in the metropolis about the efficiency of imprisonment as a punishment for juveniles are analysed in detail.

Growing concern about the need to reclaim the individual offender – to reform his or her character – along with a general resurgence in the movement for prison reform,[19] made contemporaries look long and hard at the condition of London's

---

[19] M. Ignatieff, *A Just Measure of Pain. The Penitentiary in the Industrial Revolution 1750–1850* (London, 1978); R. McGowen, 'The Well-Ordered Prison: England, 1780–1850', in N. Morris and D. Rothman (eds.), *The Oxford History of the Prison. The Practice of Punishment in Western Societies* (Oxford, 1995), 79–110; W. Forsythe, *The Reform of Prisoners 1830–1900* (London, 1987).

gaols in the early nineteenth century. They found them severely wanting. In the 1810s and early 1820s the overwhelming majority of commentators were deeply sceptical about the impact of sentences of imprisonment on the young. The 1817 parliamentary committee on London policing argued that despite much agitation about prison reform

> yet even now, in all prisons, offenders of different characters and stages of crime are mixed indiscriminately together. It is scarcely possible to devise a system better calculated to vitiate and corrupt than the mode in which juvenile offenders are thus confined . . . the greater part of these . . . some of them infants of 9, 10 and 11 years of age are mixed indiscriminately with old offenders of all ages and all of them with boys of 15 or 16, many of whom have been long practised in the commission of various acts of fraud. No one but those who have witnessed such painful exhibitions, can be aware of the pleasure which the older thieves take in corrupting those who have just entered into vicious courses.

This theme can be found in several of the statements made by witnesses to the committee. William Crawford, after commenting initially about Newgate that 'they are all confined in one yard with the men, it is scarcely possible a boy should be a single day in this prison without being contaminated', went on to generalise that 'it must be obvious . . . the tendency of confinement must be to . . . corrupt rather than reform'.[20] The Committee for Investigating the Alarming Increase of Juvenile Delinquency, of which he was an important member, actually blamed the prisons in part for the rise in juvenile delinquency. Having frequently visited the prisons of the metropolis they expressed their sorrow 'that to the defective system of discipline which exists in the prisons of London, the evil of juvenile delinquency owes in great measure its aggravation'.[21] When another committee member was asked why juvenile delinquency had increased, he replied

> I consider that the indiscriminate confinement practised in most of our prisons where the child committed for trial . . . is locked up in the same yard, and obliged constantly to associate with the hardened offender and convicted felon, is the most certain method that can be devised of increasing the number of delinquents.

Henry Grey Bennet, the chairman of the 1817 committee, having described his visits to London's gaols, concluded on similar lines that 'the union of offenders of all ages and descriptions, the want of separation . . . the union of the accused with the convicted, the young with old offenders . . . have produced the direct effect of making these establishments nurseries and schools of crime'.[22]

---

[20] *P.P.*, 1817, vii, 328–9, 430–1.
[21] *Report of the Committee for Investigating the Causes of the Alarming Increase of Juvenile Delinquency in the Metropolis* (London, 1816), 22.
[22] *P.P.*, 1817, vii, 529–40.

Similar viewpoints were expressed by less exalted witnesses. Meshack Hobbs a prisoner in Cold Bath Fields concluded that 'while these boys are continued together in the manner in which they now are . . . there does not . . . appear to be the least prospect of a reformation of any one of them . . . when they leave the prison they are more hardened in vice and immorality'. The section of the 1819 report on the state of the gaols devoted specifically to juveniles heard similar evidence. 'In the different prisons I have visited, the reformation of boys is generally considered as hopeless', one witness concluded, 'the boys have become worse and worse . . . lads going into prison for a first offence generally leave instructed in the ways of vice.'[23] The Society for the Improvement of Prison Discipline and for the Reformation of Juvenile Offenders continued to develop the same theme, and widely advertised it amongst its supporters. 'Now mark the operation on a young offender', the society's first report observed in 1818,

> he enters the prison young in vice, alarmed at the gloom of the cells, terrified with the clank of irons, with a mind necessarily prepared for good impressions. There is no classification . . . He is immediately thrown amongst the veterans in crime; his fears are derided, his rising repentance subdued, his vicious propensities cherished and inflamed . . . The very foundations of virtue are utterly sapped and destroyed . . . the prisoner enters a boy in years and a boy in vice; he departs with a knowledge of the ways of wickedness which thrice the time spent elsewhere could scarcely have conferred upon him. *These are the evils of contamination.*[24]

Such themes were increasingly taken up outside the metropolis by men such as the Warwickshire magistrate Eardley Wilmot who saw 'the early imprisonment of mere children' as 'the chief cause of the increase of crime'. Yet it was in London that the discussion initially tended to focus, aided by pamphlets such as Bennet's letter to the Common Council on Newgate and Buxton's enquiry into prison discipline.[25] In the late 1810s and early 1820s, as conviction rates rose

---

[23] *P.P.*, 1818, viii, 169; *P.P.*, 1819, viii, 149–50.

[24] *Report of the Committee of the Society for the Improvement of Prison Discipline and for the Reformation of Juvenile Offenders* (London, 1818), 18. The Society's third report, published in 1821 laid even more stress on the evils of contamination. In its discussion of 'the injurious tendency of imprisonment in the gaols of the metropolis' it told the same story of insufficient space 'for classification and employing the juvenile prisoners . . . or subjecting them to such a course of discipline as experience has proved efficacious for the reformation of criminal youth', and of young offenders confined with the hardened and thus unable to 'escape contamination' – *Report* (London, 1821), 48.

[25] J. Eardley Wilmot, *A Second Letter to the Magistrates of Warwick on the Increase of Crime in General but more Particularly of Juvenile Delinquency* (London, 1820), 6; H. C. Bennet, *A Letter to the Common Council and Livery of the City of London on the Abuses Existing in Newgate* (London, 1818); T. F. Buxton, *An Inquiry Whether Crime and Misery are Produced or Prevented by our Present System of Prison Discipline* (London, 1818), 47–8, 'He came to Newgate innocent, he left it corrupted.'

and central government regulation of such issues as classification had yet to be effectively introduced, the prison system of London (and of many provincial areas) was under tremendous strain, and facing unprecedented problems which prison administrators had failed to anticipate.[26] London's prisons in particular were seen as sources of contagion and contamination, as schools of vice and villainy with insufficient separation, classification or reformatory regimes. Once the detailed scheme for a separate juvenile penitentiary had fallen on stony ground, most commentators remained deeply ambivalent about imprisonment as a punishment for juveniles.

Although there were some dissenting voices, the majority of the small group of commentators who were positive about the use of prison sentences against juveniles tended, in the 1810s and early 1820s at least, to link such policies to the use of early, if brief, periods of solitary confinement. 'I think solitary confinement for a fortnight with a boy for his first offence is much the best punishment', one Somerset magistrate argued in 1828. Another witness before the same committee felt that 'a whipping and solitary confinement for a given number of hours' would be the best policy, 'so that the offender might avoid the contamination of gaol'. The resulting parliamentary report particularly highlighted this idea that 'corporal punishment and solitary confinement would be better than the imprisonment of them with other prisoners'.[27] It was clear to most commentators, however, that the period for which juvenile offenders could be kept in solitary confinement was very short. John Capper, superintendent of the Hulks when asked 'do you find that solitary confinement has a good effect upon boys?' replied 'not complete solitary confinement; I would give him employment though he was shut up; I would not keep him above four or five days'. Some believed even this would be far too long. 'Juvenile offenders', William Roscoe wrote in 1823, 'should not be punished by solitary confinement', even though he believed 'the policy of keeping this description of convicts completely separate from old felons is too obvious to require any arguments'.[28]

The problem at this point was less that of a clash between the principles of punishment and those of reformation, than that of a fruitless search for any effective place in which reformation might take place. The prisons, and especially those of London, were still spoken of in the early 1820s in the language of 'contagion', 'contamination', 'corruption' or 'evil communication'.[29] This

---

[26] M. De Lacy, *Prison Reform in Lancashire, 1700–1850. A Study in Local Administration* (Stanford, 1986), 63.

[27] *P.P.*, 1828, vi, 429, 458, 497.

[28] *P.P.*, 1828, vi,106; W. Pascoe, *Additional Observations on Penal Jurisdiction and the Reformation of Criminals* (London, 1823), 74.

[29] R. Evans, *The Fabrication of Virtue. English Prison Architecture, 1750–1840* (Cambridge, 1982), 6.

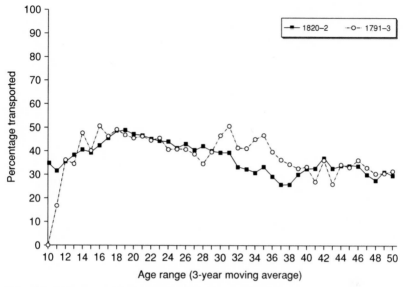

Figure 3.9 Old Bailey: percentage transported 1791–3 and 1820–2.
Note: Based on 3-year moving averages.

was bound to discourage the use of imprisonment as a post-trial sentence for juveniles and indeed it appears to have done so at the Old Bailey as early as the 1790s. Was the other major penal sanction – transportation to Australia – seen as a preferable option?

IV

Transportation was widely used at the Old Bailey (Figure 3.9). Just over 40 per cent of all convicted property offenders received this sentence. Those under fourteen were less likely to be transported (especially in 1791–3), and in both periods those between sixteen and twenty five were most likely to find themselves transported (or at least placed on the Hulks awaiting transportation). The Home Circuit usually followed the same policy towards under-fourteen year olds but focused less fully on those aged between fifteen and twenty six (Figure 3.10).

The complex supply and demand factors that lay behind these policies were rarely discussed in public in the 1810s and early 1820s. The general advantages of transportation were obvious. Offenders were removed from the home country at the same time as being offered, in theory at least, the possibility of reforming their lifestyles. As one commentator put it in the 1820s:

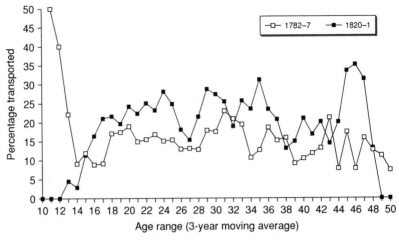

Figure 3.10 Home Circuit: percentage transported 1782–7 and 1820–1.
Note: Based on 3-year moving averages.

Of all punishments devised, that is the best which perpetually ejects the delinquent from the bosom of the society he has offended. Transportation not only holds out the best chance of criminal reform, but . . . would have two advantages; first, it would prevent the criminal calendar being swelled . . . by the names of delinquents committed for a second or greater number of offences; and, secondly it would tend to reduce the redundant population, by removing some of the worse members of society.[30]

There is certainly evidence that transportation was often seen as the highest point in the tariff-style system of punishment for non-capital offences, as can be seen from these remarks from the chairman of the Clerkenwell sessions to a boy he had just transported.

Prisoner, what can we do with you? We have done everything to reclaim you; we have imprisoned you over and over again, and given you frequent floggings, yet all is of no use: the sentence of the court is that you be transported for seven years.

[30] J. Wade, *A Treatise on the Police and Crimes of the Metropolis* (London, 1829), 21; H. Shore, 'Transportation, Penal Ideology and the Experience of Juvenile Offenders in England and Australia in the Early Nineteenth Century', *Crime, Histoire et Societes/ Crime, History and Societies*, 6 (2002), 86; S. Devereaux, 'In Place of Death: Transportation, Penal Practices and the English State, 1770–1830' in C. Strange (ed.), *Qualities of Mercy: Justice, Punishment and Discretion* (British Columbia, 1996), 52–76. By the late 1820s and early 1830s philanthropic bodies were increasingly offering forms of voluntary transportation to destitute juveniles – E. Bradlow, 'The Children's Friend Society at the Cape of Good Hope, *Victorian Studies*, 27 (1984), 155–77; E. Hadley, 'Natives in a Strange Land: The Philanthropic Discourse of Juvenile Emigration in Mid-Nineteenth-Century England', *Victorian Studies*, 33 (1990), 411–16. Among the earliest bodies to do so was the Refuge for the Destitute – P. King (ed.), *Narratives of the Poor in Eighteenth-Century Britain, Vol. iv, The Refuge for the Destitute* (London, 2006), xxi.

Asked about the Warwickshire courts' policies Eardley Wilmot replied 'it is at the option of the court to transport them for seven years or imprison them; of course, unless he is an old offender, and it is an aggravated offence, we do not give him a greater punishment than imprisonment'. In some areas magistrates moved more quickly up the scale to the transportation option and believed that they got positive results. One Yorkshire JP, for example, observed 'I only confine them for short periods . . . we agreed that wherever a boy has been brought up on one occasion, and then brought up again, he should be transported, and this has had a good effect'.[31]

As Heather Shore's work has shown, the boys' own reactions to being transported were very mixed, but amongst elite commentators in the 1810s and 1820s much was made of their indifference to, or even welcoming of, such a sentence. 'They thank you if you transport them, and very often make use of improper language' Eardly Wilmot observed. When the keeper of Newgate was asked 'do the boys in general dread transportation?' he replied 'not at all'. Bow Street's chief magistrate went further. 'A great many would like to go', he observed, 'and deem it no punishment at all.' The Reverend Bowles agreed. 'Transportation is even to many a bounty', he wrote in 1819.[32]

A sentence of transportation did not always mean a journey to Australia. The system was clogged up. Many juveniles spent a considerable part of their time on the Hulks. Some spent all of it on them. This outcome may well have been viewed very differently by younger offenders. Asked in 1818 how the young felt about transportation, the keeper of Newgate replied, 'I think there are many . . . young men . . . that are frequently more rejoiced at going than in any ways considering it as a punishment' but he then added that 'their greatest dread is going into seven years slavery, as they call it . . . going to the Hulks'.[33] The Hulks had a very unsavoury reputation. In 1819 the reformer Samuel Hoare had 'great objections to the Hulks . . . for the boys'. Even after a separate Hulk had been established for juvenile offenders in 1823, it soon became clear that conditions on it were appalling with a violent subculture of gang rule prevailing. Even the Hulks superintendent was very pessimistic about their effect on juvenile offenders. 'Eight out ten that had been liberated have returned to their old courses', he observed. To many in the 1820s the juvenile Hulk was simply 'a nursery for vice' and a place that did not even detach juvenile offenders from their old associations. As a London alderman pointed out in 1828,

[31] *Old Bailey Experience. Criminal Jurisprudence and the Actual Workings of Our Penal Code of Laws* (London, 1833), 306; *P.P.*, 1828, vi, 444 and 490.

[32] Shore, 'Transportation', 91; Shore, *Artful Dodgers*, 134; *P.P.*, 1826, vi, 37; *P.P.*, 1828, vi, 39, 54, 445; Bowles, 'Thoughts', 56.

[33] *P.P.*, 1828, vi, 183–4. On the dread of transportation see also – L. MacKay, 'Refusing the Royal Pardon: London Convicts and the Reactions of the Courts and Press 1789', *London Journal*, 28 (2003), 31–3.

the great object in the punishment of the boys, is to take them away from their friends . . . on that account the practice of sending them to the Hulks under the law for 7 years transportation, appears to be inefficient, because they have so much communication with their friends.[34]

Although the use of transportation, or of the Hulks, cannot be analysed without reference to the debates on the potential reformability of the young in such contexts, it is clear that many contemporaries involved in the judicial system were far from convinced of the efficacy of these punishments, given the poor record of the Hulks and the widespread belief (whether reflected in reality or not) that juvenile offenders might welcome transportation. Henry Grey Bennet's solution was to attack transportation. 'I propose detaining at home all those who are sent to transportation for shorter terms than for their natural lives', he wrote. However, he had to admit that imprisonment on the Hulks was completely deficient in reforming possibilities, and that this would only be achieved if strictly regulated district penitentiaries were set up. Since no such reform occurred in the 1820s, his remained a relatively isolated voice.[35] Once again the judicial authorities were deeply ambivalent about this form of punishment but were forced to use it partly by the tariff system, within which transportation was considered the highest form of punishment apart from the death penalty, and partly because the alternatives seemed even less satisfactory.

V

The courts' other main punishment options mainly involved the use of non-custodial sentences. Following the ending of branding on the hand in the late eighteenth century, this effectively meant either whipping and discharging the offender, or releasing him or her after the imposition of a fine. The Home Circuit data is not especially useful in this context since that court used non-custodial sentences very much less frequently than the Old Bailey. By the 1820s the Old Bailey was using them ten times as often as the Home Circuit (Table 3.2a), partly because the latter heard considerably fewer simple larceny cases. Within the small number of cases where non-custodial sentences were used on the Home Circuit, fines played a negligible role and the small number of whippings that were meted out were increasingly focused on juveniles.[36] The Old Bailey data

---

[34] P.P., 1819, vii, 160; Shore, *Artful Dodgers*, 129–30; P.P., 1828, vi, 53, 86, 105.

[35] H. Bennet, *Letter to Viscount Sidmouth on the Transportation Laws, the State of the Hulks and of the Colonies in New South Wales* (London, 1819), 122. Bennet's view did get some support from those who believed that if juveniles were imprisoned for longer they might be reformable – P.P., 1817, vii, 431; P.P., 1818, viii, 44.

[36] PRO, Assi 31/14–15, 23–4. In 1782–7 ten out of forty-two offenders whipped or fined were twenty-one or younger, and in 1820–1 the figure was six out of seven.

Table 3.2a *Proportion of non-custodial sentences*
Home Circuit and Old Bailey 1780s–1820s

Home Circuit	Percentage
1782–7	3.8
1821–2	1.2
Old Bailey	
1791–3	9.0
1820–2	12.3

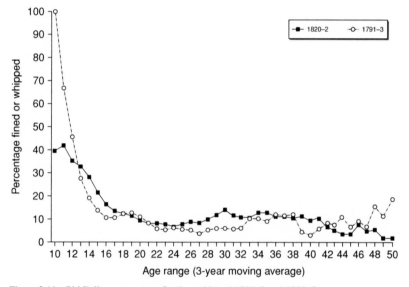

Figure 3.11   Old Bailey: percentage fined or whipped 1791–3 and 1820–2.
Note: Based on 3-year moving averages.

presented in Figures 3.11, 3.12 and 3.13 is much more useful. At that court non-custodial sentences were usually the preferred option for the very young (Figure 3.11).

Absolute numbers were very small at this stage but between 1791 and 1793 all those aged eleven or under and half of those aged under fourteen were either whipped or fined, and those in their teens also benefited from this policy to a lesser extent. 13 per cent were fined or whipped, compared to only 5 per cent of those in their twenties or early thirties. On first reading Figure 3.11 suggests this policy remained very similar in the 1820s. The very young continued to be completely covered by it. All the three seven or eight year olds convicted by the

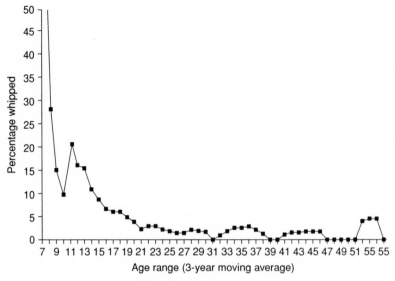

Figure 3.12 Old Bailey: percentage whipped 1820–2.
Note: Based on 3-year moving averages.

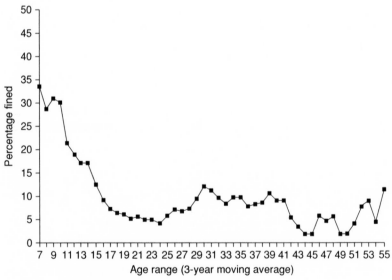

Figure 3.13 Old Bailey: percentage fined 1820–2.
Note: Based on 3-year moving averages.

Table 3.2b *Proportion of offenders fined and whipped,*
Old Bailey 1791–1822

	1791–3	1820–2
Fined	1.2	8.0
Whipped	7.8	4.3
Total of both	9.0	12.3

Sources: PRO HO 26/1-2, 26-8; Assi 31/13-15

courts 1820–2 were given non-custodial sentences. Equally over 40 per
cent of nine-to-twelve year olds benefited from such policies. Teenagers, as
figure 3.11 shows, were more likely to be fined or whipped than they had been
in the 1790s. Indeed by the 1820s they were benefiting from non-custodial sentences in large numbers. 162 out of the 324 non-custodial sentences given out
by the Old Bailey 1820–2 involved teenagers and thirteen to seventeen year
olds did especially well. 20 per cent received these relatively light sentences
compared to 7 per cent in their mid-twenties.

The Old Bailey's growing use of non-custodial sentences between the 1790s
and the 1820s was mainly due to its increasing use of fines. As Table 3.2b
indicates, by 1820–2 it used fines nearly twice as often as corporal punishment.
Between the 1790s and the 1820s the Old Bailey reduced by nearly 50 per cent
the proportion of offenders being whipped, while increasing more than sixfold
their use of fines. A new arm of penal policy, the significance of which we will
return to later, was being developed. However in both the 1790s and 1820s whipping continued to be an important part of the Old Bailey's sentencing strategies
in relation to young offenders and became more concentrated upon the young
alone. Two thirds of convicted offenders under thirteen were whipped 1791–3
and a similar pattern can be seen in 1820–2 (Figure 3.12). In both periods those
in their early to mid-teens were about four times more likely to be whipped than
those in their mid-twenties. The Old Bailey actually increased to some extent
the proportion of juvenile offenders that it sentenced to a whipping in conjunction with imprisonment. By the 1820s this policy had been developed to the
point where those under seventeen were more than 2.5 times more likely than
those over twenty to be whipped as well as imprisoned (Table 3.3). This set of
policies whereby the Old Bailey decreased the percentages subjected to whipping alone but increased the numbers being imprisoned with a whipping, whilst
focusing both policies heavily on the young, reflected contemporaries' deep
ambivalence about the use of corporal punishment. Opinion was clearly moving away from the use of corporal punishment against adults but contemporaries
were also far from unanimous about the efficacy of whipping juvenile offenders.

Table 3.3 *Percentage whipped as well as imprisoned, by age group. Old Bailey 1791–3 and 1820–2*

	1791–3		1820–2	
Age group	Total imprisoned	Percentage also whipped	Total imprisoned	Percentage also whipped
0–16	21	47.6	131	53.4
17–19	32	28.1	148	47.3
20 and over	307	25.7	681	19.4
Total	360	27.2	960	28.3

Sources: PRO HO 26/1-2, 26-8.

Some observers were very negative. A number of the witnesses questioned by the parliamentary committees of the 1810s and 1820s were very definitely against the use of corporal punishment. The report of the 1817 committee, for example, argued that flogging boys was a practice that tended 'to harden and degrade'. In this it echoed the views of the influential Committee for Investigating the Causes of the Alarming Increase of Juvenile Delinquency in the Metropolis. 'If the infliction of bodily punishment were to give way to mildness of persuasion and gentleness of reproof, if appeals were oftener made to the moral sensibility of these youths and exertions used to raise rather than degrade them in their own estimation', the committee's report argued, 'the number of juvenile deprecators would materially diminish'.[37] By the 1820s those arguing against corporal punishment had become rather less idealistic and much more pragmatic, but they were no less opposed to it as a suitable punishment for juveniles. Several contemporaries argued that boys far too frequently reoffended after being given a simple sentence of whipping alone. 'They are discharged one sessions and come in the next', the keeper of Newgate observed. Others were afraid that corporal punishment actually hardened offenders. One City of London marshall thought it a very bad plan to flog boys because 'it hardens them'. Pressed further he was similarly pessimistic about its use against the very young. The author of *Observations on the Offensive and Injurious Effects of Corporal Punishment*, published in the same decade, argued strongly that 'it has been abundantly proved that youthful delinquents are, by this discipline, more effectively matured into incorrigible criminals.' An experienced Newgate schoolmaster took the same view. 'I have ever observed', he wrote, 'the boys have become bold, daring and hardened in proportion as they have undergone the most corporal punishment.'[38]

[37] *P.P.*, 1817, vii, 330; *Report . . . Metropolis* (London, 1816), 24–5.
[38] *P.P.*, 1828, vi, 52, 89; *Observations on the Offensive and Injurious Effect of Corporal Punishment* (London, 1827), 5–7; *Old Bailey Experience*, 295.

Other observers saw corporal punishment as, at best, a mixed blessing. The London magistrate, Henry Dyer, argued that 'there are certainly cases where whipping does good, but I consider the frequent repetition of corporal punishment is by no means desirable.' Outside the metropolis the chief constable of Leeds observed that the whipping of young boys 'in many cases is of great utility, and in other cases they have appeared again during the very next sessions because it had no effect on them.'[39] Overall, however, the voices in favour of whipping for very young offenders probably still outweighed the opposition in the 1820s. It is clear that in the City of London whipping was widely used as a diversionary tactic by magistrates at the summary stage. Describing current practice in relation to six-to-ten year olds the city's Upper Marshall observed in 1816 'if the Lord Mayor can find anybody that will answer for them and give them employment he is very unwilling to commit them to Newgate . . . The Lord Mayor generally sends them to Bridewell, and has them slightly whipped and passed to their parish.' Whipping as a post-trial punishment also had other advocates in the 1810s. The Ordinary of Newgate, asked in 1818 'What is the effect produced by that punishment' (i.e. whipping), replied 'Upon young people I think it has a very good effect . . . where boys have been whipped and immediately sent home'. However he was much less sanguine about combining whipping and imprisonment. 'Where they are whipped and immediately remanded to prison . . . I think it has no effect', he observed.[40] Peel certainly supported the use of whipping and although it was banned for female offenders from 1820 onwards, the parliamentary reports of the 1820s contained more evidence in favour of it than against it. The report of the 1828 committee, which focused mainly on the provinces, concluded that 'great advantage may be derived from the application of corporal punishment to boys'. Amongst the evidence heard by the committee was that of the governor of Bury Gaol who observed that 'it is a general feeling among juvenile offenders that nothing is so much dreaded as private whipping. I have had applications from parents to save them from it . . . I confine it principally to juvenile offenders say under 20 years of age.'[41]

Opinions differed amongst those in favour of flogging about the age at which it became counter productive. One Manchester magistrate observed in 1828 that

> We have generally made a difference when the culprit is at the age of 16 or 17, and we never order the punishment of whipping to be inflicted upon persons who are upwards of 17 years of age. We do not think that it has a good effect upon the temper of such boys; but when they are under the age of 17 we think it the best means of punishing a boy.

---

[39] *P.P.*, 1828, vi, 180, 487.   [40] *P.P.*, 1816, v, 262; *P.P.*, 1818, viii, 173.
[41] Gatrell, *The Hanging Tree*, 338, 578; *P.P.*, 1828, vi, 431; *P.P.*, 1826–7, vi, 42.

Sir Thomas Baring MP argued in the same year that 'with all boys under the age of 15 or 16 years flogging would have a much better effect and deter from the repetition of the commission of the offence in a greater degree than imprisonment'.[42] The 1828 committee on London policing received a considerable amount of evidence about the effectiveness of flogging. 'What do boys dread most?', the keeper of Newgate was asked. 'Flogging I think more than anything else', he replied, although he then added 'only they soon forget it afterwards'. However, the vast majority of those in favour of it felt it should be mainly used on the very young. A Middlesex magistrate asked how he felt juvenile offenders should be dealt with, replied 'it is not a likely way to bring a lad of 7, 8, 9 or 10 years of age round to a good course of life to send him to a jail, where he shall be found in company with the most depraved boys . . . I should certainly give him a very sound whipping, and send him about his business.' Asked how 'young boys should be punished' the chief Bow Street magistrate recommended that 'more should be whipped than are'. 'A little flogging at a certain age' would, he argued 'be much more advantageous than imprisonment.' Asked 'under what age' he replied 'under 12 years of age'. The Lord Mayor of London was prepared to stretch the age upwards to some extent. 'I think for very young offenders probably corporal punishment might be useful; but . . . only for quite young children . . . perhaps under the age of 14'.[43] These opinions may well have had an effect on court policies for it was precisely against these groups – the under twelves, the under fourteens, and to a lesser extent those under sixteen or seventeen that the Old Bailey most frequently used the punishment of whipping alone. While the deepening ambivalence towards whipping resulted in an overall decline in the proportion of offenders subjected to corporal punishment alone, the continued belief amongst many practitioners that it was still a good option when the offender was young, meant that it remained an important part of juvenile justice policies in the 1820s.

VI

At the Old Bailey at least, the growing ambivalence of contemporaries towards the various punishment options available in cases involving young offenders had resulted in a major innovation by the beginning of the 1820s – the growing use of nominal fines (usually of 1 shilling) as the only recorded punishment. Although this option was used in only 8 per cent of cases between 1820–2, it made a very significant impact on juvenile sentencing patterns because its use was much more prevalent in cases involving the young (Figure 3.13). At the Old Bailey 1820–2 a nominal fine was recorded in 30 per cent of cases involving seven-to-eleven year olds and this bias continued until the mid-teens.

---

[42] *P.P.*, 1828, vi, 440 and 497.   [43] *P.P.*, 1828, vi, 38,45, 54, 66 and 239.

17 per cent of those aged eleven to fifteen received this sentence. The Old Bailey judges had introduced a new sentencing option, the most obvious beneficiaries of which were the young.

It is difficult to find any public discussion of the use of fining as a sole punishment in larceny cases. We know that magistrates quite often used fines at the summary level to deal with minor property crimes in a way that would avoid embroiling a young offender in the criminal justice system. When Colonel James Clitherow, who had been an acting Middlesex JP for twenty years, was asked in 1820 whether juvenile offenders were 'treated in the ordinary way as other offenders', he replied. 'They are trifling offences which they commit such as robbing orchards and that sort of thing; we fine them a trifle, and remand them, and frighten them as much as we can. I am very much against committing for such trifling offences; I hardly ever do.'[44] It appears that the Old Bailey judges may well have seen matters much the same way when very young offenders came before them for lesser offences. A nominal fine followed by immediate release may have been felt appropriate for a number of reasons, but in the case of young offenders it certainly meant that further contamination by the prison system would be avoided. This may well have proved increasingly attractive to the Old Bailey judges in the late 1810s and early 1820s but beneath the simple entries in the Newgate calendar recording that offenders were 'fined 1 shilling', another new policy was developing, as will be discussed more fully in the next chapter. Whilst formally recording a fine and/or that judgement was respited, the court was in fact insuring that a significant proportion of offenders, and most particularly very young offenders, were being sent to institutions which were effectively juvenile reformatories. Fining and immediate release was not the only penal option being developed by the Old Bailey and used in an increasing proportion of cases involving juveniles. The courts were also systematically developing a policy that involved covertly sentencing a growing number of young offenders to a spell in a juvenile reformatory.[45]

VII

This chapter has attempted both to analyse the many dilemmas about the punishment of juveniles which dominated contemporary discussions in the 1810s and 1820s, and to see how they were resolved and translated into action and innovation by those who ran the major courts. The late eighteenth and early nineteenth centuries, and in particular the decades of the 1810s and 1820s when juvenile delinquents flooded into the courts, were clearly periods of considerable debate, difficulty and confusion. With overcrowded and largely unregulated

---

[44] *P.P.*, 1828, vi, 231.
[45] See Chapter 4 and on the Refuge's more general history – King, *Narratives*.

prisons still the norm, the major courts of the early 1820s had to decide between a limited set of sentencing options. There were some major changes. Paradoxically, the protection that *doli incapax* afforded to those under fourteen was deeply eroded by changing attitudes amongst jurors, whose verdicts ceased to favour these groups. Yet at the same time youth brought increasing immunity for those unfortunate enough to be sentenced to death. Young offenders also gained from the major sentencing innovation of the period – the Old Bailey's use of nominal fines as either a sole punishment or as a screen behind which juvenile offenders were being siphoned off into institutions with reformatory regimes. The very young were also the major beneficiaries (if this is the right term) of court policies towards the use of whipping followed by immediate discharge. These non–custodial options, which were also used extensively by magistrates at the summary level, were often attempts at diversion – at preventing juvenile offenders from being contaminated by older offenders in the prisons or in the Hulks.

Deeply ambivalent about imprisonment for juvenile offenders, the Old Bailey used this punishment much less on the young than on those of riper age, but imprisonment (and particularly imprisonment alongside a whipping) was still an important part of penal policy towards the young. So was transportation and the Hulks, despite grave misgivings about the effectiveness of either as a deterrent or as a means of reforming young offenders. The development of a covert policy of referring a growing number of juveniles to reformatory projects such as the Philanthropic Society and the Refuge for the Destitute reflected both the optimistic attitude still being taken towards the reformability of the young in this period and the belief that these less punitive institutional regimes might be of particular benefit to the young.

Overall, attitudes to juvenile offenders and their punishment were changing in contradictory ways in the late eighteenth and early nineteenth centuries. While fewer juvenile offenders were being diverted from entering the criminal justice system, and while smaller numbers were being acquitted as the principal of *doli incapax* was eroded, once they were in the system many practitioners, magistrates and prison reformers were deeply concerned that it would contaminate them. New sentencing initiatives that might divert them away from any continuing contact with the traditional penal system were therefore gradually evolved. The period from the 1790s to the 1820s witnessed both important changes in penal policy towards juveniles – the collapse of *doli incapax*, the growth of non-custodial sentences and the emergence of experiments with juvenile reformatories – and the continuation of many long-standing penal dilemmas. If the assize circuit records used here are any guide, the major innovations began in London and then spread to the provinces. The 1810s and most of the 1820s was a period of relatively open debate. Heavily punitive approaches were not yet dominant and new options could therefore be explored. The more punitive atmosphere which led to, and probably caused the ultimate failure of, the first experiment with a juvenile prison at Parkhurst in 1838, had not yet come to dominate discussion of juvenile justice. Moreover in London, and later in Warwickshire and elsewhere experiments with reformatory institutions for juveniles were beginning to operate on principles similar to those that came to dominate discussions about the reform of juvenile offenders in the 1850s.

4. *The making of the reformatory. The development of informal reformatory sentences for juvenile offenders 1780–1830*

As we have seen in the last chapter, the English criminal justice system was struggling to find appropriate sentencing options for the rising tide of juvenile offenders that was coming into the courts by the early nineteenth century. 'In time of war', as Wade pointed out in his *Treatise on the Police and Crime of the Metropolis* in 1829, 'the sea service . . . afforded a convenient outlet for profligate youths, but now it is with great difficulty persons can be found to take them, as is proved by the experience of the Marine Society'. Wade was also clear that the alternatives were far from satisfactory. 'The methods now employed to dispose of delinquent children failing to reform them or relieve society from their presence, it is certainly expedient a new experiment should be tried', he wrote. 'This class of offenders . . . may be imprisoned and whipped, . . . (or) transported for a limited term. Neither of these punishments serves any salutary end, and when applied, the magistrates generally take occasion to remark, at the time, that they have resorted to them merely because they have no other way of disposing of the objects before them.' Wade's solution was compulsory exile, and assisted emigration in various less drastic forms did emerge as a major policy option in the late 1820s and 1830s.[1] However, although historians have paid very little attention to it and although it was not based on any statutory authority, in the first three decades of the nineteenth century the courts did evolve a new and very different sentencing option. In a significant proportion of cases involving juveniles they experimented with informal sentencing practices designed to put the offender into an institution with a reformatory regime.

---

[1] J. Wade, *A Treatise on the Police and Crimes of the Metropolis* (London, 1829), 163; E. Bradlow, 'The Children's Friend Society at the Cape of Good Hope', *Victorian Studies*, 27 (1984), 156–77; E. Hadley, 'Natives in a Strange Land: The Philanthropic Discourse of Juvenile Emigration in Mid-Nineteenth-Century England', *Victorian Studies*, 33 (1990), 411–37.

I

The formal records left by the Old Bailey and by its gaol at Newgate contain virtually no indication that juvenile offenders were being sentenced to institutions with reformatory regimes in the late eighteenth and early nineteenth centuries. *The London and Middlesex Calendar of Prisoners in His Majesty's Gaol of Newgate*, which was printed before every Old Bailey sessions and listed all those who were scheduled to appear, contain no such references when they first become available in the early 1820s. Equally, historians consulting the manuscript Home Office criminal registers for London and Middlesex, which cover much the same group of prisoners but begin three decades earlier,[2] could be forgiven for concluding that the Old Bailey was not involved in any systematic attempts to develop reformatory-based sentencing policies for young offenders. Apart from a small number of very young offenders recorded in the first years of the nineteenth century as being referred to the Philanthropic Society, there is no apparent sign that such a policy was being pursued.[3] By 1820, as we have seen in the previous chapter, a significant proportion of juvenile offenders were recorded in the Home Office criminal registers as having been given a nominal fine of one shilling. However, there is no indication in those registers, or in the parallel printed calendars, that these offenders were subjected to any other form of punishment. Unsurprisingly, therefore, most historians of crime have not portrayed the first quarter of the nineteenth century as a period when the courts were developing a new policy of sentencing a significant proportion of young offenders to reformatory-style institutions.[4]

---

[2] London Metropolitan Archive (hereafter LMA) OB/C/P 001-2 Based on a survey of 1820 and 1821. Public Record Office (hereafter PRO), HO 26. This series starts in 1791.

[3] The Philanthropic Society was set up in 1788. By 1804 its admission policies were confined almost entirely to eight- to twelve-year-olds: W. Sanders, *Juvenile Offenders for a Thousand years* (Chapel Hill, 1970), 70–90; M. Dick, 'English Conservatives and Schools for the Poor c.1780–1833; a study of the Sunday School, School for Industry and Philanthropic Society's School for Vagrant and Criminal Children'. (PhD thesis, Leicester University, 1979), 266. At least 4 offenders were recorded as being sent to the Philanthropic Society in 1806, but after this recording practice became more opaque. Samples of the first 178 offenders under 20 taken from criminal register entries in 1817 (letters A-D) and the first 352 in 1826 (A-F) reveal no overt references to sentences that directed convicted offenders to reformatory institutions. PRO HO/26/12, 23 and 32.

[4] No mention of the practice in the period before 1830 is made, for example in L. Radzinowicz and R. Hood, *A History of English Criminal Law and its Administration from 1750, Vol. v; The Emergence of Penal Policy* (London, 1986), 133–70: S. Magarey, 'The Invention of Juvenile Delinquency in Early Nineteenth-Century England', *Labour History*, 34 (1978), 11–27: M. May, 'Innocence and Experience: the Evolution of the Concept of Juvenile Delinquency in the Mid-Nineteenth Century', *Victorian Studies*, 17 (1973), 7–29; for a more nuanced discussion of voluntary societies roles which makes a very brief reference to direct sentencing – H. Shore, *Artful Dodgers. Youth and Crime in Early Nineteenth-Century London* (Woodbridge, 1999) 95–100 and especially 97. I. Pinchbeck and M. Hewitt, *Children in English Society, Vol. ii; From the Eighteenth Century to the Children Act 1948* (London, 1973), 444–5 also mentions the practice.

In reality, however, just such an experiment was taking place in the 1810s and 1820s. The Old Bailey judges, faced with the severe penal dilemmas discussed in the previous chapter, began to develop sentencing policies that would enable them to put significant numbers of young people into institutions that were designed to be reformatory. Until 1806 the number of juveniles involved was extremely limited because the only major peacetime institution available was the Philanthropic Society, which by then was only open to the tiny proportion of offenders aged twelve or under.[5] However, by the 1810s another potential reformatory with no age restrictions, the London Refuge for the Destitute, had become available. This philanthropic initiative, begun in 1804, was designed 'for the purpose of affording an opportunity of reformation to criminals, and relief to the distressed'. In its early years the Refuge took in a considerable number of adults, but it soon began to specialise and from the second half of the 1810s onwards its inmate population was dominated by juveniles.[6]

The main instrument that the Old Bailey judges mobilised in order to make use of the Refuge, and to a much lesser extent of the Philanthropic, was their tradition of recording a suspended sentence of 'judgement respited'. This had been used quite extensively in the late eighteenth century in other contexts. In May 1793, for example, at the beginning of the war against France, 17 per cent of the sentences handed out to males at the Old Bailey were recorded as either 'judgement respited for a soldier' or 'judgement respited to go to sea'. Two more sentences used the overlapping tactic of a nominal fine with a compulsory condition attached – 'fined one shilling to enlist as a soldier'.[7] This tactic was used less frequently at other times because rapid armed-forces recruitment was rarely such a high priority, but it was still used occasionally. In 1806, for example, the criminal registers include a fourteen-year-old boy given a sentence of 'judgement respited, sent to serve in the navy'. By this time the registers also make it clear that the judgement-respited procedure was being used to place a few very young offenders in the Philanthropic. In that year, one ten year old and two eleven year olds, i.e. 43 per cent of all the males under thirteen convicted in 1806, were recorded as 'judgement respited, delivered to

[5] An Account of the Nature and Present State of the Philanthropic Society (London, 1804), 9 which notes 'they are seldom taken younger than 8 or 9 or older than 12: no female has of late been received beyond that age'. In 1808 the society described 23 boys recently admitted of whom 20 were aged 8 to 12, 2 were 13 and 1 was 14. The 12 girls described were all between 8 and 11 – An Account of . . . the Philanthropic Society (London, 1808), 29: by 1828 the limits were described as 'from 9 to 12' for criminal boys – P.P., 1828, vi, 163; Dick, 'English', 266. The Marine Society may also have taken a few offenders in this way although it had moved away from taking criminal boys in the later eighteenth century.

[6] For a detailed discussion of the history of the Refuge see the introduction to my volume of documents from its archives P. King (ed.), Narratives of the Poor in Eighteenth-Century Britain. The Refuge for the Destitute (London, 2006), i–xxv; 'An Account of the Refuge for the Destitute', The Philanthropist, i (1811), 245.

[7] PRO HO 26/2.

the Philanthropic'. At this point, however, only about 1 per cent of offenders were sufficiently young to qualify for the Philanthropic – a percentage that fell still further in the 1810s when that institution ceased to accept any girls with criminal backgrounds.[8] The opening of the Refuge for the Destitute in 1806, where the only age criteria was that those under twelve were not eligible because the Philanthropic already catered for them, made it possible for the Old Bailey judges to gradually increase this particular use of respited judgements.[9] To what extent did they actually do so?

This is not an easy question to answer. The Home Office criminal registers, as we have seen, make virtually no mention of the Refuge for the Destitute. Usually by the 1810s young offenders alongside whose names a cryptic 'JR' (for 'Judgement Respited') is recorded are then put down as merely receiving a one-shilling fine before being discharged. Equally, when the printed calendars first become available in 1820 the hand-written post-trial entries that record trial outcomes are no more revealing. For a number of offenders each session the entry simply reads 'judgement respited', with the only indication of what happened after that being the printed 'Prisoners upon Orders' entry at the end of the subsequent session which sometimes offers no further information but often records that they were 'fined one shilling – discharged'.[10] Behind these opaque recording practices, however, an extensive system of referring cases to the Refuge had in fact developed. Asked directly by a parliamentary committee on London's prisons in 1818 whether the Refuge 'receive a good many persons from Newgate . . . who have been found guilty, sentenced to a fine of a shilling and discharged with the understanding that they were to be sent to that institution', a representative of the Refuge replied in the affirmative. Ten years later the superintendent of the male side of the Refuge was asked by another parliamentary committee 'Do the judges ever send persons there?' 'Yes', he replied, 'I have fifteen in the house now of that description.'[11] Although the Refuge turned away a high proportion of those who applied for admission, it made a point of advertising the fact that whatever its financial circumstances it always accepted those referred to it by the Old Bailey. (It also automatically took a smaller number who were pardoned after receiving a sentence of death or transportation on the condition that they were admitted to the institution.) This policy was orientated primarily, although not yet exclusively, towards the young. In 1819, for example, a representative of the Refuge not only told a parliamentary committee investigating juvenile offenders that many of those

---

[8] PRO HO 26/12; Dick, 'English', 266. The Marine Society by its very nature was always confined to boys.

[9] *P.P.*, 1819, vii, 156; *P.P.*, 1828, vi, 181.

[10] LMA OB/C/P 001-2. However, late in 1822 a slight change in recording practices mean that one or two references do appear.

[11] *P.P.*, 1818, viii,70; *P.P.* 1828, vi, 180.

admitted were 'recommended to the institution by the judges' but also stressed that 'some of them are so very young that it would be unreasonable to inflict upon them the punishment annexed by the law to their offences.'[12]

A rough idea of the numbers of convicts sent to the Refuge after receiving a respited judgement and a nominal fine can be gained from its sporadically surviving printed reports and its internal records. Between 1820 and 1822, for example, just under a hundred offenders who had been convicted and respited at the Old Bailey entered the Refuge. Between 1817 and 1826, which appears to have been the most important decade during which the Old Bailey made use of this judgement respited mechanism, over a quarter of the males and an eighth of the females who entered the Refuge did so by this route. In the peak years 1820–2, 43 per cent of the males admitted and 18 per cent of the females had been through that process. Because the archives of the Refuge, from the date of its move to bigger premises in 1811, have recently come to light, it is now possible to link the names in the printed Old Bailey calendars to the Refuge's own records. In December 1820, for example, these calendars list nineteen Old Bailey 'prisoners upon orders' who had been convicted in the previous two sessions and 'upon whom the judgement of the court was respited'. Of these at least twelve can be traced into the internal records of the Refuge for the Destitute including seven offenders against whose names the printed calendars specifically recorded that they were 'fined one shilling and discharged'. Split equally between the sexes, all but two of the twelve sent to the Refuge were aged between fifteen and nineteen, and only one was over twenty one. All were automatically admitted. Although there is no direct mention of the Refuge in either the printed calendars or the Home Office registers, the Old Bailey was now regularly sending batches of offenders to that institution under the cover of the judgement-respited procedure.[13] An informal system of reformatory sentencing was now in existence.

The Refuge was never dominated by those referred straight from the Old Bailey under the judgement-respited procedure. Many inmates came by other routes. A very substantial number came after they had served a term of imprisonment, a few came as a condition of being formally pardoned, and others were

---

[12] *P.P.*, 1813–4, xii, 2; *P.P.* 1819, vii, 149. In its correspondence with the Home Office, little of which survives, the Refuge always stressed that it never failed to take those referred by the judges or by the pardoning system even when its finances were extremely tight – PRO, HO 42/132/610-13; 42/137/330-8.

[13] Hackney Archives Department, (henceforth HAD) D/S 1/1-30; 2/10-14; D/S 58 2/1-9, 4/1-5. These include General Court of Governors records 1819 onwards; General Committee Female Refuge 1812 onwards (this is how it is described in the HAD catalogue but until at least 1815 these records covered some business relating to males and presumably covered all business until a separate male premises was set up in 1815). General Committee Male Refuge 1819–26, 1830–48. There appear to have been other records such as admission registers and minutes of meetings related to admissions to the temporary Refuge that have not survived. For December 1820 – LMA OB/C/P 001, PRO HO/26/26.

referred to the institution by magistrates or, more occasionally, by victims as a substitute for formal prosecution. However, Old Bailey referrals were certainly a very important part of the Refuge's operation by the early 1820s. The opening sentence of its annual printed report for 1823, which recorded that 48 per cent of the males admitted that year had been 'convicted and judgement respited', emphasised its role in taking in 'those persons, of either sex, who have been convicted of crime and pardoned by His Majesty, or respited by the judges, upon condition of their being received into the Refuge for the Destitute'.[14] By the late 1810s and early 1820s the Refuge was providing the judicial system of the metropolis with an important resource – a reformatory regime for juvenile offenders which met a series of needs but which was a particularly useful addition to the sentencing armoury of the major courts. At its peak in the later 1820s it was running two sizeable establishments, admitting nearly 180 juveniles a year and submitting them to a regime that often lasted for as long as two years. How did this come about?

The Refuge had been launched in 1806 as a purely private philanthropic initiative and anyone familiar with the unending financial difficulties experienced by such enterprises in these years will not be surprised to know that it was soon in debt and facing deep financial constraints. To understand the development of the Refuge as a central part of the reformatory sentencing strategies that were developed at the Old Bailey in the first quarter of the nineteenth century, it is therefore important to outline the general history of the Refuge in this period. In particular it is necessary to analyse the symbiotic relationship between government policy and philanthropic enterprise which shaped the Refuge's rise and decline, and which arguably turned it into the first central-state-funded juvenile reformatory.

II

The Refuge for the Destitute developed through a number of stages. Beginning as a small institution admitting about 80 inmates a year, the Refuge gradually expanded, moving to a new site in Hackney Road, Shoreditch in 1811. Begun in 1804 on the initiative of an Anglican minister, its first committee of nine was far from impressive, including as it did three minor clergymen, two members of a banking family, a lieutenant colonel and a clerk at the Exchequer Office. However, it quickly struck a chord, attracting a range of philanthropic activists including evangelicals such as Zachary Macaulay, more traditional churchmen such as the lawyer Stephen Lushington, and commercial men such as the Rousseau-influenced Thomas Furly Forster. These men quickly garnered many influential connections and its subscription lists grew

---

[14] *Short Account of the Refuge for the Destitute* (London, 1824), 17.

fivefold in just over ten years. By 1806, the Duke of York was its president, and the Prime Minister, Lord Grenville, was a vice president – as was another PM, Spencer Percival, at the time of his assassination in 1812. By the later 1810s many key government figures such as the Home Secretary, Sidmouth, and the Chancellor of the Exchequer, Vansittart, as well as the Prime Minster, Lord Liverpool, were playing similar roles.[15] Its subscription lists were packed with the great and the good. In 1821, for example, they included more than seventy individuals of the rank of duke, marquis, viscount, earl, or lord, as well as six bishops, thirty-six MPs and a number of other influential figures such as Wilberforce, Ricardo and Baron Rothschild. In 1815, after consulting with the Home Secretary, it expanded into two separate establishments – one for males and one for females, and in 1818 two further 'Temporary Refuges' were added with finance partly provided by members of 'The Committee for Investigating Juvenile Delinquency'. By the mid-1820s it was admitting an average of 180 inmates a year, more than seven times the annual number being taken by the Philanthropic.[16]

At its inception, the Refuge had two broad aims – to offer 'an opportunity of reformation to the criminal and relief to the distressed'. These were primarily to be achieved by 'receiving within its walls persons discharged from penal confinement, penitent prostitutes, and others who, from loss of character and extreme indigence cannot procure an honest maintenance.'[17] However, within a decade or so the institution was beginning to change its focus in three ways. First, from a non-age-specific remit it increasingly specialised in the treatment of juveniles alone. As early as 1816, 88 per cent of the males admitted to the Refuge were under twenty. By the period 1826–8, when systematic information first becomes available on the whole of the inmate population, the Refuge was essentially a juveniles-only institution and 96 per cent of the males were under twenty. The focus was increasingly on those in their mid-teens, the peak age for boys being fourteen and for girls sixteen (Figure 4.1). In 1828, asked about the ages of the inmates, the superintendent of the male side of the Refuge replied that 'I have hardly any but boys; I have no more men than what I require as servants in the house . . . I have only four above

---

[15] For a more detailed discussion of the Refuge's early stages and of the activists involved on its committees etc. – see King, *Narratives of the Poor*, i–xxv; the Refuge has not been given much attention by historians of juvenile delinquency but brief discussions can be found in M. May, 'A Child's Punishment for a Child's Crime: The Reformatory and Industrial School Movement in Britain c. 1780–1880', (PhD thesis, London, 1981), 230; D. Andrew, *Philanthropy and Police. London Charity in the Eighteenth Century* (Princeton, 1989), 192–3; *A Short Account of the Refuge for the Destitute* (1816), 22–70. Surprisingly there is no real discussion of the Refuge in M. Roberts, *Making English Morals. Voluntary Association and Moral Reform in England, 1787–1886* (Cambridge, 2004).

[16] *A Short Account of the Refuge for the Destitute* (1821), Appendix 1–55; HAD D/S 4/4, 106 and D/S 58/2/12, 47–8; Dick, 'English', 262.

[17] 'An Account', *Philanthropist*, 1 (1811), 245.

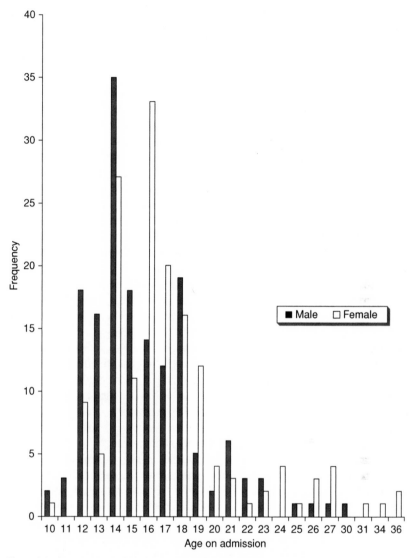

Figure 4.1   Age structure, admissions to the Refuge for the Destitute 1826–8.

twenty, and I do not think that I have more than seven that are as much as seventeen.'[18]

Secondly, the Refuge started to move away from a general focus on the destitute and increasingly concentrated most of its resources on those who

---

[18] *P.P.*, 1819, vii, 161; *P.P.*, 1828, vi, 183; *A Short Account of the Refuge for the Destitute* (1828).

had actually committed offences.[19] In 1818, for example, the printed *Account* published by the Refuge, whilst it continued to stress its joint aims 'to succour the destitute, and to reform the vicious', also described itself specifically as an 'asylum for penitent criminals'. By 1823 the Refuge's annual report underlined just how far this change had gone by stressing that 'During the last year, the committee have adhered to the *primary* views of the institution, and have applied its provisions to *criminal objects* only'.[20] Finally, at the same time as the Refuge was increasingly focusing on offenders it was also moving, as we have seen, towards a more significant pre-incarceration rather than post-incarceration role. Those who set up the Refuge had originally envisaged that its main functions in relation to offenders would be 'to provide a place of refuge and reformation for persons who have been discharged from prison or the Hulks'. However, as the Old Bailey judges and a number of magistrates' courts began to use the Refuge as an alternative to a prison sentence this emphasis changed. As early as 1816 the Refuge was reporting that 'the greater number (of inmates) were received at the instance of judges and magistrates', and figures supplied to a 1819 parliamentary committee indicate that over half of all the males admitted to the Refuge between 1816 and 1818 were sent there either after having been 'convicted and judgement respited' or after an informal decision in the magistrates courts.[21] Rather than just acting as an aftercare institution for destitute exprisoners, by the late 1810s and 1820s the Refuge had begun to play a significant role within the sentencing process itself. By the early 1820s the managers of the Refuge were stressing that it was 'so constituted in its design, as to impose its beneficial provisions between the infliction of punishment upon convicted offenders against the laws of the land and their possible recovery to society', and were congratulating themselves that their endeavours 'have afforded means to the judicial and executive powers of mitigating the . . . severities of general laws towards the juvenile delinquent.'[22]

'The Refuge for the Destitute' never formally changed its name, but it had gradually moved from refuge to reformatory, from the destitute to the delinquent, from a non-age-specific admissions policy to a complete focus on juveniles, from the relieving of distress to the use of 'rational principles of Remedy and Prevention' in order to arrest 'the progress of crime'.[23] By the late 1820s it saw itself first and foremost as a juvenile reformatory which 'for more than 20 years had proved that a great number of youthful offenders might be reformed'[24]

---

[19] *A Short Account of the Refuge for the Destitute* (1823), 15.
[20] *A Short Account of the Refuge for the Destitute* (1818), 18 and 34; and *A Short Account of the Refuge for the Destitute* (1824), 17 – italics as in the original.
[21] *A Short Account of the Refuge for the Destitute* (1812), 3; *A Short Account of the Refuge for the Destitute* (1816), 8; *P.P.*, 1819, vii, 161.
[22] *A Short Account of the Refuge for the Destitute* (1823), 15; HAD, D/S 4/1, 36.
[23] *A Short Account of the Refuge for the Destitute* (1823), 15.   [24] HAD, D/S 58/2/12, 60–1.

and its annual reports were soon simplifying its history along those lines by suggesting that it was founded 'with the design of counteracting the progress of youthful delinquency by providing an asylum for young persons of both sexes'. This clearly distorted to some extent the much more general motives and aims of those who had originally set up the Refuge. However, in 1840 (when juvenile delinquency was attracting even greater attention) this did not prevent the committee from boasting with some justification that 'they may lay claim to the credit of having been the first to rouse the attention of the British public to the vast practical importance of providing efficient remedies for the serious and widespread evil of juvenile delinquency'.[25]

The managers of the Refuge did not necessarily move from refuge to reformatory, from a post-incarceration to a partially pre-incarceration facility, entirely of their own volition. In its early years the Refuge was seriously short of cash and often in deep debt to its treasurer and this was particularly the case after its move to new premises in 1811. When the courts, and particularly the Old Bailey, started to use the Refuge informally as a sentencing option its managers seem to have quickly realised that this was their main hope of getting state funding. As they began to use their extensive contacts within the government in an attempt to obtain a regular central grant they made great play of the fact that they were providing an important service to the courts and the government by always accepting all of the offenders referred to them both by the Old Bailey under the judgement-respited system, and by other routes. Initially they made considerable mileage out of the small number of offenders they automatically accepted after they had received a formal royal pardon. The minutes of the General Committee, for example, after reporting that 'your committee have made an earnest appeal to His Majesty's Government for pecuniary assistance', partly based their hopes that they would soon get 'some support' on the positive testimony about the 'beneficial provisions of the Refuge' provided by the Prince Regent after it had accepted four capital offenders recently pardoned by him 'on the express condition of their being admitted into the Refuge'.[26] Increasingly, however, the committee's requests for funding played on its role in servicing the needs of the Old Bailey justices and of the magistracy for a reformatory sentencing option. In the memorial they sent to the Home Office in February 1813 asking for a 'National Grant of Pecuniary assistance', they first stressed the fact that both these groups 'have deemed it expedient to arrest the sentence' of many offenders by 'recommending them as fit objects for the support and restraint which this establishment provides'. They then highlighted their policy of always acceding to these requests despite the costs involved. 'Such recommendations', they wrote,

---

[25] *The Annual Report of the Refuge for the Destitute for the Year 1832* (1833), 5: HAD, D/S 58/2/12, 73.
[26] HAD, D/S 4/3, 188.

have been always regarded, by your memorialists, as applications made by authority, in the name of the country at large; and therefore, having with them, the most imperative claim on their attention; so that they have never suffered the lowest state of the funds of the refuge, to furnish them with a plea for the rejection of any object so recommended.[27]

This argument that the Refuge was providing a vital sentencing option and, of course, saving the costs that would have accrued if these offenders had been imprisoned or transported,[28] soon bore fruit. The Refuge received its first grant of £1,500 in 1814 and by 1817 it was in regular receipt of a substantial annual sum. Between 1819 and 1826, the peak period of the judgement-respited procedure, it received a grant of £5,000 per year, although this was then reduced to some extent in the later 1820s. This grant more than doubled the income of the charity, and it covered around half of the costs of the Refuge.[29] In applying each year for the renewal of this state subsidy, the managers of the Refuge continued to lay great emphasis on their role as a sentencing option. In 1821, for example, they claimed that among the 281 persons who had been afforded the benefit of the institution in the previous year 'a very large proportion has been recommended by His Majesty's judges and magistrates, several having received the royal pardon . . . and many others respited by the judges for the express purpose of being sent to the Refuge for the Destitute'. In 1822 their application not only stressed that they performed an 'essential service' in admitting 'criminals recommended by His Majesties justices' but also suggested that this procedure was being widely adopted outside London. 'Seldom a session passes at the Old Bailey', they wrote in their memorial to the secretary of state, Robert Peel, 'but the judges recommend some of the individuals there tried, to be sent to the Refuge; and in the same manner persons are constantly admitted by the desire of the judges of assize, and the courts of quarter sessions in the country.'[30]

By developing its role as a reformatory offering an important sentencing option to the courts in the later 1810s and early 1820s, the Refuge had been able to shore up its precarious finances and greatly expand its operations. The journey of this institution from refuge to reformatory had complex causes, but it was clearly a very useful institutional survival strategy. The key period between 1813 and 1817 during which the Refuge sought to obtain financial backing from the government was one of rapidly growing anxiety about crime, and most especially about juvenile crime.[31] The Refuge was able to mobilise these concerns

---

[27] *P.P.*, 1813–14, xii, 3; PRO, HO 42/137/330–8.

[28] HAD, D/S 4/6 10 Feb. 1821 notes 'considerable expense is saved to the country, by maintaining within its walls very many who otherwise would be confined at the public charge in gaols and bridewells, and some who would, at a large expense be sent out of the kingdom.'

[29] HAD, D/S 58/2/12, appendix. [30] HAD, D/S 4/6 10 Feb. 1821 and 26 Jan. 1822.

[31] See chapters 2 and 3.

to support its case for funding by reorientating its operation in two ways. First, at precisely the point, in 1815, when demobilisation meant that the capital was overflowing with young males it proposed opening a separate male refuge which would enable it to reverse its previous wartime policy of admitting more females than males.[32] Second, as the number of juvenile offenders reaching the courts rapidly expanded it also reorientated its policy about prioritising young offenders. In 1815 less than half the males admitted into the Refuge were under twenty. In 1816 this rose to over 85 per cent and remained at or above that level from then onwards.[33] The Refuge turned itself into a juvenile reformatory at precisely the right time to cash in on, and in its own way reinforce, the growing focus on juvenile delinquency as a major social problem which rapidly gained momentum in the mid-1810s.

In the later 1810s it also gained from an alliance with the influential 'Committee for Investigating the Alarming Increase of Juvenile Delinquency in the Metropolis' formed in 1815. For the first two years of its existence this charitable body, which drew its core support from Quaker and evangelical circles and from those involved in the fight against the slave trade and the capital code, was not intimately involved with the operations of the Refuge. At the beginning of 1816, only three of the Refuge's committee members were also members of the Juvenile Delinquency Committee.[34] However, this changed rapidly in the next few years. By 1818 the committee, which had now evolved into the 'Society for the Improvement of Prison Discipline and for the Reformation of Juvenile Offenders', had been instrumental in building a temporary refuge in the grounds of the Refuge for the Destitute which considerably increased the latter's capacity.[35] Moreover, the key players in the Prison Discipline Society – its treasurer, chairman and two secretaries – were all highly active members of the committee that ran the Refuge for the Destitute. The Juvenile Delinquency Committee had attempted to persuade the Home Secretary of the need to build a separate 'Juvenile Penitentiary' and had presented detailed plans for such an institution to a parliamentary committee in 1817, but these initiatives were unsuccessful and the increasing involvement of key Quaker activists such as Samuel Hoare and Peter Bedford in the affairs of the Refuge may not have been unrelated to that failure. The most active role in the governance of the Refuge was played by the 'visitors' and by 1821 half of the visitors involved in the day-to-day running of the male Refuge were leading members of the Society

---

[32] HAD D/S 58/2/12, appendix – In 1828–30 the Refuge admitted more males than females. Between 1807 and 1815 only 32 per cent of those admitted were males. For opening the male establishment the Refuge was given a £2,000 grant by parliament – *P.P.*, 1817, vii, 450.

[33] *P.P.*, 1819, vii, 160–1.

[34] *A Short Account of the Refuge for the Destitute* (1816), 1–3: *Report of the Committee for Investigating the Causes of the Alarming Increase of Juvenile Delinquency in the Metropolis* (London, 1816), 2; Roberts, *Making English Morals*, 104–5.

[35] *P.P.*, 1819, vii, 156

for the Improvement of Prison Discipline and for the Reformation of Juvenile Offenders. That society, which also boasted an illustrious group of vice presidents, had considerable influence in the early 1820s and provided both positive publicity for the Refuge and continuing financial support for its temporary refuges.[36]

By 1820 the Refuge had therefore managed to ally itself not only with the government but also with the most important philanthropic body working within its chosen field of operations. Neither of the other English early juvenile reformatory experiments that were operating in the first quarter of the nineteenth century – the Philanthropic and the tiny Warwick Asylum opened in 1818 – managed to get central state funding in this period. Indeed it is not clear that there were any other juvenile reformatories in Europe that did so. In the long term, the Refuge's partial dependence on state funding was a two-edged sword. It became increasingly important that each successive Home Secretary be persuaded of the value of the institution and the two reductions that Peel introduced in the Refuge's grant suggest that this proved particularly difficult in his case. Although the institution attracted considerable praise from various commentators in the 1830s, in the following decade – after the Refuge's governors had repeatedly turned down the Home Secretary's proposals for a merger with the Philanthropic – the government withdrew its grant support and the male Refuge had to be closed almost immediately.[37] However, in the first three decades of the nineteenth century a complex and informal set of interactions between a body of philanthropists, a group of judges wishing to expand their sentencing options in cases involving juveniles and a government that was responding to growing fears about juvenile delinquency, created both a new informal system of reformatory sentencing and what appears to have been Europe's first centrally funded juvenile reformatory.

---

[36] *Report of the Committee of the Society for the Improvement of Prison Discipline and for the Reformation of Juvenile Offenders* (London, 1818), 1–4; and The Fourth Report (London, 1822), 46; *P.P.*, 1817, vii, 524–30; *A Short Account of the Refuge for the Destitute* (1821), 3; R. McGowen, 'The Well-Ordered Prison: England, 1780–1850', in N. Morris and D. Rothman (eds.), *The Oxford History of the Prison. The Practice of Punishment in Western Societies* (Oxford, 1995), 96–7; Roberts, *Making English Morals*, 103–6.

[37] King, *Narratives of the Poor*, i–xxv. Peel deliberately probed very critically every aspect of the Refuge's operations during the 1820s, perhaps because, as Devereaux has suggested, he had very little time for the notion that criminals could be reformed – S. Devereaux, 'Peel, Pardon and Punishment: The Recorder's Report Revisited' in S. Devereaux and P. Griffiths (eds.), *Penal practice and Culture 1500–1800: Punishing the English* (Basingstoke, 2004), 274. On the amalgamation debates PRO, HO 45/1000; For examples of the praising of the Refuge – Anon, *Prison Discipline with Hints on other Preventive and Remedial Measures Required to Diminish Crime . . . Written by a County Magistrate* (London, 1835), 37–8 which observes 'Is not the Refuge for the Destitute the most useful society in this country?' and also contains high praise from the Chaplain of Cold Bath Fields Prison; T. Wontner, *Old Bailey Experience: Criminal Jurisprudence and the Actual Working of our Penal Code of Laws* (London, 1833) was very critical of voluntary efforts in this area but made an exception of the Refuge – 355, 393.

III

How was this new sentencing option used in the first quarter of the nineteenth century? Did the courts, and more specifically the Old Bailey, only resort to this option when faced with certain very particular kinds of offenders? It is far from easy to work out precisely how the judgement-respited system was used in practice. The Old Bailey judges did not formally record their selection criteria. Moreover, the process was informal and was rarely recorded at all. However, the surviving internal records of the Refuge, despite their patchy and sometimes inconsistent nature, are rich in qualitative material, particularly when they are used to trace offenders already identified in the Old Bailey records. One dimension of admissions policy is immediately clear from such an exercise. Although the court occasionally sent older offenders to the Refuge for a brief stay, the great majority of those who were subjected to the full one-to-two-year programme organised by the Refuge were juveniles. A systematic survey of all those reported in the Refuge records as having been admitted after having judgement against them respited in the period 1820–2 (Figure 4.2) indicates that the peak age was sixteen and that about 70 per cent were aged nineteen or less.[38] Moreover, as we have seen, by the mid-1820s almost the entire inmate population of the Refuge was under twenty years old (Figure 4.1).

It is much more difficult to work out what other characteristics persuaded the Old Bailey judges to single out particular offenders for reformatory treatment. If the brief descriptions taken down by the Refuge at their admission are any guide, the backgrounds of those placed in the institution by the Old Bailey judges were very varied. The judges almost certainly favoured those offenders who had both aroused their sympathy and seemed to exhibit signs of potential reformability, but did this mean that they mainly selected those young people who could present themselves as having been driven into crime by economic and social forces beyond their control?

There is considerable evidence that this was an important set of criteria. A core theme in many of the brief narratives recorded in the early 1820s was family breakdown. Ann Smith's father had 'run away from her' when she was seven. Her mother was dead. James McBride was deserted at the age of fourteen by his father, 'a dissipated man and fond of strong drink'. Thomas Hill, thirteen, was the son of a shoemaker who had 'left his family 4 years since and went to America with another woman'. Phrases such as 'his parents are dead' or 'he has no parents' pepper the reports.[39] So do references to young offenders who had spent time in their parish workhouse because their parents had deserted them. One sixteen-year-old ex-inmate of St Clement Danes workhouse, for

[38] Based on HAD, D/S 4/5, 6, 23, and 24 and on LMA OB/C/P 001–2.
[39] HAD, D/S 4/5 30 Dec. 1820; 4/23, 396; 4/24, 27.

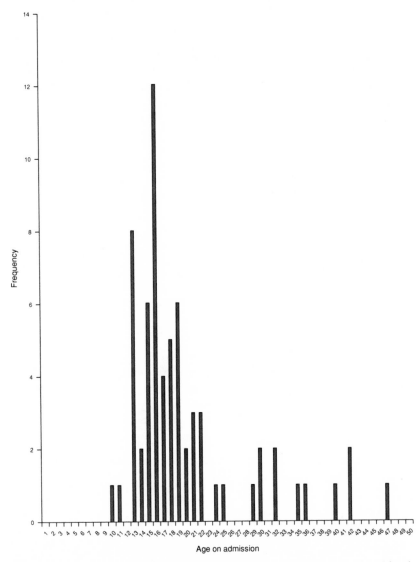

Figure 4.2   Age structure, judgement-respited offenders, Refuge for the Destitute male and female combined 1820–2.

example, told the committee he believed his mother was still living but 'he knows not where'. These young people were easily exploited and had precious few resources to fall back upon when times were hard. The entry for the ten-year-old, John Hill, poignantly illustrates this. 'He has no friends', the clerk at the Refuge recorded. 'He was brought up in Marylebone workhouse, whence he was taken by one Raspberry, of Witham Essex, a chimney sweeper, who having no work, discharged him.'[40]

The court may also have recognised that even those with some limited family networks available to them became highly vulnerable when they lost their main source of employment. Examples of young offenders whose appropriational activities appear to have begun when they could not find work occur regularly in the Refuge archives. Mary McGraham, a fifteen year old from Connaught, was fairly typical having fallen into crime after losing her place as a servant. Others were badly affected by the casual nature of the labour market. Elizabeth Johnstone, seventeen, lived with her grandmother and 'did waistcoat work', but 'being out of work and in much distress she stole 4 shoes' from a shop in Back Lane and was convicted.[41] Harriet Summers, fifteen, having had to leave home 'because her father in law would not keep her', went to her cousins who obtained her lodgings with a laundress. However, 'she had no employment for her' and she soon stole and pledged some gowns.[42] Some of the young offenders who came to the Refuge under the judgement-respited system still had parents who were alive and potentially sympathetic, but their family could be of little help to them because they were long-distance migrants who had failed to find a survival strategy in the big city. Thomas Harris, for example, the eighteen-year-old son of 'a very poor' Coventry ribbon weaver, 'came to London about six months since to seek employment, but has found no work, except a few jobs as porter'. David Tyndale, sixteen, whose parents lived in Ramsgate, had worked as a painter and glazier until, 'being out of employ he stole a prayer book and was convicted'.[43]

The Old Bailey judges did not, however, confine their referrals to the Refuge to those whose crimes might in part be excused by the fact that they lacked family support and/or had fallen into distress through unemployment. A very considerable proportion of those who were sent to the Refuge as an alternative to either imprisonment or transportation were in regular employment and still had frequent contact with their parents and other relatives. William Thacker, nineteen, worked for a hat-maker before his arrest, and was described by the latter as 'a very indifferent character'. His father was a sawyer and his parents lived just round the corner from William's workplace but were described as living an 'improbous life'.[44] Sarah Richards, sixteen and the daughter of a jeweller, had recently returned to her parents' house after living for nine months as servant to her uncle who kept 'a ham and beef shop'. She then 'went to Bow fair, where she

[40] HAD, D/S 4/23, 66 and 202.   [41] HAD, D/S 4/5, 7 Oct. 1820; 4/6, 66–7.

[42] HAD, D/S 4/5 7 Oct. 1820; Harriet was not the only young offender who had been driven out of the family home by the behaviour of her parents. Frances Ottaway, for example, left home at 15 'her father-in-law having used her ill'. 4/5, 30 Dec. 1820.

[43] HAD, D/S 23, 59 and 176. The Refuge (D/S 4/5, 183,) some put him to work repainting the premises.

[44] HAD, D/S 4/5, 86.

was seduced' and fell into crime.[45] The majority of young female offenders had recently been in, or were still in, service when they committed their offences and most of the boys sent to the Refuge also had some form of employment when they were arrested. Some were respectable apprentices – one was apprenticed to a bookbinder after being 'educated in Christ's Hospital'. Some were still schoolchildren. James Ewan and Samuel Rushton (aged thirteen and fourteen) were pupils at the St Pancras National School when they were arrested.[46] However, at the other end of the spectrum several boys clearly followed highly marginal occupations. One was an errand boy, another had 'usually gone about town with pipes and a drum', while James McBride, sixteen, made a precarious living 'lighting Whitecombe Street with torches'.[47] While many had problematic or non-existent families, in a considerable number of cases it is clear that the young offenders referred to the Refuge came from reasonably functional family backgrounds. Moreover, their fathers' occupations suggest that a considerable proportion had not been brought up in households from the very poorest groups in the metropolis. Some of their fathers were probably on the lowest and most vulnerable rungs of the occupational hierarchy – a bricklayer's labourer, a poor ribbon weaver, a dealer in old clothes in Petticoat Lane – but others appear to have been well established in skilled or semi-skilled trades –a locksmith, a gunmaker, a fanmaker, a cabinetmaker, a jeweller, a master bricklayer, a manufacturer of scouring paper, a customs house officer, an exciseman.[48]

Lacking any equivalent depth of information about a parallel sample of young offenders whom the Old Bailey did not refer to the Refuge, it is impossible to work out whether particular kinds of offender were being singled out for reformatory treatment. However, the Old Bailey judges clearly did not reserve reformatory sentences only for those who could claim that acute distress and family breakdown had been major factors in their offences. Nor did they only offer this alternative sentence to offenders who came from relatively respectable backgrounds. They sent a broad spectrum of different types of young offender to the Refuge.

There is not space here to discuss in detail the reformatory regime experienced by those who were admitted to the Refuge for the Destitute in the early nineteenth century, although the survival of detailed internal records does make this possible.[49] Broadly speaking, however, the regime was based on very similar principles to those on which a number of other reformatory institutions established in the early nineteenth century were founded[50] – the idea that

---

[45] HAD, D/S 4/5 7 Oct. 1820.   [46] HAD, D/S 4/23, 54–5, 203.

[47] HAD D/S 4/23, 111, 241 and 396.

[48] Based on HAD, D/S 4/5, 1820–2 sample. The only trades to occur two or three times in a sample of under fifty were bricklayer, tailor, gardener and shoemaker.

[49] King, *Narratives of the Poor.*

[50] W. Forsythe, *The Reform of Prisoners 1830–1900* (London, 1987), 4.

most individuals are reclaimable; a stress on 'lenient and persuasive' treatment rather than harsh physical punishment combined with a focus on orderly habits and strict conformity to regulations; the use of individualised treatment plans and of incentives to produce correct responses (such as returning part of the income earned by labour); the importance of providing religious and educational instruction; the centrality of constant employment; and the high priority given to instruction in a trade and to ensuring that inmates would be able to maintain themselves once they have left the institution. In practice, by the mid-1810s this meant a tightly regulated, work-orientated day, daily prayers, basic instruction, and a reasonably good diet. Classification was rudimentary and was mainly based on work roles. Boys started in the wood-cutting shed and then graduated to a trade – tailoring, shoemaking, bookbinding, etc. Female employment was increasingly dominated by washing, for the stronger girls at least.[51] Discipline was mainly via dietary deprivations, short periods in solitary confinement or a temporary return to hard labour in the woodshed. The average stay was two years, but if a suitable situation – an apprenticeship, regular employment with relatives or friends, a place aboard ship, or latterly an emigration opportunity – became available, many inmates stayed for shorter periods. The core emphasis was on retraining and the re-establishment of a good character so that the inmate could be self-supporting as soon as possible.[52]

The Refuge's founders had not originally intended to formally enclose the institution in order to prevent inmates from leaving without permission, but during the 1810s it effectively become a prison, with bars being fitted in a number of places to prevent further escapes.[53] Inmates were allowed visitors on a fairly regular basis and after six months they were permitted to visit family or respectable friends for brief, one day, 'holidays' provided that their behaviour had been good. However, partly, no doubt, as a result of its growing role as a sentencing option for the Old Bailey, the Refuge had almost all the attributes of a prison establishment by the 1820s. Asked about this by a parliamentary committee in 1828 the superintendent of the male Refuge admitted that the inmates could not get out and that the Refuge was 'like a prison' and 'quite secure, surrounded with walls'.[54] The Refuge's legal position when an offender

---

[51] See for example *A Short Account of the Refuge for the Destitute* (1806, 1816, 1828); 'An Account', *The Philanthropist*, 1 (1811), 244–51; *P.P.*, 1818, viii, 365–7; *P.P.*, 1819, vii, 149–72; *P.P.*, 1828, vi, 180–6; May, 'A Child's Punishment', 230–5; F. Hill, *National Education* (London, 1836), 31–5.

[52] *P.P.*, 1819, vii, 151; *P.P.*, 1828, vi, 181–2. Emigration gradually developed as a potential outcome HAD, D/S 4/1, 70–1. In 1822 two thirds of males went to apprenticeships *A Short Account of the Refuge for the Destitute* (1823), 18.

[53] *P.P.*, 1828, vi, 181; *P.P.*, 1831–2, vii, 115. Many inmates still managed to abscond – HAD, D/S 4/23, 12, 43–4, 101, 127.

[54] *P.P.*, 1819, vii, 154–7; In 1821 the committee decided that apprentices should have leave of absence on alternative Sundays – HAD, D/S 4/23, 189; *P.P.*, 1828, vi, 181.

absconded was highly problematic. In law the respited judgement could only hang over the offender until the next sessions of the Old Bailey, i.e. about a month and a half. After that, as the Refuge's treasurer made clear in 1817, the institution did not have any legal power to restrain the person. 'We have no power to detain them', Samuel Hoare admitted in 1819, whilst at the same time observing that by then very few inmates left until they were formally released – presumably because the premises had been made secure. Another witness before the 1819 committee, the lawyer and long-serving committee member Stephen Lushington, was well aware that the Refuge had little legal foundation for many of its operations. 'Though we have no power of detention', he observed,' we should not think it right to set a boy at liberty sent to us by government . . . though perhaps we are not justified by strict law to detain them'.[55] The legal position of those who absconded after being sent to the Refuge by the Old Bailey continued to cause difficulties. In 1822 the Refuge agreed to admit Charlotte Duckitt, who 'had been convicted at the Old Bailey of . . . robbery and judgement was respited in order that she might be sent to the Refuge', but when problems arose and they took legal advice they found themselves in a difficult position. When the superintendent went to confirm the legal position with the judges he was informed in no uncertain terms by the Common Sergeant that 'the committee cannot send her back to Newgate; and that he is aware that they cannot keep her in the refuge against her will.' He therefore 'recommended to the committee to be very circumspect'.[56] Although the Old Bailey was making extensive use of the judgement-respited procedure to place juvenile offenders in the Refuge, and to a lesser extent in the Philanthropic, there was no formal legal or statutory authorisation for the practice. All those involved had to be very circumspect, which may explain the courts' reluctance to formally record the existence of the practice in their printed calendars or in the criminal registers. The Refuge, although itself effectively part of the legal system, was operating right on the edges of illegality.

IV

Despite the almost complete silence of the formal court records on the subject, there can be no doubt that the London courts gradually developed a system of informal reformatory sentences in the first quarter of the nineteenth century and then used it extensively to deal with juvenile offenders. This centred mainly on the Refuge for the Destitute and to a lesser extent on the Philanthropic. After 1825 it may also have included the Chelsea School of Discipline opened in that

[55] *P.P.*, 1819, vii, 151, 166.
[56] HAD, D/S 4/6, 135 and 141. Charlotte had been convicted on 5 December 1821, so that by the time the judge was consulted another Old Bailey Sessions had already taken place and she could not therefore be sent back to the court for sentencing – LMA OB/CP/2.

year.[57] This judicial change was not initiated by government and at no point in this period did it receive legislative backing. Indeed its legal foundations were extremely shaky. It was created by the dynamic interaction at ground level between a group of philanthropists, the Old Bailey judges, and the formal government authorities. The personnel involved in these groups sometimes overlapped and each played an important role. However, the main momentum behind the development of this informal reformatory sentencing system arose from the creation of institutions with reform-based regimes capable of being used as sentencing alternatives, and then from the courts' increasing desire to use them as they became aware that all other sentencing options were inadequate when juveniles were involved. Once the latter started to use charitably financed institutions as reformatories this then allowed the Refuge in particular to gain financial assistance from the government and this in turn enabled it to further expand its operations. By 1835 the Refuge was being described in the *Times* as 'almost a government concern'[58]. The first partially state-funded juvenile reformatory in England had come of age.

---

[57] May, 'A Child's Punishment', 235. Other experiments in providing places of incarceration/asylum for juvenile offenders and destitute young people had, of course been attempted well before 1800, although they rarely if ever concentrated so completely on juveniles. The London Workhouse, opened in 1699, was originally intended for vagrants and children found in the streets – J. Beattie, *Policing and Punishment in London 1660–1750* (Oxford, 2001), 29. In the sixteenth century, the London Bridewell initially aimed to set aside some space to offer industrial training to impoverished boys – J. Innes, 'Prisons for the Poor: English Bridewells 1555–1800', in F. Snyder and D. Hay, *Labour, Law and Crime. An Historical Perspective* (London, 1987), 56. Provincial Bridewell policies were also sometimes youth focused – P. Griffiths, 'Masterless Young People in Norwich, 1560–1660', in P. Griffiths, A. Fox and S. Hindle (eds.), *The Experience of Authority in Early Modern England* (Basingstoke, 1996), 160.

[58] *The Times*, 30 Jan. 1835.

Part II

Gender

5. Gender, crime and justice in late eighteenth- and early nineteenth-century England

Current work on gender, crime and justice in eighteenth- and nineteenth-century England includes remarkably little research on the impact of gender at two of the fulcrum points of the criminal justice system – the verdicts and sentences passed by the major courts. The general texts on crime and punishment in this period give no clear indication about whether these decisions were affected by the sex of the accused, and even the recent books written by Conley and Zedner, which foreground gender issues, offer only occasional insights into the core question this paper is concerned with – to what extent did gender affect trial outcomes?[1] Although his much quoted article on 'The criminality of women in eighteenth-century England' did not cover these issues, John Beattie's pathbreaking monograph *Crime and the courts in England 1660–1800* does, however, provide a number of significant, if scattered, insights based on the Surrey evidence.[2] The first section of this study follows Beattie's work in

Acknowledgement: The author would like to thank Garthine Walker, Deirdre Palk, Bob Shoemaker, Loraine Gelsthorpe, Barry Godfrey, and all those who offered comments on this paper when it was given at Nene College, at the Cambridge Early Modern Seminar and at the Institute of Historical Research. I would also like to thank Joan Noel and Cris Gostlow for their assistance in data collection and processing. The work for this article was funded by the ESRC as part of its Crime and Social Order initiative (L210252020).

[1] C. Emsley, *Crime and Society in England 1750–1900*, 2nd edn (London, 1996) does have a separate chapter on gender. J. Briggs *et al.*, *Crime and Punishment in England: an Introductory History* (London, 1996) contains virtually no discussion. There is also remarkably little on gender and justice in D. Philips, *Crime and Authority in Victorian England: the Black Country 1835–1860* (London, 1977); D. Jones, *Crime, Protest, Community and Police in Nineteenth-Century Britain* (London, 1982); D. Jones, *Crime in Nineteenth-Century Wales* (Cardiff, 1992); V. Gatrell, 'Crime, Authority and the Policeman State', in F. M. L. Thompson (ed.),*The Cambridge Social History of Britain 1750–1950* (Cambridge, 1990); G. Rudé, *Criminal and Victim: Crime and Society in Early Nineteenth-Century England* (Oxford, 1985); and L. Radzinowicz and R. Hood, *A History of English Criminal Law and its Administration from 1750*, [5 vols.] (London, 1948–1986). The exceptions are C. Conley, *The Unwritten Law: Criminal Justice in Victorian Kent* (Oxford, 1991); and L. Zedner, *Women, Crime and Custody in Victorian England* (Oxford, 1991).

[2] J. Beattie, *Crime and the Courts in England 1660–1800* (Oxford, 1986); J. Beattie, 'The Criminality of Women in Eighteenth-Century England', *Journal of Social History*, 8 (1975), 80–116.

concentrating primarily on property crime and on the major courts, but it uses a much larger sample of over 11,000 cases and focuses on a different and shorter period by using selected years between the 1780s and the 1820s. The core data was collected directly from the records of the Old Bailey, which covered London and Middlesex, and from those of the Home Circuit, which covered Essex, Surrey, Sussex, Kent and Hertfordshire.[3] This was then supplemented by evidence from Lancashire and the Northern Assizes Circuit, the only jurisdictions which supplied the early nineteenth-century parliamentary committees with separate data on male and female offenders.[4] The second section of this chapter then briefly uses work on other crimes and other courts to assess the typicality of these results, before moving on to use early modern and twentieth-century research as a means of exploring elements of continuity and change in the relationship between judicial outcomes and gender. Finally, the paper discusses the potential relevance of the explanatory frameworks developed by modern criminologists and then briefly explores a number of factors that need to be more deeply researched before any attempt can be made to explain the highly gendered nature of trial outcomes visible in the period 1780–1830.

I

Both the courts chosen for detailed study here were near the apex of the criminal justice system. The county assizes and their rough equivalents in London and Middlesex, the Old Bailey sessions, had jurisdiction over all capital offences. They also heard a very considerable proportion of non-capital property crimes. The precise division of responsibility for grand- and petty-larceny cases (hereafter referred to as simple larceny) between the quarter sessions and the assizes courts differed between counties[5] and these differences are reflected in the proportion of simple larceny cases among the Old Bailey and assizes accused, seen in Table 5.1. In the late eighteenth and early nineteenth centuries an average of around two fifths of those tried on the Home Circuit were indicted for simple, non-capital larcenies, whilst the equivalent figure at the Old Bailey was three

---

[3] HO 26/1-2 and 26/26-28, Public Record Office (henceforth PRO) – London and Middlesex data for October 1791 – September 1793 and October 1820 – September 1822, i.e. 4 full court years; Old Bailey cases only were inputted from these records. Assi 31/13–15 (Summer assizes 1782 to 1787 inclusive), Assi 31/18-19 (Summer 1799 – Lent 1801), Assi 31/23-24 (1820–21), Assi 31/25 (1827), PRO.

[4] P.P. 1819, viii, 228–35; 260–62.

[5] In Surrey and Sussex just under a third of simple larceny cases were heard at the assizes. Beattie, *Crime*, 284; in Essex, where the quarter sessions did not decide to take on grand-larceny cases until the 1780s, 56 per cent of property crime cases 1790–9 were heard at the assizes, 35 per cent at quarter sessions, 9 per cent in the five borough courts. P. King, 'Crime, Law and Society in Essex 1740–1820' (PhD thesis, Cambridge University, 1984), 33.

Table 5.1 *Gender and types of property-crime indictment. Old Bailey and Home Circuit, 1780s–1820s*

	Old Bailey		Home Circuit	
Type of crime	Male (%)	Female (%)	Male (%)	Female (%)
Simple theft	63.3	64.2	41.3	37.0
Private stealing	12.3	19.5	1.9	13.1
Stealing from dwelling house	3.4	3.4	3.7	6.9
Sheep and cow stealing	0.4	0.1	5.6	0.9
Horse stealing	0.8	0.0	6.6	0.0
Burglary/housebreaking	5.7	1.0	21.7	17.7
Robbery	6.3	4.6	11.6	7.5
Receiving	1.9	3.1	2.4	6.9
Coining/uttering	1.2	1.5	1.3	4.9
Fraud/indirect appropriation	4.6	2.7	4.0	5.3
Total	99.9	100.1	100.1	100.2
Sample size	5096	1515	3988	452

Sources:
Old Bailey: PRO HO26/1-2 and 26/26-28. Sample years October 1791 – September 1793: October 1820 – September 1822. Crimes not involving direct or indirect appropriation are excluded. Data collected for Old Bailey London and Middlesex prisoners only.
Home Circuit: PRO Assi 31/13-15 (Summer assizes 1782 to Summer 1787); Assi 31/18-19 (Summer 1799–Lent 1801); Assi 31/23-24 (1820–1); Assi 31/25 (1827).

fifths.[6] However, although the information available from these two sources is not identical, and was created at slightly different stages in the trial process, they are broadly comparable since each was the major criminal court in its region.[7]

The Old Bailey data on verdicts (see Table 5.2) indicates clearly that female property offenders awaiting trial in London had much better prospects than their male counterparts. The majority of men (61 per cent) were convicted. The majority of women were not. Only 44 per cent of the female accused were found guilty. Women were nearly twice as likely to avoid public trial completely, either because their victims failed to turn up and prosecute them or because the grand jurors brought 'not found' verdicts, thus dismissing the prosecution case before it could be presented in open court. Women also attracted a considerably higher percentage of not guilty verdicts. The combined effects of these two processes meant that males accused of property crime in late eighteenth- and

[6] The Old Bailey registers do not usually indicate which cases involved 'petty' rather than 'grand' larceny.
[7] The Old Bailey (or Newgate) registers appear to have been based on a list made up before the trial process (grand or petty jury) began. The Home Circuit agenda books were created, it seems, after the grand-jury deliberations but before the petty-jury public trial. The Old Bailey records therefore include the subgroup of offenders who were confined for property crime but were never actually tried in public, either because their prosecutor failed to turn up, or because the grand jury brought in a 'not found' verdict.

Table 5.2 *Old Bailey property offenders. Verdicts analysed by gender, 1791–1822*

Outcome	All property offenders		Simple larceny		Private stealing		Robbery	
	Male (%)	Female (%)	Male (%)	Female (%)	Male (%)	Female (%)	Male (%)	Female (%)
Failed to reach court/died in gaol	1.9	1.0	1.2	0.7	0.0	0.0	8.8	5.8
Discharged – no prosecution or 'Not found'	12.9	25.1	13.3	23.4	16.1	41.0	16.6	14.5
Not guilty	23.9	30.2	21.7	28.8	20.5	28.5	36.9	49.3
Guilty	61.0	43.7	63.8	47.1	63.0	30.5	37.8	30.4
Verdict unknown	0.2	0.0	0.1	0.0	0.5	0.0	0.0	0.0
Total	99.9	100.0	100.1	100.0	100.1	100.0	100.1	100.0
Sample size	5096	1515	3225	972	629	295	320	69

Sources: see Table 5.1.

early nineteenth-century London were 40 per cent more likely than their female equivalents to be convicted.

Once convicted, male offenders were also subjected to a harsher range of punishments than females (see Table 5.3). 8 per cent of women were fined and immediately released compared to 5 per cent of males. Whipping had long been used predominantly against men and after 1820 the law no longer permitted the whipping of women.[8] Imprisonment (which seldom lasted more than a year) was the most popular sentence for women, while transportation (which would usually be for seven to fourteen years) was the court's most frequent sentencing strategy for male offenders. 8 per cent of women were sentenced to death compared to 13 per cent of men but in reality the death penalty itself was reserved almost exclusively for men. Only one female property offender actually reached the gallows in the years sampled here (i.e. 0.15 per cent). Eighty-nine males met that fate (2.85 per cent). Amongst those sentenced to imprisonment women got only a marginally better deal than men, but nearly half spent six months or less in gaol and only a fifth were incarcerated for more than a year. Transportation may have been considered a better option by some younger prisoners – a number of contemporaries certainly feared that it was.[9] However, since most of those sentenced to transportation spent many months in gaol or on the hulks awaiting shipment, a sentence of transportation usually involved a longer period of incarceration than one of imprisonment – as well as separation from family and friends and the prospect of being subjected to the variety of often harsh regimes being developed in Australia.[10] Transportation would rarely have been a better option than imprisonment from the convict's point of view and those in charge of sentencing clearly saw the former as a heavier sanction.

The impact of gender on sentencing policies can be overemphasised. Many women were subjected to tough penalties. Nearly two-fifths of female convicts were either sentenced directly to transportation or given that punishment after being reprieved from a death sentence. The early nineteenth-century ban on the whipping of women did mean that, while many men were sentenced to whipping and imprisonment, women did not have to suffer this double penalty. However, although the Old Bailey increasingly used fines instead of whipping for female offenders, some female convicts who would have been whipped and released in the eighteenth century almost certainly suffered imprisonment instead, once the whipping of women became unlawful in 1820. Thus the impact

---

[8] The public whipping of women was abolished in 1817, private whipping in 1820. Radzinowicz, *A History*, i, 578. Whipping was already used less frequently for female than for male property offenders by the 1780s – Beattie, *Crime*, 611–13.

[9] Radzinowicz, *A History*, 1, 31–2; 5, 474–6.

[10] R. Hughes, *The Fatal Shore: a History of the Transportation of Convicts to Australia 1787–1868* (London, 1987); Zedner, *Women, Crime and Custody*, 174–5.

Table 5.3 *Old Bailey property offenders. Sentences analysed by gender, 1791–1822*

Sentence	All property offenders		Simple larceny		Private stealing		Robbery	
	Male (%)	Female (%)	Male (%)	Female (%)	Male (%)	Female (%)	Male (%)	Female (%)
Fined	5.4	8.3	7.5	11.1	2.3	3.3	0.0	0.0
Whipped (publicly or privately)	6.2	1.1	8.5	0.9	4.3	2.2	0.0	0.0
Imprisoned	32.3	50.0	41.0	60.1	18.8	43.3	4.1	4.8
Transported	42.5	32.6	40.5	26.0	71.9	47.8	12.4	33.3
Sentence to death and reprieved	10.4	7.9	2.2	2.0	1.5	3.3	57.0	57.1
Hanged	2.9	0.2	0.3	0.0	0.5	0.0	26.5	4.8
Punishment unknown	0.3	0.0	0.2	0.0	0.8	0.0	0.0	0.0
Total	100.0	100.1	100.2	100.1	100.1	99.9	100.0	100.0
Sample size	3127	662	2054	458	399	90	121	21

Sources: See Table 5.1.

of changes in both legal frameworks and sentencing attitudes was often complex and contradictory, but significant gender-based differences in sentencing policy are clearly observable. By the 1820s almost all female property offenders were avoiding the direct physical punishments of whipping and hanging, whilst finding it relatively easy to attract sentences such as fining or imprisonment, which were usually regarded as much less intrusive and punitive than transportation. Amongst property offenders at least, the great intrusion, death, was reserved almost entirely for men in late eighteenth- and early nineteenth-century London.

Since the first two columns in Tables 5.2 and 5.3 all relate to a very broad category of offences, i.e. all types of property theft, from stealing a loaf of bread to highly lucrative robberies accompanied with violence, it remains possible that women received more lenient treatment from the courts because they less frequently committed the most serious offences. As Table 5.1 indicates, the proportions of both male and female offenders being indicted for simple larceny were very similar, but women were considerably under-represented among offences such as housebreaking, horse stealing and robbery, which attracted the heaviest sentences. It is therefore necessary to look at verdict and sentencing patterns for a number of individual offences. Once we control for type of offence do women still get noticeably more lenient treatment from the courts? The data on simple larceny alone in Tables 5.2 and 5.3 suggests that they do.[11]

The pattern of verdicts is very similar to that found for all property offenders. Women were much more likely to avoid public trial and more likely to be found not guilty if they were tried by a petty jury in open court. While 64 per cent of male larcenists were convicted, only 47 per cent of females indicted for simple larceny suffered the same fate. Sentencing patterns showed parallel similarities. Males were as likely to be transported as to be imprisoned.[12] Only a quarter of females were transported while three fifths were imprisoned. Did women also receive more favourable treatment when they were accused of capital crimes? Since the only categories of capital crime in which more than sixty female offenders were involved were privately stealing (from the shop or person) and highway robbery, these were the two selected for detailed scrutiny.

---

[11] Unfortunately the records used here do not describe the stolen goods consistently enough to enable the 'simple larceny' category to be broken down in this way. Other court records such as indictments may make it possible to control for type of goods stolen but the amount of work involved would be huge and the resulting sample sizes would be very small.

[12] The fact that 2 per cent of male and female 'simple larceny' accused were sentenced to death alerts the historian to the fact that offence definitions are not always detailed enough in the Old Bailey registers. A capital sentence could not have been passed if these larcenies had not been accompanied by behaviour such as pickpocketing which could turn a simple theft into a capital charge. In this 2 per cent of cases at least, offence definition clearly was not complete.

In London women accused of shoplifting or of picking pockets[13] received remarkably lenient treatment compared to men (Tables 5.2 and 5.3). They were two-and-a-half times more likely to be discharged before public trial and a third more likely to attract a 'Not guilty' verdict if they reached that stage. 63 per cent of males accused of private stealing were found guilty. 31 per cent of females suffered the same fate. Sentencing policies were slightly less polarised but the pattern was equally clear. While men were three times more likely to be transported than to be either imprisoned or fined, women's chances were roughly equal. In robbery cases (Tables 5.2 and 5.3) gendered differences were much smaller at the verdict stage. The relatively small number of women indicted for robbery (sixty nine) were only slightly less likely than the men to avoid public trial. The main differences in robbery cases came in sentencing and pardoning policy. 38 per cent of women but only 17 per cent of men were sentenced to either transportation or imprisonment – presumably because the jury had brought in a partial verdict. 57 per cent of both men and women were sentenced to death but then reprieved. 27 per cent of males (thirty-two individuals) went to the gallows for robbery in the four years sampled. One woman (4.8 per cent) found herself unable to avoid the fatal tree.

Were trial outcomes equally gendered on the Home Circuit 1782–1827? Tables 5.4 and 5.5 suggest that the pattern was remarkably similar. Since the Home Circuit agenda books did not systematically record cases discharged before public trial, female offenders' capacity to obtain much more lenient treatment at this stage – seen clearly in the Old Bailey evidence (Table 5.2) – cannot be analysed outside London but the Home Circuit pattern of 'Guilty – Not guilty' verdicts for all property offenders (Table 5.4) is very similar to that found at the Old Bailey (Table 5.2). Female property offenders were 40 per cent more likely than their male equivalents to attract a 'Not guilty' verdict. The Home Circuit data also indicates that they were more than 50 per cent more likely to attract a partial verdict (in which the jury downgraded the charge and then convicted on a lesser one)[14] rather than a full conviction. The Home Circuit judges used fining and whipping much less frequently than their Old

[13] Shoplifting and pickpocketing – the legal terms for which were 'privately stealing from a shop' and 'privately stealing from the person' – were, by definition, secret acts that involved no violence. They were therefore generally regarded as less serious and the statutes that made them capital offences were virtually the only substantial and widely used parts of the 'bloody code' that were repealed, or extensively revised, in the first twenty years of the nineteenth century. Radzinowicz, *A History*, i, 554, 580, 636–7. Picking pockets and stealing goods valued over a shilling was made non-capital in 1808. Most acts of shoplifting were made non-capital in 1820 when the threshold was raised from 5 shillings to 15 pounds. All were non-capital by 1823. Although these two forms of 'private' stealing were put together here in order to create sample sizes large enough for gender comparisons to be made, it must be remembered in interpreting these figures that they were not necessarily similar types of offence apart from the 'private' nature of the act involved.

[14] Beattie, *Crime*, 424 on partial verdicts and their use.

Table 5.4 *Home Circuit. All property offenders. Verdicts analysed by gender, 1782–1827*

Outcome	All property offenders Male (%)	Female (%)	Simple larceny Male (%)	Female (%)	Housebreaking Male (%)	Female (%)	Robbery Male (%)	Female (%)	Private stealing Male (%)	Female (%)	Stealing in dwelling house Male (%)	Female (%)
Not guilty	27.7	38.9	28.0	37.1	19.8	30.0	32.6	61.8	32.0	37.3	24.5	29.0
Guilty	57.2	44.3	62.9	58.0	48.0	28.8	58.8	17.7	40.0	39.0	38.1	29.0
Partial verdict	9.3	14.4	3.3	4.2	25.9	31.3	5.2	20.6	24.0	23.7	33.3	41.9
Unknown / failed to reach trial	5.8	2.4	5.8	0.6	6.3	10.0	3.5	0.0	4.0	0.0	4.1	0.0
Total	100.0	100.0	100.0	99.9	100.0	100.1	100.1	100.1	100.0	100.0	100.0	99.9
Sample size	3988	452	1645	167	864	80	463	34	75	59	147	31

Sources: See Table 5.1.

Table 5.5 *Home Circuit, all property offenders. Sentences analysed by gender, 1782–1827*

Sentence	All property offenders		Simple larceny		Housebreaking		Robbery		Private stealing		Stealing in dwelling house	
	Male (%)	Female (%)	Male (%)	Female (%)	Male (%)	Female (%)	Male (%)	Female (%)	Male (%)	Female (%)	Male (%)	Female (%)
Fined	1.4	1.1	2.9	2.9	0.2	0.0	0.0	0.0	0.0	0.0	0.0	0.0
Whipped (publicly or privately)	1.2	3.4	2.5	7.7	0.5	0.0	0.0	0.0	2.0	2.6	0.0	0.0
Imprisoned	33.9	61.9	63.5	81.7	13.5	35.4	5.3	46.2	57.1	50.0	24.8	45.5
Transported	19.8	12.8	26.3	6.7	16.7	16.7	6.3	7.7	28.6	18.4	25.7	18.2
Sentence to death and reprieved	29.1	17.7	0.9	1.0	48.9	43.8	47.2	23.1	8.2	26.3	45.7	36.4
Hanged	11.6	2.6	0.4	0.0	18.4	4.2	38.6	23.1	4.1	2.6	3.8	0.0
Punishment unknown	3.0	0.4	3.6	0.0	1.8	0.0	2.6	0.0	0.0	0.0	0.0	0.0
Total	100.0	99.9	100.1	100.0	100.0	100.1	100.0	100.1	100.0	99.9	100.0	100.1
Sample size	2726	265	1128	104	651	48	303	13	49	38	105	22

Sources: See Table 5.1.

Bailey counterparts.[15] They also used the death sentence more often than the London court – presumably because a much higher percentage of those indicted before them were accused of major capital crimes (Table 5.1). Despite these factors gender made a very similar impact on sentencing policies at both the Home Circuit assizes and the Old Bailey (Tables 5.5 and 5.3). More than three-fifths of Home Circuit female property offenders were imprisoned, and only a fifth were sentenced to death. A third of males were imprisoned and two fifths sentenced to death. As at the Old Bailey, capitally convicted women found it very much easier to get a reprieve. Seven female property offenders reached the gallows in the ten years sampled (2.6 per cent of the female convicted), compared to 317 males (11.6 per cent).

The similarities are equally marked when the Home Circuit data is analysed for specific categories of crime (Tables 5.4 and 5.5). At both the Old Bailey and on the Home Circuit females accused of simple larceny gained about a third more acquittals than the males. Sentencing policies in Home Circuit simple-larceny cases (Table 5.5) once again favoured imprisonment more for women than for men and reserved transportation mainly for the latter. In robbery cases the assizes pattern was even more polarised than that found at the Old Bailey. Females received nearly twice as many acquittals as males and were four times more likely to attract a partial verdict. The combined effect of these two processes was that only 18 per cent of women were found guilty as charged compared to 59 per cent of men (Table 5.4). Jurors appear to have been trying to avoid convicting women on the full charge knowing that highway robbery attracted fewer pardons than any other form of theft. Because of this, three of the thirteen female robbers found guilty (23 per cent) were actually hanged. In the same years 117 males (39 per cent) went to the gallows. The Home Circuit data on housebreaking and stealing in the dwelling house follows similar lines, and only the relatively small number indicted for privately stealing do not show highly gendered sentencing patterns.[16] Overall, therefore, the pattern is clear. At the Old Bailey and at the Home Circuit assizes women were less likely to be convicted and more likely to be given a range of sanctions which both judges and juries considered to be more lenient.

[15] Fining alone was rare in property crime cases in the eighteenth century. Between 1 and 2 per cent of property offenders, whether male or female, Home Circuit or Old Bailey, were simply fined in the 1780s and 1790s. However, in London, but not on the assizes circuit, it had been adopted as a significant option by 1820 – especially for females and for the young.

[16] The exceptional finding that sentencing policies did not favour females in private stealing cases on the Home Circuit may be related to the tiny proportion of male Home Circuit offenders accused of private stealing (1.9 per cent compared to 13.1 per cent of females). This was not repeated at the Old Bailey where the percentages were 12.3 and 19.5 respectively (see Table 5.1). It is possible that the few males accused of this crime on the Home Circuit were particularly likely candidates for leniency, or that gender ratios amongst shoplifters and pickpockets were different on the Home Circuit. The repealing of the capital statutes relating to these offences may also have had an effect and further research on this is clearly required.

Table 5.6 *County Palatine of Lancaster. Conviction and execution rates for capital crimes analysed by gender, 1798–1818*

Offence	Percentage of committals leading to conviction		Percentage of convicted that were hanged		Sample sizes (committals)	
	Male (%)	Female (%)	Male (%)	Female (%)	No. male	No. female
Shooting, etc. intent to murder	34	–	20	–	29	0
Murder	12	2	100	100	86	44
Rape	33	–	25	–	12	0
Sodomy	35	–	100	–	17	0
Arson	43	0	83	–	14	1
Burglary and theft in dwelling house	64	39	19	7	248	36
Horse, cow and sheep stealing	74	0	5	–	108	1
Highway robbery	60	45	38	0	135	11
Private stealing from person/shop	23	30	0	0	13	23
Croft breaking	72	0	15	–	36	2
Coining and uttering	88	90	0	0	8	10
Forgery	47	47	58	14	189	30
Miscellaneous offences	94	100	18	0	18	5
All types of capital crime	54.5	33.7	29.9	7.3	913	163

Source: *P.P.*, 1819, viii, 228–35.

Was this pattern also found in other parts of England? The limited data available on Lancashire and on the Northern Circuit assizes[17] suggests that it was. In Lancashire between 1798 and 1818, 54.5 per cent of the male accused committed for capital crimes were described as convicted, compared to 33.7 per cent of women (see Table 5.6). 30 per cent of the capitally convicted men went to the gallows in Lancashire. 7 per cent of the women went with them. This pattern is particularly marked amongst those accused of highway robbery, housebreaking and stealing from the dwelling house, while in forgery cases male and female conviction rates were very similar, but men were four times as likely to be hanged if they were capitally convicted. Unfortunately the Northern Circuit returns (which covered Yorkshire, the City of York, Newcastle, Northumberland, Cumberland and Westmorland) were only compiled for one year, 1804. They do, however, include information on the proportion of male and female offenders discharged before public trial and they confirm that women

[17] *P.P.*, 1819, viii, 228–35, 260–62.

Table 5.7 *Northern Circuit assizes: verdicts and punishments analysed by gender, 1804 only*

(a) Verdicts	Male (%)	Female (%)
Discharge, no prosecutor or 'Not Found'	18	29
Not guilty	26	21
Guilty of capital charge	44	36
Partial verdict	12	14
Total	100	100
Sample size	34	14
(b) Punishment given to capitally convicted convicts		
Punishment	Male (%)	Female (%)
Imprisonment	20	40
Transportation	60	60
Hanging	20	0
Total	100	100
Sample size	15	5

Source: *P.P.*, 1819, 8, 260–2.

were much more likely than men to get positive decisions at this stage (see Table 5.7). Men were about 25 per cent more likely to be found guilty as charged, and amongst those who were capitally convicted women once again avoided hanging while men did not. There can be very little doubt, therefore, that the relatively favourable treatment given to women in London and the South-east was not a regional but a national phenomenon.[18]

II

Technical problems, such as the inadequacy and catch-all quality of some offence definitions, mean that the findings in Tables 5.1–5.7 need to be interpreted with care.[19] Moreover, it would require a separate chapter to review in detail the myriad ways in which the criminal justice system was changing between the 1780s and the 1820s and the impact of those changes on the

[18] Since the Lancashire data is drawn almost exclusively from a wartime period it also confirms that the patterns found in Tables 5.1–5.7 were not confined to peacetime periods alone. The London and Home Circuit samples were drawn largely from peacetime years because they were originally chosen in order to analyse the changing age structure of offenders in two similar periods. Since wartime recruitment severely depressed the numbers of juveniles and young adults reaching the courts, this was thought to be best achieved by sampling mainly before and after the period of the French wars 1793–1815.

[19] More work needs to be done, for example, on variations between counties and time periods in the proportions of non-capital offenders tried outside the assizes or the Old Bailey.

verdicts and sentencing policies experienced by women and men.[20] A preliminary comparison of the pre-1793 period and the 1820s suggests that the
tightening-up of aspects of the criminal justice system between these periods (seen, for example, in the decline of acquittal levels for both male and
female accused)[21] may have affected females slightly more than males.[22] However, there was no fundamental change in the overall pattern of trial outcomes.
Throughout the period from the 1780s to the 1820s, in every area investigated
and for almost every type of property crime indicted in the major courts, female
offenders had a considerably greater chance of obtaining more lenient treatment
than their male counterparts.

Since these findings on the relative leniency experienced by women were
confined to property crimes, to the major courts and to a relatively brief period,
it is necessary to use the limited research available on other crimes, other courts,
and other periods to explore the typicality of these findings and their broader
implications for the study of gender and justice. This will be done by asking
three questions. First, was the pattern of leniency summarised in Tables 5.1–5.7
confined primarily to property crime? Very few of the felonies tried at either the
assizes or the Old Bailey were non-property offences and those that were were
often sex specific. Only a man could be indicted for rape or sodomy, while almost
all those accused of infanticide were women.[23] Virtually the only frequently
used categories of non-property felony indictment were murder and infanticide.
Even here, however, women represented only a tiny proportion of the accused.
9 per cent of those accused of murder in Surrey 1660–1800 were female. At the
Old Bailey 1791–3, thirty one of the thirty-three offenders indicted for murder
were men. Neither of the two women accused was convicted, whereas twelve
of the men (39 per cent) were found guilty. John Beattie's Surrey homicide

[20] D. Philips, 'A New Engine of Power and Authority: the Institutionalisation of Law-Enforcement
in England 1780–1830', in V. Gatrell, B. Lenham, G. Parker (eds.) *Crime and the Law: the
Social History of Crime in Western Europe since 1500*, (London, 1980), 155–89. The proportion
of indicted offenders who were female also fell in this period: M. Feeley and D. Little, 'The
Vanishing Female: the Decline of Women in the Criminal Process, 1687–1912', *Law and Society
Review* 25 (1991), 719–57.

[21] National figures first appeared in *P.P.*, 1819, viii, 126–7. The proportion of indicted offenders
acquitted fell from 23.7 per cent in 1805 to 19.3 per cent in 1818.

[22] To summarise briefly: at the Old Bailey in 1791–3 slightly under a third of women avoided
public trial, slightly over a third were acquitted and 31 per cent were found guilty. By 1820–2
the equivalent proportions were a fifth avoiding trial, a quarter acquitted and 53 per cent found
guilty. Men also suffered adverse changes but they were not quite as great. The proportion of
males found guilty rose from 50 to 68 per cent. At the Home Circuit assizes the proportion of
men found guilty rose 9 per cent while the proportion of females rose 18 per cent. Gendered
differences in sentencing policies altered comparatively little, although sentencing policies in
general changed in diverse ways as hanging and whipping declined, imprisonment grew to be
more central and transportation re-emerged after the 1780s crisis. Imprisonment remained the
most popular sentence handed out to women throughout the period from the 1780s to the 1820s
in both jurisdictions.

[23] Beattie, *Crime*, 6, 74–139; Conley, *The Unwritten Law*, 81–95, 187–8.

evidence suggests a similar pattern: 75 per cent of the female accused were either discharged by the grand jury or acquitted by the trial jury, compared to half of the male accused.[24] The Lancashire data in Table 5.6 is problematic both because murder and infanticide were not differentiated in the parliamentary returns and because the proportion of murderers found guilty is extremely low, suggesting that a conviction was only recorded when neither an acquittal nor a partial verdict of manslaughter was returned.[25] Nevertheless the Old Bailey and Surrey patterns are clearly confirmed by the fact that in Lancashire females accused of murder were six times less likely to be convicted and hanged than their male counterparts.

In theory the law by no means favoured women. If a wife was convicted of murdering her husband, for example, her action was defined as petty treason and until 1790 she was sentenced to death by burning. When a husband murdered his wife he was simply hanged. Equally, until 1803, in infanticide cases involving unmarried mothers the normal legal presumption of innocence was reversed if an attempt was made to conceal the birth.[26] However, in practice the limited evidence available suggests that violent female offenders received relatively lenient treatment in the eighteenth century. In Surrey between 1720 and 1802 only one of the thirty-five women indicted for infanticide was found guilty and sentenced to death, while in Staffordshire the figures were zero out of thirty-nine.[27] Although no firm conclusions can be drawn until further comparative work has been done on the types of murder indictments brought against men and women and the relative strength of the evidence against them,[28] the aggregated data currently available for Surrey, London and Lancashire suggests that women accused of murder clearly had a better chance of obtaining a lenient verdict than

---

[24] Beattie, *Crime*, 97; PRO, HO 26/1-2 – same sample periods as Table 5.1.

[25] The Old Bailey documents make it difficult to trace partial verdicts of manslaughter directly, but if sentencing is used as a guide, the figures come out as very similar to those recorded in Lancashire. Three of the thirty-one males accused of murder were sentenced to death (9.7 per cent), none of the females was. In London all those fully convicted and therefore sentenced to death were hanged – an identical pattern to that found in Lancashire.

[26] This provision was repealed in 1803 by Lord Ellenborough's Act (42 Geo. 2, c. 58) after which infanticide was tried in the same way as other murders except that in infanticide cases a jury could bring in a lesser verdict of 'concealment of birth' which carried a maximum penalty of two years' imprisonment.

[27] Radzinowicz, *A History*, i, 209–13; this was changed in 1803. L. Rose, *Massacre of the Innocents: Infanticide in Great Britain 1800–1939* (London, 1986), 70–87; M. Jackson, *New-born Child Murder: Women, Illegitimacy and the Courts in Eighteenth-Century England* (Manchester, 1996), 168–77; Beattie, *Crime*, 130; R. Malcolmson, 'Infanticide in the Eighteenth Century', in J. Cockburn (ed.), *Crime in England 1550–1800*, (London, 1977), 196–7.

[28] See the brief discussion of wilful murder in Beattie, *Crime*, 97, and his warnings about comparability, 437. Women accused of poisoning their husbands or masters (a crime which was sometimes portrayed as a potential threat to patriarchy) may also have found it particularly difficult to obtain merciful verdicts from the middle-aged, propertied, male jurors of this period.

their male counterparts. The pattern is therefore fairly similar to that found in major-court property-crime cases.

Unfortunately, even less information is currently available to answer the second key question: was the more lenient treatment given to female offenders confined only to the major courts, to the assizes and to the Old Bailey? The stakes were very high in the courts that provide the data for Tables 5.1–5.7. Public trial and full conviction meant an automatic sentence of death in many cases. Even though the judges often reprieved the vast majority of those they sentenced to death, the jurors who sat on the grand and petty juries could not predict, or even directly affect, those decisions. To be sure of preventing a female (or a male) offender from being hanged they had to find a favourable verdict themselves. At the lower jury trial court – the quarter sessions – the stakes were not nearly as high. The justices in these courts had no power to hang offenders and the range of sentences they handed out was much less severe. Did this reduce the jurors' inclinations to acquit or find partial verdicts in cases involving females? The limited research available suggests that it may have done to some extent. At Surrey quarter sessions 1660–1800, 62 per cent of the females accused of non-capital property crimes were found guilty as charged compared to 66 per cent of males. The difference in cases involving long-established capital property crimes (where hanging was a very real possibility) was vastly greater, the figures being 22 and 51 per cent respectively. The verdicts of Essex jurors followed a similar pattern: relatively little difference between male and female acquittal and partial verdict rates in petty-larceny cases (which were mainly tried at quarter sessions) but much larger differences in favour of females in capital property crime cases such as burglary and highway robbery.[29]

The possibility that the quarter-sessions courts were less inclined to favour women than the assizes or the Old Bailey remains open to question, however. Shoemaker's study of early eighteenth-century London misdemeanour cases indicates both that grand jurors were more sympathetic to female defendants and that, on average, women received lower fines than men. Recent work on assault prosecutions at the Essex quarter sessions 1748–1821 suggests that female offenders were treated considerably more leniently. 32 per cent of females were acquitted compared to 17 per cent of males.[30] Since the vast majority of assault cases were dealt with informally at the petty-sessions level, it is interesting to note that Barry Godfrey's preliminary work on the late nineteenth-century Exeter summary courts suggests a similar pattern of

[29] Beattie, *Crime*, 437; P. King, 'Crime, Law and Society', 308.

[30] R. Shoemaker, *Prosecution and Punishment: Petty Crime and the Law in London and Rural Middlesex c. 1660–1725* (Cambridge, 1991), 149–59; Chapter 7. It should be noted that the gender of the victim, by contrast, made virtually no difference to trial outcomes.

relative leniency towards females in assault cases.[31] Unfortunately, however, while summary-court records survive in relatively large quantities for the late nineteenth century those of earlier periods do not. Since these courts only dealt with relatively minor forms of illegal appropriation (wood stealing, poaching, false reeling of yarn, etc.) and had only limited sentencing powers, this might not be seen as a major problem given that our primary aim here is to assess the gendered nature of trial outcomes in property crime cases. However, in other ways it makes a full history of gender and justice in this period very difficult to write. The summary courts dealt with a variety of ill-defined but important categories of lawbreaking which were used to discipline women. They regularly punished nightwalkers, bastard bearers, lewd women, idle and disorderly persons, and keepers of disorderly houses, for example. They were also the main formal judicial forum in which disputes relating to marital violence were settled. At the very least, therefore, an awareness that we know very little about the policies pursued towards men and women in these lower courts should warn us against overgeneralising from the assizes and Old Bailey evidence. However, that data, and the more fragmentary quarter-sessions evidence currently available, remains extremely suggestive given the consistency of findings across several regions and across many categories of both property crime and violent crime. It is therefore necessary to explore a third question. Was the more lenient treatment accorded to women in the major courts confined to the period from the 1780s to the 1820s?

It is difficult to answer this question. Methods of recording sentences, of trying offenders and of categorising offences change over time as do legal frameworks, policing policies and sentencing alternatives. Moreover the official statistics collected in the nineteenth century did not usually record the verdicts and sentences given to men and women separately. However, the later twentieth-century statistics do and these, along with the very limited data collected by early modern historians, can be used to make a preliminary survey of continuity and change in the treatment of female and male offenders.

Existing published work on crime and justice in the two centuries before 1780 contains relatively little systematic data on the gendered nature of trial outcomes. The main sources for the pre-1680 period are the brief tabulations in Cynthia Herrup's work on Sussex 1592–1640 and in Jim Sharpe's work on Essex 1620–80.[32] Since women could not plead benefit of clergy at all before the early 1620s, and were not granted completely equal access to this legal means of avoiding capital punishment until 1691, female property offenders

---

[31] See B. Godfrey, 'Prosecuting Violence in the Cities of England 1888–1908', paper presented to the Department of Criminology seminar, Keele University, April 1997.

[32] C. Herrup, *The Common Peace: Participation and the Criminal Law in Seventeenth-Century England* (Cambridge, 1987); J. Sharpe, *Crime in Seventeenth-Century England: a County Study* (Cambridge, 1983).

Table 5.8 *Essex assizes and quarter sessions, all property offenders and housebreakers only, 1620–80. Verdicts analysed by gender*

	All property offenders		Housebreakers	
Outcome	Male (%)	Female (%)	Male (%)	Female (%)
Not found	21.1	24.6	11.6	10.1
Not guilty	28.5	33.8	27.5	39.4
Guilty	50.4	41.5	60.9	50.5
Total	100	99.9	100	100
Sample size	1953	337	440	99

Source: J. Sharpe, *Crime in Seventeenth-Century England: a County Study* (1983), 95, 100. Excluding those categorised as 'no details', 'other', or 'at large'.

stealing goods worth over a shilling were severely disadvantaged by the law in the seventeenth century in ways that were no longer the case between 1780 and 1830.[33] However, when the decisions actually made by the courts are analysed elements of continuity do emerge. In Sussex before 1640 men and women experienced much the same conviction rates in non-capital (i.e. petty-larceny) cases, but once again in cases involving more serious crimes a highly gendered pattern emerges. Men were 75 per cent more likely to be convicted of capital thefts and two thirds more likely to be convicted of murder. They were also nearly 50 per cent more likely to be convicted of grand larceny – an offence which the growth of benefit of clergy had effectively reduced to a non-capital charge for men but not for women. Moreover, although the overall hanging rates for men and women indicate only a slight favouring of the latter, when individual offences are analysed the differences in both the categories of property crime Herrup uses are stark. 66 per cent of the men convicted of capital thefts were hanged, compared to 20 per cent of the women. For grand larceny the percentages were 12 and 7 per cent respectively.[34]

Sharpe's early study of Essex 1620–80 does not include any sustained discussion of the impact of gender on trial outcomes, but it does contain data on all property offenders and on housebreakers which can be reworked to provide further insights (see Tables 5.8 and 5.9). This data brings together both

[33] Beattie, *Crime*, 424, 485; Herrup, *The Common Peace*, 48. Thefts of under a shilling were not felonies and could not usually therefore result in a capital conviction. The history of benefit of clergy is complex (Beattie, *Crime*, 141–7) but this plea, if successful, meant that the offender was branded and then released rather than sentenced to death.
[34] Herrup, *The Common Peace*, 150, 176.

Table 5.9 *Essex assizes and quarter sessions, all property offenders and housebreaking only, 1620–80. Sentences analysed by gender*

Sentence	All property offenders		Housebreaking	
	Male (%)	Female (%)	Male (%)	Female (%)
Whipped	40.0	68.6	9.7	22.0
Read, a clerk, branded	49.3	27.9	37.3	30.0
Hanged	10.6	3.6	53.0	48.0
Total	99.9	100.1	100	100
Sample size	984	140	268	50

Source: Sharpe, *Crime*, 95, 109. Excluding those categorised as 'no details', 'other', or 'at large'.

quarter-sessions and assizes accused.[35] Thus, if our earlier assumption that the quarter-sessions courts produced less polarised patterns is correct, gender differences should be less stark. They are, but they are also still apparent – both in the figures on all property offenders and in the evidence for housebreakers alone. The proportion of men found guilty was around 20 per cent higher in both data sets, while the proportion of women sentenced to hang was consistently lower. Garthine Walker's thesis on early modern Cheshire also suggests that sentencing was weighted against men in both housebreaking and burglary cases, and that, after branding was introduced for women in the 1620s, no woman was hanged for housebreaking while the majority of men continued to go to the gallows.[36]

The various tables containing gendered data which can be found in John Beattie's book on the Surrey courts 1660–1800 suggest similar continuities. 14 per cent of male property offenders had their indictments dismissed by the grand jury compared to 18 per cent of females.[37] Petty jurors showed the same tendencies, acquitting 38 per cent of females but only 33 per cent of males as well as using partial verdicts much more liberally in cases involving women. While only a quarter of the women sentenced to death 1660–1800 went to the gallows, 43 per cent of the men made the same journey.[38]

The apparent continuity of relatively lenient trial outcomes in cases involving females accused of major property crimes from the late sixteenth century to the

---

[35] Sharpe, *Crime in Seventeenth-Century England*, 95–109.

[36] G. Walker, 'Crime, Gender and Social Order in Early Modern Cheshire' (PhD thesis, Liverpool University, 1994), 190.

[37] Beattie, *Crime*. 404. Figures based on totals produced by adding the four categories of property offence listed together (i.e. capital, non-capital, forgery, fraud).

[38] *Ibid.*, 437–8.

early nineteenth clearly requires further investigation. It is very possible, for
example, that this period witnessed a substantial rise in more lenient sentencing
policies towards women. Walker's work certainly suggests that the introduction
of branding for women in the 1620s was an important watershed in property-
crime cases, and that before that decade sentencing policies can by no means
be assumed to have favoured women.[39] Nor can it be assumed, until further
research has been published, that females found guilty of murder or infanticide
in the seventeenth century necessarily received as favourable treatment as they
seem to have done by the end of the eighteenth.[40] Given that women were the
main recipients of the extremely heavy sentencing policies pursued towards
those convicted of witchcraft in the sixteenth and seventeenth centuries, and
that they were no longer subjected to such prosecutions or penalties in later
centuries,[41] it would clearly be dangerous to overemphasise the theme of continuity. However, in property crime cases at least, a brief review of the extensive
late twentieth-century research on pre-trial processes, verdicts and sentences
does raise the possibility that the pattern of relative leniency towards women
seen between 1780 and 1830 may well have survived, albeit in changing forms
and with many short-term variations and exceptions, from the early modern
period to the 1980s and 1990s.

In the late 1970s and early 1980s about 70 per cent of the girls but only 45 per
cent of the boys dealt with by the police for indictable offences were let off with
a caution. In 1985 the equivalent figures for indictable and summary offenders
of all ages were 27 per cent of women cautioned compared to 20 per cent of
men.[42] Modern verdict patterns are more difficult to study than eighteenth-
century ones because plea bargaining and guilty pleas are now so common.

---

[39] Walker, 'Crime', 187, 190.
[40] The evidence currently available leaves this issue open to debate. Sharpe, *Crime in Seventeenth-Century England*, 124, contains figures that suggest (using the same method as that used for Tables 5.8–5.9) that 39 per cent of male murderers in Essex were convicted compared to 29 per cent of females. The proportions of convicted offenders actually hanged were 52 and 50 per cent respectively. Herrup, *The Common Peace* (150), suggests Sussex women were less likely to be convicted of murder but the sample size is very small. Walker's book *Crime, Gender and Social Order in Early Modern England* (Cambridge, 2003) suggests that while women were more likely to be acquitted of murder, once convicted they were considerably more likely to hang. Infanticide cases certainly suggest a different pattern in the seventeenth century when Herrup (p. 150) suggests 53 per cent were convicted and Sharpe (p. 135) notes that 37 per cent of the female accused went to the gallows. In Surrey 1660–1719, 30 per cent of infanticide accused were sentenced to death and 11 per cent were hanged. In the period 1720–1802 the figures were 3 per cent in both cases (Beattie, *Crime*, 116).
[41] J. Sharpe, *Instruments of Darkness: Witchcraft in England 1550–1750* (London, 1996) esp. 105–27, 169–89. For a European-wide overview of the predominance of women amongst those accused of witchcraft, of the high execution rates and of the decline of prosecutions after the mid-seventeenth century, see for example, B. Levack, *The Witch-Hunt in Early Modern Europe*, 2nd edn (London, 1995), 23, 134, 190. All English witchcraft statutes were repealed in 1736.
[42] F. Heidensohn, *Women and Crime* (London, 1985), 53; A. Morris, *Women, Crime and Criminal Justice* (Oxford, 1987), 81.

Table 5.10 *England and Wales: sentences for indictable offences analysed by gender, 17–20 year olds and offenders aged 21 or over, 1983*

Outcome	17–20 year olds		21 years and over	
	Male (%)	Female (%)	Male (%)	Female (%)
Conditional discharge	8	21	9	21
Probation	9	21	6	17
Fine	45	46	47	46
Community service order	15	4	7	2
Imprisonment/youth custody	21	7	31	12
Other	1	3	1	1
Total	99	102	101	99
Sample size	115,600	14,800	216,100	40,500

Source: A. K. Bottomley and K. Pease, *Crime and Punishment: Interpreting the Data* (Milton Keynes, 1986), 88.

However, it is interesting to find *The Times* reporting in March 1997 that a recent study had shown that 'women accused of serious crimes are far more likely to walk free from court than men . . . and in some areas of Britain they are twice as likely to be acquitted'.[43] The yearly Criminal Statistics for England and Wales issued by the Home Office make it possible to analyse sentencing policies for all indictable offences by gender and the figures for 1983 found in Table 5.10 are not untypical.[44] Care must be taken in interpreting these figures. Sentencing options were not identical. There were no detention centres for females, for example, and community-service orders seem to have been perceived by both the courts and the probation officers making recommendations to them as primarily a male-sentencing option.[45] However, the overall pattern seems remarkably similar to that found for property crime cases between 1780 and 1830. Whatever their age, women were more than twice as likely to be conditionally discharged or put on probation, equally likely to be fined, but two or three times less likely to be given the severest punishment – imprisonment. If they were given a custodial sentence, women were also much more likely both to be given suspended sentences and to suffer shorter terms in prison.[46]

Thus a surface reading of the data available from the late sixteenth to the late twentieth century appears to draw the reader in the direction of continuity as a

[43] *The Times*, 2 Mar. 1997.
[44] Table 5.10 is based on the 1983 figures quoted in A. Bottomley and K. Pease, *Crime and Punishment: Interpreting the Data* (Milton Keynes, 1986), 88. Broadly similar figures for 1991 and 1995 can be found in C. Hedderman and L. Gelsthorpe (eds.), *Understanding the Sentencing of Women* (London, 1997), 2.
[45] Bottomley and Pease, *Crime*, 88–92.
[46] Morris, *Women*, 85–7; Heidensohn, *Women*, 60–62.

key theme in the study of the impact of gender on judicial outcomes.[47] However, even a brief review of the forces that lay beneath the apparent continuation across more than 400 years of more lenient prosecution, verdict and sentencing policies towards women brings forth some rather different perspectives. Patterns of trial outcomes may appear relatively static, but did the reasons that lay beneath those patterns change fundamentally in the period being briefly surveyed here?

III

To examine the possibilities of change, of discontinuity, it is necessary to look beneath the statistics on trial outcomes and explore some of the potential ways in which we might try to explain them. This is a complex subject which can only briefly be touched on here. It is also an extremely difficult one. Eighteenth- and early nineteenth-century observers and criminal justice administrators have left virtually no record of their reasons for favouring women. Indeed, there are few indications that contemporaries were aware that the patterns of leniency towards women seen in Tables 5.2–5.7 were a feature of their criminal justice system. It was clear to most contemporaries that very few women were hanged, particularly for property crimes. However, apart from an occasional aside by an assize judge who, in leaving a condemned woman to hang, made reference to the fact that her crime was too great to allow the normal immunity of women from hanging to apply in this case,[48] contemporaries rarely referred to this issue in public. It may yet be possible to find documents and contexts in which the reasons for these gendered patterns of trial outcomes are discussed, but they are proving difficult to uncover. Modern criminologists by contrast have produced a considerable amount of research on this issue, partly by observing and interviewing the criminal justice practitioners themselves. Some of the explanatory frameworks created by this work will be very briefly reviewed here in order to test their applicability to the evidence available for late eighteenth- and early nineteenth-century England.[49]

[47] For an introduction to a broader debate on continuity or change as key themes, see B. Hill, 'Women's History: a Study in Change, Continuity or Standing Still?', *Women's History Review* 2 (1993), 5–22; J. Bennett, 'Women's History: a Study in Continuity and Change', *Women's History Review* 2 (1993), 173–84.

[48] Anon., *An Authentic Narrative of the Celebrated Miss Fanny Davis* (London: 1786) includes a record of the judge remarking in passing sentence that she should not expect that her sex would protect her from the hand of justice 'on this occasion'.

[49] For overviews of some of this work, see, for example, A. Edwards, 'Sex/Gender, Sexism and Criminal Justice: Some Theoretical Considerations', *International Journal of the Sociology of Law* 17 (1989), 165–84; Morris, *Women*, 79–103; Heidensohn, *Women*, 31–68; I. Nagel, 'Sex Differences in the Processing of Criminal Defendants', in A. Morris and L. Gelsthorpe (eds.), *Women and Crime* (Cambridge: Cropwood Conference Series No. 13, 1981), 104–21.

Although recent criminological research in this area has followed a number of complex and interwoven themes,[50] much of the work relevant to this study has revolved either implicitly or explicitly around one key question: were women treated differently because they were women or because, as a group, they were more likely to exhibit other attributes (such as fewer previous convictions) which induced those involved in deciding trial outcomes to look on them more favourably? The findings of most recent research have overwhelmingly emphasised the latter explanation. Work on cautioning, for example, has suggested that women are not more frequently cautioned because they are women, but because of the nature of their offences or because the police see them as less troublesome.[51] Equally Farrington and Morris's recent work on the Cambridge courts concluded that, while women appeared to get more lenient treatment, once allowance was made for the fact that women committed less serious offences and were less likely to have previous convictions, 'the sex of the defendant did not have any direct influence on the severity of the sentence'.[52] Other studies, which have attempted more sophisticated levels of analysis by making allowance for factors such as race, age and socioeconomic status as well as crime, previous convictions, general demeanour, etc., have led to further diminutions in the perceived importance of the sex of the accused as a key influence on judicial decision-making.[53] Some specific circumstances in which female offenders may be more harshly treated have been uncovered – the most central finding being that female offenders who do not conform to notions of respectable female behaviour (especially sexual behaviour) are more likely to receive heavier punishment.[54] However, the overall trend of much recent criminological work seems to have reached the point, to quote Anne Edwards' recent overview, where it is almost 'the expectation that continued and careful investigation will eliminate the influence of sex/gender altogether as an independent

---

[50] A large literature has recently grown up around this subject. Much of it gives little space to the type of findings expressed in Table 5.10, focusing more frequently on issues not directly within the purview of this chapter, including rape trials, the judicial treatment of prostitutes, the police processing of young girls perceived to be in danger and a rich variety of other issues that reveal the gendered nature of judicial decision-making. See, for example, S. Walklate, *Gender and Crime: an Introduction* (London, 1995); P. Carlen and A. Worrall (eds.), *Gender, Crime and Justice* (Milton Keynes, 1987); S. Edwards, *Women on Trial* (Manchester, 1984); C. Smart, *Women, Crime and Criminology: a Feminist Critique* (London, 1976); N. Naffine (ed.), *Gender, Crime and Feminism* (Aldershot, 1995); L. Gelsthorpe and A. Morris, *Feminist Perspectives in Criminology* (Milton Keynes, 1990); A. Worrall, *Offending Women: Female Lawbreakers and the Criminal Justice System* (London, 1990); R. Dobash, R. P. Dobash, L. Noaks (eds.), *Gender and Crime* (Cardiff, 1995).
[51] Morris, *Women*, 80.
[52] Heidensohn, *Women*, 44, quoting D. Farrington and A. Morris, 'Sex, Sentencing and Reconviction', *British Journal of Criminology*, 23 (1983), 245–6.
[53] Edwards, 'Sex/Gender', 170–1.
[54] Edwards, *Women*, 185; Heidensohn, *Women*, 43–50; Morris, *Women*, 82–101.

variable with statistical significance'.[55] This raises an important question for the historical work presented here – could the same have been true in the late eighteenth and early nineteenth centuries or in the early modern period? Are there hidden variables unrelated to the gender of the accused which explain the apparently lenient treatment given to women seen in Tables 5.2–5.7?

Unfortunately the data historians have to work with in the late eighteenth and early nineteenth century is much less complete than that available to modern criminologists. Accurate information on socioeconomic status or even on occupations is particularly hard to come by,[56] and in the era before the arrival of professional police forces information on previous convictions is also highly fragmentary. It must also be remembered that the legal categories used in Tables 5.1–5.5, such as simple larceny, housebreaking and private stealing, encompass a wide range of crimes, and that within these categories women may have tended to commit crimes which were less lucrative, less violent, or less likely to be labelled as serious. However, where information on potential hidden variables does exist it tends, on balance, to favour discontinuity rather than continuity. Although the seriousness of the offence can only be very crudely controlled for by studying broad sets of legal categories such as private stealing, it remains significant that when this is done (Tables 5.2–5.5) almost every type of female offender can be seen to receive much more lenient treatment. The fragmentary evidence available about the number of previous convictions males and females brought to the early nineteenth-century courts also provides no grounds for believing that this was the hidden variable behind the relatively lenient treatment received by females. While less than 61 per cent of male transportees to Australia were recorded as having previous convictions, the equivalent figure for females was 65 per cent.[57] Moreover, when national data was first collected in 1857, 40 per cent of women admitted to local prisons had had previous commitments compared to 26 per cent of men.[58] It seems highly unlikely, therefore, that if Farrington and Morris' work on 1980s Cambridge could be repeated for

---

[55] Edwards, 'Sex/Gender', 171.

[56] Women's occupations are very rarely recorded and men's status is also inaccurately stereotyped on most indictments. Exceptionally men's occupations are fairly systematically given in the Old Bailey records of the early 1790s but women are usually described in terms of their relationship to men – spinster, wife, widow.

[57] Based on data for the period 1787–1852 in L. Robson, *The Convict Settlers of Australia* (Melbourne, 1965), 176–185. Information is not available for a considerable proportion of convicts – A. Shaw, *Convicts and the Colonies* (London, 1981), 149–52 – and these findings are therefore very tentative. The figure for women with previous convictions quoted by Oxley is lower than Robson's. This may reflect different ways of treating unknowns or the fact that Oxley's data is drawn from the period after 1826. D. Oxley, *Convict Maids* (Cambridge, 1996), 41. Oxley does not quote any figures for men which would allow comparisons to be made. Transportees are, of course, an untypical sample of all prosecuted offenders (*ibid.*, 110) and this evidence must therefore be treated with caution.

[58] Zedner, *Women*, 318–20.

early nineteenth-century England, their conclusions would be the same. Controlling for type of offence and previous convictions would almost certainly not eliminate the patterns of relative leniency towards female offenders seen in Tables 5.2–5.7.

Although information is difficult to come by, it also seems unlikely that controlling for age or race would have that effect. Indeed, since offenders in their early and mid-teens undoubtedly attracted more lenient verdicts and sentences and since, in London at least, a higher proportion of male than of female accused fell into that age group,[59] controlling for age might well have the effect of increasing the gendered differentials in trial outcomes. Race is only an issue in a tiny proportion of cases in the late eighteenth and early nineteenth centuries. Even in London, Norma Myers' research on 'the black presence' at the Old Bailey 1780–1830 has revealed that only about four people of African descent per year were indicted (i.e. 0.2 per cent). Only 10 per cent of this small group were female and the verdicts and sentences received by accused blacks were very similar to those given to all offenders.[60] Until research on a large sample of cases involving groups such as Irish-born offenders is completed the broader impact of ethnicity on male or female trial outcomes is difficult to evaluate,[61] but race alone was clearly not a central factor in this period. Thus many of the hidden variables modern criminologists have used to explain away the apparently lenient treatment given to women by the courts do not hold the same explanatory power for the historian of late eighteenth- and early nineteenth-century England.

While many of the other concepts and interpretative frameworks developed by modern criminologists may well be useful starting points for historians attempting to explain the patterns found in Tables 5.2–5.7, it cannot be assumed

---

[59] P. King, 'Decision-makers and Decision-making in the English Criminal Law, 1750–1800', *Historical Journal*, 27 (1984), 25–58, especially 36–41; King, 'Female offenders'; P. King and J. Noel, 'The Origins of 'the Problem of Juvenile Delinquency': the Growth of Juvenile Prosecutions in London in the Late Eighteenth and Early Nineteenth Centuries', *Criminal Justice History*, 14 (1993), 17–41, especially 21–7. Since women were over-represented among the relatively small number of offenders in their thirties and early forties (who also received relatively lenient treatment) the juvenile effect may have been counteracted to some extent.

[60] London and slave ports such as Bristol and Liverpool were the main centres of black communities in Britain in the late eighteenth and early nineteenth centuries: P. Linebaugh, *The London Hanged* (London, 1991), 35; D. Killingray, 'The Black Presence and Local History', *The Local Historian*, 19 (1989), 8–15, especially 8. The great majority were men: J. Walvin, 'Blacks in Britain: the Eighteenth Century', *History Today* (September 1981), 37–8; N. Myers 'The Black Presence Through Criminal Records 1780–1830', *Immigrants and Minorities*, 8 (1988), 292–307; N. Myers, *Reconstructing the Black Past: Blacks in Britain 1780–1850* (London, 1996), 82–103.

[61] For a few years after 1791 the place of birth of the accused is given for the Old Bailey accused and trial outcomes involving Irish-born offenders (a substantial minority) can therefore be studied. I hope to eventually publish this data. Early samplings have yet to reveal any significant harshening of trial outcomes in cases involving Irish accused but larger samples are clearly required before this can be confirmed and gendered differences have yet to be identified.

automatically that those frameworks will hold water when applied to the years between 1780 and 1830. A recurring theme in recent criminological work, for example, is that female defendants who are not considered to be 'normal', 'conventional' or 'respectable' women (i.e. female defendants whose lifestyles violate conventional notions of women's proper roles) are more likely to receive harsher treatment within the criminal justice system.[62] However, some of the limited evidence available suggests that considerable caution needs to be used in applying such assumptions to the half century before the 'bloody code' was repealed in the 1830s. A detailed reconstruction of the backgrounds of all the female property offenders whose trials were reported in the Old Bailey Sessions Papers in 1792 indicates that a considerable proportion of them were prostitutes who had stolen their client's property before or after they offered their sexual services.[63] Surprisingly, however, these women were not more harshly treated by the courts. They achieved the same or slightly higher acquittal rates and similar sentencing outcomes as all other female accused.[64] Equally, while some modern criminologists have argued that violent female offenders are treated more harshly than female thieves, because they are effectively being punished for a breach of role expectations as much as for breaking the criminal law, this was not usually the case in the later eighteenth and early nineteenth centuries. Although attitudes to violence were gradually changing, the great majority of women accused of assault between 1770 and 1820 were fined rather than imprisoned, whereas even in minor property crime cases very few women were fined, and imprisonment, transportation or whipping was the norm.[65] The same was true for males accused of assault, but females achieved considerably higher acquittal rates than their male counterparts in both assault and murder cases. They also received much more lenient treatment from judges and jurors alike when they committed the main form of property crime which involved violence – highway robbery (see Tables 5.2–5.5). In these contexts Zedner's conclusion for the Victorian years that 'the seriousness of female crimes was

[62] Heidensohn, *Women*, 43; Edwards, *Women*, 1–4, 185; Morris, *Women*, 101; P. Carlen, 'Women, Crime, Feminism and Realism', reprinted in Naffine, *Gender, Crime and Feminism*, 433.
[63] See King, 'Female Offenders.'
[64] Sample based on all female property offenders appearing in the Old Bailey Sessions Paper trial reports January to December 1792 using HO26/1–2 for further information. A third of prostitutes and just under a third of all female offenders whose trials were reported were found not guilty. This pattern may not have been true earlier in the century but as lawyers increasingly infiltrated criminal trials at the Old Bailey in the late eighteenth century a considerable number of prostitutes hired them to orchestrate their defence. The lawyers in turn soon developed a very effective defence tactic, attacking the male victim's character and thus turning the public hearing into a trial of the prosecutor himself. The parallel with the fate of many female victims in rape trials, who also effectively ended up in the dock themselves, is fascinating and ironic. The effect, however, was to get a significant number of prostitutes off. See, for example, the case of Sophia Tilly, December 1792, *Old Bailey Sessions Papers*.
[65] Morris, *Women*, 88; Edwards, *Women*, 177, chapter 7. See also simple larceny figures in Tables 5.3 and 5.5 and King, 'Crime, Law and Society', 336.

measured primarily in terms of women's failure to live up to the requirements of the feminine ideal'[66] is difficult to apply to earlier periods. Neither sexual propriety nor non-violent behaviour were absolute preconditions for achieving better trial outcomes for the women who appeared before the courts between 1780 and 1830.

A number of the other structures of explanation found in late twentieth-century criminological work might conceivably provide helpful starting points in analysing the favourable treatment given to female offenders. For example, if most women were seen as 'troubled' and in need of 'treatment' or 'protection', while most men were perceived as 'troublesome'[67] and in need of 'deterrence' and punishment; or equally if male crime were construed as decisive planned action while women's crimes were construed primarily as understandable, almost involuntary, responses to social, economic or psychological problems, a gendered pattern of trial outcomes would almost certainly have resulted. Not all of these notions would automatically have produced greater leniency towards women. Protectionism, for example, is a two-edged sword particularly where the policing of young women's sexuality is concerned. However, in routine property-crime cases these underlying attitudes and patterns of action would almost certainly have resulted in trial outcomes that would have been generally favourable to women.[68] Unfortunately the extent to which these, and other, late twentieth-century attitudes and modes of action were paralleled in the late eighteenth and early nineteenth centuries remains difficult to gauge since few contemporaries or criminal justice practitioners wrote letters, diaries or pamphlets that recorded their motives or actions. Research on the eighteenth and nineteenth centuries therefore has to begin less ambitiously by investigating a group of potential influences that are more susceptible to analysis, although it is important to keep these potentially useful modern explanatory frameworks in mind.

Perhaps the most obvious potential influence was the legal principle of *feme covert* by which a woman committing an offence with her husband could gain an acquittal on the grounds that she was acting under her husband's orders (i.e. that she was coerced by him against her will). Although the majority of female offenders were single in the eighteenth century, this strange outgrowth of the

---

[66] L. Zedner, 'Women, Crime and Penal Responses: a Historical Account', in M. Tonry (ed.), *Crime and Justice. A Review of Research*, 14 (1991), 307–62, especially 320.

[67] Hedderman and Gelsthorpe, *Understanding the Sentencing of Women*, 26–9.

[68] Edwards, *Women*, 187. For an interesting discussion of the ambivalent effects of some of these notions, see Worrall, *Offending Women*, 165–7; Walklate, *Gender*, 140, who also discusses the ways female defendants are frequently denied a sense of responsibility for their actions and therefore placed in a 'compassion trap' in which they are presumed to have qualities associated with femininity, presumed to be more caring, nurturing and domestic. On the ways young girls can be over-policed and on the sexualisation of female deviance: Morris, *Women*, 96–100; Heidensohn, *Women*, 48–51.

logic of patriarchy undoubtedly saved a considerable number of wives from prosecution or conviction for theft.[69] However, the proportion of wives (and non-wives) who were successful in claiming immunity by using this principle remains unclear, and it is possible that its usefulness may have declined to some extent in the early nineteenth century.[70] Whatever its direct impact, *feme covert* almost certainly expressed and reinforced a broader set of discursive formations that often portrayed women as weaker, as less culpable, or as more easily led astray – attitudes which could have resulted in more lenient trial outcomes for a wide range of female offenders.

Alternatively, more material considerations may have played the most important role in these decisions. Pleas of poverty, unemployment and economic vulnerability made by women may have received a more sympathetic hearing in the courts because women were highly marginalised in the employment market during this period, forced into lower-paid and less secure types of work.[71] Judges and jurors may therefore have been more willing to treat economic hardship as a real mitigating factor in cases involving females, particularly if they were mothers. Imprisoning or transporting women with young children to support not only punished the children as well as the offender, but also produced a costly and often permanent breakdown in family life that increased the burden on the rates, and the eighteenth-century courts, like their twentieth-century counterparts, may have been particularly reluctant to remove women perceived to be 'good mothers' from their families and children.[72] Equally pragmatically, but in a different way, female offenders may simply have been perceived as less of a threat. Women formed a relatively small and declining proportion of property offenders in the late eighteenth and early nineteenth centuries. They also tended to be concentrated in types of crime such as petty larceny and shoplifting which were not felt to be particularly threatening or dangerous. They posed, to quote John Beattie, 'a less serious threat to lives, property and order'.[73]

---

[69] 'A feme covert shall not be punished for committing any felony in company with her husband; the law supposing she did it by the coercion of her husband' commented Anon., *The Laws Respecting Women* (London, 1777), 70. See also: W. Blackstone, *Commentaries on the Laws of England* 4 vols. (Oxford, 1765–9), iv, 22–4. For further discussion see King, 'Female Offenders'; Beattie, *Crime*, 414. For a further discussion of potential causes of the relative leniency experienced by women in the eighteenth century, see P. King, *Crime, Justice and Discretion: Law and Society in England 1740–1820* (Oxford, 2000).

[70] Deirdre Palk's current research on Bank of England prosecutions for forgery in the first quarter of the nineteenth century suggests that *feme covert* by no means always saved wives who acted with their husbands. For the mid-nineteenth century, see B. Godfrey, 'Workplace Appropriation and the Gendering of Factory "Law": West Yorkshire 1840–1880', in M. Arnot and C. Usborne (eds.), *Gender and Crime in Modern Europe* (London, 1999), 137–50.

[71] Discussed in more detail in King, 'Female Offenders'.   [72] Edwards, *Women*, 7–8.

[73] Feeley and Little, 'The Vanishing Female'; Rudé, *Criminal and Victim*, 45–6, 50–1, 60–3; Beattie, *Crime*, 240, 439.

Pregnant women had long been able to 'plead their belly' and avoid the gallows (not just temporarily in most cases),[74] but a range of less specific but equally powerful taboos about the punishments that could legitimately be inflicted on women may also have been developing in the later eighteenth and early nineteenth centuries. This period witnessed an increased sensitivity towards, and questioning of, the use of judicial violence[75] and the resulting movement away from physical and public punishments seems to have manifested itself particularly early and particularly strongly in relation to women. The 1790s witnessed the abolition of burning women at the stake. The 1810s saw the ending of the public whipping of women. After 1820 women could no longer be whipped at all, while men remained vulnerable to such punishment well into the second half of the nineteenth century.[76] Allied to this there also seems to have been a growing reluctance to send women to the gallows unless an extreme affront to patriarchy (such as the poisoning of a husband or master) had been committed.[77] Female offenders were still being hanged occasionally in the early decades of the nineteenth century but as arguments about the reform of the capital statutes gathered momentum wrongly judged or overharshly punished women were increasingly used by the anti-hanging lobby to add emotional resonance to their campaign. From the 1780s, Vic Gatrell has argued,

> women's physical punishment became a delicate matter. Anxiety about executing women, about burning their bodies . . . or about whipping them . . . now tended to be activated by the sense that even at their worst women were creatures to be pitied and protected from themselves, and perhaps revered.[78]

However, the precise relationship between these developments and the emergence of middle-class ideals about womanhood, such as the idealised vision of 'the angel in the house', still remains to be elucidated. Although Zedner has begun to explore the implications of those changes for attitudes to female offenders, further work is clearly needed to establish in what ways, if any,

---

[74] Beattie, *Crime*, 430–1. The use of this plea was declining, however: J. Oldham, 'On Pleading the Belly: a History of the Jury of Matrons', *Criminal Justice History*, 6 (1985), 1–43.

[75] M. Foucault, *Discipline and Punish* (London, 1977); R. McGowen, 'Punishing Violence, Sentencing Crime', in N. Armstrong and L. Tennenhouse (eds.), *The Violence of Representation: Literature and the History of Violence*, (London, 1989), 140–55. R. McGowen, 'A Powerful Sympathy: Terror, the Prison, and Humanitarian Reform in Early Nineteenth-Century Britain', *Journal of British Studies*, 25 (1986), 312–34.

[76] Radzinowicz, *A History*, i, 209–13, 578.

[77] A relative reluctance had existed, as we have seen, since the seventeenth century (if not before). In the late seventeenth and eighteenth centuries the proportion of capitally convicted female offenders who were hanged fluctuated. The Surrey figures were 1663–94, 27 per cent; 1722–48, 52 per cent; 1749–63, 10 per cent; 1764–75, 0 per cent; 1776–87, 29 per cent; 1788–1802, 19 per cent: Beattie, *Crime*, 454, 514, 532–3. By 1827–30 only four of the fifty-nine people executed in London were women and all of these had committed murder: V. Gatrell, *The Hanging Tree* (Oxford, 1994), 8.

[78] Gatrell, *The Hanging Tree*, 336–7.

the growth of ideas about separate spheres had an effect on judicial decision-makers.[79]

At this early stage of research, therefore, any attempt to explain the patterns of judicial leniency towards women found in the late eighteenth and early nineteenth centuries inevitably remains extremely tentative. However, two preliminary conclusions can perhaps be advanced on the basis of the work presented here. First, it is necessary to reappraise Zedner's observation that:

> Although male criminals were also seen as sinners, women who offended provoked a quite different response, not least an extraordinary sense of moral outrage. The moralising approach to crime that predominated in the early nineteenth century clearly distinguished, therefore, according to sex. While the male offender was merely immoral, his female counterpart was likely to be seen as utterly depraved irrespective of any actual, objective difference between them.[80]

Although she goes on to point out that 'just how far such attitudes affected judgements made about women actually on trial . . . remains unknown' the implication of these remarks is that female offenders were likely to provoke a particularly outraged, and therefore presumably harsher, response from the courts. The fact that Tables 5.2–5.7 imply strongly that the opposite was the case suggests that further exploration of the relationship between broader gendered attitudes and gendered patterns of judicial decision-making is required. In particular Zedner's implicit assumption that in the period up to the mid-nineteenth century female offenders were in double jeopardy because 'women's crimes not only broke the criminal law but were viewed as acts of deviance from the 'norm' of femininity' certainly requires further refinement in the light of the more lenient verdict and sentencing policies women received in the major courts between 1780 and 1830.[81]

---

[79] C. Hall, 'The Early Formation of Victorian Domestic Ideology' in her book *White, Male and Middle Class: Explorations in Feminism and History* (Oxford, 1992), 75–94; L. Davidoff and C. Hall, *Family Fortunes: Men and Women of the English Middle Class 1780–1850* (London, 1987); Zedner, *Women, Crime and Custody*, 1–18 focuses on the Victorian period primarily but argues that the ideal of the angel in the house 'affected all but the very lowest stratum of society'. It should be noted, of course, that early modern historians have found many of the constructs associated with nineteenth-century attitudes to women's roles in earlier periods. The extent of change in the late eighteenth and early nineteenth centuries may have been overemphasised. See, for example, M. Wiesner, *Women and Gender in Early Modern Europe* (Cambridge, 1993), 240–52; A. Vickery, 'Golden Age to Separate Sphere? A Review of the Categories and Chronology of English Women's History', *Historical Journal*, 36 (1993), 383–414.

[80] Zedner, 'Women, Crime and Penal Responses', 321.

[81] Zedner, 'Women, Crime and Penal Responses', 308. Zedner does not refer directly to the concept of 'double jeopardy' in this passage but her language comes close to paralleling modern work which does; Edwards, *Women*, 216 – 'women defendants are on trial both for their legal infractions and for their defiance of appropriate femininity and gender roles'; F. Heidensohn, *Crime and Society* (London, 1989), 102.

Secondly, the more lenient treatment given to female offenders in this period cannot, it seems, be explained simply by reference to the independent variables which twentieth-century criminologists have found to be so important. As more evidence becomes available some of these variables may well turn out to be relevant. The women accused of crimes in the major courts of England between 1780 and 1830 may, on average, have had shorter criminal records, better character references or have been perceived for other reasons as less 'hardened' offenders. More important, however, the men who made all the key decisions in the criminal justice system in this period[82] almost certainly perceived female offenders very differently, and as a result felt that a different range of verdict and sentencing options was appropriate when the accused was a woman. The deeper patterns of thinking that lay beneath these perceptions and assumptions are difficult to unravel, but it is clearly inadequate to appeal simply to notions of 'an often instinctive chivalry' as historians such as Elton have done.[83] Paternalism, protectionism, practicality and prejudice, not to mention growing perceptions of the differences between public and private spheres, may all have had a role to play. However, what seems clear is that somewhere within the complex contradictions of patriarchy, the interaction of various forces meant that female offenders accused of crimes in the major courts of late eighteenth- and early nineteenth-century England frequently succeeded in obtaining much more lenient treatment than their male counterparts.

[82] Between 1780 and 1830 all jurors, magistrates, assize and Old Bailey judges and Home Office officials involved in pardoning decisions were men.
[83] G. Elton, 'Crime and the historian', in Cockburn, *Crime in England*, 13.

6. Gender and recorded crime. The long-term impact of female offenders on prosecution rates across England and Wales 1750–1850

Two contradictory views about the impact of female offenders on prosecution rates for major indictable crimes can be found in the current literature. Whilst almost all historians and criminologists agree that women usually represent a smaller proportion of indictable offenders than men and tend to commit less violent offences and to be involved in more petty property offences,[1] there is much less agreement about patterns of change over time. On the one hand many criminological texts stress continuity. Alison Morris recently observed,

> Sex differences in crimes have been described as so sustained and so marked as to be, perhaps, the most significant feature of recorded crime. Certainly historical records reveal a disparity between the sexes and more recent statistics in a variety of jurisdictions demonstrate that recorded crime is overwhelmingly a male activity.[2]

Frances Heidensohn's widely used textbook not only concluded that 'men's excessive contribution to criminality has been observed for almost as long as crime has been recorded' but also spoke of the 'stubbornly stable ratio' of men to women amongst recorded offenders.[3]

Historians working on major indictable crime were, like most criminologists, slow to pick out gender as an important variable. However, starting with John Beattie's pathbreaking work in 1975 this has gradually become a focus of attention and in particular two recent articles by Feeley and Little have posited a completely different model – one of discontinuity rather than continuity. In their pathbreaking article in 1991 entitled 'The Vanishing Female: the Decline of Women in the Criminal Process 1687–1912', which focused almost entirely on English data, and in a follow up piece by Feeley alone on 'The Decline of Women in the Criminal Process: a Comparative History' which also used data from various Dutch and Belgium cities, the authors turned the conventional view on its

---

[1] A Morris, *Women, Crime and Criminal Justice* (Oxford, 1987), 1; J Beattie, 'The Criminality of Women in Eighteenth-Century England', *Journal of Social History*, 7 (1975), 80–116.

[2] Morris, *Women, Crime*, 18–19.

[3] F. Heidensohn, *Crime and Society* (London, 1989), 94 and 87.

head.[4] Attacking the view recently posited by two criminologists, Gottfredson and Hirschi, that 'Gender differences appear to be invariant over time and space', Feeley argued that this 'consensus within the field', this 'taken for granted' fact, was fundamentally mistaken.[5] Instead, based mainly on evidence taken from the Old Bailey Session Papers, he argued that 'at periods in the seventeenth and eighteenth centuries, women constituted 30 to 50 per cent of the cases in the criminal process, and that by the late nineteenth and throughout the twentieth century this figure dropped to 5 to 15 per cent', i.e. that there was a 'two and one-half to fourfold decrease in women's involvement'.[6] In particular Feeley and Little's article concentrated on the period up to 1850 by talking of 'the marked decrease in women's criminal involvement that appears to have taken place over the course of the eighteenth and early nineteenth centuries'.[7]

Since the Old Bailey dealt almost exclusively with felony cases, Feeley and Little's argument is fundamentally an argument about major indictable crimes – property crime, murder, etc., but the authors not only posited it with very few reservations (at least until the mid-nineteenth century when they did admit that major jurisdictional changes altered the balance of cases at the Old Bailey), but also went on to explain it in terms of a number of broader social changes. Having carefully dealt with and set aside potential long-term explanations relating to demographic patterns in London, to the changing role of distinctively female offences such as witchcraft and infanticide, to the possibility that distinctively male offences were increasingly criminalised, and to 'a fourth possibility that the high percentage of women defendants in the eighteenth century was due to women following men into crime'[8] they looked instead to broader issues for their long-term explanations. Significant shifts in the roles accorded to women in the economy, in the family and in society meant, they argued, that 'women became less inclined and able than men to engage in activity defined as criminal, and women were less subject to the criminal sanction as other forms of more private control emerged'.[9] In 1994 Feeley argued that during the same period as women's participation in recorded crime fell two-and-a-half- to fourfold 'an intensification of "private" patriarchy' occurred. By this he meant that as

> women's participation as more or less equal participants in household production . . . diminished; men became primarily economically responsible for wives and children. Women were excluded from much of developing industry or segregated into fewer and fewer low-wage occupations . . . changes . . .

---

[4] M. Feeley and D. Little, 'The Vanishing Female: the Decline of Women in the Criminal Process 1687–1912', *Law and Society Review*, 25 (1991), 719–57; M. Feeley, 'The Decline of Women in the Criminal Process: A Comparative History', *Criminal Justice History*, 15 (1994), 235–74.

[5] Feeley, 'The Decline of Women', 235.   [6] *Ibid.*

[7] Feeley and Little, 'The Vanishing Female', 720.   [8] *Ibid.*, 733–8.   [9] *Ibid.*, 741.

generally regarded as having been harmful to women's status. The loss of their economic functions led to a loss of power and autonomy within their family; male head of household authority was solidified. By the end of the nineteenth century, there was a clear separation of home and work, a firmer sexual division of labour, the exclusion of women from the public sphere and from productive work, and the confinement of women to reproductive and domestic work in the home.

Thus he concludes (giving too little attention to the complex arguments women's historians continue to have about the nature and extent of these changes) that

> throughout the eighteenth and nineteenth centuries . . . a new version of the family was constituted, one that was far more private and patriarchal. Over this same period, women's criminality appears to have declined. We cannot, of course, say conclusively that women began to commit fewer criminal offences. But patriarchal control theory would suggest that the numbers we have found reflect real differences in female criminality as well as men's willingness to involve them in public criminal justice institutions.[10]

Much has therefore been hung on the quantitative conclusions Feeley and Little came to about the 'vanishing female' offender. Moreover, their work is now widely quoted in broader work on crime and justice in this period. David Taylor's recent overview *Crime, Policing and Punishment in England 1750–1914*, for example, quotes their conclusions widely in discussing the diminishing significance of women amongst recorded criminals. Robert Shoemaker's *Gender in English Society 1650–1850* uses their work as the basis for his conclusion that 'the proportion of defendants accused of serious crime who were female declined dramatically over the course of this period' and goes on to add that between 1750 and 1850 'this basic trend is also found in studies for other parts of the country.'[11] Martin Wiener has quoted Feeley and Little's figures to support his interesting argument about the criminalisation of men in the nineteenth century, and recent work on nineteenth-century Russian criminal statistics has used their conclusion as a comparative starting point. Their work was also considered important enough to be included in a volume reprinting

---

[10] Feeley 'The Decline of Women', 260. For an example of critiques of oversimplistic models of changing gender relations see A. Vickery, *The Gentleman's Daughter. Women's Lives in Georgian England* (Yale, 1998) who suggests 'The saga of progressive female incarceration is as inconsistent with the social history of the eighteenth century, as it is incompatible with the new history of the indefatigable Victorians'. See also however other excellent recent work such as D. Valenze, *The First Industrial Woman* (Oxford, 1995); A Clark, *The Struggle for the Breeches. Gender and the Making of the British Working Class* (London, 1995); R. Shoemaker, *Gender in English Society 1650–1850: The Emergence of Separate Spheres?* (London, 1998).

[11] D. Taylor, *Crime, Policing and Punishment in England 1750–1914* (London, 1998), 47. Shoemaker, *Gender in English Society*, 302; Clive Emsley is more careful, quietly suggesting there may be problems – C. Emsley, *Crime and Society in England 1750–1900* (London, 2nd edn, 1996) 152.

seminal essays in the social history of crime recently edited by Robert Weiss.[12] This chapter seeks not to debate the links Feeley and Little made between various broad social changes and changing levels of female recorded crime, but rather to take a fresh and critical look at the concept of the 'vanishing female' itself. Having done so it will argue that this is a highly problematic way of thinking about female involvement in recorded crime once evidence from a wide range of English and Welsh counties is analysed for the period from the early eighteenth century to the 1850s.

I

It is extremely difficult to gather consistent evidence about long-term trends in indictable crime. Before official statistics began to be collected in 1805 we are reliant on the records of the courts themselves – on indictments, on minute books and process books of indictments, on assize and quarter-sessions calendars, etc. These sources all have their intrinsic problems and have been used by historians in slightly different ways. Indictment counts, for example, which are the nearest most historians have got to an index of recorded crime before the coming of the professional police, have been done in a small group of counties. However, apart from the fact that some historians did not systematically record gender ratios when counting recorded crimes,[13] there are other technical problems. In some counties 'not found' indictments, i.e. those that were rejected by the grand jury and therefore never went on to public trial, have not systematically survived. In others they have. Similarly some counties contained boroughs with quarter-sessions jurisdiction and although a particular county's quarter-sessions and assizes indictments may have survived intact the borough ones may not have done so. Record survival also changes over time. Although these changes do not necessarily cause major distortions in the proportions of females found amongst the accused, they need to be kept in mind when comparisons are made. Similarly the national figures produced after 1805 did not consistently include a proper county-by-county gender dimension until 1834, and were themselves extracted from the centrally collected criminal registers in ways which require careful scrutiny. The precise group of offences being covered also needs constant thought. Whilst the vast majority of felonies were property

[12] M. Wiener, 'The Victorian Criminalisation of Men', in P. Spierenburg, *Men and Violence. Gender, Honor, and Rituals in Modern Europe and America* (Ohio, 1998), 209; S. Frank, 'Women and Crime in Imperial Russia 1834–1913: Representing Realities', in M. Arnot and C. Usborne (eds.), *Gender and Crime in Modern Europe* (London, 1999), 95. The editors of that volume also discuss Feeley and Little's findings relatively uncritically in their introduction – 'Why Gender and Crime? Aspects of an International Debate', 7. R. Weiss (ed.), *Social History of Crime, Policing and Punishment* (Aldershot, 1999).

[13] No systematic information on gender appears, for example, in B. Davey, *Rural Crime in the Eighteenth Century: North Lincolnshire 1740–1780* (Hull, 1994).

crimes, care needs to be taken in comparing data on property crimes alone to that on all felonies which would include small numbers of cases involving murder, rape, sodomy, etc. In England and Wales in 1818, for example, 2.5 per cent of the felony cases committed for trial as recorded in the official statistics did not involve acts of property appropriation.[14] Since much of the eighteenth century data is based on property crimes alone, a very small distortion is therefore introduced when comparisons are made with post-1805 information on all felonies. However, using a variety of eighteenth-century county-based research studies and information available for every county from contemporary reports for 1805–7 and for every year from 1834 onwards, it is possible to look at gender ratios among recorded offenders for a variety of counties for the period from the early eighteenth century to the mid-nineteenth.[15]

Probably the most useful county to begin a survey of long-term recorded crime is Essex, because it has been subjected to the greatest scrutiny by historians of different periods. Here all the borough court records survive from the 1740s and 'not found' indictments also survive in an almost complete series at both the quarter sessions and the assizes. This means that figures produced by an indictment count pre-1805 will be based on almost exactly the same documents as those that were counted when the post-1805 criminal registers (which included borough and 'not found' indictments) were made up. Those registers in turn form the basis of all the printed statistics on indictable crime produced after 1805. My own study of property-crime indictments at the Essex borough sessions, quarter sessions and assizes forms the basis of the figures in Table 6.1 for 1740–59, 1760–79 and 1780–1804.[16] The official parliamentary papers offer no information about the gender ratios for individual counties for indicted offenders until 1834 but for the period 1805–7 these can be recovered from other contemporary printed sources.[17] These figures, along with samples taken from the first half decade when full information is available (1834–8) and from the last half decade before the first formal legislative transfer of felony cases into summary jurisdiction (1843–7), make possible a survey of change from the mid-eighteenth century to the mid-nineteenth.

The picture that emerges from the Essex data is of very little if any long-term decline over the relevant century (Table 6.1). The mid-eighteenth-century

[14] *P.P.*, 1819, viii, 131 (including the small 'felony and misdemeanour' category for which no description of the offence is given).

[15] For the best guide to the gradual improvement in the quality of government crime records see – V. Gatrell and T. Hadden, 'Criminal Statistics and their Interpretation' in E. Wrigley (ed.), *Nineteenth-Century Society. Essays in the Use of Quantitative Methods for the Study of Social Data* (Cambridge 1972), 336–96.

[16] P. King, *Crime, Justice and Discretion in England 1740–1820* (Oxford, 2000), 133 and Table 5.1 for a full list of the sources on which this data is based.

[17] J. Neild, *State of the Prisons in England, Scotland and Wales* (London, 1812), 639; Anon, 'A Statement of the Number of Criminal Offenders' Essex Record Office Q/SBb 412.

Table 6.1 *The proportion of female offenders amongst Essex indictments 1740–1847*

Period	Females indicted	Total indicted	Percentage female
1740–59	175	1156	15.1
1760–79	184	1331	13.8
1780–1804	387	3161	12.2
1805–07	58	431	13.5
1834–8	284	3121	9.1
1843–7	417	3065	13.6

Sources: For first three periods sources are Essex assizes, quarter sessions and borough records as listed in footnote to Table 5.1 in King, *Crime, Justice and Discretion*, 133: Figures for 1805–7 from J. Neild, *State of the Prisons in England, Scotland and Wales* (London, 1812) 639; Anon, 'A Statement of the Number of Criminal Offenders' Essex Record Office Q/SBb 412. For 1834–8 – *P.P.*, 1835, xlv, 113; *P.P.*, 1836, xli, 115; *P.P.*, 1837 xlvi, 115; *P.P.*, 1838, xliii, 113; *P.P.*, 1839, xxxviii, 113; For 1843–1847 *P.P.*, 1852–3, lxxxi, 57. First three periods = property crime only. Final three include other felonies.

figure of 15 per cent, which was swelled by a higher percentage during the wartime years 1740–8, was never regained, but the figure for the period 1760–79 is almost exactly the same as for the years between 1843 and 1847. A considerable decline occurred between the wartime period 1805–7 and the peacetime years 1834–8 – a pattern found elsewhere – but by the 1840s recovery to mid-eighteenth-century levels had effectively occurred. The eighteenth and early nineteenth centuries, highlighted in Feeley and Little's article[18] as a great period of decline, seem to have witnessed no discernible long-term change in gender ratios among indictable offenders in Essex. Indeed the same may well be true of the period from the early seventeenth century to the mid-nineteenth. Jim Sharpe's study of indictments in Essex between 1620 and 1680 concluded that 14.4 per cent of theft suspects at the assizes and quarter sessions were female.[19] If Joel Samaha's rather less reliable work on the period 1559–1602 is any guide the trend may even have been an upward one since he found only 10.3 per cent of indictable offenders were female during that period. He also studied a smaller sample from the period roughly between Sharpe's study and my own (1668–1713) and came up with a figure of 13.5 per cent for those years.[20]

---

[18] Feeley and Little, 'The Vanishing Female', 740.

[19] J. Sharpe, *Crime in Seventeenth-Century England. A County Study* (Cambridge, 1983), 95.

[20] J. Samaha, *Law and Order in Historical Perspective. The Case of Elizabethan Essex* (New York, 1974), 170 and 140. For a critique of Samaha's methodology – L. Knafla, 'Crime and Criminal Justice. A Critical Bibliography', in J. Cockburn (ed.), *Crime in England 1550–1800* (London, 1977), 285.

Table 6.2 *The proportion of female offenders amongst Berkshire indictments 1740–1847*

Period	Females indicted	Total indicted	Percentage female
1740–59	127	800	15.9
1780–9	68	635	10.7
1805–7	30	150	20.0
1834–8	153	1204	12.7
1843–7	221	1460	15.1

Sources: First two columns from R. Williams, 'Crime and the Rural Community in Eighteenth-Century Berkshire 1740–1789' (PhD thesis, Reading, 1985) 293. These related to theft accusations only. Final three periods, for sources see Table 6.1. These include all types of felony.

There is no such thing as a typical county and Essex was certainly not typical when it came to the gender ratios of its indictable offenders. In 1805–7, for example, the Essex figure of 13.5 per cent was very low compared to a national average of more than twice that proportion (Appendix 6.1). Gender ratios varied widely across different regions as we will see later in this analysis, and despite its proximity to the metropolis Essex was in the subregion, the Home Counties, with the lowest female percentages in 1805–7. However, the Essex figures are in many ways a stronger indication of possible trends than those for the Old Bailey alone because the Essex data includes county quarter-sessions and borough-sessions indictments as well as those brought to the assizes, whereas the Old Bailey data does not. In London the Middlesex quarter sessions and the City of London and the Westminster sessions all handled at least some property crime cases but these are not included in Feeley and Little's calculations.

The only other county for which full indictment-based quarter-sessions and assizes information on gender and recorded crime is available from the mid-eighteenth century onwards is Berkshire (Table 6.2). Here Richard Williams' study of theft prosecutions gives us a figure for the mid-eighteenth-century decades of 15.9 per cent.[21] This was followed by a lower figure of 10.7 per cent for the largely peacetime decade of the 1780s. The percentage of offenders who were female then rises to 20 per cent for the wartime years 1805–7 before once again following the Essex pattern after the end of the Napoleonic wars by declining to a low of 10.6 per cent in the mid-1830s. It then recovers to almost exactly the same level as the mid-eighteenth century by the years

[21] R. Williams, 'Crime and the Rural Community in Eighteenth-Century Berkshire 1740–1789' (PhD thesis, Reading University, 1985), 293. Like the equivalent figures in Essex this is again buoyed up by higher percentages for the 1740s – a decade almost entirely of war.

Table 6.3 *The proportion of female offenders amongst Somerset indictments 1725–1847*

Period	% Female quarter sessions	Period	% Female assizes and quarter sessions
1725–9	16		
1730–4	17		
1740–4	20		
1750–4	18		
1766–70	17		
1786–90	16		
1800–4	19	1805–7	21.8
1816–20	14	1834–8	15.5
		1843–7	16.8

Sources: periods of quarter-sessions data – S. Pole, 'Crime, Society and Law-Enforcement in Hanoverian Somerset' (PhD thesis, Cambridge, 1983) 139; Larceny only. Sources for 1805–7, 1834–8, 1843–7 see Table 6.1. These include all types of felony.

1843–7. The many similarities in the data for these two counties are striking. A mid-eighteenth-century rate which falls in the later eighteenth century, recovers in the Napoleonic wars, declines after the end of those wars and then recovers by the 1840s to much the same level as that seen in the 1750s and 1760s suggests that gender ratios were subject to quite complex changes in the short term (especially in relation to war) but that between the mid eighteenth and mid-nineteenth centuries no significant long-term decline whatsoever is observable. Is the same pattern apparent in counties further away from London?

The information we have available elsewhere is less easy to interpret, but for two south-western counties good data is available on quarter-sessions prosecutions up to 1820. This overlaps with the nationally collected quarter-sessions, borough-sessions and assizes data available from 1805 onwards, thus allowing some discussion of trends over a century or more. Such data must be handled with care. Each county had its own policies and patterns concerning the proportion of theft cases that were heard at quarter sessions and female offenders may, in some areas, have been better represented among the petty thieves tried at quarter sessions than among the property offenders taken to the assizes. However, the Somerset quarter-sessions data in Steve Pole's thesis shows a remarkable consistency with the nationally collected Somerset data on all courts available after 1805 (Table 6.3). All Pole's seven sample periods taken from the years 1725 to 1804 produced figures of between 16 and 20 per cent – the only period reaching 20 per cent being once again the wartime mobilisation period

Table 6.4 *The proportion of female offenders amongst Cornwall indictments 1740–1847*

Period	% Female quarter sessions	Period	% Female assizes and quarter sessions
1740–54	21.4		
1760–74	29.7		
1780–94	34.4		
1800–14	30.3	1805–7	25.0
		1834–8	17.8
		1843–7	23.1

Sources and Notes: 1740–54 to 1800–14 figures based on sample of first and last five years in each period, property crime only. Cornwall Record Office QS 1/1–10. For 1805–7, 1834–8, 1843–7 see Table 6.1. These include all types of felony.

1740–4. For rest of the period 1725 to 1804 between 16 and 19 per cent of those indicted for property crime at the Somerset quarter sessions were women. The nationally collected county figures which would have included both assizes and borough-court indictments followed a familiar parallel path. The 1805–7 Somerset figure of 21.8 per cent was very slightly higher than its 1800–4 quarter-sessions equivalent. The figure then fell to 15.5 per cent in the mid-1830s (only slightly higher than the 14 per cent Pole calculated for the post-war period 1816–20) before recovering to nearly 16.8 per cent in 1843–7. This figure for 1842–7 is exactly the same as the average percentage, which Pole found at the quarter sessions alone for the period 1725–90 if the wartime years 1740–4 are excluded.

My own work on England's most far-flung county, Cornwall, indicates that it had a considerably higher proportion of female offenders amongst its quarter sessions property-crime indictments than some other areas. This rose from 21.4 per cent 1740–59 to 30.3 per cent 1800–14 (Table 6.4).[22] The equivalent Cornwall figure for quarter sessions, borough sessions and assizes in the nationally gathered statistics for 1805–7 was 25.0 per cent. This declined after the end of the Napoleonic wars to 17.8 per cent before rising again by 1843–7 to 23.1 per cent – a figure remarkably close to, and slightly higher than, the quarter-sessions figure a hundred years earlier.

The consistency of this late eighteenth-century and early nineteenth-century pattern (of rising female involvement in indictment percentages during the French wars and then decline followed by revival) can also be seen in the data collected on Gloucestershire for my project on juvenile delinquency, although

[22] Cornwall, as so often, had its own specific pattern despite following the same general lines, as the peak in 1780–94 of over 34 per cent indicates.

Table 6.5 *The proportion of female offenders amongst Gloucestershire indictments 1789–1847*

(i) Period		Female indicted	Total indicted	Percentage female
	Figures based on assizes and quarter sessions calendars (excluding Bristol)			
1789–93		40	245	16.3
1806–11		92	386	23.8
1817–18		64	608	10.5
1820–2		57	549	10.4
1825–7		61	632	9.7
(ii)	Nationally collected statistics (including Bristol by 1838)			
1805–7	Gloucestershire	65	271	24.0
1805–7	Bristol	40	138	29.0
1805–7	Gloucestershire and Bristol	105	409	25.7
1834–8	Gloucestershire and Bristol	642	4347	14.8
1843–7	Gloucestershire and Bristol	994	5162	19.3

Sources for (i): Gloucestershire Record Office QSG/2. *Sources for (ii)*: see Table 6.1. Bristol was unique in that until the mid-1830s its figures were given separately in the county returns.

the precise periods surveyed were not chosen with this in mind. This work covered the period 1789 to 1827 and was based on intermittently surviving assize and quarter-sessions calendars which are less all inclusive than indictment series but represent a reasonably consistent sample of all indicted offenders (including non-property offenders). Starting from an average of around 16 per cent in the pre-war period 1789–93, the proportion of offenders who were female rises abruptly during the Napoleonic wars to nearly 24 per cent before plummeting to around 10 per cent for the post-war years 1817–27 (Table 6.5).[23] These figures excluded Bristol, which, unusually, has its own assizes as well as quarter-sessions jurisdiction in this period. The nationally gathered statistics available for 1805–7 also differentiated between Gloucestershire and Bristol giving an almost exactly similar figure for the whole county 1805–7 as that found in the Gloucestershire goal calendars for 1806–11 (see Table 6.5), the Bristol figure for 1805–7 being about 5 per cent higher. Unfortunately, by 1838 Bristol and Gloucestershire had been amalgamated in the printed county-based crime statistics. However, even allowing for the fact that, if 1805 is a good guide, the inclusion of Bristol would increase the overall Gloucestershire figure by 1.7 per cent (Table 6.5), the pattern is clear. There was a collapse after the

[23] For a fuller discussion of sources see Chapter 2.

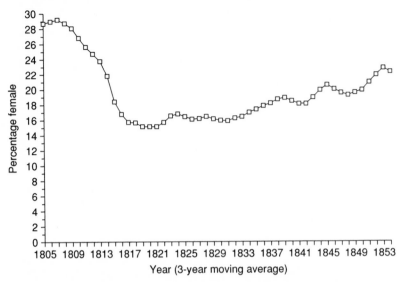

Figure 6.1 Percentage of major court accused who were female: England and Wales 1805–56. *Note*: Based on 3-year moving averages.

Napoleonic wars followed by a rise in the percentage of offenders who were female to around the figure for 1789–93.[24]

Evidence from five diverse counties therefore points to a common pattern of very little if any long-term change between the mid-eighteenth century and the mid-nineteenth century in the proportion of indictable offenders who were female, and for the second half of this period this pattern is very much confirmed by the national data for England and Wales as a whole that becomes available in various parliamentary reports. Although these gave no ratios for individual counties until 1834 they did include one national figure for male and female indictable offenders for each year from 1805 onwards and these figures form the basis of Figure 6.1.[25] This clearly indicates that the national pattern followed those of all the five counties we have just studied in depth. The years 1805–7, a period of extensive mobilisation as the French wars once again gathered momentum after a brief lull, produced a very high female proportion among indicted offenders of around 29 per cent. This fell very rapidly as the war came towards its end to a low point of around 15 per cent in the half

[24] The comparison of the two peacetime periods 1789–93 and 1843–7 suggests a slight growth in percentages but this slight inflation is almost certainly due mainly to the fact that the 1843–7 figures include Bristol which the 1789–93 ones do not.

[25] These figures are based on Gatrell and Hadden, 'Criminal Statistics', 392, information on male and female 'indictable committals for trial' collected by them from the parliamentary papers.

decade immediately after the coming of peace (1816–20). It then rose only a fraction in the 1820s and very early 1830s. However, a more sustained long-term increase to nearly 23 per cent then occurred over the next two decades – a phenomenon that was attracting considerable attention from Home Office statisticians by the 1840s. Thus the national data clearly confirms the county-based work already presented. By only graphing this national data for the years 1805–1818, Feeley and Little gave an impression of decline, but by extending the data on to the 1850s a completely different picture emerges. The second quarter of the nineteenth century, in particular, emerges as a period of rising female involvement in recorded crime and the government was aware of this. In 1846 the Home Office's annual commentary on the criminal statistics noted that 'there appears to be an almost uninterrupted increase in the proportion of female offenders.'[26]

II

To what extent does the evidence for London look different to the patterns so far discussed? One major source is the evidence on Surrey's urban parishes produced by John Beattie and quoted by Feeley and Little. Since the area concerned was effectively part of London, this is a good place to begin to unravel the knotty problem of what was happening in the metropolis itself. Beattie's data is reproduced in twenty-year periods in Table 6.6 along with the later, post-1805, data for the whole of Surrey which includes, of course, a considerable rural area as well. Beattie found that in the long eighteenth century female property offenders formed twice as high a proportion of all property offenders in urban/neo-metropolitan Surrey as they did in the rest of the county[27], so the figures available after 1805 will inevitably be somewhat lower than they would have been if they had covered urban Surrey alone.[28] However, even as they stand the Surrey figures suggest a considerable amount of continuity. The late seventeenth and very early eighteenth century stands out as a period of peculiarly high female participation rates, but overall the picture is not one of decline. The 1843–7 figure of 21.9 per cent (which would probably have been nearer 24 or 25 per cent if it had referred only to metropolitan Surrey) is slightly

---

[26] Feeley and Little, 'The Vanishing Female', 731. S. Redgrave, 'Criminal Tables for the Year 1845', *Journal of the Statistical Society*, 9 (1846), 182 also observed that 'The increasing proportion of female offenders, which has been remarked in former tables continues' and provided figures suggesting that the proportion had risen 4 per cent between 1837 and 1845. For the fact that 'the proportion of female to male offenders is on the increase' was still being commented on in the later 1850s, see Anon, 'The Statistics of Female Crime'. *The Economist*, Sept. 11, 1858, 1010–1.

[27] Beattie, 'The Criminality of Women', 97.

[28] Although it should be noted that 1660–1800 over two thirds of Surrey offenders came from urban areas – *ibid*.

Table 6.6 *The proportion of female offenders amongst indictments in urban Surrey and Surrey as a whole 1661–1847*

(i) Period	Urban Surrey, property offenders		
	Females indicted	Total indicted	Percentage Female
1661–80	113	477	23.7
1681–1700	127	314	40.4
1701–20	149	404	36.9
1721–40	189	680	27.8
1741–60	338	1036	32.6
1761–80	154	727	21.2
1781–1805	335	1531	21.9
(ii)	All of Surrey, all felonies		
1805–7	145	546	26.6
1834–8	967	4888	19.8
1843–7	1102	5023	21.9

Sources: Feeley and Little, 'The Vanishing Female', 757 (quoting Beattie) and for section (ii) see Table 6.1.

higher than that for urban Surrey 1761–80 and only very slightly lower than that for the period 1661–80. Once again the post 1805 data shows that this county witnessed the familiar high figure during the Napoleonic wars followed by a considerable fall and then a recovery, but apart from the exceptional years 1680–1710, both the figures for urban Surrey and those for Surrey in general provide no clear evidence of a long-term decline in female participation rates. The only way that such a decline can be put forward is by starting the series in that brief late seventeenth- and early eighteenth-century period of very high female participation and here may lie one of the major problems that Feeley and Little's study accidentally created.

What was happening at the centre – in London and Middlesex? For the period after 1805 this can be ascertained because, unlike any other region, statistics about London offenders' gender ratios were fairly regularly published in various parliamentary reports and an almost complete series of figures for 1805–55 can therefore be gathered for this area (see Figure 6.2).[29]

The overall pattern is not dissimilar to that found in Figure 6.1. From a high point of over 38 per cent in 1805–7 the percentage of indicted offenders who were female halved to just under 19 per cent in 1820 but then rose again to over

[29] This is based on a 3-year moving average. Sources are 1805–7, Neild, *State of the Prisons*, 639; Anon, 'A Statement of the number of Criminal Offenders', Essex Record Office, Q/SBb, 412; 1811–27 *P.P.*, 1828, vi, 288–9; 1828–31 *P.P.*, 1831–2, xxxiii, 5; 1834–8. As listed in footnotes to Table 6.1; for 1839–42 *P.P.*, 1840, xxxviii, 113; *P.P.*, 1841, xviii, 55; *P.P.*, 1842, xxxii, 55; *P.P.*, 1843, xlii, 55; for 1843–52 *P.P.*, 1852–3, lxxxi, 57 for 1853–5 *P.P.*, 1856, xlix, 59.

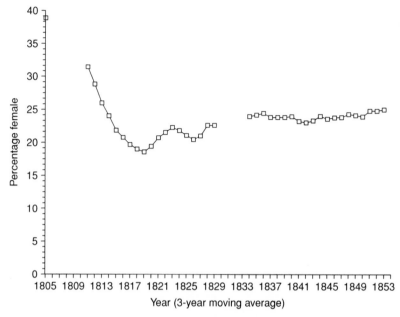

Figure 6.2   Percentage of major court accused who were female: London 1805–55.
Note: Based on 3-year moving averages.

25 per cent by the beginning of the 1850s. Since this data included information
from all of the courts in London dealing with felony cases rather than just
the Old Bailey it must be regarded as the most reliable guide. How does it
compare to Feeley and Little's Old Bailey Sessions Paper data? For the years
1805–1840 there are marked similarities. Since they took samples at five-year
intervals[30] their data can be compared to the statistics for all London courts for
most dates from 1805–7 onwards. They follow an almost exactly similar pattern
(Table 6.7). Both are in the mid to high 30s in 1805, then there is the usual huge
drop so that by 1815 both figures are at a level of 24 per cent. A further fall
to 17 and 18.6 per cent respectively then occurs by 1820 but between 1825
and 1840 both sets of figures range between 21 and 24 per cent and are usually
very similar. Thus in the thirty-five-year period 1805–1840 there is a very strong
suggestion that the Old Bailey Sessions Papers subset of cases produced figures
roughly in line with those for the London courts as a whole. However, after 1840
the figures diverge. The Old Bailey percentage continues to decline to 15 per
cent by 1855 whilst the overall London courts figure remains high and rises
slightly to over 25 per cent. This was almost certainly due to jurisdictional

---

[30] Feeley and Little, 'The Vanishing Female', 756, Appendix Table 2a.

Table 6.7 *The proportion of females amongst indicted offenders in the Old Bailey sessions papers and the full parliamentary returns for all London courts 1805–1855*

	Old Bailey sessions papers	All courts (three-year moving average)
1805	35	38.8
1810	28	–
1815	24	24.1
1820	17	18.6
1825	24	22.0
1830	23	22.9
1835	21	24.1
1840	24	24.1
1845	19	24.2
1850	18	24.4
1855	15	25.3

Sources: Feeley and Little, 'The Vanishing Female', 756, for Column 1. For Column 2 see *Parliamentary Papers* listed in footnote 29. Column 2 figures are a three-year moving average centred on the relevant year.

changes. Feeley and Little's breakdown of the types of case heard at the Old Bailey shows that larceny formed a steady proportion of cases throughout the period 1735–1835 (50–59 percent), but this figure fell from 58 per cent in 1835 to 31 per cent in 1855 and 13 per cent by 1875.[31] The caseload of the Old Bailey rose steadily until 1835 but after 1850 it then plummeted rapidly. It became a differently designed jurisdictional entity. 'It may be' therefore, as Feeley and Little themselves pointed out 'that jurisdictional changes removed offences that disproportionately involved women from the Old Bailey and into the lower courts' and that 'these jurisdictional changes account for much of the reduction in women at the Old Bailey throughout the second half of the nineteenth century'.[32] Jurisdictional changes almost certainly also account for the fact that the parliamentary statistics covering all London's courts for the period 1840–55 show not a decline but a slight rise in the percentage of offenders who were female while the Old Bailey Sessions Papers show another drastic decline.

Do we get a picture of large-scale long-term decline if we compare the accurate parliamentary statistics on female percentages available for the mid-nineteenth century, when around a quarter of offenders were female, with the situation at both the Old Bailey and the Middlesex Sessions a hundred years earlier? Feeley and Little's article supplies us with data for the mid-1750s which helps to answer this question in relation to both those courts. At the Old Bailey

[31] *Ibid.*, 725.   [32] *Ibid.*, 724.

in 1750, 26 per cent of offenders were female, the equivalent figure in 1755 being 30 per cent – offering a notional average of 28 per cent. Similarly Norma Landau's figures for three Middlesex Sessions in 1753 and 1754 average out at 26 per cent.[33] A full London figure for all courts might therefore have been somewhere between 26 per cent perhaps at the beginning of the 1750s and a figure of around 28 per cent by the mid-1750s. There are many unknown variables of course – the typicality of the years chosen, the possibility that figures from the Westminster and City of London sessions would have been different from those Landau found in Middlesex, the precise ratio of cases between the Old Bailey and the three sessions. However, the early 1750s were peacetime years so in comparing them with the later 1840s and early 1850s we are comparing two peacetime periods. The result is very interesting. Even here in the metropolis the hundred years from the 1750s to the 1850s saw virtually no decline in the proportion of indicted offenders who were female.

The late seventeenth century and the early eighteenth was clearly a highly exceptional period. As John Beattie's recent work has shown, in the decade or so on either side of 1700, female involvement amongst those indicted at the Old Bailey for crimes committed in London seems to have reached heights never recorded either before or since. In the period 1690 to 1713 women actually outnumbered men among the London indicted.[34] However, rather than being the start of a long-term decline, Beattie's work also makes it clear that this was a brief and highly exceptional peak which coincided with a period of warfare and of particular concern about offences in which women were involved. In both the preceding period (1670–89) and the following one (1714–50) the proportion of females amongst the accused was very much lower. Between 1670 and 1689, for example it was only 32.9 per cent compared to 51.2 between 1690 and 1713. Almost all the evidence so far collected from outside London also suggests very strongly that the late seventeenth and early eighteenth centuries were exceptional times. Both the urban Surrey and the Essex evidence indicate extensive continuities between the mid-seventeenth- and mid-eighteenth-century figures, for example, and over a longer period Walker's recent work on Cheshire also indicates tremendous long-term stability. Between 1590 and 1669, 22 per cent of Cheshire theft suspects were female. In both 1805–7 and 1843–7 the figure was just over 20 per cent.[35] Thus, for the period 1750–1850

---

[33] *Ibid.*, 730 and 756; N. Landau, 'Indictment for Fun and Profit: a Prosecutor's Reward at Eighteenth-Century Quarter Sessions', *Law and History Review*, 17 (1999), 507–36.

[34] J. Beattie, *Policing and Punishment in London 1660–1750* (Oxford, 2001), 65; J. Beattie, 'Crime and Inequality in Eighteenth-Century London', in J. Hagan and R. Peterson (eds.), *Crime and Inequality* (Stanford, 1995), 134–5.

[35] On the introduction of capital punishment for two offences – shoplifting and thefts by servants – in which women were greatly involved and for a discussion of the late seventeenth and very early eighteenth century as a period of high anxiety in London about crime – see J. Beattie, 'London Crime and the Making of the "Bloody Code", 1689–1718', in L. Davison *et al.* (eds.), *Stilling*

and very probably for the period 1650–1850 there is very little evidence of any long-term decline in female involvement in the criminal process as persons accused of indictable crimes. All the evidence appears to be pointing the other way.

III

The pattern we have found from the mid-eighteenth to the mid-nineteenth century of long-term stability but of short-term changes raises a number of questions. Some relate to the inner rhythm of the century between 1750 and 1850, i.e. to the rising female involvement in recorded crime during the French wars followed by an extended period of some twenty years when female percentages remained low before recovering to mid-eighteenth-century levels by the late 1840s. Another question grows out of this context – what was the general impact of war on the percentage of offenders who were female? Other questions arise out of the need to assess the spatial aspect of these changes. How exceptional or typical was London and to what extent were there regional differences in changing experiences of female recorded crime? Finally it may be briefly worth reassessing the periods on either side of the years 1750–1850 to analyse their contribution to the idea of the vanishing female offender.

The large rises in the proportion of offenders who were female during the French wars is hardly surprising. The Napoleonic war period in particular witnessed mobilisation on a massive scale peaking at about half a million men around 1810 – two and a half times the number mobilised in any other eighteenth-century conflict.[36] The removal of such a large proportion of the country's young, mobile, marginal and often underemployed or unemployed males inevitably cut down male recorded crime levels. This was, after all, the group most vulnerable to prosecution for property crime.[37] More important the widespread practice of compulsorily enlisting accused young fit male offenders before they came to formal trial could greatly depress male prosecution rates as I have argued in detail elsewhere.[38] This was particularly noticeable at the beginning of the nineteenth century because the numbers mobilised were so huge, but in the earlier conflicts of 1740–8, 1756–62, 1777–82, a similar effect was observable as the data from Essex in Table 6.8 makes clear. The percentage of all property offenders who were female rose from 12 or 13 per cent to 20 per cent during both the Seven Years War and the American War of

---

the Grumbling Hive. The Response to Social and Economic Problems in England 1689–1750 (Stroud, 1992), 49–76; G. Walker, Crime, Gender and Social order in Early Modern England (Cambridge, 2003), 135 and 159. This comparison is problematic because the nineteenth-century figures included a small number of non-property crimes but homicide percentages in 1590–1669 were very similar. One fifth were women.

[36] King, Crime, Justice and Discretion, 154.   [37] Ibid., 169–217.

[38] P. King, 'War as a Judicial Resource. Press Gangs and Prosecution Rates, 1740–1820' in N. Landau (ed.), Law, Crime and Society 1660–1840 (Cambridge, 2002), 71–96.

Table 6.8 *The proportion of Essex property offenders who were female.*
Wartime and peacetime compared 1740–92

	Total no. of property offenders	No. of female property offenders	Percentage female all types of property crime	Percentage female petty larceny only	
1740–8	525	83	15.8	18.6	War
1749–54	392	50	12.7	15.8	Peace
1755–62	367	75	20.4	32.9	War
1763–76	1047	130	12.4	18.7	Peace
1777–82	439	90	20.5	29.8	War
1783–92	1383	170	12.3	17.2	Peace

Sources: As for 1740–1805 in Table 6.1.

Independence, i.e. increased by about two thirds. War also had a fundamental impact on overall crime rates, but just as mobilisation reduced them drastically so it also almost always increased very considerably the proportion of females amongst those accused of felony.[39] This pattern helps to explain why the percentage of indicted offenders who were female failed to recover for so long after the drastic fall we have observed in all of England and Wales after the French wars ended in the 1810s. Unlike the eighteenth century in which another war usually occurred within about a decade to boost female offender ratios, no significant conflict emerged in the nineteenth century until after 1850.

This does not explain, however, the peculiar depth of the collapse of female-offender percentages in the years between 1805–7 and the later 1820s and early 1830s. The difference between peacetime and wartime female-involvement figures was not 60 per cent as it had been in the eighteenth century according to the Essex figures, but was around 100 per cent. In London, for example, female percentages were cut from 38.8 to 18.6 per cent (Table 6.7) while in the national figures the change was from 29.3 to 15.2. In Lancashire they fell from 30.2 in the period 1801–5 (which included a brief demobilisation period before hostilities began again in 1805) to 17.9 in 1820–2.[40] Why was this drop so much greater than the previous ones brought about by transitions from war to peace? The years following the end of the Napoleonic Wars witnessed two important changes which may be relevant here – a very rapid rise in the number of young offenders being prosecuted, and a simultaneous trend towards the deeper gendering of juvenile delinquency. The proportions of London and

[39] This pattern was not repeated, however, in every single war, – see for example the first part of the French wars in P. King, 'Crime, Law and Society in Essex 1740–1820', (PhD thesis, Cambridge University 1984), 67.

[40] For Lancashire sources see footnote 9 in Chapter 2.

Manchester offenders under eighteen more than doubled between 1790 and 1820, and by the 1820s 48 per cent of Manchester offenders and 38 per cent of London ones were aged under twenty (Chapter 2)[41]. However, just as juvenile delinquency began to have a major impact on overall recorded crime rates for the first time, it also become, for a brief period at least, an almost exclusively male preserve. As I hope to show in detail elsewhere, in many urban areas virtually all the increase in juvenile indictments was due to the growing prosecution of males. In both Manchester and London, the proportion of juvenile offenders who were female declined rapidly between 1815 and the mid-1820s, although the trend then gradually reversed in the 1830s.[42] Given that juveniles constituted such a substantial proportion of all the indicted, this almost certainly played a part in depressing the overall proportion of urban offenders who were women in the period 1815–30.

The prosecution of juvenile delinquents did not rise rapidly everywhere in England (Chapter 2). In many rural areas there was still little change in the proportion of indicted offenders who were juveniles in the late 1820s. However London and Lancashire alone accounted for 28 per cent of all indictments in England and Wales 1834–8 and since other urban areas such as Birmingham and Bristol also had very high percentages of juveniles by the 1820s the impact of the gendering of juvenile delinquency on the national statistics would clearly have been important. The spatially differentiated pattern in the growth of juvenile delinquency does, however, raise another important question in relation to the patterns of gendered change under scrutiny in this chapter. To what extent and in what ways did the percentage of all indicted offenders who were female differ between regions? And did this change across time?

IV

The scattered information already used from eighteenth-century studies of individual counties has shown that there were wide variations in the proportion of offenders who were female. John Beattie's research led him to conclude that 'women in the city were . . . much more likely to be accused of . . . theft than women in the rural parishes and small towns of Surrey and Sussex and the urban–rural disparity was much greater for women than for men'.[43] This close relationship between the degree of urban involvement in a county and its percentage of female offenders was also confirmed by my own work on the assizes

---

[41] *Ibid.*, and for figures for 0–16 year olds in London see H. Shore, *Artful Dodgers. Youth and Crime in Early Nineteenth-Century London* (Woodbridge, 1999), 165.

[42] P. King 'The Gendering of Juvenile Delinquency in Early Nineteenth-century England' (forthcoming) and for further discussion H. Shore, 'The Trouble with Boys: Gender and the Invention of the Juvenile Offender in Early Nineteenth-Century Britain' in Arnot and Usborne (eds.), *Gender and Crime*, 75–92.

[43] Beattie, 'The Criminality of Women', 97.

records of the five Home Counties. Surrey had the highest proportions, followed by Kent (which also contained some extensive neo-metropolitan parishes) and then Essex (which had a few). Hertfordshire and Sussex, the most purely rural of the five counties, had much lower percentages of female offenders.[44] However, this neat correlation in the South-east between the degree of urban involvement and the percentage of offenders who were female did not necessarily hold for the rest of England. The picture was much more complicated. Cornwall, far away from the metropolis, produced a quarter sessions figure for female offenders twice that of Sussex or rural Surrey. Here the growing reliance of the region on mining which employed many women, may have been a factor[45] as it may also have been in the North-east. Gwenda Morgan and Peter Rushton's work on the North-east has upheld the strong impact of the urban context. Their startling finding that 50 per cent of all the thieves tried at the Newcastle quarter sessions or assizes were women 1719–1800 makes the overall London figures seem low. Their figures for two other counties affected by mining – Durham and Northumberland – each recording that just under a third of theft offenders were women[46] – are also extremely high compared to Sussex's 10 per cent. The North-east may even be an exceptional area in which there was some long-term decline in female participation. There are no equivalent figures for Newcastle alone in the nineteenth century but although the Northumberland and Durham figures hold up well for 1805–7 and although by the 1840s they were still above the national average, the early-to-mid-nineteenth-century figures (Appendices 6.1, 6.2 and 6.3) were lower than those found by Morgan and Rushton for the eighteenth century.

The existence of figures for every county for 1805–7 and then from 1834 onwards makes a regional analysis possible for this key period (Table 6.9) and reveals some surprising contrasts which show the need for a more complex model of spatial variations in female involvement in recorded crime. It is interesting to note, for example, that in 1805–7 the five counties with the highest percentages of female offenders among those committed for trial in the major courts were Carmarthen, Flintshire, Northumberland, Pembroke and Radnor (Appendix 6.1). While this rightly raises questions about our tendency to see high female involvement in indictable crime as solely an urban phenomenon, there are many problems with such figures. Four of these five far-flung counties processed incredibly small numbers of offenders through their major courts (in Radnor eight, in Pembroke twenty, in three years) and all that can be said is that in certain areas where there was clearly a deep reluctance to formally indict either men or women in the major courts, women had as good a chance as

---

[44] King, *Crime, Justice and Discretion*, 199.   [45] See chapter 8.

[46] G. Morgan and P. Rushton, *Rogues, Thieves and the Rule of Law. The Problem of Law-Enforcement in North-East England 1718–1800* (London, 1998), 67.

Table 6.9 *The proportion of female offenders amongst those committed for trial in different regions of England and Wales 1805–47*

	1805–7 (%)	1834–8 (%)	1843–7 (%)
1. Northern counties	39.5	22.1	23.1
2. Lancashire	40.2	22.6	24.7
3. Yorkshire	27.4	17.0	18.6
4. West Midlands	24.4	15.4	19.1
5. East Midlands	20.2	10.3	12.5
6. Eastern counties	22.0	11.8	16.0
7. South-eastern counties	19.2	14.3	17.7
8. London and Middlesex	38.9	24.1	23.6
9. South-central counties	22.0	14.6	16.5
10. South-west	24.9	22.9	23.4
11. Wales	31.4	18.8	21.2
12. All England and Wales	28.8	17.3	19.7

Key: 1. Northumberland, Cumberland, Westmorland, Durham,
4. Cheshire, Derby, Notts, Stafford, Shropshire, Hereford, Worcester, Warwick, Monmouth, Gloucester, Bristol,
5. Notts, Leicester, Northants, Rutland, Bedford, Oxford, Bucks,
6. Lincs, Hunts, Cambs, Norfolk, Suffolk,
7. Herts, Essex, Kent, Surrey, Sussex,
9. Berks, Hants, Wilts, Dorset, Somerset,
10. Devon, Cornwall.

men of getting through the various pre-trial processes which filtered out almost all of the accused before they could be officially recorded as indicted offenders. Nineteenth-century commentators made much of variations in crime rates between counties and used them naively in lengthy debates about, for example, the impact of education and literacy on crime.[47] Such debates were dogged by problems, however, not the least being the assumption that indictment rates reflected differences in real crime levels rather than, as seems more likely, differences in the ways victims and committing magistrates used the criminal justice system. Too much should not therefore be read into either the individual county figures in Appendices 6.1, 6.2 and 6.3 or the regional figures in Table 6.9. However, the latter, based as it is on much larger sample sizes, does suggest one or two tentative conclusions about spatial differences in female involvement in recorded crime.

[47] For example J. Fletcher, *Summary of the Moral Statistics of England and Wales* (London, no date), T. Plint, *Crime in England*, (London 1851). 'The counties, taken separately, exhibit many irregularities', Rawson observed: R. Rawson, 'An Inquiry into the Statistics of Crime in England and Wales', *Journal of the Statistical Society*, 2 (1839), 343.

Looking at the 1805–7 figures first – the nearest we have to a spatial picture for the central part of the period under review here – three patterns emerge. First, urbanisation was clearly a factor. Lancashire and London, which contained the two greatest conurbations, had very high female-participation rates. So did the northern counties which included Newcastle where we know female-involvement was very high in the eighteenth century. Secondly, however, areas still dominated by rural economies – especially Wales – also had very high female-involvement rates. The four Welsh counties amongst the top five already quoted were exceptional, but not that exceptional. Wales as a whole had much higher rates than the national average or than those of the Midlands or Yorkshire. Third the south-east counties including Surrey, Kent and Essex which involved considerable areas in or on the very edge of the metropolis had the lowest percentage of female involvement of any part of England and Wales. Areas like Norfolk (27 per cent) and Devon (25 per cent) had much greater percentages of female offenders than Hertfordshire and Essex (14 and 13 per cent). Indicted offenders in far-flung areas like rural Wales and Cumberland (37 per cent) were much more likely to be women than those in the Home Counties (Appendix 6.1).

The later data on the 1830s and 1840s indicates that the large disparities seen in the eighteenth-century evidence and in the 1805–7 data were greatly reduced by mid-century. In 1805–7 London's percentage of female offenders was ten percentage points above the national average. In the northern counties it was 11 per cent. By 1843–7 these figures were 4 per cent and 3 per cent (Table 6.9). This mainly reflected a general fall in the percentage of indicted offenders who were women. However, when combined with the very considerable growth in the number of offenders coming to court in the more rural areas, it also suggests that as the criminal justice system was used more frequently in areas such as rural Wales so female percentages may have fallen.

The general pattern of differentials between regions remained fairly similar in the 1840s to those found in 1805–7. London, Lancashire, the northern counties and Wales remained above the national average. Yorkshire, the Midlands, central and eastern England all remained below the national average. The only region which changed sides – from being four percentage points below the national average 1805–7 to nearly four points above it 1843–7 – was the far South-west (both Devon and Cornwall). Once again, as with rural Wales and Cumberland, the far-flung regions of England and Wales seem to have followed their own distinctive path, maintaining a higher female involvement in recorded indictable crime than areas such as the Midlands and the south-eastern counties. Lacking any information on real levels of crime, on the differential impact of economic changes, and most importantly on the changing attitudes of victims and committing magistrates, it is almost impossible to explain these differences. They do however, serve as a warning against making too simplistic a model of links between levels of urbanisation and levels of female involve-ment in recorded crime. Urbanisation on a massive scale in the London and Manchester area, for example, did raise female participation rates amongst indictable offenders, but so (in many cases) did distance from the centre – the far-flung areas a long way from the capital or from the major conurbations also showed a relative tendency to draw females into the formal criminal justice system.

From the point of view of evaluating Feeley and Little's work this regional data can be helpful in answering the question – how typical was London? Clearly in 1805–7 it was highly untypical – its level of female involvement in indicted crime was a third higher than the national average and more than double that of the counties immediately surrounding it (Table 6.9). However, its exceptional role in boosting national female percentages was eroded in the first half of the nineteenth century. In part this was because, as other large cities grew up, London's offenders declined from nearly 27 per cent of the national total 1805–7 to less than 17 per cent by the mid-1840s, but more importantly it was because the difference between London's female-participation rate and the national one fell from 35 per cent to 20 per cent. London had been highly exceptional but was gradually falling into line. Indeed by the years 1843–7 the percentage of females amongst indicted offenders was almost exactly the same in London as it was in Devon and Cornwall (Appendix 6.3). Ironically, therefore, the London figures come closest to being a useful guide to possible national levels of female involvement at precisely the time, the mid-1840s, when the Old Bailey data used by Feeley and Little becomes a very inaccurate guide to the situation in London itself (Table 6.7).

What happened after 1850? Feeley and Little's data on the period from the 1850s to the 1890s is clearly deeply suspect given the jurisdictional changes already outlined and noted by them, but, ironically, their picture of decline matches the patterns found in the national and county data more closely for this period than for the years 1750–1850. The new statistical series begun in 1857, and quoted by Gatrell and Hadden, shows that the proportion of indictable committals for trial that involved females fell from 22.2 per cent 1857–9 to 15.3 per cent 1890–2, i.e. that female involvement fell by a third.[48] There are many possible reasons for this decline. It may, for example, have had more to do with the 'rationing of crime' recently discussed by Howard Taylor[49] than with changes in the nature of patriarchy or the other long-term shifts in social and economic life emphasised by Feeley and Little. However, there can be no

---

[48] Gatrell and Hadden, 'Criminal Statistics', 394 – based on three-year averages. Zedner using individual years comes up with a similar extent of decline but different individual figures L. Zedner, *Women, Crime and Custody in Victorian England* (Oxford, 1991), 36.

[49] Howard Taylor, 'Rationing Crime: The Political Economy of Criminal Statistics since the 1850s', *Economic History Review*, 101 (1998), 569–90.

Table 6.10 *The proportions of males and females
amongst London prisoners 1816*

Crime	Male	Female
Felony	76.5	23.5
Assault	76.1	23.9
Other misdemeanours	61.7	38.3
Average percentage	70.3	29.7
Sample size	11293	4768

Source: P.P., 1817 vii, 548–53. Based on Giltspur-Street Prison and House of Correction, Newgate, Tothill Fields Bridewell, New Prison at Clerkenwell, House of Correction Cold Bath Fields, County Gaol of Surrey Horsemonger Lane. Debtors excluded.

doubt that, to quote Zedner, 'women formed a declining proportion of those proceeded against by indictment' between the 1850s and the 1890s.[50]

V

Studying crime via indictable offences alone is, of course, highly problematic in itself. A large number of men and women were committed to prison or otherwise punished by the summary courts while others were indicted at the quarter sessions for misdemeanours such as assault, but they have not been included in this survey because they were not formally accused of felony. They would not therefore have been included in the Old Bailey Sessions Papers, in the county-based work on crime rates done by eighteenth-century historians or in the post-1805 criminal statistics gathered by government. Females were almost certainly better represented amongst those imprisoned for non-felonies than amongst those in prison for felony. Detailed information on London's prison population in 1816, for example, shows that females represented 23.5 per cent of those held in relation to felonies, 23.9 per cent of those held in relation to assault and 38.3 per cent of those held for other misdemeanours such as vagrancy or being idle and disorderly (Table 6.10). Similarly while information collected in 1819 on prisoners in all English gaols reveals that 18.7 per cent were women, in the same year only 15.8 per cent of indictable felons in England and Wales were female. In order to put the notion of the vanishing female to rest for the period 1750–1850, however, this discussion has focused only on indictable crime because this was the basis on which Feeley and Little's research was founded.[51]

[50] Zedner, *Women, Crime and Custody*, 36.
[51] *P.P.*, 1819, xvii, 1–55. Women may also have been better represented amongst those tried summarily than amongst the indicted. In 1857 it was reported that women constituted 28 per cent of those tried summarily and 21 per cent of those committed for trial – *Economist*

What conclusions does this survey of a wide variety of new material from across England and Wales suggest about Feeley and Little's thesis? Detailed investigation of the period up to 1850 has revealed a number of very significant problems with Feeley and Little's view of a two-and-a-half to fourfold decrease in women's involvement in crime in the eighteenth and nineteenth centuries. The data for many counties suggests long-term stability in female involvement in recorded crime between 1750 and 1850 and the data for London itself during this period suggests a very small decline and possibly no decline at all. The late seventeenth and early eighteenth century undoubtedly saw a massive peak in female recorded crime in London, but although we have no comparable mid-seventeenth-century figures for the metropolis, the evidence from urban Surrey and Essex suggests this was a very temporary phenomenon. Much further research is needed on this earlier period but there appear to be extensive continuities between the mid-seventeenth century and the mid-eighteenth, just as there were between the mid-eighteenth and the mid-nineteenth.

The picture is complicated by spatial variations and the complex geography of female involvement in indictable crime, but until the period 1850–1900, at least, there appears to be very little evidence of a long-term decline. Only by using the exceptional period around 1700 as a starting point and by ignoring the evidence from both a series of county studies and from the national and county statistics published after 1805 can the period of the eighteenth and early nineteenth centuries be portrayed as one of decline. From 1750 to 1850, and almost certainly from the mid-seventeenth to the mid-nineteenth century the proportion of females to be found amongst indicted offenders showed very little, if any, sign of significant long-term change. On closer inspection therefore, the vanishing female offender vanishes.

Sept. 11, 1858, 1011. In their introduction to J. Kermode and G. Walker, *Women, Crime and the Courts in Early Modern England* (London, 1994), 4, the authors rightly point out that 'studies of crime which focus primarily upon felonies prosecuted at the courts of assize and quarter sessions under-represent the degree and nature of women's involvement'. They also rightly call for a movement towards considering women's actions within the legal process in context as an antidote to mere quantification. Because 'women have been the minority of those officially prosecuted' they point out 'an emphasis on quantification has resulted in women being duly counted and then discounted'. Whilst agreeing with the need for qualitative studies to balance the quantitative, I hope that this foray into the purely quantitative dimension has helped to put women back into the picture. They were not vanishing and we need detailed qualitative work to understand the significant and changing role they played.

Appendix 6.1 *Females as a percentage of indicted offenders 1805–7*

County	Males	Females	All	% Female
Anglesey	8	2	10	20.00
Bedford	47	11	58	18.97
Berks	120	30	150	20.00
Brecknock	24	13	37	35.14
Buckingham	102	15	117	12.82
Cambridge	84	16	100	16.00
Cardigan	8	2	10	20.00
Camarthen	15	12	27	44.44
Carnarvon	14	3	17	17.65
Chester	209	53	262	20.23
Cornwall	102	34	136	25.00
Cumberland	37	22	59	37.29
Denbigh	9	2	11	18.18
Derby	89	14	103	13.59
Devon	271	90	361	24.93
Dorset	94	27	121	22.31
Durham	60	22	82	26.83
Essex	373	58	431	13.46
Flintshire	8	6	14	42.86
Glamorgan	32	11	43	25.58
Gloucester	206	65	271	23.99
Bristol	98	40	138	28.99
Hants	330	112	442	25.34
Hereford	99	26	125	20.80
Hertford	125	21	146	14.38
Huntingdon	36	5	41	12.20
Kent	472	113	585	19.32
Lancaster	663	445	1108	40.16
Leicester	100	32	132	24.24
Lincoln	148	45	193	23.32
Merioneth	1	0	1	0.00
Middlesex	2187	1390	3577	38.86
Monmouth	36	11	47	23.40
Montgomery	31	10	41	24.39
Norfolk	303	114	417	27.34
Northampton	99	25	124	20.16
Northumberland	59	63	122	51.64
Nottingham	168	48	216	22.22
Oxford	97	21	118	17.80
Pembroke	10	10	20	50.00
Radnor	4	4	8	50.00
Rutland	12	6	18	33.33
Salop	128	50	178	28.09
Somerset	230	64	294	21.77
Stafford	211	64	275	23.27
Suffolk	276	59	335	17.61
Surrey	401	145	546	26.56
Sussex	204	38	242	15.70
Warwick	302	122	424	28.77
Westmorland	14	4	18	22.22
Wilts	182	37	219	16.89
Worcester	131	41	172	23.84
York	472	178	650	27.38
TOTAL	9541	3851	13392	28.76

Appendix 6.2 *Females as a percentage of indicted offenders 1834–8*

County	Male	Female	Total	% Female
Bedford	700	56	756	7.41
Berks	1051	153	1204	12.71
Buckingham	1062	80	1142	7.01
Cambridge	1049	131	1180	11.01
Chester	2503	525	3028	17.34
Cornwall	956	207	1163	17.80
Cumberland	492	145	637	22.76
Derby	936	115	1051	10.94
Devon	2141	714	2855	25.01
Dorset	942	157	1099	14.29
Durham	724	168	892	18.83
Essex	2837	284	3121	9.10
Gloucester	3705	642	4347	14.77
Hants	2386	439	2825	15.54
Hereford	751	136	887	15.33
Hertford	1362	120	1482	8.10
Huntingdon	302	46	348	13.22
Kent	3781	680	4461	15.24
Lancaster	10135	2956	13091	22.58
Leicester	1517	183	1700	10.76
Lincoln	1705	297	2002	14.84
Middlesex	13348	4242	17590	24.12
Monmouth	595	129	724	17.82
Norfolk	2989	373	3362	11.09
Northampton	1063	132	1195	11.05
Northumberland	574	207	781	26.50
Nottingham	1373	207	1580	13.10
Oxford	1199	136	1335	10.19
Rutland	90	14	104	13.46
Salop	1047	173	1220	14.18
Somerset	3417	626	4043	15.48
Stafford	3094	583	3677	15.86
Suffolk	2202	258	2460	10.49
Surrey	3921	967	4888	19.78
Sussex	1855	239	2094	11.41
Warwick	3280	628	3908	16.07
Westmorland	113	21	134	15.67
Wilts	1456	206	1662	12.39
Worcester	1577	242	1819	13.30
York	5479	1125	6604	17.04
Anglesea	46	13	59	22.03
Brecon	116	19	135	14.07
Cardigan	60	5	65	7.69
Carmarthen	153	49	202	24.26
Carnarvon	134	25	159	15.72
Denbigh	273	36	309	11.65
Flint	105	9	114	7.89
Glamorgan	367	118	485	24.33
Merioneth	38	10	48	20.83
Montgomery	175	34	209	16.27
Pembroke	170	66	236	27.97
Radnor	69	12	81	14.81
TOTAL	91415	19138	110553	17.31

Appendix 6.3 *Females as a percentage of indicted offenders 1843–7*

County	Male	Female	Total	% Female
Anglesey	78	24	102	23.53
Bedford	810	98	908	10.79
Berks	1239	221	1460	15.14
Brecknock	196	36	232	15.52
Buckingham	1361	116	1477	7.85
Cambridge	1151	173	1324	13.07
Cardigan	129	26	155	16.77
Camarthen	395	73	468	15.60
Carnarvon	172	27	199	13.57
Chester	3285	836	4121	20.29
Cornwall	1125	338	1463	23.10
Cumberland	444	188	632	29.75
Denbigh	305	77	382	20.16
Derby	1112	166	1278	12.99
Devon	2943	902	3845	23.46
Dorset	1003	202	1205	16.76
Durham	1128	279	1407	19.83
Essex	2648	417	3065	13.61
Flintshire	224	38	262	14.50
Glamorgan	694	273	867	31.49
Gloucester/Bristol	4168	994	5162	19.26
Hants/Southampton	2594	563	3157	17.83
Hereford	856	208	1064	19.55
Hertford	1184	130	1314	9.89
Huntingdon	335	70	405	17.28
Kent	3637	786	4423	17.77
Lancaster	12008	3942	15950	24.71
Leicester	1760	251	2011	12.48
Lincoln	1986	433	2419	17.90
Merioneth	56	14	70	20.00
Middlesex	17219	5324	22543	23.62
Monmouth	950	284	1234	23.01
Montgomery	281	77	358	21.51
Norfolk	3075	608	3683	16.51
Northampton	1200	179	1379	12.98
Northumberland	849	282	1131	24.93
Nottingham	1352	245	1597	15.34
Oxford	1243	217	1460	14.86
Pembroke	284	78	362	21.55
Radnor	106	17	123	13.82
Rutland	133	24	157	15.29
Salop	1429	356	1785	19.94
Somerset	3624	730	4354	16.77
Stafford	3714	942	4656	20.23
Suffolk	2213	385	2598	14.82
Surrey	3921	1102	5023	21.94
Sussex	1887	414	2301	17.99
Warwick	3723	782	4505	17.36
Westmorland	186	35	221	15.84
Wilts	1891	322	2213	14.55
Worcester	2455	545	3000	18.17
York	7133	1633	8766	18.63
TOTAL	107894	26482	134276	19.72

Part III

Non-lethal violence

7. Punishing assault: the transformation of attitudes in the English courts

In early modern England physical violence was regarded as an acceptable instrument of social policy and of individual and group interaction by almost all sectors of society. There were dissenting voices and differences of emphasis, but violence was accepted as the primary means by which the state punished offenders. It was also an intrinsic part of many popular recreations, and was usually seen as a legitimate way to resolve interpersonal disputes. This atmosphere of acceptance changed rapidly, if by no means uniformly, in the late eighteenth and early nineteenth centuries, but research on this vital transition has been confined largely to the first two of these three dimensions.

Many historians have identified the later eighteenth and early nineteenth centuries as a period of fundamental change in attitudes to judicial violence. The replacement of public and physically violent punishments such as hanging, whipping, and branding by new carceral strategies has been subjected to detailed analyses, as have the parallel attacks of the authorities on such forms of popular recreation as cudgelling and bull-baiting, which involved physical violence against either people or animals. However, virtually no research has been undertaken on the changing ways in which the courts punished interpersonal violence. These judicial policies form the main focus of this paper.[1]

Murder and rape, which were capital felonies, have been studied fairly extensively. Here the sentencing options were relatively clear cut. Full conviction

---

[1] See, for example, M. Ignatieff, *A Just Measure of Pain: The Penitentiary and the Industrial Revolution* (London, 1978). The vast relevant literature of historical work and social theory is given innovative treatment in D. Garland, *Punishment and Modern Society* (Oxford, 1990). On popular recreations, see R. Malcolmson, *Popular Recreations in English Society, 1700–1850* (Cambridge, 1973). On the important notion of 'sympathy' and the growing sensibility about violence, see R. McGowen, 'Punishing Violence, Sentencing Crime', in N. Armstrong and L. Tennenhouse (eds.), *The Violence of Representation: Literature and the History of Violence* (London, 1989), 140–56; R. McGowen, 'A Powerful Sympathy: Terror, the Prison, and Humanitarian Reform in Early Nineteenth-Century Britain', *Journal of British Studies*, 25 (1986), 312–34. For an excellent overview that touches briefly on interpersonal disputes, see J. Beattie, 'Violence and Society in Early-Modern England', in A. Doob and E. Greenspan (eds.), *Perspectives in Criminal Law* (Aurora, Ontario, 1985), 36–60.

meant a capital sentence, and only by various forms of partial verdict could other sentences be used. Because the vast majority of assaults and other acts of violence were not defined as felonies, court procedures and sentencing patterns were more diverse and informal. Within that diversity, however, a major transformation can be identified in sentencing policies and court procedures for cases involving assault or assault and battery. Moreover, the timing of that transformation suggests that the magistrates, who were its instigators, were influenced as much by contemporary changes in sentencing policies, by the prison reform movement, and by the growing demand for a reformation of manners amongst the poor, as they were by any general changes in sensibilities about interpersonal violence.[2]

I

The detailed study of interpersonal violence that did not either result in death, or have any overtly sexual content, has been largely neglected by historians. In part, this neglect is related to the fact that most of these disputes were intra- rather than interclass in nature. Historians wanting to use the criminal records to study the nature of the elite's authority and the relationship between the propertied and the poor therefore turned to property crime or to so-called social crime rather than to assault. Equally, whereas murder indictments proved attractive to the quantifying instincts of early historians of crime – because the dark figure of unrecorded crime was thought likely to be a less debilitating problem, and because all murderers were indicted in the major courts where record survival was good – assault cases had none of these advantages. Those who wished to study assault found themselves having to tread the difficult and shifting boundaries between the civil and the criminal law. The eighteenth-century legal textbooks make it clear that most forms of assault could be dealt with under either civil or criminal procedures. The entry under 'Assault and Battery' in Burn's classic magistrates' manual, *The Justice of The Peace and Parish Officer*, for example, observed that

---

[2] See, for example, T. Gurr, 'Historical Trends in Violent Crime. A Critical Review of the Evidence', in M. Tonry and N. Morris (eds.), *Crime and Justice*, 3 (1981), 295–353; L. Stone, 'Interpersonal Violence in English Society 1300–1900', *Past and Present*, 101 (1983), 22–33; J. Sharpe, 'The History of Violence in England: Some Observations', *Past and Present*, 108 (1985), 206–15 and Stone's 'Rejoinder', *ibid.*, 216–24; J. Cockburn, 'Patterns of Violence in English Society: Homicide in Kent 1560–1985', *Past and Present*, 130 (1991), 70–106. On rape, see, for example, A. Clark, *Women's Silence, Men's Violence: Sexual Assault in England, 1770–1845* (London, 1987). For the intermediate offence of manslaughter, which was not a capital felony, see J. Beattie, *Crime and the Courts in England, 1660–1800* (Oxford 1986), 81–113. This work suggests that a similar harshening of punishments occurred in relation to manslaughter as that seen in this article for assault.

There is no doubt that the wrong-doer is subject both to an action at the suit of the party, wherein he shall render damages; and also to an indictment at the suit of the king, wherein he shall be fined according to the heinousness of the offence.[3]

Blackstone's *Commentaries* took a similar approach, dealing with assault both in the third volume, on private wrongs, and in the fourth, on public wrongs. Further problems follow from the fact that assault and battery had an extremely broad definition in law. The actions that lay behind an assault indictment could vary from a threatening gesture to a major nearly fatal beating. Although Burn insisted that 'Notwithstanding the many ancient opinions to the contrary, it seems agreed at this day, that no words whatsoever can amount to an assault', he went on to point out that the threat of violence alone, under certain conditions, constituted an assault. 'Assault,' he wrote, 'is an attempt to offer, with force and violence, to do a corporal hurt to another; as by striking at him with or without a weapon . . . or by holding up one's fist at him; or by any other such like act, done in an angry, threatening manner. And from hence it clearly follows, that one charged with an assault and battery, may be found guilty of the assault, and yet acquitted of the battery.' The definition of battery was equally loose:

Battery seemeth to be, when any injury whatsoever, be it never so small, is actually done to the person of a man, in an angry, or revengeful, or rude, or insolent manner, as by spitting in his face, or any way touching him in anger, or violently justling him out of the way, and the like.[4]

Even setting aside other forms of interpersonal violence, such as riot, property damage, etc. (which might be dealt with under different legal categories), assault and battery alone covered a huge variety of minor acts of aggression. It is not difficult to imagine the customers in a crowded alehouse jostling, pushing, threatening, and hitting each other often enough in one evening to keep the local quarter sessions busy for weeks, if all such acts ended in an indictment.

Any attempt to count assault cases across time and use them as an index of changing levels of interpersonal violence is clearly fraught with difficulty. The dark figure of unrecorded crimes is so huge that it engulfs the relatively small number of acts that reached the courts. Furthermore, since either civil or criminal proceedings could be started by the victim, any increase in criminal

[3] For an overview of the historiography, see J. Innes and J. Styles, 'The Crime Wave: Recent Writing on Crime and Criminal Justice in Eighteenth-Century England', *Journal of British Studies*, 15 (1986), 380–435. Assault, for example, makes virtually no impact on the key volumes such as D. Hay, P. Linebaugh, *et al.* (eds.), *Albion's Fatal Tree* (Harmondsworth, 1975); R. Burn, *The Justice of the Peace and Parish Officer* (London, 1766; 10th edn), i, 100–3; W. Blackstone, *Commentaries on the Laws of England* (Oxford, 1765–1769), iii, 120; iv, 217, 356–7.
[4] Burn, *Justice*, ii, 100–3.

prosecutions could be considered as much a reflection of the changing strategies of victims or constables as a result of variation in the frequency of interpersonal violence.

Assault hearings are also difficult to analyse quantitatively because the vast majority of them never went beyond the summary level. As the justicing note-books of Hunt, Norris, and Whitbread show, only a tiny proportion of assault cases were sent on to the major courts to become formal indictments. Instead, magistrates used a variety of strategies. They often bound over the accused in ways that did not result in indictments, but even more commonly, they either dismissed the case as unfounded or settled it by informal arbitration, which usually resulted in compensation and/or the payment of costs. Out of a sample of nearly a hundred assault-related, petty-sessions examinations recorded at the Lexden and Winstree hundreds in northern Essex in the late eighteenth century, only one appears to have led to formal indictment at the Essex quarter sessions. Since adequate and consistent summary-court records do not survive over extended time periods in any part of England for the eigh-teenth century, quantitative work on summary accusations for assault is rarely rewarding.[5]

The almost complete neglect of assault prosecutions by historians of crime has recently begun to change, as those interested in gender-related issues have started studying domestic violence. However, almost all the detailed work pub-lished so far relates to the later nineteenth century, when the rich vein of divorce-court records became available. There is, as yet, no detailed study of domestic violence in eighteenth-century England, although Hunt and Clark wrote articles in 1992 using small groups of eighteenth-century cases. Apart from a short sec-tion of Sharpe's book on seventeenth-century Essex and a useful and suggestive overview by Beattie, there is also no overall research on interpersonal violence in early-modern England, except for the debate on the nature of homicide and on changing homicide rates across many centuries.[6]

---

[5] Beattie, *Crime*, 74–5. On constables settling assault informally, see L. Radzinowicz, *A History of English Criminal Law and Its Administration from 1750* 5 vols. (London, 1948–1986), ii, 258; P. King, 'Crime, Law and Society in Essex, 1740–1820', PhD Cambridge University, 1984; E. Crittall (ed.), *The Justicing Notebook of William Hunt, 1744–1749* (Wiltshire, 1982); R. Paley (ed.), *Justice in Eighteenth-Century Hackney: The Justicing Notebook of Henry Norris* (London, 1991); A. Cirket (ed.), *Samuel Whitbread's Notebooks, 1810–11, 1813–14* (Bedfordshire, 1971). Assault also came before the manorial court, but, by this period, most of these courts had declined and no longer heard such cases.

[6] M. Hunt, 'Wife-Beating, Domesticity and Women's Independence in Eighteenth-Century London', *Gender and History*, 4 (1992), 10–33; A. Clark, 'Humanity or Justice? Wife beating and the Law in the Eighteenth and Nineteenth Centuries', in C. Smart (ed.), *Regulating Womanhood* (London, 1992), 187–206; M. Doggett, *Marriage, Wife Beating and the Law in Victorian England* (London, 1992); A. Hammerton, *Cruelty and Companionship: Conflict in Nineteenth-Century Married Life* (London, 1992); J. Sharpe, *Crime in Seventeenth-Century England: A County Study* (Cambridge, 1983), 115–23; Beattie, 'Violence and Society'.

The court records can be used in a number of ways to explore the evolving nature of disputes that ended in an assault prosecution. The availability of good petty-sessions and/or quarter-sessions depositions over extended periods would make it possible to develop a typology and then analyse changes in the mixture of cases across time. However, any such system of categorisation would entail problems, and, since neither assault depositions nor petty-sessions examinations were treated as formal documents of record during the period of this study, their survival is extremely fitful. Other types of record – diaries, newspaper reports, prison calendars, justice of the peace notebooks, and police records – could also provide important insights. Davis' work on the later nineteenth-century disputes, for example, has shown the value of the newspaper reports about petty-sessions and police-court hearings that begin to become available around the middle of the nineteenth century. For the eighteenth and early nineteenth centuries, however, the most readily available and most consistent records that have survived are the indictments and recognizances that were created when cases were brought to the major courts. Since the vast majority of these cases went to the quarter sessions rather than to the assizes, the quarter-sessions records are the key sources.[7]

Recognizances, as Shoemaker's work on London has shown, can demonstrate the different strategies that victims and magistrates adopted in dealing with assault-related disputes. Moreover, in counties such as Essex, where the clerks systematically recorded the victim's occupation on the recognizance, these records show that the labouring poor, as well as the middling sort, made extensive use of the assault prosecuting process. For the purposes of this article, however, the quarter-sessions indictments serve as the key source, because they record the verdict and the punishment. The indictments are not informative about the context or nature of the assault, but they can be used to divide the offences into four categories – simple assaults, assaults on officials (usually constables), assaults related to a sexual attack, and assaults indicted as part of a broader accusation of riot. (The last have been excluded from this analysis because the court was reacting primarily to the act of riot rather than to the accompanying assault.) The former three categories and the gender and occupation of the accused have been used here to highlight different aspects of changing verdict and punishment patterns over time. The results – preliminary though they are, since they relate to only one county – suggest that sentencing policies in assault cases have received far too little attention from historians.

[7] J. Davis, 'Prosecutions and their Context: The Use of the Criminal Law in Late Nineteenth Century London', in D. Hay and F. Snyder (eds.), *Policing and Prosecution in Britain 1750–1850* (Oxford, 1989). See also N. Tomes, 'A Torrent of Abuse: Crimes of Violence between Working-Class Men and Women in London, 1840–75', *Journal of Social History*, 11 (1978), 328–45.

Table 7.1 *Punishment structure for all types of assault, Essex quarter sessions, 1748–1821*

Sentence receiced	1748–52	1770–4	1793–7	1819–21	Average Percentage for all sample periods
Not guilty (%)	12.5	16.7	18.7	20.8	17.7
Fined 1/- or less (%)	73.2	61.9	34.1	13.2	42.2
Fined over 1/- (%)	5.4	3.8	7.7	13.2	7.8
Imprisoned (%)	3.6	13.1	31.9	51.6	27.6
Removed by *certiorari* (%)	5.4	4.8	7.7	1.1	4.6
Total known (%)	*100.1*	*100.3*	*100.1*	*99.9*	*99.9*
(Sample size)	*(56)*	*(84)*	*(91)*	*(91)*	*(322)*
(Unknown)	*(22)*	*(12)*	*(13)*	*(7)*	
(Total sample size)	*(78)*	*(96)*	*(104)*	*(98)*	

Notes: All raw data are shown in italicised form and placed in parentheses. 'Removed by *certiorari*' meant that the case was removed to a higher court.
Source: Essex Record Office, process book of indictments, Q/SPb, 10–19.

Fundamental changes were taking place, and the nature of those changes raises a number of questions requiring detailed research.[8]

II

The pattern of outcomes in assault cases at the Essex quarter sessions, as recorded in the process book of indictments, was very different in the mid-eighteenth century from that found in 1820 (see Table 7.1). Four subperiods, usually of five-years duration, were sampled at roughly twenty-five-year intervals. During the first of these periods, 1748–52, virtually the only punishment imposed on those found guilty of assault was a nominal fine of one shilling or less, reflecting the essentially civil mode of proceedings in such cases. Assaults, as Beattie has pointed out, were treated more as private than as public concerns. Once offenders were convicted, they normally reached a settlement with their victims, the magistrates simply recording a nominal fine and dismissing the case. Only when this routine was not followed did magistrates impose substantial fines, or, in exceptional instances, resort to imprisonment. By the final sample period, 1819–21, this pattern had reversed: 13 per cent of cases were resolved by nominal fines, as opposed to the 73 per cent seventy years earlier;

[8] R. Shoemaker, *Prosecution and Punishment: Petty Crime and the Law in London and Rural Middlesex c. 1660–1725* (Cambridge, 1991); P. King, 'Decision-makers and Decision-making in the English Criminal Law, 1750–1800', *Historical Journal*, 27 (1984); Beattie, *Crime*, 459.

Table 7.2 *Punishment structure for plain assault, Essex quarter sessions, 1748–1821*

Sentence received	1748–52	1770–4	1793–7	1819–21	Average Percentage for all sample periods
Not guilty (%)	18.4	17.2	19.8	27.0	21.0
Fined 1/- or less (%)	60.5	65.5	37.0	15.9	42.1
Fined over 1/- (%)	7.9	1.7	8.6	12.7	7.9
Imprisoned (%)	5.3	13.8	25.9	42.9	24.2
Removed by *certiorari* (%)	7.9	1.7	8.6	1.6	5.0
Total known (%)	*100.0*	*99.9*	*99.9*	*100.1*	*100.2*
(Sample size)	*(38)*	*(58)*	*(81)*	*(63)*	*(240)*
(Unknown)	*(12)*	*(6)*	*(12)*	*(6)*	
(Total sample size)	*(50)*	*(64)*	*(93)*	*(69)*	

Notes: All raw data are shown in italicised form and placed in parentheses. 'Removed by *certiorari*' meant that the case was removed to a higher court.
Source: Essex Record Office, process book of indictments, Q/SPb, 10–19.

Table 7.3 *Punishment structure for assault upon an official, Essex quarter sessions, 1748–1821*

Sentence received	1748–52	1770–4	1793–7	1819–21	Total Percentage for all sample periods
Not guilty (%)	0.0	8.7	0.0	7.7	5.4
Fined 1/- or less (%)	100.0	56.5	14.3	7.7	45.9
Fined over 1/- (%)	0.0	8.7	0.0	15.4	8.1
Imprisoned (%)	0.0	13.0	85.7	69.2	36.5
Removed by *certiorari* (%)	0.0	13.0	0.0	0.0	4.1
Total known (%)	*100.0*	*99.9*	*100.0*	*100.0*	*100.0*
(Sample size)	*(18)*	*(23)*	*(7)*	*(26)*	*(74)*
(Unknown)	*(10)*	*(6)*	*(0)*	*(1)*	
(Total sample size)	*(28)*	*(29)*	*(7)*	*(27)*	

Notes: All raw data are shown in italicised form and placed in parentheses. 'Removed by *certiorari*' meant that the case was removed to a higher court.
Sources: Essex Record Office, process book of indictments, Q/SPb, 10–19.

Table 7.4 *Punishment structure for assault with intent to ravish, Essex quarter sessions, 1748–1821*

Sentence received	Percentage for all sample periods
Not guilty	37.6
Fined 1/- or less	12.6
Fined over 1/-	0.0
Imprisoned	50.0
Removed by *certiorari*	0.0
Total known	*100.2*
(Sample size)	*(8)*
(Unknown)	*(1)*
(Total sample size)	*(9)*

Notes: All raw data are shown in italicised form and placed in parentheses. 'Removed by *certiorari*' meant that the case was moved to a higher court.
Source: Essex Record Office, process book of indictments, Q/SPb, 10–19.

slightly more than 50 per cent of those convicted were imprisoned, compared with the 4 per cent in the mid-eighteenth century; and fines that were not nominal doubled from 5 to 13 per cent. This pattern obtained in cases involving assaults on private individuals, as well as in cases involving assaults on officials, such as constables (see Tables 7.2 and 7.3).

By the late eighteenth century, the latter tended to be punished more heavily. The small number of cases involving assault with intent to ravish indicate that an even higher proportion of convicted offenders were imprisoned (see Table 7.4). Overall, therefore, the period between 1750 and 1820 saw a clear shift from a nominal fine to imprisonment for all types of assault.[9]

This change was accompanied by a parallel shift in pleas and jury verdicts. As Table 7.1 indicates, the proportion of offenders found not guilty rose substantially between 1750 and 1820. However, this development was less a reflection of new jury attitudes than of a sea change in how the accused chose to plead. Between 1748 and 1752, more than three quarters of the accused confessed to the offence (see Table 7.5). By 1819–21, however, only 13 per cent did so. Most trials in the mid-eighteenth century ended before they had begun, no doubt reflecting the likelihood of an informal agreement between victim and accused. As assault indictments were treated more and more in the manner of criminal rather than civil proceedings, fewer of the accused were willing to

[9] See Beattie, 'Violence', 42, for a discussion of nominal fining. This pattern of movement toward imprisonment continued after 1820, if the Black Country figures are any guide. D. Philips, *Crime and Authority in Victorian England* (London, 1977), 268.

Table 7.5 *Verdicts for all types of assault, Essex quarter sessions, 1748–1821*

Sentence received	1748–52	1770–4	1793–7	1819–21	Total Percentage for all sample periods
Guilty (%)	9.1	18.8	44.2	66.7	38.2
Not guilty (%)	12.8	17.5	19.8	20.4	18.2
Confessed (%)	78.2	64.0	36.0	13.0	43.6
Total known (%)	*100.1*	*100.3*	*100.0*	*100.1*	*100.0*
(Sample size)	*(55)*	*(80)*	*(86)*	*(93)*	*(314)*
(Unknown)	*(23)*	*(16)*	*(18)*	*(5)*	
(Total sample size)	*(78)*	*(96)*	*(104)*	*(98)*	

Note: All raw data are shown in italicised form and placed in parentheses.
Source: Essex Record Office, process book of indictments, Q/SPb, 10–19.

risk confession. Jurors' attitudes did not, as Table 7.1 seems to imply, incline increasingly toward mercy as more serious penalties were introduced. Instead, the ratio of guilty to not-guilty verdicts increased from near parity in the third quarter of the eighteenth century to more than three to one in 1819–21 (see Table 7.5). Both judges and juries were getting tougher on those accused of assault.

These parallel transformations in sentencing policies, verdicts, and pleas began slowly in the third quarter of the eighteenth century, but the greatest changes appear to have occurred between the sample periods 1770–4 and 1793–7. Confessions and nominal fines fell from around two thirds to just over one third of trial pleas and trial outcomes, while the proportion of offenders imprisoned rose 250 per cent. Although all of these trends continued to gather pace well into the nineteenth century, assault cases at the Essex quarter sessions seem to have lost their essentially civil character in the period between the American War of Independence and the beginning of the French wars.

This change did not coincide with a decline in assault indictments. In 1748–52, the Essex process book recorded an average of sixteen such cases per year. In the three-year period 1819–21, this figure had doubled to nearly thirty three per year, indicating that indictment levels had more than kept up with population increase. The process book excluded indictments that were 'not found' by the grand jury and therefore never came to public trial, but, even when these are included in the count, along with the small number of assault accusations that were heard at the assizes, the same pattern of increasing indictment levels emerges (see Table 7.6). After a decline between the 1750s and 1760s, the number of assault indictments brought to the Essex courts more than doubled in the next thirty years. Unlike murder rates, which were

Table 7.6 *Assault indictments, Essex quarter sessions and assizes, 1750–1800*

Decade	Number of indictments
1750–9	185
1760–9	130
1770–9	178
1780–9	224
1790–9	279

Sources: Essex Record Office, Q/SPb, 10–17; and, for 1776–82 when no process book is available, quarter-sessions rolls. Occasional damage to some of these rolls may have caused slight undercounting in these years. For the assizes: Public Record Office, Assi 35/190–240.

in long-term decline during this period, assault indictments were rising fairly rapidly from 1750 to 1820, providing a cautionary note to those who wish to use murder rates as a guide to more general changes in levels of interpersonal violence.

The verdicts and sentences analysed in Tables 7.1–7.4 do not represent the typical outcome of assault cases in this period. The vast majority of cases continued to be heard informally at the petty-sessions level, where the magistrates had no formal powers to imprison the accused until after the period studied here. However, although the cases analysed in Tables 7.1 to 7.4 represent the tip of the iceberg above a broader petty-sessions-based system that was not formally empowered to imprison offenders, the importance of the transformations observed at the Essex quarter sessions should not be underestimated. This phenomenon was not confined to Essex. Beattie's less detailed work indicates that a similar change was occurring in Surrey. Almost all those convicted of assault before 1750 were fined, but from 1780 to 1800, nearly one fifth of Surrey assault convicts were imprisoned. Why did these quarter-sessions benches turn away from token fines and embrace imprisonment so wholeheartedly? Why did jurors harshen their verdicts and offenders abandon confessions?[10]

III

To what extent was this transformation related to changes in the nature of the offences or offenders coming before the courts? It was certainly not confined

[10] See footnote 2 for the participants in the debate about murder rates. These murder rates may be less interesting than the changing contexts in which murder occurred. For a suggestive study, see A. Parrella, 'Industrialisation and Murder: Northern France, 1815–1914, *Journal of Interdisciplinary History*, 22 (1992), 627–54. For the Surrey data, see Beattie, *Crime*, 609.

Table 7.7 *Punishment structure by gender for all types of assault, Essex quarter sessions, 1748–1821*

Sentence received	Total male	Total female
Not guilty (%)	16.7	31.8
Fined 1/- or less (%)	42.3	40.9
Fined over 1/- (%)	8.3	0.0
Imprisoned (%)	28.0	22.7
Removed by *certiorari* (%)	4.7	4.5
Total known (%)	*100.0*	99.9
(Sample size)	*(300)*	*(22)*
(Unknown)	*(48)*	*(6)*
(Total sample size)	*(348)*	*(28)*

Notes: All raw data are shown in italicised form and placed in parentheses.
'Removed by *certiorari*' meant that the case was removed to a higher court.
Source: Essex Record Office, process book of indictments, Q/SPb, 10–19.

to one type of assault; it can be observed in both plain assault cases and those involving violence against officials (see Tables 7.2 and 7.3). Although it is conceivable that the proportion of indictments for plain assault that arose from particularly dangerous or frightening forms of violence had increased between 1750 and 1820, there is no evidence that this increase occurred. Indeed, if Place's observation was right – that the population was getting less 'gross and brutal' in this period – then the opposite may well have been true. Further research on depositions and contemporary diaries is required, but it seems unlikely that the increasingly harsh sentencing policies in Table 7.2 were a reaction to a major change in the types of assault cases being sent on to the quarter sessions by committing magistrates. Did the nature of the offenders and victims involved in these cases change?[11]

The gender of the accused did not alter significantly. Only 8 per cent of the offenders indicted for assault in the four sample periods were women, and this percentage remained steady throughout. Women did obtain a higher proportion of not-guilty verdicts than men and, as a result, were slightly less likely to be imprisoned (see Table 7.7); but the sample size is too small to conclude with any certainty that assaults by females were treated less seriously or more leniently. The gender of the person assaulted made even less impact on sentencing policy (see Table 7.8). The proportion of female victims did decline to some extent, from 26 per cent in the 1770s to 17 per cent in 1819–21, but since those who assaulted women received treatment from the courts similar to that of those who assaulted men (Table 7.8), this change

[11] M. Thale (ed.), *The Autobiography of Francis Place* (Cambridge, 1972), 82, quoted in Beattie, *Crime*, 137.

Table 7.8 *Punishment structure for plain assault by gender of victim, Essex quarter sessions, 1770–1821*

Sentence received	Total male	Total female
Not guilty (%)	18.6	19.5
Fined 1/- or less (%)	31.3	36.6
Fined over 1/- (%)	7.6	4.9
Imprisoned (%)	27.9	24.4
Removed by *certiorari* (%)	4.7	2.4
Unknown (%)	9.9	12.2
Total (%)	100.0	100.0
(Sample size)	*(172)*	*(41)*

Notes: All raw data are shown in italicised form and placed in parentheses. 'Removed by *certiorari*' meant that the case was removed to a higher court. No data on gender of victim is available in the process book of indictments for 1748–52.
Source: Essex Record Office, process book of indictments, Q/SPb, 10–19.

would not account for the transformation in sentencing policies. Indictments for domestic violence were rare. Only a handful of husbands were indicted for this offence by the Essex quarter sessions during the last third of the eighteenth century. It appears that, like the Wiltshire and London justices of the peace, William Hunt and Henry Norris, whose justicing books have survived, the Essex magistrates dealt with almost all such assaults informally at the petty sessions. Hence, at the quarter-sessions level, changing attitudes to domestic violence, which by the mid-nineteenth century had resulted in special legislative initiatives designed to discipline violent husbands more severely, did not have any significant impact on sentencing policies between 1750 and 1820.[12]

Did the social status of victims or accused change significantly in ways that might have affected sentencing policy? The occupational structure of the prosecutors bound by recognisances in assault cases did not change significantly between 1760 and 1800 (see Table 7.9). During this period, approximately 26 per cent of those whose occupations are known were labourers, nearly another

[12] The decline in the proportion of assault offenders who were women is of interest in itself of course. Were women being attacked less, or being less protected by the law when they were attacked? Were magistrates dealing with a greater proportion of minor assaults on women at the summary stage? In Essex, the sources give little indication of how these questions might be answered. M. May, 'Violence in the Family: An Historical Perspective', in J. Martin (ed.), *Violence in the Family* (Chichester, 1978), 143–5; Clark, 'Humanity or Justice', 199–201.

Table 7.9 *Occupations of prosecutors for assault, Essex quarter sessions, 1760–1800*

Occupation	1760–9: (%)	1770–9: (%)	1780–9: (%)	1790–9: (%)	Total 1760–99: (%)
Gentlemen	3.0	1.9	3.2	3.4	3.0
Professionals	0.0	0.0	1.6	1.1	0.8
Farmers/yeomen	24.2	15.4	22.2	25.0	22.0
Husbandmen/gardeners	0.0	1.9	3.2	5.7	3.4
Tradesmen and artisans	45.5	46.2	42.9	36.4	41.5
Sea trades	3.0	3.8	3.2	3.4	3.4
Labourers	24.2	30.8	23.8	25.0	25.8
Number in sample	33	52	63	88	236

Note: Those whose occupations are unknown are excluded, as are women (10 per cent) and officials/military men/servants (8 per cent).
Source: Essex Record Office, Q/SMg, 19–28.

22 per cent were farmers, nearly half were tradesmen or artisans, and 3 per cent were gentlemen.[13]

Information about the occupations of the accused is much more difficult to ascertain. Unfortunately, in the second half of the eighteenth century, the Essex quarter-sessions clerks gradually changed their methods of recording the occupation or social status of the accused. After 1750, they began to adopt the normal assizes practice of using the three stereotyped terms, labourer, yeoman, and gentlemen. As a result, the proportion of accused males placed under these three headings rose from 30 per cent in 1748–52 to 51 per cent in 1770–4 and to 72 per cent in 1792–7. This system eventually eradicated the range of occupations found in the earlier period. The proportion of those accused of assault called labourers rose threefold, the proportion labelled yeomen rose two-and-a-half times, and the proportion listed as artisans declined from nearly two thirds to one quarter of the entries in the process book of indictments. The clerks clearly were using the terms 'labourer' and 'yeoman' more frequently, presumably transferring the poorer artisans into the former category and the richer tradesmen – such as millers and innkeepers (who were often minor land-holders) – into the latter category. Although the occupations in the indictments appear to suggest that an increasing proportion of assault prosecutions were directed against yeomen and labourers, there is no evidence that this was the

[13] Essex Record Office (ERO), recognizances to prosecute, Q/SMg, 19–28. A minority of those bound by recognizance to prosecute for assault settled out of court or failed to appear. Thus, this is not exactly a sample of those who actually indicted someone. It is possible, for example, that a higher proportion of lower-status prosecutors dropped out at this stage.

case. As the indirect evidence of the recognizances shows, artisans did not suddenly become less aggressive or litigious. Until the early nineteenth century at least, prosecution for assault was not an experience confined to the poor.[14]

Given the increasingly problematic nature of the occupational information in the indictment books, the impact of the social status of the accused on verdicts and punishments is difficult to measure. However, it is interesting to note that, although the courts never put gentlemen in jail and were more likely to imprison perpetrators of low status, by the 1790s, even those regarded as yeomen could find themselves in prison if their assaults were regarded as particularly heinous.[15]

IV

If neither the gender nor the social status of victims and accused help to explain the transformation of sentencing patterns in assault cases, what were the influential variables? Unfortunately, there is little direct evidence available about the motives and thoughts of the quarter-sessions magistrates who were behind the changes. Quarter-sessions trials were not formally recorded and were rarely reported in the newspapers or in printed trial reports. Moreover, the private papers of the Essex gentry say little about the magistrates' awareness of this change, let alone their reaction to it.

However, by the second half of the eighteenth century powerful legal voices were calling for an end to the use of nominal fines in assault cases. The final volume of Blackstone's *Commentaries,* published in 1769, contained the following pointed critique:

It is not uncommon, when a person is convicted of . . . a battery . . . for the court to permit the defendant to *speak with the prosecutor*, before any judgement is pronounced; and, if the prosecutor declares himself satisfied, to inflict but a trivial punishment. This is done, to reimburse the prosecutor his expenses, and make him some private amends, without the trouble and circuity of a civil action. But it surely is a dangerous practice: and, though it may be intrusted to the prudence and discretion of the judges in the superior courts of record, it ought never to be allowed in local or inferior jurisdictions, such as the quarter-sessions; where prosecutions for assaults are by this means too frequently commenced, rather for private lucre than for the great ends of

---

[14] ERO, process books of indictments. Q/SPb, 10–19. Single woman's occupations were never given, either before or after this change, and so they have been excluded. The occupations of the husbands of married women were usually given, and they suffered from the trend toward stereotyping.

[15] During the three sample periods, 1748–52, 1770–4, 1793–7, the overall percentages were labourers 32 per cent; yeomen 19 per cent; gentlemen nil; artisans, tradesmen, seatraders, and all others not in the former three categories, 67 per cent. Five of the seven yeomen who were imprisoned received their sentences in the period 1793–7.

public justice. . . For, although a private citizen may dispense with satisfaction for his private injury, he cannot remove the necessity of public example. The right of punishing belongs not to any one individual in particular, but to the society in general, or the sovereign who represents that society: and a man may renounce his own portion of this right, but he cannot give up that of others.[16]

This demand for the transfer of assault cases from the private to the public sphere, backed as it was by copious quotes from Cesare Beccaria, was published and widely read at the very time when those accused of assault in the quarter sessions were beginning to experience a transformation of precisely this kind. Whether in response to Blackstone or not, in the final third of the eighteenth century, the quarter-sessions bench in Essex and in Surrey acted increasingly along the lines that he was advocating by abandoning nominal fines and using imprisonment in a growing number of cases. By the late 1790s, this trend was noted by Colquhoun in his brief references to assault, and he clearly wanted the trend toward heavier punishments for interpersonal violence to continue. 'It is the triumph of liberty', he wrote, quoting Montesquieu,

> when the criminal laws proportion punishments to the particular nature of the offence . . . In offences which are considered by the legislature as merely personal and not of the class of public wrongs, the disproportion is extremely shocking. If, for instance, a personal assault is committed of the most cruel, aggravated, and violent nature, the offender is seldom punished in any other manner than by a fine and imprisonment, but if the delinquent steals from his neighbour secretly more than the value of twelve pence, the law dooms him to death.[17]

Both Blackstone's and Colquhoun's arguments were centred on legal issues rather than on emotional or psychological ones, but, by the mid-nineteenth century, the work of another eminent legal writer, Stephens, suggested that a much less distanced reaction had become the norm. 'That sharp pain should be inflicted on anyone under any circumstances', he wrote in 1860, 'shocks and scandalises people in these days.' Many historians of crime and law in Britain have argued that the period from the mid-eighteenth to the mid-nineteenth century witnessed a fundamental shift in attitudes toward interpersonal violence and a growing sensitivity to, and repugnance of, overt acts of aggression. The cessation of public physical punishments, the decline in the murder rate, and the withering of support for violent forms of recreation all strongly suggest such a shift. Beattie, for example, has argued cogently that the high tolerance of physical violence exhibited by most sectors of society until the mid-eighteenth century was replaced by a growing antipathy toward cruelty or violence:

---

[16] Blackstone, *Commentaries*, iv, 356–7.
[17] P. Colquhoun, *A Treatise on the Police of the Metropolis* (London, 1796; 2nd edn), 265–6.

'Attitudes towards violence and the character of violence itself both appear to have changed in some significant ways in the later eighteenth century each no doubt encouraged by the other.'[18]

These persuasive arguments fit well with Elias' generalised model centring on a longer term 'civilising process' that, he suggests, was producing growing levels of self-restraint and an ever-stronger and more wide-ranging set of cultural assumptions that rejected open displays of aggression. However, it is difficult to account for the transformation of judicial attitudes to assault indictments, as seen in Table 7.1, purely by reference to a new repugnance toward violence, because it does not explain the timing of the change. The growing distaste for interpersonal violence was far from complete by 1820. As Conley's work on Kent has shown, even after 1850 many men and women from a broad range of social backgrounds still believed that it was legitimate to retaliate physically to verbal provocations.[19]

Nor was the decline in violent punishments a unilinear process. Cockburn recently suggested that levels of judicial violence were higher in the eighteenth century than they had been in the early modern period, pointing to major elements of continuity in the attitudes of the courts toward violent punishments before the mid-nineteenth century. A fairly broad consensus on the desirability and effectiveness of corporal punishment survived, he argues, well into the nineteenth century, with further revivals of interest in later periods. In 1862, for example, an act of parliament reintroduced flogging as an extra punishment for armed robbers, and, as late as 1875, the Kent magistrates were urging that the use of flogging be increased against juvenile offenders and those convicted of assault. Although sentencing policies in assault cases were transformed between 1750 and 1790, many parallel changes in other parts of the judicial system did not occur until considerably later. The Essex courts continued to make extensive use of hanging between 1750 and 1790. The proportion of capital convicts who were hanged remained relatively stable and began to decline decisively only after 1800. It took a further three decades before parliament finally swept away most of the capital code.[20]

---

[18] J. Stephens, *Essays by a Barrister* (London, 1862), 142–9, quoted in M. Wiener, 'Changing Attitudes to Violence in Nineteenth-Century Britain', paper presented at the International Association for the History of Crime and Criminal Justice (IAHCCJ) Conference (Paris, 1994). Beattie, *Crime*, 138; Clark, 'Humanity or Justice', 189.

[19] N. Elias, *The Civilising Process* (Oxford, 1978–1982; originally published 1939); Garland, *Punishment*, 213–47; C. Conley, *The Unwritten Law: Criminal Justice in Victorian Kent* (Oxford, 1991), 48–9.

[20] J. Cockburn, 'Punishment and Brutalization in the English Enlightenment', *Law and History Review*, 12 (1994), 155–79. Although the rate of assault prosecutions declined in the late Victorian period, it remained remarkably high at mid-century, compared with other types of offence. V. Gatrell, 'The Decline of Theft and Violence in Victorian and Edwardian England', in V. Gatrell, B. Lenman, and G. Parker (eds.), *Crime and the Law: The Social History of Crime in Western Europe since 1500* (London, 1980), 288: King, 'Crime', 334–88.

Moreover, there were no substantial legislative changes concerning the treatment of violent offenders between 1750 and 1790. Apart from the 1803 Act that increased the penalties for those who attempted to murder or seriously injure, the period 1790–1820 was also largely devoid of legislative change. Not until 1828 did any major enactment substantially affect the law of assault. Significantly, this act was directed mainly at the magistrates in petty sessions and did little more than formalise existing practice by empowering two justices 'to hear and determine' assault cases and impose fines of up to £5. Although the 1828 Act enabled magistrates to imprison those unable to pay their fines for up to two months, not until the early 1860s were they formally given the right to decide between a fine and imprisonment in the first instance. This delay did not prevent the transfer of the vast majority of assault cases to the petty-sessions courts. Almost all of the small number of assaults formally indicted at the Essex quarter sessions by the 1840s either were committed against officials or involved some other form of aggravated circumstance. Indictments for plain assault, which were increasing in number in the quarter century before the 1828 Act, had virtually disappeared from the quarter-sessions indictment book by the mid-1840s.[21]

The absence, before 1820, of any significant legislative enactment that would have made it easier to punish those accused of assault, and the failure of parliament to make significant inroads into the capital code until after that date, suggests that the growing sensitivity toward violence was by no means uniform across the criminal justice system. Why did the quarter-sessions magistrates start to take assault cases seriously half a century before significant legislative initiatives emerged, and, indeed, several decades before the courts themselves made a decisive turn away from hanging and public whipping in the first few years of the nineteenth century? Clearly questions about timing cannot be answered simply by reference to the gradual development of sensibilities in the eighteenth and nineteenth centuries. Although this trend forms the necessary background, several other factors need to be considered in order to explain the transformations in sentencing policies toward assault.

V

Those convicted of assault were not the only ones who found themselves in danger of incarceration by the Essex quarter sessions after 1750. The bench

---

[21] S. Stone, *The Justice's Pocket Manual* (London, 1842; 2nd edn), 18–19; S. Stone, *The Justice's Manual or Guide to the Ordinary Duties of a Justice of the Peace* (London, 1873; 16th edn), 62–3, for details of 9 Geo.4.c.31, and 24 and 25 Vict.c.100. The former act replaced, and built on, Lord Ellenborough's Act of 1803. Gatrell, 'Decline', 358, indicates that by 1850, more than 99 per cent of common assaults were tried summarily rather than committed for trial. ERO, Q/SPb, 23–4. This was also the pattern in the Black Country – Philips, *Crime and Authority*, 262.

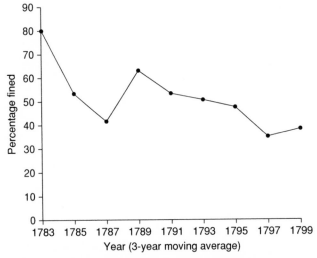

Figure 7.1 Percentage of assault convicts given a nominal fine 1783–99 (Essex).
Note: Based on 3-year moving averages taken every two years.
Source: Essex Record Office, Q/SPb, 8–17.

was also turning to imprisonment to deal with an increasing number of petty-larceny convicts. At first, their policies toward minor thieves and violent offenders developed along similar lines. In the period 1748–52, only 4.9 per cent of those convicted of petty larceny in Essex were imprisoned, whereas 3.6 per cent of those accused of assault and 4.1 per cent of those found guilty of that offence were given prison sentences. By 1770–4, the figures rose to 14.8 per cent of petty-larceny convicts and 13.7 per cent of assault convicts. In the 1780s, as the transportation crisis deepened, imprisonment became the customary punishment for petty larceny. By 1793–7, 89 per cent of petty-larceny convicts were imprisoned and, similarly, if less decisively, 40 per cent of assault cases now drew prison sentences. However, Figures 7.1– 7.3 suggest that the main change from fines to imprisonment for assault cases occurred between 1784 and 1788, whereas the sudden increase in imprisonment for petty-larceny cases occurred five years earlier, between 1779 and 1784. It seems likely that, during the later 1780s, the precedent already set for petty larceny was an important influence on the quarter-sessions propensity to confer prison sentences in assault cases. As incarceration became an increasingly appropriate and useful sanction against petty thieves, those who wanted to move assault proceedings away from their predominantly civil mode could now point to the existence of a viable and flexible alternative.[22]

---

[22] ERO, Q/SPb, 8–17. For detailed analysis of changing sentencing policies toward petty offenders, see King 'Crime', 334–9.

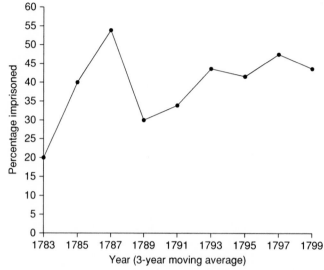

Figure 7.2 Percentage of assault convicts imprisoned 1783–99 (Essex).
Note: Based on 3-year moving averages calculated every two years.
Source: Essex Record Office, Q/SPb, 8–17.

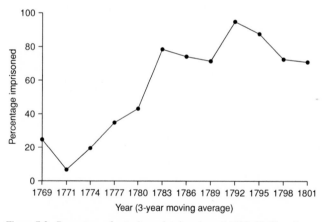

Figure 7.3 Percentage of petty larcenists imprisoned 1783–99 (Essex).
Note: Based on 3-year moving averages calculated every two years.
Source: Essex Record Office, Q/SPb, 8–17.

Flexibility was certainly part of the attraction of imprisonment. Although three quarters of those found guilty of assault received sentences of three months or less, the range of sentences varied from a few days to two years (see Table 7.10). The length of imprisonment for assault was remarkably similar to imprisonment for petty larceny and, from the later 1780s, when the quarter-sessions

Table 7.10 *Range of imprisonment sentences for assault, petty and grand larceny, Essex quarter sessions, 1770–1820*

	Assault			Petty larceny		Grand larceny
Length of Imprisonment	1770–4	1793–7	1819–21	1776–85	1786–1804	1786–1804
Up to 1 month (%)	30	42	41	50	51	42
1.1 to 3 months (%)	50	30	43	33	33	30
3.1 to 6 months (%)	10	15	9	9	12	17
6 months or more (%)	10	12	9	7	3	12
(*Sample size*)	(*10*)	(*26*)	(*47*)	(*96*)	(*274*)	(*113*)

Note: The Period, 1748–52, was excluded from the sample because only two assault convicts were imprisoned. Of petty thieves, 37 per cent were also whipped in 1776–85, and 18 per cent in 1786–1804; in 1776–1804, 28 per cent of grand-larceny convicts were also whipped.
Source: Essex Record Office, Q/SPb, 9–19. Sentences in which length is unknown have been excluded. For further details, see King, 'Crime, Law and Society in Essex, 1740–1820', unpub. PhD thesis (Cambridge, 1984).

jurisdiction expanded, for grand larceny also, the only major difference being that many petty thieves were subjected to the additional penalty of whipping. A parallel form of flexibility might have been achieved in assault cases had the courts instituted a sliding scale of fines – as they had, to some extent, in the seventeenth century – instead of the single, nominal fine. However, by the eighteenth century, those involved in assault cases were much more plebeian than they had been a century earlier, and a graded system of fines was less appropriate when a growing proportion of those convicted hardly had the resources to pay even a minimal sum. Hence, imprisonment provided a much more practical form of flexibility.[23]

The availability of sufficient prison accommodation may also have influenced the Essex magistrates' decision to move toward imprisonment in assault cases. The county's main gaol had been rebuilt in the 1770s, following an outbreak of gaol fever, and, by the mid-1780s, a large new house of correction was being constructed at Halstead after the old one had been destroyed by fire. More important, however, the nature of the regimes to which prisoners were to be subjected came under intense review during this period, as a movement for prison reform began to gain momentum. The writings of Howard, Hanway, and others, which claimed that hygienic, highly regulated prison regimes – including regular religious instruction, strict work schedules, and an element of solitary confinement – offered a way of reforming offenders, were gaining influence. By the early 1780s, the new climate of reform, which these writings

[23] Sharpe, *Crime in Seventeenth-Century*, 119.

both reflected and helped to create, was affecting not only decisions about prison construction and prison systems, but also more general attitudes toward offenders. Magistrates and county benches were considering the possibility that minor offenders could be reformed by stricter imprisonment policies. As one commentator noted at the beginning of the decade, solitary confinement, work, and religious instruction were particularly appropriate for offenders who 'from their age, infirmities, or the slight nature of their crimes [were] improper objects for any severer punishments'.[24]

Although Essex was not in the forefront of the prison reform movement, this major rethinking of attitudes toward imprisonment by no means passed the county by. It was in the forefront of the magistrates' minds from the mid-1780s onward, and resulted in the introduction of solitary cells in the county gaol and in two houses of correction in 1786. The impetus behind this attempt to introduce what Hanway called 'the humane rigour of solitary confinement' had largely dissipated by the mid-1790s. However, for seven or eight years after the initial decision to build solitary cells, the Essex quarter-sessions bench was clearly involved in the wave of enthusiasm for solitary confinement and prison reform, which resulted in a more extensive programme of prison rebuilding in counties such as Sussex, Norfolk, Lancashire, and Gloucestershire. Between 1788 and 1793, the Essex quarter sessions sentenced an average of six offenders a year to solitary confinement. Moreover, these sentences were not applied to property offenders alone. One quarter of them went to those found guilty of particularly heinous assaults, including one sentence of a year's solitary confinement that was well publicised by the *Chelmsford Chronicle* in 1789.[25]

Thus, the very rapid increase in the use of imprisonment against assault convicts that occurred in the mid and later 1780s (Figure 7.2) coincided with a brief wave of enthusiasm for prison reform in Essex. The magistrates began to move toward imprisonment in assault cases not only because they had recently done so in relation to petty larceny, but also because they were involved in a wave of prison reform which, for a brief period at least, widened their sense of the usefulness of confinement. The experiment with solitary confinement implied a broader vision of the uses of imprisonment, and the fact that, from the beginning, it was used against both thieves and violent offenders adds

---

[24] J. Howard, *The State of the Prisons in England and Wales* (London, 1777); Ignatieff, *Just Measure*; M. DeLacy, *Prison Reform in Lancashire, 1700–1850: A Study of Local Administration* (Stanford, 1986); Beattie, *Crime*, 574–5.

[25] P. King, *Crime, Justice and Discretion in England, 1740–1820* (Oxford, 2000). See also N. Briggs, *John Johnson, 1732–1814: Georgian Architect and County Surveyor of Essex* (Chelmsford, 1991), 113–20. DeLacy, *Prison Reform*; J. Hanway, *The Defects of the Police* (London, 1775), i–xxv; Ignatieff, *Just Measure*, 78–120. ERO, Q/SPb, 16–17; *Chelmsford Chronicle*, 17 July 1789.

an interesting dimension to current historical debates about the origins of the penitentiary.

Historians differ widely in the relative importance that they attach to the various motivations that lay behind the prison reform movement. Some link reform primarily to the pragmatic imperatives created by gaol fever outbreaks and by the government's failure to find an alternative destination for those sentenced to transportation between 1775 and 1787. Others view reform as driven by philanthropic, religious, and philosophical changes, combined – in some analyses – with the industrial elite's desire to impose new forms of labour discipline on the poor.[26]

Fisher recently argued that the new prisons were designed primarily to punish young petty thieves and that 'the adoption of a corrective penology in the last decades of the eighteenth century' can be portrayed as a 'juvenilisation of the criminal law'. Although his point cannot be evaluated fully in this chapter, the possibility that the newly reformed prison regimes applied to both violent offenders and young petty thieves tends to undermine rather than reinforce Fisher's argument. The age structure of the two criminal groups was entirely different. No age information is available for violent offenders in Essex, but in Shropshire, where ages were recorded, less than 7 per cent of those in prison for violent offences were younger than twenty. Since information about the ages of prison inmates does not survive for late eighteenth-century Lancashire, whence all of Fisher's evidence is drawn, Fisher had to develop his argument without any information about the proportion of prisoners who were in their teens. This fact raises major questions about his conclusions in relation to petty thieves, since work on both London in the early 1790s and the Home Counties from 1782 to 1787 suggests that relatively few indicted property offenders were juveniles. It also raises questions about his decision to marginalise and virtually ignore assault. The parallel growth of imprisonment for violence in the 1780s meant that a growing number of prisoners were being drawn from a type of offender that largely excluded the young.[27]

The fact that violent offenders never formed a large proportion of prison inmates in these years by no means wholly undermines Fisher's argument,

[26] M. Foucault, *Discipline and Punish: The Birth of the Prison* (London, 1977); DeLacy, *Prison Reform*; Ignatieff, *Just Measure*; M. Ignatieff, 'State, Civil Society and Total Institutions: A Critique of Recent Social Histories of Punishment', in D. Sugarman (ed.), *Legality, Ideology and the State* (London, 1983), 183–211; W. Forsythe, *The Reform of Prisoners, 1830–1900* (London, 1987), 1–14.

[27] G. Fisher, 'The Birth of the Prison Retold,' *Yale Law Journal*, 104 (1995), 1235–1316; Shropshire Record Office, Calendars of Assizes and Quarter Sessions, I, 1786–94 (n = 106); King, 'Decision-makers'; P. King and J. Noel, 'The Origins of the Problem of Juvenile Delinquency: The Growth of Juvenile Prosecutions in London in the Late Eighteenth and Early Nineteenth Centuries', *Criminal Justice History*, 14 (1993), 17–41.

particularly if that argument is confined to Lancashire alone. However, the knowledge that in other areas the new prisons were being used increasingly against assault convicts as well as against those found guilty of property crime does add weight to Ignatieff's very different emphasis on the importance of placing prison reform in the context of a much more general attack on the manners of the poor. As Ignatieff argued in his discussion of the 1780s,

> To many, the times called for a reassertion of social authority, a vindication of the moral legitimacy of the state, and a renewed effort to reform the morals of the disobedient poor. Since men like Hanway . . . defined crime as part of a wider pattern of insubordination among the poor, they were fascinated by the thought of an institution that would give them total control over the body, labour, and even the thought processes of a poor man. The penitentiary, in other words, was more than a functional response to a specific institutional crisis. It exerted a hold on men's imaginations because it represented in microcosm the hierarchical, obedient, and godly social order, which they felt was coming apart around them.

The relationship between the rise of the prison reform movement and the rapid growth of imprisonment for assault manifested in the Essex data, had little connection, it seems, to any crisis about 'youth' or to the 'juvenilisation' of the criminal justice system. It was, however, intimately connected with the constellation of changes that Ignatieff highlights – the desire of the authorities for control over the lives of labouring men and women, whatever their age.[28]

VI

The prison reform initiatives of the mid-1780s complemented, and in some ways formed part of, a more general movement for the reformation of manners that was gathering momentum throughout this period. By the mid-1780s, magistrates in many counties – including Essex – were involved in a host of activities designed to attack 'the vices of the poor' as they conceived them.

The *Chelmsford Chronicle* began to carry a considerable number of articles devoted to these subjects. In 1786, it published William Mainwaring's Middlesex grand jury address, which linked 'the great increase of thieves' to such issues as unregulated alehouses, idleness, gaming, and vagrancy. A month after the King's June 1787 proclamation 'for discouraging vice and immorality', the *Chronicle* published a letter demanding that magistrates immediately put into force 'the laws against drunkenness . . . profaneness . . . and obscene books

---

[28] Ignatieff, *Just Measure*, 84.

and pamphlets'. In the next two months, the Essex magistrates responded by issuing orders about the better regulation of alehouses and by publishing an abstract of the laws relating to Sunday observance, profane swearing, tippling, and drunkenness. At the same time, the vestry at Wanstead – led by the rector Samuel Glasse, who was soon to be a prominent member of the Proclamation Society – issued detailed orders about the suppression of idle and disorderly conduct on the sabbath, of illegal alehouses and excessive drinking, of vagrancy, of the selling of licentious publications, and of all 'dissolute, immoral and disorderly behaviour'. The ensuing flurry of letters about this matter fed into a larger parish-based campaign against vagrancy early in 1788, and led to further debate about the repression of alehouses.[29]

Although these debates contained no specific references to assault cases, the widespread Essex movement for the reformation of manners may well have had an impact on this area of judicial practice. Figure 7.2, which is based on a three-year moving average calculated every two years, indicates that the years when the debate about this issue was most intense (1786–8) were also the years when prison sentences for assault were rapidly increasing. The annual figures reveal that the greatest change occurred in 1786 and 1787. In 1785, five assault offenders were imprisoned. In 1786 and 1787, the number rose to fifteen and sixteen, respectively, before falling back to a yearly average of seven cases between 1788 and 1793.

Assault may not have been listed specifically as a concern, but contemporary letters in the *Chronicle*, such as that written by an 'old magistrate' in 1787, clearly implied that reform was needed across the whole spectrum of cases coming before the quarter-sessions bench:

> The police of England is excellent the execution of it of late years weak, timid and mean. Is there a fault from vagrancy to murder that has not its plain and adequate punishment; yet except those that are within the purview, or bordering upon, felony is there scarcely an offence that is not daily committed under the unconcerned view of the magistracy . . . A firm magistracy would soon teach vice that there is no want of vigour in the laws.[30]

[29] J. Innes, 'Politics and Morals: The Reformation of Manners Movement in Later Eighteenth-Century England', in E. Hellmuth (ed.), *The Transformation of Political Culture in Late Eighteenth Century England and Germany* (Oxford, 1990), 57–118; D. Andrew, *Philanthropy and Police: London Charity in the Eighteenth-Century* (Princeton, 1989), 165–73. For a brief discussion of the reformation of manners movement in the context of an earlier 'birth of sensibility,' see P. Langford, *A Polite and Commercial People: England 1727–1783* (Oxford, 1992), 461–505. *Chelmsford Chronicle*, 21 Apr. 1786; 15 Sept. 1786; 12 and 26 Jan. 1787; 6, 20 and 27 July 1787; 10, 17, 24 and 31 Aug. 1787; 7 Sept. 1787; 28 Dec. 1787; 11 Jan. 1788; 1, 8, 15 and 22 Feb. 1788.

[30] *Chelmsford Chronicle*, 10 Aug. 1787.

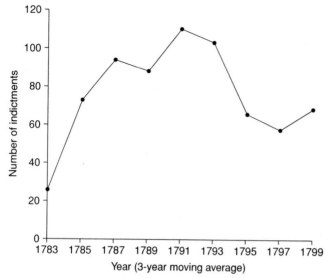

Figure 7.4   Average annual level of assault indictments 1782–1800 (Essex).
Note: Based on 3-year moving averages calculated every two years.
Source: Essex Record Office, Q/SPb, 8–17.

The firmer policies that this correspondent and other contributors explicitly demanded in response to drunkenness and illegal sports also had implications for policies toward assault. Many accusations of interpersonal violence came from drunken pub brawls or recreational activities that had got out of hand. Magistrates determined to crack down on such behaviour may well have been inclined to deal more harshly with assault accusations that arose from these contexts. This disposition, in conjunction with the magistrates' general desire to show 'no want of vigour' in their treatment of cases that offered opportunities to reform the manners of the poor, may well explain the sudden increase in imprisonment in 1786 and 1787.

The magistrates' willingness to take assault seriously may also have caused the escalation in the number of assault indictments brought to the court in the mid-1780s (see Figure 7.4). This timing matches almost exactly the pattern for property-crime indictments, which rose rapidly after the 1783 peace and fell when the armed forces remobilised at the beginning of the French wars a decade later. In the case of assault, however, it would be dangerous to argue – as some historians have argued in relation to property crime – that this increase reflected a growth in lawbreaking due to the problems experienced by the poor in the transition from war to peace. In the early 1780s, only a tiny minority of assault cases were sent on by the magistrates to be tried by formal indictment. Even if the debates of the mid-1780s, and the general clamour about the regulation of the poor, increased the proportion sent on for trial only by a few percentage points, virtually the entire increase in indictments could have been caused by that change. Thus, the rapid growth of imprisonment as a sanction in assault cases during the mid-1780s was almost certainly not a reaction to an actual increase in the number of violent assaults, as Figure 7.4 might, at a casual glance, suggest. Rather, the sudden rise in assault indictment rates and the rapid growth in the use of imprisonment as a punishment for assault were both produced by changing attitudes among the magistracy.

The mid-1780s witnessed a pronounced leap in recorded property crimes and an extended period of panic among the propertied about 'the rapid increase in robberies' and 'the vagrant banditti,' who were always felt to pose a threat during such post-demobilisation periods. This situation in turn both fed into, and stimulated, a broader movement for the reformation of the manners of the poor, which was at its height in the second half of the 1780s, precisely when the drive for prison reform was gathering momentum. The steep, short-term rise in the proportion of assault offenders who were imprisoned between 1786 and 1787 was part of a long-term trend continuing well into the early nineteenth century (Table 7.1); but, in the mid-1780s, this particular conjunction of events seems to have propelled the Essex quarter-sessions bench toward sanctions against violent criminals similar to those already in use against petty thieves.[31]

As Gatrell has argued in his recent work about the rise of 'the policeman state,' anxiety about the lawlessness of poor people intensified late in the eighteenth century, helping to launch a 'disciplinary assault' on those who were thought to threaten the dominant order. The impact of this state of affairs on prosecutions for assault, however, remains largely unexplored. The evidence presented here suggests that a major transformation took place well before the creation of the professional police and even before the onset of the social fears that accompanied the growth of radicalism in the decades after the French Revolution. In the mid-eighteenth century, most magistrates treated interpersonal violence as a civil rather than a criminal matter, but, by the late eighteenth century, their tolerance toward violent action by the poor – and, to some extent, even by the middle classes – had been fundamentally eroded. Although the great majority of assault-related disputes in 1820 were still being processed at the summary level, a significant minority resulted in public

---

[31] Beattie, *Crime*, 214–21; D. Hay, 'War, Death and Theft in the Eighteenth-Century: The Record of the English Courts', *Past and Present*, 95 (1982), 117–60; *Chelmsford Chronicle*, 28 Dec. 1787.

trials at which ritual confessions and nominal fines were no longer the expected outcome. Those convicted of interpersonal violence became subject to legal procedures similar to those experienced by petty thieves. Without any formal changes in the law the quarter-sessions bench in Essex and elsewhere during the period 1750 to 1820 transferred assault decisively away from the civil toward the criminal sphere. This change reflects not only new attitudes to violence but also new attitudes to the manners and reformability of the poor.[32]

The long-term impact of the transformation of attitudes identified here is difficult to evaluate because little research has yet been completed. For example, it is not yet possible to define the extent to which the harsher punishments imposed on those committing assault affected the propensity of various social groups to resort to violence in certain situations. Nor is it yet clear whether the criminalisation of assault hearings persuaded members of the middle class to transfer their disputes to the civil courts. Until detailed studies of the records of various civil tribunals, of the depositions created before major court hearings, and of petty-sessions examinations books are available, it will not be possible to determine how patterns of violence changed in the eighteenth and nineteenth centuries. Even then, a thorough analysis of economic, social, and ideological trends will be necessary before the impact of the transformation in sentencing policies can be put in proper perspective.[33]

Much has been written about 'the rise of respectable society' after 1830 and about 'the decline of theft and violence in Victorian and Edwardian England', but these themes have not been well researched for the preceding era. In particular, the reformation of manners movement that first took shape in the 1780s has been strangely neglected, in comparison with the similar campaign that occurred between the 1690s and the 1730s. The half century that immediately preceded the policing, poor-law, and capital-statute reforms of the 1820s and 1830s saw few major centralised initiatives directed at controlling the lives of the poor. At a lower level, however, county, divisional, and parish authorities had wide discretionary powers and the role that their changing responses played in reshaping social policies and social attitudes should not be underestimated. In the matter of assault, as in many other areas of social policy during this period, historians can easily be misled by an overemphasis on legislative activity. Although parliamentary acts offering formal legal protection to the victims of various kinds of assault were passed in the mid- and late nineteenth century, the criminal justice system had altered its attitudes and policies toward assault

[32] V. Gatrell, 'Crime, Authority and the Policeman State', in F. M. L. Thompson (ed.), *The Cambridge Social History of Britain, 1750–1900* (Cambridge, 1990), 3, 243–65.

[33] The impact of the new police force on assault prosecution patterns, for example, requires close analysis.

long before then. Victorian legislation tended to formalise changes that had begun more than half a century earlier.[34]

Whereas historians of penal change have, of necessity, focused considerable attention on the late eighteenth and early nineteenth centuries, historians of crime have concentrated on either the eighteenth century or the Victorian period. However, the period from the late 1770s to the early 1830s, with all its complex local initiatives and ideological currents, witnessed important changes in its own right; it deserves to be regarded not just as a problematic borderland but as a rich territory for historical investigation.[35]

[34] F. M. L. Thompson, *The Rise of Respectable Society: A Social History of Victorian Britain, 1830–1900* (London, 1988); Gatrell, 'Decline'; Innes, 'Politics'; R. Shoemaker, 'Reforming the City: The Reformation of Manners Campaign in London, 1690–1738', in L. Davidson *et al.* (eds.), *Stilling the Grumbling Hive: The Response to Social and Economic Problems in England, 1689–1750* (Stroud, 1992), 99–120; D. Eastwood, *Governing Rural England: Tradition and Transformation in Local Government* (Oxford, 1994); G. Rude, *Criminal and Victim, Crime and Society in Early Nineteenth Century England* (Oxford, 1985).

[35] For a rich study of this period that was published just after this one was completed and that also points out that cultural explanations stressing the inevitable impact of the rise of sensibility are not enough, see V. Gatrell, *The Hanging Tree: Execution and the English People 1770–1808* (Oxford, 1994).

8. Changing attitudes to violence in the Cornish courts 1730–1830

While there can be little doubt that attitudes to interpersonal violence were changing in the eighteenth and early nineteenth centuries, it has proved remarkably difficult for historians to analyse precisely when, why and with what consequences those changing attitudes occurred. An extensive debate about murder rates, which are virtually the only quantifiable measure of violence levels (and a very problematic one at that) has arisen,[1] and on the other side of the coin extreme judicial violence in the form of hanging has also recently been subjected to considerable analysis.[2] However, the vastly more frequent number of acts of everyday violence which did not lead to murder and, in the other direction, the very frequent use by the courts of violent punishment not resulting in death, have only just begun to receive attention. Through Landau, Shoemaker and Smith's work on London, and through King and Beattie's work on Essex and Surrey,[3] major changes in attitudes to assault indictments and to the use of

---

[1] See for example, T. Gurr, 'Historical Trends in Violent Crime. A Critical Review of the Evidence', in M. Torry and N. Morris (eds.), *Crime and Justice* (1981), 3, 295–353; L. Stone, 'Interpersonal Violence in England: Some Observations', *Past and Present*, 108 (1983), 22–33; J. Sharpe, 'The History of Violence in England: Some Observations', *Past and Present*, 108 (1985), 206–15 and Stone's 'Rejoinder', *ibid.*, 216–24; J. Cockburn, 'Patterns of Violence in English Society: Homicide in Kent 1560–1985', *Past and Present*, 130 (1991), 70–106; H. Taylor, 'Rationing Crime: the Political Economy of Criminal Statistics since the 1850s', *Economic History Review*, 101, (1998), 560–90; J. Archer, 'The Violence we have Lost? Body Counts, Historians and Interpersonal Violence in England', *Memoria y Civilizacion*, 2 (1999), 171–90; M. Eisner, 'Modernisation, Self-Control and Lethal Violence: The Long-term Dynamics of European Homicide Rates in Theoretical Perspective', *British Journal of Criminology* 41 (2001), 618–38; see also articles by E. Monkkonen, B. Cavarlay, R. Roth, H. Thorne and P. Spierenburg in the section on 'Long-term trends in Violence' in *Crime, Histoire et Sociétés (Crime, History and Societies)*, 5 (2001), 7–106.

[2] Most recently in the formidable V. Gatrell, *The Hanging Tree. Execution and the English People 1770–1868* (Oxford, 1994).

[3] N. Landau, 'Indictment for Fun and Profit: a Prosecutor's Reward at Eighteenth-Century Quarter Sessions', *Law and History Review*, 17 (1999), 507–36; G. Smith, 'The State and the Culture of Violence in London 1760–1840' (PhD thesis, University of Toronto, 1999); G. Smith, 'Civilised People Don't Want to see that Kind of Thing: The Decline of Public Physical Punishment in London 1760–1840', in C. Strange (ed.), *Qualities of Mercy: Justice, Punishment and Discretion*

255

public whippings (and whippings in general) have been uncovered but this work has been extremely restricted geographically. The criminalisation of assault and the declining use of public whipping have been effectively documented for the area in and immediately adjacent to London but not for any other region. This paper attempts to broaden that analysis by using the records of a county almost as far away from London as any other part of England and Wales – Cornwall.

Historians continue to argue about precisely how 'separate' Cornwall was,[4] but there is no doubt that while London and the Home Counties were at the centre of the eighteenth-century state – were the privileged location where key military, administrative, economic and cultural resource-holders most frequently met – Cornwall was very much at the opposite end of the spectrum.[5] To call it part of the 'periphery' may be doubtful, but it may perhaps be usefully seen, as some historians have portrayed it, as part of the 'inner periphery' of the British Isles along with Wales and parts of north-east England.[6] This did not mean, of course, that Cornwall was marginal economically. Quite the opposite. During the period being studied here the region underwent a fundamental economic transformation as tin mining increased and copper mining became a huge industry. Cornwall's industrialisation may have been 'imperfect, incomplete and overspecialised' but its capacity to rapidly increase production cannot be doubted. Cornish copper production, for example, rose much faster throughout the eighteenth century than GNP as measured by Craft's recent calculations.[7] The years being studied here were the great period of economic growth in Cornwall. At its peak in the second decade of the nineteenth century Cornwall was producing more than two thirds of the world's fine copper. However, that figure had fallen to less than 25 per cent by the 1850s,[8] for by the second quarter of the nineteenth century foreign competition was eroding the strength of Cornish mining, and a period of adjustment and massive out-migration was

(Vancouver, 1996), 21–51; R. Shoemaker, 'Streets of Shame? The Crowd and Public Punishments in London 1700–1820', in S. Devereaux and P. Griffiths (eds.), *Penal Practice and Culture, 1500–1800: Punishing the English* (Basingstoke, 2004), 232–57; J. Beattie, 'Violence and Society in Early-Modern England', in A. Doob and E. Greenspan (eds.), *Perspectives in Common Law* (Aurora, Ontario 1985), 36–60; J Beattie, *Crime and the Courts in England 1660–1800* (Oxford, 1986); P. King, *Crime, Justice and Discretion in England 1740–1820* (Oxford, 2000); Chapter 7.

4 For a good discussion see P. Payton, *The Making of Modern Cornwall* (Redruth, 1992), 1–40.

5 Despite road improvements during the eighteenth-century Cornwall remained relatively remote. A. Guthrie, *Cornwall in the Age of Steam* (Padstow, 1994), 103–15. J. Rowe, *Cornwall in the Age of the Industrial Revolution* (Liverpool, 1953), 29. A Hamilton Jenkin, *Cornwall and its People* (London, 1970), 137–46.

6 Payton, *The Making*, 18, quoting Unwin who saw the outer periphery as Scotland and Ireland.

7 B. Deacon, 'Proto-industrialisation and Potatoes: A Revised Narrative for Nineteenth-Century Cornwall', *Cornish Studies*, 5 (1997), 65.

8 Rowe, *Cornwall in the Age*, 128.

beginning.[9] However, during the period studied here Cornwall was at the height of its own very particular industrialisation process with nearly a third of its population employed in mining. It may, as some historians have suggested, have been a capitalistic industrial economy accompanied by a proto-industrial society, but the social and economic life of Cornwall was undoubtedly undergoing massive change.[10] It is within this context that this paper analyses how the Cornish courts reacted both to the cases of violent assault brought before them, and to their own separate options about how frequently they should use physical violence to punish property offenders.

Since there were no major legislative changes in relation to these matters until the nineteenth century, and no apparent attempt to direct policy from the centre, it is possible to use the surviving court records to test the extent to which judicial decision-makers in different parts of the country (primarily magistrates on the quarter-sessions bench and trial jurors) changed policies towards violence at their own discretion. To what extent and in what ways did the Cornish courts alter their key policies towards violence?

I

The vast majority of eighteenth-century assault cases were resolved informally at a summary level without going on for jury trial. In Wiltshire in the 1740s, for example, William Hunt JP immediately dismissed, or (more commonly) resolved by agreement, over 80 per cent of the assault cases brought before him and in north Essex in the later eighteenth century this figure was even higher.[11] However, a very significant number of assault prosecutions were brought to the quarter sessions in every county each year and it is in those courts that the most important changes in judicial policy can be observed.[12] The summary courts had very limited powers in assault cases. Technically they were not allowed to impose formal fines until the Offences against the Person Act of 1828, although they not infrequently made 'orders' for compensation payments that were effectively fines. They also had no powers of imprisonment although once again they did sometimes imprison those unable to find sureties to keep the peace or unable to enter into recognizances guaranteeing their appearance for jury trial

[9] P. Payton, 'Reforming Thirties and Hungry Forties – the Genesis of Cornwall's Emigration Trade', *Cornish Studies*, 4 (1996), 107–27; B. Deacon, 'A Forgotten Migration Stream: The Cornish Movement to England and Wales in the Nineteenth Century', *Cornish Studies*, 6 (1998), 96–117; I. Soulsby, *A History of Cornwall* (Chichester, 1986), 97–9.

[10] Deacon, 'Proto-industrialisation', 61.

[11] R. Shoemaker, *Prosecution and Punishment. Petty Crime and the Law in London and Rural Middlesex c.1660–1725* (Cambridge, 1991), 46–7; Chapter 7.

[12] The absolute number of quarter-sessions assault cases cannot, of course, be used as any guide to changing levels of violence – see Chapter 7.

in a higher court.[13] The quarter sessions, by contrast, could directly either fine or imprison or both. They could exact nominal fines or huge ones. They could also exact large fines and then imprison the offender until the fine was paid. While summary-court policies towards assault were therefore important (and still await their historian), it was at the quarter sessions that policy options were broadest in the long eighteenth century and the potential for local initiatives and locally driven policy changes was therefore greatest.

It is fortunate, therefore, that the minute books of the Cornish quarter sessions survive from 1737 making it possible to study what happened in Cornwall in the century before the late 1820s, when the major changes produced by the 1828 Act had a tendency to transfer all but a few plain assault cases out of quarter-sessions jurisdiction.[14] To what extent did the Cornish quarter sessions change their attitude to assault cases over the period between the 1730s and the 1820s?

Work on Essex, Surrey and London, and most recently Landau's detailed discussion in the *Law and History Review*, have shown that in the mid-eighteenth century in areas near the centre, assault prosecutions, although technically crown (i.e. criminal) prosecutions, were in fact civil suits.[15] To quote a charge given to the Middlesex grand jury in 1770,

> Injuries to the persons of the King's subjects, by assaults or battery, are the lowest offences subject to your enquiry. These partake in a great measure of the nature of a civil action, inasmuch as the fine upon conviction, though nominally given to the King, is in most instances imposed with a view to a pecuniary satisfaction to the injured party . . . though in many cases the injury complained of, may be so small as hardly to entitle the sufferer to a recompense.[16]

In these circumstances victims usually indicted their assailants not in order to get them punished but as a means of obtaining compensation. The court either allowed them to make a settlement before the trial or, if the case came to trial, it usually imposed a nominal fine provided the accused had made a settlement with the victim.[17]

---

[13] The higher court was almost always the quarter sessions but occasionally assault cases were heard at the assizes. For a good newspaper report on such a case see *West Briton* 23 Aug. 1811 quoted in R. Barton (ed.) *Life in Cornwall in the Early Nineteenth Century* (Truro, 1997), 22–3.

[14] Unfortunately the rest of the core Cornish quarter-sessions archive has been destroyed and no indictments, recognizances, etc. therefore survive. The core of this paper is based on the Cornish quarter-sessions minute books – Cornwall Record Office (henceforward CRO) QS 1/1–11 which cover all the years 1737–1830. Other useful material has survived via private archives notably CRO AD 604 and DDX 460/1.

[15] King, 'Punishing Assault', 49; Beattie, *Crime*, 457–9; Landau, 'Indictment for Fun'.

[16] G. Lamone (ed.), *Charges to the Grand Jury 1689–1803*, (Camden Fourth Series, xliii, London, 1992), 426–7.

[17] Lawyerly involvement may often have been crucial. In 1787 the sessions minute books record 'hearing what could be alleged by advocates on either side', CRO QS 1/5, 267. For a very rare

Table 8.1 *Sentences imposed in assault cases, Cornwall quarter sessions analysed by decade, 1737–1821*

Period	Fined 1/- or less (%)	Fined over 1/- (%)	Imprisoned (%)	Imprisoned till fine paid (%)	Unknown or other (%)	Sample size
1737–49	86.46	8.33	2.08	2.08	1.05	96
1750–9	92.00	6.00	0.00	2.00	0.00	121
1760–9	95.21	1.37	2.74	0.68	0.00	154
1770–9	92.50	4.17	2.50	0.83	0.00	142
1780–9	85.90	3.85	9.62	0.00	0.63	180
1790–9	87.96	3.70	7.41	0.00	0.93	119
1800–9	58.33	11.90	20.24	9.52	0.00	104
1810–21	53.96	6.74	30.94	7.19	1.17	153

Source: CRO QS 1/1–10. The period 1737–49 witnessed the only case in which the accused was sentenced to the pillory (for assault and false imprisonment).

It is clear from Table 8.1 that this was very much the pattern in Cornwall in the middle of the eighteenth century. In the period from 1737 to 1779, for example, at least 96 per cent of those convicted of assault were fined and almost all of these offenders were given nominal fines of a shilling or less. Given the very wide legal definition of an assault, which included both simply holding up a fist in an angry manner and doing great physical damage to another just short of murder,[18] those cases would have arisen from a huge variety of contexts. Unfortunately the surviving Cornish records only give any indication of the severity of the assault in a few very exceptional cases. However, whether they arose from trivial disagreements or major physical assaults, it is clear that in the mid-eighteenth century the vast majority of cases were settled in a civil manner, a nominal fine being recorded once a settlement or compensation had been agreed. In the mid-eighteenth century only a very small proportion of the accused even waited to be tried before making a settlement. Between 1737 and 1759, 71 per cent of all the accused confessed (Table 8.2), thus making the trial little more than a place to formally register a pre-agreed settlement. At its height in the 1760s this approach to quarter-sessions indictment for assault involved more than three quarters of defendants pleading guilty and 97 per cent of those who either confessed or were found guilty being given a nominal fine of a shilling or less. This form of quarter-sessions assault trial was slow to change in Cornwall and the figures for the entire period 1737–1821

example of newspapers reporting this civil form of assault case proceedings *Ipswich Journal*, 17 July 1762.
[18] See chapter 7; R. Burn, *The Justice of the Peace and Parish Officer* (10th edn, London, 1766), i, 100–1.

Table 8.2 *Confessions and verdicts in assault cases, Cornwall quarter sessions, analysed by decade 1740–1820*

Period	Guilty (%)	Not guilty (%)	Confessed (%)	Unknown (%)	Sample
1737–49	9.40	17.95	71.79	0.85	117
1750–9	11.57	17.36	71.07	0.00	121
1760–9	16.88	5.84	75.97	1.30	154
1770–9	18.31	15.49	66.20	0.00	142
1780–9	21.11	13.33	65.00	0.56	180
1790–9	19.23	9.24	71.43	0.00	119
1800–9	37.50	19.23	41.35	1.92	104
1810–21	45.10	8.50	43.79	2.61	15

Notes: Source – CRO QS 1/1-10. These records do not systematically record grand-jury verdicts (although they do refer on occasions to 'not found' verdicts or prosecutions abandoned because the prosecutor failed to turn up) and all tables and graphs refer only to cases which reached the petty-jury trial stage.

reflect this. During these years nearly two thirds of the accused confessed,[19] and more than four fifths of sentences were nominal fines – a further 5 per cent of those found guilty being given substantial fines. The tiny fraction of cases (2.1 per cent) involving assaults on officials were the major exception.[20] In these cases only 25 per cent of those convicted were fined, and imprisonment, or at least imprisonment until an often sizeable fine was paid, was the more usual outcome.

This mid-eighteenth century civil and confessional pattern of dealing with normal assault cases was the same for every social stratum. However, from the 1780s onwards the pattern began to change very gradually towards a more criminal, less confession-based, and more socially and sexually differentiated system. Very slowly at first, and increasingly rapidly after 1800, sentences of imprisonment began to play a more significant role in trial outcomes (Figure 8.1). In the 1780s and 1790s between 7 and 10 per cent of all those guilty of assault were imprisoned. This was hardly a large change but given that a further 4 per cent of cases now resulted in substantial fines, the range of outcomes was beginning to broaden and nominal fines were no longer a virtually guaranteed outcome in normal assault cases as they had been since the 1730s.

[19] Sometimes the court almost certainly persuaded them to do so, as they are recorded as changing their plea from not guilty to guilty for example, CRO QS 1/4, 406–8.
[20] 93.58 per cent of cases were described as plain assault or assault and battery, 2.39 as assault and misdemeanour, 0.46 (5 cases) as assault with intent to ravish, 0.28 as assault and trespass, 0.83 per cent as assault and wrongful imprisonment, 0.28 as assault and attempted rescue (presumably from arrest), 1 case involved assault and attempted sodomical practices, CRO QS 1/1–10.

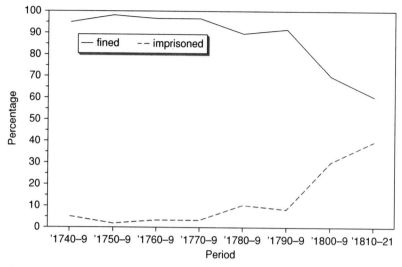

Figure 8.1   Assault cases, Cornish quarter-sessions sentences 1740–1820.

The most significant changes came, however, very late in the period being studied here. Between 1800 and 1821 nominal fines, which were now normally a shilling rather than the six pence usually used at mid-century, declined to just over 50 per cent of sentences. Meanwhile larger fines increased significantly (Table 8.3 and Figure 8.2) and imprisonment rose to one third of sentences 1800–9 and nearly two fifths 1810–21. The criminalisation of assault was rapidly advancing and the willingness to confess declined equally rapidly as a result. In the 1790s more than 70 per cent of the accused still confessed, but in the first quarter of the nineteenth century this went down to just over 40 per cent (Table 8.2). A fundamental change was occurring, but it was one which affected men and women differently and which was also partly dependent on the social class of the accused.

Although only 10.7 per cent of those tried for assault in Cornwall were women – a figure similar to that found elsewhere[21] – the impact of gender on trial outcomes was highly significant and sometimes contradictory (Tables 8.4, 8.5 and 8.6). Women were more than 50 per cent more likely to be found not guilty if they chose not to confess (Table 8.4) but those found guilty of assault were nearly twice as likely to be given direct prison sentences (Table 8.5). While 17.2 per cent of women were given simple imprisonment sentences, only 8.9 per cent of men suffered a similar fate. Imprisonment until an often substantial fine was paid or sizeable sureties were provided (which could be a harsh sentence or a light one depending on the convicted person's financial

[21] Chapter 7.

Table 8.3 *Size of fines in assault cases, Cornwall quarter sessions, 1737–1821*

Size of fine	1737–49 (%)	1750s (%)	1800–09 (%)	1810–21 (%)
1d	0.00	1.02	1.35	0.00
2–3d	2.13	0.00	0.00	0.00
4–6d	74.47	88.78	8.11	6.72
7d to 1/-	13.83	4.08	67.57	73.11
1/1d to 5/-	3.19	0.00	0.00	2.52
5/1d to 10/-	3.19	6.12	0.00	0.00
10/1d to £1	0.00	0.00	2.70	1.68
£1.0.1d to £2	1.06	0.00	2.70	5.88
£2.0.1d to £5	1.06	0.00	14.86	4.20
£5.0.1d to £10	1.06	0.00	1.35	2.52
£10.0.1d to £20	0.00	0.00	0.00	2.52
£20.0.1d to £100	0.00	0.00	1.35	0.84
Total	99.99	100.00	99.99	99.99
(*Sample Size*)	(*94*)	(*98*)	(*74*)	(*119*)

Sources: As for Table 8.1.

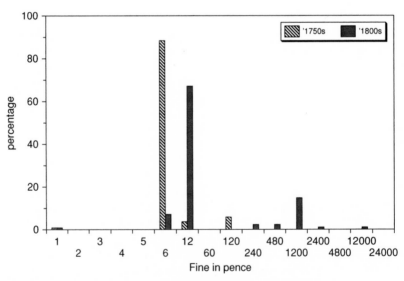

Figure 8.2 Size of fines, assault cases 1750s and 1800s compared (Cornwall).

Table 8.4 *Verdicts and confessions analysed by gender, assault cases, Cornwall quarter sessions, 1737–1821*

Verdict	Males (%)	Females (%)
Guilty	22.61	22.22
Not guilty	12.13	19.66
Confessed	64.34	57.26
Unknown	0.92	0.85
(Sample size)	*(973)*	*(117)*

Sources: as for Table 8.1.

Table 8.5 *Sentences in assault cases analysed by gender, Cornwall quarter sessions, 1737–1821*

Sentence	Males (%)	Females (%)
Fined 1/- or less	82.24	79.57
Fined over 1/-	5.61	2.15
Imprisoned	8.88	17.20
Imprisoned till fine paid	2.80	0.00
Unknown/other	0.47	1.08
Total	100.00	100.00
(Sample)	*(856)*	*(93)*

Sources: as for Table 8.1.

circumstances) was inflicted on a further 2.8 per cent of men but was not used against women. The court also completely avoided imposing substantial fines on women (Table 8.6). No woman was fined more than one pound while 6.5 per cent of men suffered this fate. Two per cent – mainly gentlemen and yeomen – were fined £20, £50 or even in one case £100. The court may have felt that women did not have the resources to pay such fines and this fact may have also increased their willingness to imprison women. However, despite the relatively small numbers involved, the greater use of imprisonment against women (Table 8.5) raises important questions about the courts' motives. Why did the Cornish courts come down so hard on violent women in this way?

One of the Cornish courts' main concerns may well have been the relative independence enjoyed by many single young women in various parts of the county. Cornish women were in quite considerable demand at various times of the year as field workers – particularly in weeding in May and June, haymaking

Table 8.6 *Size of fines in assault cases by gender, Cornwall quarter sessions, 1737–1821*

Size of Fine	Male (%)	Female (%)
1d	14.00	20.00
2–3d	2.58	3.53
4–6d	54.67	50.59
7d to 1/-	19.04	22.35
1/- to 5/-	1.35	1.18
5/1d to 10/-	1.11	1.18
10/1d to £1	0.74	1.18
£1.0.1d to £2	1.35	0.00
£2.0.1d to £5	2.33	0.00
£5.0.1d to £10	0.86	0.00
£10.0.1d to £20	1.11	0.00
£20.0.1d to £50	0.74	0.00
£50.0.1d to £100	0.12	0.00
Total	100.00	100.01
(*Sample size*)	(814)	(85)

Sources: as for Table 8.1.

in July and harvesting in August and early September.[22] 'The women, everywhere in the county, perform a large part of the rural labours, particularly the harvest work, weeding the crops, hoeing turnips and potatoes etc. and attending the threshing machines' observed the author of *The General View of the Agriculture of the County of Cornwall* in 1811.[23] More important however, a large number of young women were employed as 'balmaidens', within the rapidly growing mining industry. Women were virtually never employed underground but large numbers were employed on the surface in 'spalling', breaking up the ore with hammers and sorting or washing it. In the eighteenth century girls often began work at the mine at the age of eight or nine and in 1851, 36 per cent of the female labour force in the copper mines was under fifteen and at least 75 per cent were under twenty five.[24] Since married women were strongly discouraged from working at the mine, the vast majority of the balmaidens would have

[22] S. Schwartz, 'In Defence of Customary Rights; Labouring Women's Experience of Industrialisation in Cornwall 1750–1870', *Cornish Studies*, 7 (1999), 10–11; On one of the few farms whose accounts have been analysed in detail their inputs in these months were often greater than men's. N. Pounds, 'Barton Farming in Eighteenth-Century Cornwall', *Journal of the Royal Institute of Cornwall*, New Series 7 (1973), 62.

[23] G. Worgan, *General View of the Agriculture of the County of Cornwall* (London, 1811), 159; Schwartz, 'In Defence'.

[24] On balmaidens – L. Mayers, *Balmaidens* (Penzance, 2004); S. Schwartz, ' "No Place for a Woman": Gender at Work in Cornwall's Metalliferous Mining Industry', *Cornish Studies*, 8 (2000), 69–96; Rowe, *Cornwall in the Age*, 28; Guthrie, *Cornwall in the Age of Steam*, 73; G. Burke, 'The Decline of the Independent Bal Maiden: The Impact of Change in the Cornish

been both young and single. It is therefore interesting to note the different ways in which the Cornish courts dealt with accusations of violence against single women rather than those who were, or had been married. A survey of the status information given about female assault convicts in the years from 1780 to 1821, which was the period in which a range of sentencing options were used for the first time, reveals two patterns. First single women were twice as likely to be found guilty as married women or widows were. Secondly, and more important, while no widow was imprisoned for assault and only 14 per cent of married women suffered this sentence, 44 per cent of single women were incarcerated. Despite the patchiness of the status information available, single women appear to have comprised the vast majority of female assailants against whom a prison sentence was imposed. Given that single women also had an equal predominance amongst the balmaidens, who by their late teens often gained a degree of independence from the wages they received for their hard physical labour as surface workers, the courts may well have been specifically cracking down on this group. Many early-nineteenth-century observers certainly felt the balmaidens were too forthright, too independent and too ostentatious in their clothing. This general sense that the balmaidens were getting ideas above their station and were too coarse and immoral in their habits may well have influenced the ways the courts dealt with them, although since the court records never describe women's occupations but only their status in relationship to men, it is impossible to be sure that this was what was happening. The justices may equally, of course, have been reluctant to imprison married women or widows with children to support given the poor law burdens this might create. Overall, however, it is clear that the courts' preference for imprisoning female rather than male assailants was at least partly linked to their perception that violent young single women needed to be particularly strictly disciplined.[25]

Occupational or status information is only available for about 60 per cent of all offenders but an analysis of verdicts and punishments for male assault convicts by social status between 1780 and 1821 suggests that the court was using its growing willingness to criminalise assault highly selectively. Verdicts show a slightly differentiated pattern. Tinners were the group most likely to be found guilty followed closely by labourers. However, these differences were partly affected by the relative willingness of various groups to confess, and the courts' policies show up most clearly in its sentencing structures. The proportion of convicted offenders sentenced directly to imprisonment varied very greatly according to the social status of the accused (Table 8.7). While 34 per cent of

Mining Industry', in A. John (ed.), *Unequal Opportunities. Women's Employment in England 1800–1918* (Oxford 1986).

[25] Schwartz, 'No Place', 70; J. Rule, 'The Labouring Miner in Cornwall 1740–1870' (PhD thesis, University of Warwick, 1971), 12; Schwartz, 'In Defence', 18. Mayers, *Balmaidens*, 17–23. The number of female surface workers in the mining industry grew to more than 5,000 by the early nineteenth century and some estimates put it as high as 14,000 at its peak.

Table 8.7 *Sentences for assault analysed by social status, Cornish quarter sessions, 1780–1821*

Sentence	Gentlemen total	Gentlemen percentage	Yeoman total	Yeoman percentage	Labourers total	Labourers percentage	Tinners total	Tinners percentage	Artisans total	Artisans percentage
Fined 1/-or less	7	63.64	44	67.69	40	45.98	5	33.33	21	53.85
Fined over 1/-	1	9.09	12	18.46	5	5.75	1	6.67	2	5.13
Imprisoned	1	9.09	7	10.77	38	43.68	5	33.33	11	28.21
Imprisoned till fine paid	2	18.18	1	1.54	4	4.60	2	13.33	5	12.82
Enlisted	0	0.00	0	0.00	0	0.00	1	6.67	0	0.00
Unknown	0	0.00	1	1.54	0	0.00	1	6.67	0	0.00
Total		100.00		100.00		100.01		100.00		100.01
(*Sample size*)		(*11*)		(*65*)		(*87*)		(*15*)		(*39*)

Sources: as for Table 8.1.

tinners, a third of labourers, and 28 per cent of artisans and tradesmen were given direct prison sentences, only 10 per cent of yeomen and one gentleman (9 per cent) were treated in a similar way. A further 13 per cent of tinners and 4 per cent of labourers were imprisoned until their fines were paid and/or sureties were found – both things which the poorest of them may have found very hard to do. The tinners were very widely involved in the regular outbreaks of food rioting in Cornwall throughout the eighteenth century and John Rule has argued that they probably used this type of direct action more frequently that any other occupational group. Moreover, during the key period when increasing numbers of assault convicts began to be imprisoned by the Cornish quarter sessions the tinners, along with many labourers, played a particularly leading role in the numerous Cornish riots of 1793, 1795, 1796, 1801 and 1812. In 1795, for example, when high bread prices coincided with a major fall in the price of tin, several bodies of riotous tinners were involved in such widespread unrest that the authorities in various parts of Cornwall were forced not only to put measures in place to ensure that wheat was available at reasonable prices but also to ask the Home Office for some quite novel forms of assistance. Alongside the usual requests for a military presence, for example, the Home Office also received a letter in March 1795 asking that 'the East India Company be persuaded to ship 200 tons of tin to each of the markets of Bengal and Madras' in order to 'to quiet the minds of the people'.[26] Thus the courts' harsher attitude to these particular occupational groups when they appeared before them on assault charges may well have been affected by the tinners' reputation for disorderliness and by their well-known riotous inclinations, although the few cases where assault accusations were specifically linked to riots have been left out of the sample analysed here.

It cannot always be assumed that juries and quarter-sessions magistrates had similar motivations. All of the small number of excise officers who pleaded not guilty to assault were found guilty by quarter-sessions petty juries composed mainly of yeomen and tradesmen – groups who were not renowned for their love of customs officers, yet none of the seven men concerned were imprisoned by the magistrates and all but one received a nominal fine. Equally, even the cryptic quarter-sessions minute books indicate that there were certain special types of assault that were harshly dealt with simply because of their very nature. As early as 1769, for example, Edward Physick, a yeoman, was imprisoned for three months and fined twenty pounds for an assault 'on the body of Agnes Fetherstone' his apprentice.[27] Equally in 1822, John Tanson, uniquely in this period, received violence for violence, in the form of a whipping as well as a

---

[26] Rule, 'The Labouring Miner', 116–176; PRO, HO 42/34/108,110,116,120,123. On the role of tinners in the extensive riots of 1773 see *London Chronicle*, 2–4, 4–6 and 10–12 Mar. 1773 and *Sherbourne Mercury* 29 Mar. 1773.
[27] Jenkin, *Cornwall and its People*, 1–7; CRO QS 1/3 334.

year's imprisonment for assaulting a girl 'under the age of 10' with the intention of having carnal knowledge of her.[28] Similar motivations may well have lain behind the heaviest sentence the court gave out in an assault case during this period. In 1799 a Blisland yeoman convicted of assaulting Philippa Coleman was fined £100, imprisoned for a year and forced to enter into a recognizance of £500 to keep the peace towards her in future.[29] However, in the 94 per cent of cases which involved assault without any aggravating circumstances, the pattern was clear. The court was selective. When it came to dealing with independent single young women, tinners and labourers the courts' policies appear, despite small sample sizes in some cases, to have been considerably harsher. As will be indicated in the concluding section, when broader geographical comparisons will be made, the Cornish quarter sessions came late to the use of imprisonment in routine assault cases, but when it did so there can be little doubt that the criminalisation of assault was applied in a way that targeted groups whose behaviour the magistrates and middling jurors were particularly concerned to control.

II

The courts' use of whipping as a punishment for petty larceny also underwent fundamental changes in this period. At mid-century the Cornish quarter sessions, like the equivalent courts in most other counties, dealt with petty larcenists primarily in two ways. They either whipped them or transported them.[30] Table 8.8, which is based on a five-year sample of all petty-larceny cases taken from each decade, indicates clearly that at mid-century nearly three quarters were whipped and just under a quarter transported, with just a handful being imprisoned as well as whipped. This pattern continued unaltered through the 1760s and 1770s (Table 8.8) and then changed dramatically and fundamentally.[31] As elsewhere, imprisonment rapidly rose to complete dominance.

70 per cent of convicted property offenders were sentenced to imprisonment alone, 1780–99; a further 10 per cent to imprisonment and whipping. This partly reflected the transportation crisis of the 1780s and was also related to the availability from 1779 onwards of the newly built gaol at Bodmin,[32] but it primarily reflected a country-wide change in thinking about punishment for minor larceny, for which imprisonment was increasingly felt to offer a

[28] CRO QS 1/10, 337.
[29] CRO QS 1/6, 547–8. By the beginning of the nineteenth century the Cornish courts may well have been exhibiting an increasing sensitivity towards violence by men on women. An increased number of husbands were put in bridewell, or otherwise punished, for assaulting their wives.
[30] King, Crime, Justice and Discretion, 265; Beattie, Crime, 507.
[31] Table 8.8 may slightly delay showing the change because the five years sampled in every decade were the first five. 1775–9 may have witnessed the beginning of the move towards imprisonment so obvious in the following column.
[32] The new gaol at Bodmin was declared ready to receive prisoners in July 1779 CRO QS 1/4, 240.

Table 8.8 *Sentences for property crimes, Cornwall quarter sessions,
1740–1820*

Sentence	1740s and 1750s (%)	1760s and 1770s (%)	1780s and 1790s (%)	1800s and 1810s (%)
Fined	0.00	0.00	2.13	0.00
Whipped only	72.45	77.23	4.96	3.70
Whipped and imprisoned	3.06	0.00	9.93	14.07
Imprisoned only	0.00	0.00	69.50	69.63
Transported	23.47	22.77	5.67	9.63
Imprisoned till enlists	0.00	0.00	7.80	2.22
Unknown	1.02	0.00	0.00	0.74
Total	100.00	100.00	99.99	99.99
(*Sample size*)	(*98*)	(*101*)	(*141*)	(*135*)

Sources: as for Table 8.1. First five years of each decade sampled.

flexible and, some hoped, a reformatory alternative.[33] Whipping alone became
a residual punishment from the 1780s onwards – 4 to 5 per cent of offenders
now received this sentence. However, whipping accompanied by imprisonment grew in importance. 10 per cent of property offenders were given such
sentences 1780–99 and 14 per cent 1800–19 (Table 8.8). Corporal punishment
both in public and in private remained an important part of Cornish penal strategies. Indeed analysis of the different types of whipping sentences handed out to
property offenders 1737–1824 suggests not only the development of a highly
gendered strategy, but also the possibility that the late eighteenth century, while
it witnessed a decline in the absolute number of whippings, may also have
seen a surprising but widespread change in the context within which corporal
punishment was administered.

Throughout the period 1740–1819 the Cornish quarter-sessions' policies
towards males and females in property-crime cases showed important differences (Table 8.9) which back up, to a limited extent, recent work on the relative leniency shown to female property offenders by the eighteenth-century
courts.[34] Jurors found 44 per cent of females not guilty but only 32 per cent
of males. Equally males were twice as likely to receive the heaviest sentence,
transportation, and nearly 10 per cent were subjected to imprisonment and
whipping whereas less than one per cent of females received this punishment.
Males were also slightly more likely to receive a whipping as their only punishment, although nearly a third of women also received this sentence. By contrast
females were much more likely to receive a sentence of simple imprisonment.

[33] Beattie, *Crime*, 520–618; M. Ignatieff, *A Just Measure of Pain. The Penitentiary in the Industrial Revolution 1750–1850* (London, 1978).
[34] Chapter 5.

Table 8.9 *Sentences in property crime cases by gender, Cornwall quarter sessions, 1740–1819*

Sentence	Male (%)	Female (%)
Fined	0.28	1.63
Whipped only	35.04	30.08
Whipped and imprisoned	9.97	0.81
Imprisoned only	34.19	58.54
Transported	15.95	8.94
Imprisoned till enlists	3.99	0.00
Unknown	0.57	0.00
Total	99.99	100.00
(*Sample size*)	(*351*)	(*123*)

Sources: as for Table 8.1.

For the purposes of this study however, perhaps the most important dimension of penal policy was the willingness of the authorities to use violence in public against the bodies of those convicted of minor property crimes[35] whether they were male or female. How did this change over the period studied here?

The Cornish quarter-sessions minute books vary greatly in the amount of information they offer about the physical punishments they meted out whether in public or in private. The number of lashes is never specified although some sense of this can be garnered from two cases heard before the borough court of Launceston. In 1783 this court sentenced Charity Witherige, who had stolen some beef, 'to receive 30 lashes on her bare back by 12 o'clock . . . during which time she is to be loo round the town from the town hall to the town end from there to the town hall by way of the fish market'. Three years later a male thief was sentenced 'to receive six and thirty lashes, 12 in the market place, 12 opposite the old shambles and 12 in the new shambles'.[36] The Cornish quarter sessions gave out no such numbers but occasionally they did record that an offender should be 'severely whipped'. On three specific occasions, by contrast, they recorded that an offender should be 'moderately' whipped. The courts' motives for these variations is unclear, although it is interesting to find that in July 1741 it ordered the wife of a yeoman to be moderately whipped, but made no such merciful stipulation in the following case which involved a Redruth spinster who had committed her offence with two labourers and who was almost certainly therefore of much lower social status.[37]

---

[35] Almost all the property crimes tried at the Cornwall quarter sessions were petty larceny cases (97 per cent). In addition 1 per cent involved receiving and 2 per cent involved fraud, false pretences and embezzling.
[36] CRO B/LAUS/688.   [37] CRO QS 1/1, 114.

Table 8.10 *Timings of public whippings, Cornish quarter sessions, 1737–1824*

Time (hours)	Earliest time stipulated (%)	Latest time stipulated (%)
08.00	1.02	0.00
09.00	9.18	0.00
10.00	29.59	1.02
11.00	10.20	0.00
12.00	37.76	44.90
13.00	5.10	8.16
14.00	0.00	20.41
15.00	1.02	15.31
16.00	6.12	2.04
17.00	0.00	8.16
(Sample size)	(98)	(98)

Sources: as for Table 8.1.

When a public whipping was decided upon the Cornish courts, like their counterparts elsewhere,[38] frequently set out very carefully the day, time and place. The tinner Humphrey Tonkin, for example, was sentenced to two whippings, one 'on Saturday next between 10 and 12 in the market place Truro' and the other the following Friday between 10 and 12 in the public market at Redruth.[39] Since Saturday was market day in Truro and Friday was market day in Redruth[40] the aim was clearly to give maximum publicity to the punishment by choosing a time when the town centres concerned would be full not only of their own inhabitants but also of those from the surrounding area. Other sentences specified not a particular day but simply that the whipping should be done on market day. In 1811, for example, the labourer Francis Pinch, was given two-months hard labour and ordered to be 'publicly whipped from the Butter Market in Bodmin up the Fore Street for 200 yards on some market day.[41] Timing was clearly linked to maximum exposure. Between 10 a.m. and 2 p.m. were the peak times for obvious reasons although other timings were also stipulated (Table 8.10). Usually a two-hour period was given but longer

---

[38] Beattie, *Crime*, 545; G. Morgan and P. Rushton, *Rogues, Thieves and the Rule of Law* (London, 1998), 135–6. Shoemaker, 'Streets of Shame', 234; This careful planning of routes and timing can also be observed at certain points in earlier periods – P. Griffiths, 'Bodies and Souls in Norwich: Punishing Petty Crime 1540–1700', in Devereaux and Griffiths, *Penal Practice*, 91–2; D. Postles, 'The Market Place as Space in Early Modern England', *Social History*, 29 (2004), 42–54.

[39] CRO QS 1/1, 170.

[40] R. Brookes, *The General Gazetteer or Compendious Geographical Dictionary* (London, 1812); Worgan, *General View of the Agriculture of the County of Cornwall*, 163.

[41] CRO QS 1/7, 693.

periods were allowed which may have given those involved a certain flexibility, allowing them to pick their time carefully according to the rhythm of market day or of the working day.

Timings might relate to the place where the whipping was to occur – an aspect that was given particular attention by the Cornish quarter sessions on a large number of occasions. Although nearly two thirds of public whippings were ordered to be administered in the town where the quarter sessions had taken place (usually Lostwithiel, Liskeard, Bodmin or Truro) 35 per cent took place elsewhere. Sometimes the whipping was inflicted in the town nearest to the place of the crime itself. Indeed there is evidence that victims could pay to have a convicted thief whipped at or very near the scene of the crime. In 1740, for example, the quarter-sessions minute book records not only that Joseph Vincent, a St Austell tinner, was to be given a public whipping but also that he was 'to be carried at the expense of the prosecutor to the town of St Austell on Friday 25th July there to be whipped between 12 and 2' (Friday was market day in St Austell).[42] Two years later Elizabeth Parsons was similarly conveyed by the gaoler to Camelford for her public whipping 'at the expense of the prosecutor'.[43] If the prosecutor could not or would not pay, the community might do so instead. In 1741 John Giles of St Austell was whipped in the town after being conveyed there 'at the expense of the inhabitants of the parish'.[44] It is difficult to know how frequently these practices went on,[45] but it is clear that the quarter sessions were willing to tailor the place of punishment to local needs and this was particularly so when offences had been committed by those working in the mines.

No less than 10 per cent of the public whippings about which information is available concerning the place of punishment occurred at the specific mine where the offence took place. Although few of the Cornish magistrates were involved directly in the management or running of the mines,[46] many were 'adventurers' (i.e. part owners, investors or profit sharers in the mines), and in any case landowners received a significant share of the ore produced.[47] The quarter-sessions bench was clearly in no doubt about the usefulness of public examples when mining equipment or materials had been stolen or various forms of appropriation had been practised by miners. Indeed the need to use

[42] CRO QS 1/1, 80; Worgan, *General View of the Agriculture of the County of Cornwall*, 163.
[43] CRO QS 1/1, 149.   [44] CRO QS 1/1, 94.
[45] The minute books of later years may simply not have bothered to record who paid for whippings to be arranged at the places victims or vestries wanted them to occur.
[46] Deacon, 'Proto-industrialisation', 67 argues as late as 1856 only 8 per cent of Cornish magistrates were not landed or clerical gentry.
[47] On the adventurers system, Guthrie, *Cornwall in the Age of Steam*, 66; Rowe, *Cornwall in the Age*, 50–1, argues that landowners took great care that mines remained productive since 'their usual share of a sixth part of the value of the minerals raised was often a considerable part of their income'.

all the means available to discourage mine-related thefts was a theme dwelt on at length in the chairman of the quarter-sessions addresses to the grand jury. 'I was in hopes' the chairman announced to the grand jury on one such occasion

> that by the endeavours of those who have acted before now in your office, the public spirit which the concern in mines have shown in not regarding expense in prosecuting offenders who have robbed them of their property, and the assistance of magistrates, I should have been able to congratulate you upon having expunged from our calendar, this species of offence, the stealing of materials from mines, where ingratitude is added to the turpitude of the crime – for surely nothing can be more ungrateful than where the hand of the person is put forth to purloin the property of the benefactor who provides his mouth with bread. I am sorry that our united endeavours have not been attended with all the success we could have wished. However, I trust we shall in time by perseverance in our conduct be able to preserve property of this kind more free from depredation at least, if we cannot entirely pluck up the evil by the roots.[48]

Clearly a key part of the courts' attempts to control mine-related theft were strategically placed whippings. Public whippings were arranged at many of the main mines in Gwennap, for example – Poldice Mines saw five public whippings, Consolidated Mines three. Other mine-based whippings were spread out across the mining areas, a total of fourteen mines being involved in all. Sometimes the location was very specific. John Morcom of Gwennap, was publicly whipped for stealing candles 'at the United Mines near Symon's Engine house,' while Samuel Martin was whipped 'near the account house at Free Kirby Mine' for the same offence.[49] The time of day chosen for these public whippings sometimes appears to have coincided with the changing of shifts and it is clear that the Cornish magistracy were willing to put considerable effort into orchestrating these mine-based whippings. Occasionally shoes or clothes had been stolen, which could have been the property of fellow workers, but the main items that the accused had stolen were almost certainly the property of the mines themselves – tallow candles, copper ore, tin, brass sieves, timbers, etc.[50] James Johns and James Manger, for example, were whipped at Wheel Breage mine for stealing 50 lbs of tin-stuff from Lord Godolphin and others (presumably his fellow capital adventurers in the mine).

---

[48] CRO AD 604.

[49] CRO QS 1/8, 221, 260. For a newspaper report advertising Morcom's flogging – Barton, *Life in Cornwall*, 55.

[50] For a discussion of forms of pilfering and sanctions against mineworkers who appropriated materials – J. Rule, 'The Perfect Wage System? Tributing in the Cornish Mines', in J. Rule and J. Wells (eds.), *Crime, Protest and Popular Politics in Southern England 1740–1850* (London, 1997), 61–4.

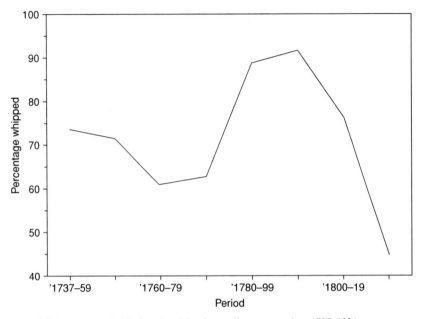

Figure 8.3 Percentage of whippings in public, Cornwall quarter sessions 1737–1824.

The vast majority of these mine-based whippings occurred in the 1780s and 1790s and they therefore fitted into the broader pattern of change revealed in Figure 8.3. Although the absolute number of sentences involving whipping declined in the late eighteenth century, the use of public whipping, which had begun to fall in the third quarter of the century, increased in the 1780s and 1790s to a point where at the turn of the century over 90 per cent of whippings were in public (Figure 8.3).[51] This then fell again towards the end of the period studied here, but even between 1810 and 1824, 45 per cent of whippings remained public, indeed the court produced another flurry of mine-based public whippings in 1815–16.[52] However, this renaissance of public whipping was highly gendered (Figure 8.4). For just as the percentage whipped in public was rising to new heights from the 1780s onwards, the public whipping of women was being abandoned completely. 50 per cent of women had been publicly whipped in the years 1737 to 1769, but this percentage fell to a third in the 1770s and the public whipping of women had ceased completely by 1790. Thus while the Cornish quarter sessions increased their relative use of public whipping against

[51] A similar change occurred in the North-east – Morgan and Rushton, *Rogues*, 134 – and to a lesser extent in Essex – King, *Crime, Justice and Discretion*, 272–3.

[52] CRO QS 1/8, 221, 228, 260, 580.

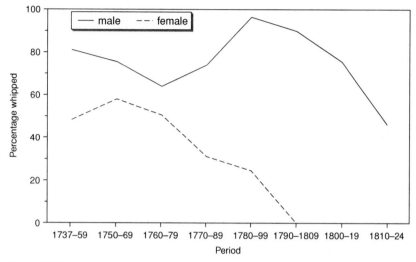

Figure 8.4 Percentage of whippings in public, male and female, Cornwall quarter sessions 1737–1825.

men in the 1780s and 1790s and persisted with the use of public whipping in nearly half of whipping sentences through until the 1820s, they pursued exactly the opposite policy towards women well before the public whipping of women was made illegal in 1817.

III

How does this Cornish evidence illuminate our understanding of changing attitudes and policies towards violence between the 1730s and the 1820s? Given the lack of any significant legislative change in relation to normal assault prosecutions in this period, local courts maintained immense discretion. Did courts well away from the metropolis make similar changes in their policies towards assault cases as those in and around London? The Cornish evidence suggests both important differences and some overall similarities in policies towards assault over this period. In the mid-eighteenth century, like their metropolitan counterparts, the Cornish quarter-sessions handling of assault cases very much suggests an institution designed to ensure that most disputes were settled outside court.[53] Confessions following out-of-court settlements were the norm here as in Middlesex, Essex, Surrey and elsewhere. However, this pattern remained dominant for much longer in Cornwall than in the other areas that

---

[53] Landau, 'Indictment for Fun', 533.

have so far been studied. No change at all is observable in Cornwall before the 1780s whereas by the 1770s in both Essex and the City of London significant proportions of assault convicts (up to one fifth) were being imprisoned.[54] Things began to change very slowly in Cornwall between 1780 and 1800 but this change was minimal compared to that occurring in London. In the 1790s only 7.4 per cent of Cornish assault convicts were being imprisoned, whereas in Essex more than a third were being incarcerated and in Surrey, London and Middlesex the figure was around a fifth.[55]

Confessions also remained the norm a lot longer in Cornwall. Only 36 per cent of the accused confessed in Essex between 1793 and 1797 whereas for the 1790s as a whole the equivalent figure for Cornwall was 71 per cent.[56] Only at the beginning of the nineteenth century did the Cornish pattern shift decisively towards the criminalisation of assault which elsewhere had been gathering pace for more than a quarter of a century. Imprisonment and large fines became likely outcomes for the first time and confessions fell to less than 50 per cent as a response. Research on other areas has not analysed which social groups became the targets of this criminalisation of assault, but in Cornwall the tinners, labourers and single women, a significant proportion of whom were almost certainly mineworkers, were clearly the main although not the sole targets.

The pattern in relation to the use of whipping as a punishment for petty crime is more complex. The use of whipping alone as a key punishment remained until the 1770s and was slightly more dominant than in some other counties,[57] but in Cornwall, as elsewhere, imprisonment rose to dominate petty-larceny sentences in the final two decades of the eighteenth century and continued to do so until 1820 (Table 8.8). Every county so far studied used public and private whipping slightly differently over this period but it is clear that the policies of the Cornwall quarter sessions differed from those of other counties in a number of ways. First while there is evidence that the balance of public to private whippings moved very slightly towards the former for a few years in the 1790s in Essex and in London, in Cornwall public whipping underwent a major renaissance in the period from 1780 to 1800.[58] Second, public whippings continued to be used in a very significant proportion of whipping sentences in Cornwall well into the 1820s, whereas evidence from elsewhere suggests that public whipping was gradually becoming a residual practice by this time. The Cornish newspapers

---

[54] Chapter 7; Smith, 'The State and the Culture of Violence', 310.
[55] Beattie, 'Violence and Society', 50; Smith, 'The State and the Culture of Violence', 310, which indicates that change was slightly slower in Middlesex than in the City of London.
[56] Chapter 7.   [57] Beattie, *Crime*, 507, 546, 578, 597.
[58] King, *Crime, Justice and Discretion*; Shoemaker, 'Streets of Shame', 239, which shows a slight rise from 23 to 26 per cent in the proportion of London whippings done in public between the 1780s and the 1790s. In the North-east a similar if less marked increase also occurred – Morgan and Rushton, *Rogues*, 134.

continued to give positive and quite extensive coverage to public whipping without any adverse comment or criticism about this use of public space.[59] Most public whippings still seem to have been seen, for men at least, as a means of humiliating and identifying the untrustworthy and of destroying their reputation in their local community.[60] Londoners may have been feeling that public whippings no longer performed these functions, metropolitan crowds may have been less willing to participate or local businessmen may have been increasingly unwilling to put up with the disruption to commerce and traffic which the crowds drawn to public whippings might create.[61] In the smaller market towns of Cornwall, however, it seems to have taken a lot longer for these pressures against public whipping to develop. Moreover, the Cornish courts, manned by gentry and jurors who often still perceived the local miners as unruly and in need of public exemplary punishment, continued to use public whippings at the workplace well into the nineteenth century – a practice that had been rare elsewhere even in the eighteenth century.[62]

This general tendency for the Cornish quarter sessions to be much more willing to display acts of judicial violence in public than counties nearer London was, however, gender specific. The Cornish abandoned the public whipping of women by the 1780s, and although this was somewhat later than the similar change in Essex, it was roughly in line with the chronology of metropolitan practice.[63] The Cornish courts may well have used processes other than indictment to make a fairly concerted attack on wife-beating at the beginning of the nineteenth century[64] and their attitude to violence against women requires further study. However, despite the fact that the Cornish magistrates were by no means out of contact with their metropolitan counterparts – they sent three representatives to the Proclamation Society's meeting in London in the late 1780s for example[65] – there is no doubt that the chronology of change was different in Cornwall. The Cornish quarter sessions began the process of criminalising

[59] *West Briton*, 18 Oct. 1811; 26 Apr. 1816, for whippings in towns. 20 Jan. 1815 for a mine-head whipping – Barton (ed.), *Life in Cornwall*, 24, 55, 68.

[60] The exception here may have been the whipping of those caught pilfering from mines. Here workmates may have been less likely to revile the whipped offender and more likely to identify with him if he had stolen company property. These whippings appear more likely to have been designed as physical deterrents.

[61] Smith, 'The State and the Culture of Violence', 402–3; Shoemaker, 'Streets of Shame'.

[62] This is not to say it did not occur – Morgan and Rushton, *Rogues*, 136, for example, mentions one offender sentenced to be whipped at the Crawley Iron Works. In London thieves who had stolen from ships and warehouses were sometimes whipped on the docks in the late eighteenth century – Shoemaker, 'Streets of Shame', 235.

[63] King, *Crime, Justice and Discretion*, 286.

[64] CRO QS 1/7, 357, 553, 605; 1/8, 75, 135, 271, 672; 1/9, 74, 75. The author is currently working on a paper for publication entitled 'The Cornish Courts and Gender Relations 1730–1850'.

[65] *Resolutions of the Magistrates Deputed from the Several Counties of England and Wales . . . by Desire of the Society for Giving Effect to His Majesty's Proclamation Against Vice and Immorality* (London, 1790), 4.

assault much later than areas around the metropolis and kept public whipping as a significant part of punishment policy towards male offenders for rather longer, and in a more diverse set of circumstances, than their counterparts in areas in or around the metropolis. The implications of this chronology for our understanding of spatial variations in attitudes to violence in this period are difficult to unravel. Without further studies of other regions it remains unclear whether these differences between Cornish and metropolitan area procedures can be mainly ascribed to the Cornish 'particularism' that Dr Johnson and other contemporaries found so remarkable[66], or whether Cornwall was simply one of a number of areas of England and Wales which responded less quickly to new sensibilities about violence. If, as John Carter Wood has recently argued, this period witnessed both the growth of a more 'civilised' mentality which was more sensitive to violence and demanded greater self-restraint, and the survival of an older 'customary' mentality which continued to legitimise direct physical action, it could be argued that Cornwall's relatively slow adoption of these policies reflected the continued purchase of the latter mentality.[67] Did an older set of 'customary' notions, which accepted the positive role of violence in certain situations, hold its power as a discursive framework and as a basis for action longer amongst the magistrates and jurors of courts on the periphery than it did nearer the centre? Only detailed work in other regions will fully answer this question, but the Cornish evidence suggests that there were almost certainly significant spatial variations in criminal justice practices in relation to both the punishment of non-lethal violence and the use of violent punishments in late eighteenth- and early nineteenth-century England and Wales.

[66] P. Payton, *Cornwall* (Fowey, 1996), 185.
[67] J. Carter Wood, *Violence and Crime in Nineteenth-Century England: The Shadow of our Refinement* (London, 2004).

Part IV

The attack on customary rights

9. *Legal change, customary right, and social conflict in late eighteenth-century England: the origins of the Great Gleaning Case of 1788*

In 1788 the Court of Common Pleas, after lengthy deliberations, came to a judgement in *Steel v. Houghton et Uxor*, concluding that 'no person has, at common law, a right to glean in the harvest field'. Gleaning was of considerable importance to many labouring families in the eighteenth century; therefore, both the provincial and the London-based newspapers reported the 1788 judgement at length, as well as covering the 1786 case of *Worlledge v. Manning* on which it was partly based. The 1788 case not only stimulated a widespread public debate over the gleaners' rights,[1] but also established an important legal precedent. From 1788 onward, every major legal handbook from Burn's *New Law Dictionary* of 1792 to the early twentieth-century editions of Wharton's *Law Lexicon* used it as the standard case law reference. It is quoted in a wide variety of law books written for farmers such as Williams's *Farmers' Lawyer* and Dixon's *Law of the Farm*, as well as inspiring long footnotes in the post-1788 editions of Blackstone's *Commentaries*. By 1904, it was being referred to in the law reports as 'the great case of gleaning'.[2]

Acknowledgements: I would like to thank Clive Paine of the Suffolk Record Office, who is writing a general history of the Culford estate, for his generous advice, the University of Liverpool for the research fellowship that made this work possible, and Edward Thompson for the question that spurred me to look at the link between Cornwallis and these cases.

[1] *English Reports* (Common Pleas), 126: 32–9; Chapter 10; P. King, 'Customary Rights and Women's Earnings: The Importance of Gleaning to the Rural Labouring Poor 1750–1850', *Economic History Review*, 44 (1991), 461–76; *The Times*, 13 June 1788; *Norwich Gazette*, 21 June 1788; *Cambridge Chronicle*, 21 June 1788; *Chelmsford Chronicle*, 9 June 1786, 13 June1788; *Bury and Norwich Post*, 17 May 1786 to 7 June 1786 and 18 June 1788 to 17 Sept.1788; *Northampton Mercury*, 2 Aug. 1788; *Ipswich Journal*, 20 May 1786, 3 June 1786, 14 June 1788; *Annals of Agriculture* 9, 13–15, 164–7, 636–46; 10, 218–27.

[2] R. Burn, *A New Law Dictionary* (London, 1792); J. Wharton, *The Law Lexicon or Dictionary of Jurisprudence*, 4th edn (London, 1867), 426; 10th edn (1902), 347. See also T. Williams, *The Farmers Lawyer* (London, 1819), 207; G. Clark, *Memoranda Legalia; or an Alphabetical Digest of the Laws of England* (London, 1800), 217; T. Tomlins, *The Law Dictionary* (London, 1820); T. Williams, *Every Man His Own Lawyer* (London, 1812), 553; *An Abridgement of Cases Argued and Determined in the Courts of Law during the Reign of George III* (London, 1798), i: 205–7; H. Dixon, *A Treatise on the Law of the Farm* (London, 1858), 244; W. Blackstone, *Commentaries*

Steel was not an isolated case. During the eighteenth and early nineteenth centuries, the labouring poor in many parts of England not only endured irregular employment and inadequate wages, but also suffered a series of attacks on their customary rights. Even those fortunate enough to live in parishes untouched by enclosure and the wholesale transformation of property rights and customary practices it usually entailed, might still become involved in extensive legal battles that sometimes resulted in adverse judgements in the higher courts. As Edward Thompson has observed, 'during the eighteenth century one legal decision after another signalled that the lawyers had become converted to the notions of absolute property ownership and that (whenever the least doubt could be found) the law abhorred the messy complexities of use right.'[3] In his influential article on 'The grid of inheritance' he quotes a Chancery decision in 1741 disallowing the right of turbary, a 1788 decision disallowing the taking of dead wood, and 'the famous decision against gleaning' in the same year.[4]

Historians interested in the relationship between social and legal change have so far concentrated almost all their attention on the consequences rather than on the origins of these central-court decisions. Indeed, the effects of these legal changes on local practice and on the poor's access to customary rights remains the subject of much debate. As David Sugarman has recently pointed out, many social historians have come dangerously close to conflating the existence of a legal ruling with the separate question of its operation, mediation, and enforcement in practice. The Hammonds, for example, concluded that from 1788 onward the Common Pleas judgement enabled the farmers to take control of the gleaning activities of the poor. However, a detailed investigation of the 1788 case suggests strongly that the gleaners' rights were not fundamentally affected by this central-court judgement. The farmers were rarely able to mobilise formal legal sanctions against the gleaners. The vigorous collective protests of the gleaners, the continued strength of local customary law, the legal difficulties that prevented the farmers from using the more accessible courts against the gleaners, and the greater sympathy toward the gleaners' case often shown by magistrates, jurors, clergymen, and others, combined to make it almost impossible for the farmers to control the gleaners through legal sanctions either before or after the 1788 judgement. Thus while it is clear that the indefinite use rights of the poor and the fringe benefits of the communal grid

on the Laws of England, 18th edn (London, 1829), 212–13; H. Theobald, *The Law of Land*, 2nd edn (London, 1929), 151; *Law Reports* (H. L. App. Cas., 1904): 476; see also *ibid.*, (H. L. App. Cas., 1882), 8: 156; *ibid.* (Chapter, 1891), 2: 703, *ibid.*, (Chapter, 1901), 2: 400–1.

[3] E. P. Thompson, *Whigs and Hunters* (London, 1975), 241.

[4] E. P. Thompson, 'The Grid of Inheritance', in J. Goody, J. Thirsk and E. P. Thompson (eds.), *Family and Inheritance* (Cambridge, 1976), 340.

were frequently attacked by the propertied, these attacks were not automatically successful. In eighteenth-century Cumbria, for example, the tenants managed to resist repeated attempts by manorial lords to erode their use rights and impose arbitrary fines upon them.[5]

While the long-term effects of these legal judgements clearly raise a number of important issues, it is unfortunate that little work has been done on the conjunction of forces that gave rise to these cases. This neglect is partly due to the nature of the court records. The extended summary of *Steel v. Houghton* in the *English Reports* contains an eclectic mixture of general legal arguments. Against Judge Gould, who supported the gleaners, Lord Loughborough and the other judges argued, among other things, that gleaning was not a universal common law right because it was unknown in some places; that it was uncertain who could claim the right; that the law should not turn acts of charity into legal obligations; that Gould's supporting authorities – Mosaic Law and the progleaner pronouncements of Hale, Blackstone, Gilbert, and others – were either irrelevant or insubstantial; that granting the right to glean would 'raise the insolence of the poor' as well as being against their own interests since, by reducing the farmers profits, it would reduce the ratepayers' capacity to contribute to the poor rates; and finally that, to quote Lord Loughborough's opening remarks, 'it was inconsistent with the nature of property which imports absolute enjoyment'.[6]

However, at no point are these general legal arguments related to the specific circumstances from which the case arose. To examine the origins rather than the broader consequences of *Steel v. Houghton*, it is therefore necessary to use local sources. These sources allowed exploration of the genesis of the 1786 and 1788 judgements and the construction of a social history of these cases through an analysis of the changing nature of social and economic relations in the tiny Suffolk parish of Timworth from which they both arose.[7] This article is a case study of the reciprocal relationship between law, land, and property

[5] D. Sugarman and G. Rubin, (eds.), *Law, Economy and Society: Essays in the History of English Law 1750–1914* (Abingdon, 1984), 33; see also Chapter 10; R. Malcolmson, *Life and Labour in England 1700–1780* (London, 1981), 144; J. L. and B. Hammond, *The Village Labourer* (London: Longman, 1978), 67–9; Thompson, 'The Grid of Inheritance', 340–1; K. Snell, *Annals of the Labouring Poor* (Cambridge, 1985), 179–80. For discussions of gleaning (mainly post-1788) see also B. Bushaway, *By Rite: Custom, Ceremony and Community in England 1700–1880* (London, 1982), 144 and D. Morgan, 'The Place of Harvesters in Nineteenth-Century Village Life', in R. Samuel (ed.), *Village Life and Labour* (London, 1975), 57; C. Searle, 'Custom, Class Conflict and Agrarian Capitalism: The Cumbrian Customary Economy in the Eighteenth Century', *Past and Present*, 110 (1986).

[6] *English Reports* (C.P.), 126, 32–9. Minor extra detail is contained in Williams, *An Abridgement of Cases*, 1: 205–9.

[7] Timworth's population in 1801 was 149. *The Victoria History of the Counties of England: Suffolk*, 2: 692.

and of the way that legal precedent is shaped by specific and highly localised social and economic conflicts.[8] In the process, it illustrates the intimate link between these legal cases and three of the most important social processes that have been highlighted by social historians of this period – the proletarianisation of the rural poor, the closure of the parish, and the enclosure of the land.

I

The precise nature of the conflict that sparked off the first Timworth gleaning case, *Worlledge v. Manning*, is difficult to reconstruct because the court records contain virtually nothing about the origins of the case, and the main participants do not appear to have left any correspondence relating to it.[9] However, the 1786 case clearly arose from a disagreement about gleaning during the 1785 harvest. After the barley crop had been cut and cleared, the Timworth shoemaker, Benjamin Manning, had gone onto the lands of the parish's richest farmer, John Worlledge, to glean and had carried away a quantity of barley. Worlledge disputed his right to do so and brought an action for trespass in the Court of Common Pleas. After a considerable delay the court finally decided in Worlledge's favour in May 1786 and awarded him just over £26 in damages and costs.[10]

What were Worlledge's aims and motives in bringing his case? Most eighteenth-century disputes between farmers and gleaners revolved around certain limited issues such as the gleaners' refusal to wait until the crop was cleared, but Worlledge's case was more general. It fundamentally challenged the poor's right to glean certain crops and in doing so it broke new ground. As the local newspapers pointed out in June 1786 'this was the first time the right of gleaning was ever reduced to a legal question.'[11]

Worlledge was not acting alone. In a letter to the *Bury and Norwich Post* published immediately after the 1786 judgement, a correspondent signing himself 'X.Y.' (who was almost certainly Arthur Young) vehemently attacked 'those who instituted' the case. He was in no doubt that some form of association

---

[8] Although the *English Reports* provide a distorted view of these cases, this narrowly defined legal source has been virtually the only evidence used to discuss their characteristics. We need an interdisciplinary history of law and material society in order to understand legal history, and this article is intended as a contribution toward such a history. Sugarman and Rubin, *Law, Economy and Society*, 123.

[9] I have been unable to find any detailed documents among the records of the Court of Common Pleas in the Public Record Office apart from brief one-line entries in PRO Ind. 6552 and 6554 and CP 40/3785. Contemporary newspapers and law reports record legal arguments at length but offer only fragments about the disputes themselves.

[10] PRO Ind. 6552; *Ipswich Journal*, 3 June 1786; *Bury and Norwich Post*, 15 May 1786; *English Reports* (C.P.), 126, 34; Suffolk Record Office, Bury St Edmunds FL641/9/1.

[11] *Ipswich Journal*, 3 June 1786; *Chelmsford Chronicle*, 9 June 1786. For the nature of gleaning conflicts in this period see chapter 10.

or joint subscription had backed Worlledge. His letter expressed the hope 'that those who have by their subscriptions supported the present litigation, will withdraw them and retain in their memory the . . . lines of the immortal Thomson', whose poetry advocating a generous-hearted approach to the gleaners was then quoted at length.[12] Unfortunately, this subscription does not appear to have left any record of its activities,[13] but whoever the subscribers were, they were going to need considerable perseverance to obtain the kind of judgement they were looking for. Although technically Worlledge had won the 1786 case, obtaining substantial costs and damages, his victory was a hollow one. The initial announcement about the case, which appeared in the first edition of the *Bury and Norwich Post* after the 1786 judgement, reported that the court had come down strongly against Manning's plea that the poor had 'a general right to glean all kinds of corn'.[14] However, this report, which was almost certainly printed at the instigation of the subscribers, considerably distorted the nature of the 1786 judgement and was attacked by the gleaners' main advocate, the Suffolk justice of the peace and parliamentary reformer Capel Lofft, who insisted that the paper immediately print a more accurate account of the legal arguments involved.[15] This account cast a different light on the case. Manning, it emerged, had lost on a technicality. He had failed to assert plainly that he was a resident of Timworth at the time of the alleged trespass. The Court of Common Pleas had, to quote one of its judges, 'given no sort of opinion on the right' as it related to inhabitants of the parish in which the gleaning had occurred. It had been established 'that there was no general right of gleaning', in the sense that 'the poor and indigent could not glean on land distant from their own parishes' but if this had been the precedent the subscribers had wanted to establish, they would surely have prosecuted a non-resident gleaner. Benjamin Manning, however, was definitely a resident of Timworth. He had a settlement there, and his family received relief from the parish officers.[16]

---

[12] *Bury and Norwich Post*, 7 June 1786. The quote is from James Thomson's 'Seasons' written in the late 1720s, which advocated that the farmers 'fling from the full sheaf . . . the liberal handful' to the gleaners.

[13] A growing number of prosecution associations were in evidence in the three hundreds around Timworth during the 1780s, but no resident of Timworth or of the neighbouring parishes of Ingham or Culford appear in their printed subscription lists. *Bury and Norwich Post*, 28 Dec. 1785, 19 Apr. 1786, 9 Oct. 1790.

[14] *Bury and Norwich Post*, 17 May 1786.

[15] Lofft, who later distanced himself from the gleaners, probably helped Manning considerably in 1786. Five years earlier he had inherited estates near Timworth and became a justice of the peace, *Dictionary of National Biography*; 'Particulars Relative to the Life of Capel Lofft esq', in *The Monthly Mirror* (June 1802 and the following volume). Lofft trained as a barrister and wrote various legal works as well as poetry and political tracts. In 1780 he was a founding member of the Society for Constitutional Information. *Bury and Norwich Post*, 24 May 1786, 31 May 1786.

[16] *Chelmsford Chronicle*, 9 June 1786; *Ipswich Journal*, 3 June 1786; *Bury and Norwich Post*, 31 May 1786; SRO Bury St Edmunds FL641/7/1.

The subscribers had therefore won the battle but not the war, for no general precedent had been established. Even more damaging from the farmers' point of view was the possibility that the judgement could be interpreted as confirming the right of the local poor to glean. As the *Ipswich Journal* pointed out:

The court however, did not seem to entertain a doubt, but that the poor and indigent had a right to glean, after the harvest was cut, taken and carried away, in their own parish. At least as they did not deny the principle it is fair to conclude they allowed it.[17]

The 1786 case therefore proved counterproductive from the subscribers' point of view. It probably strengthened the gleaners' position rather than weakening it – provided that they stayed within their own parish. Many of the Timworth poor clearly refused to change their gleaning practices after the 1786 judgement. Benjamin Manning probably went back to Worlledge's land to glean, for at the Bury quarter sessions immediately after the 1786 harvest, John Worlledge was indicted by Manning for assault, a tactic that the East Anglian poor often used to counter the farmers' attempts to stop them gleaning.[18]

It is hardly surprising, therefore, that despite XY's passionate plea that they abandon their attempts to contest 'this truly charitable and godlike institution', the subscribers refused to let the matter drop. After the harvest of 1786, a new case was begun in the Court of Common Pleas against another Timworth gleaner, Mary Houghton, whose husband was also a shoemaker. The plaintiff in this case was James Steel, one of the four largest farmers in Timworth who lived in the neighbouring parish of Ingham.[19] It was nearly two years before a final judgement was reached, during which time Lofft was involved in a heated defence of the gleaners' rights both in the *Annals of Agriculture* and elsewhere. However, despite his careful use of Blackstone, Hale, and Old Testament precedent, he was unsuccessful. Judgement was found in favour of Farmer Steel. John Houghton, Mary's husband, had to find £35 5s. for the plaintiff's damages and costs.[20]

---

17 *Ipswich Journal*, 3 June 1786.
18 SRO Ipswich, B105/2/48, 9 Oct. 1786. Unfortunately, no record survives of the outcome or the context in which the assault occurred. For gleaners' use of assault accusations see Chapter 10.
19 *Bury and Norwich Post*, 7 June 1786. Steel was the fourth largest ratepayer in Timworth 1786–7 and had considerable holdings in Ingham. SRO Bury St Edmunds FL594/3/26, 641/7/1; 'Survey of the Estates of Culford, Ingham, and Timworth . . . the Property of Marquis Cornwallis' 1793 shows Steel's homestead just over the Timworth/Ingham boundary.
20 *The Monthly Magazine and British Register*, 4 (July–Dec., 1797), 432–3. For Lofft's debate with the poor law writer Thomas Ruggles see, *Annals of Agriculture* 13–15, 164–7, 636–46; *ibid.*, 10: 218–27; J. Gilbert, *The Law of Evidence*, ed. C. Lofft (London, 1791), 11: 508–12. On the legal costs, see PRO Ind. 6554. The £35 did not include the Houghtons' own legal costs, which would have been large. Two barristers had been briefed and had pleaded on their behalf. It remains unclear how much they received from Capel Lofft or from other sources. Lord Campbell's *Lives of the Chancellors* refers to a 'benevolent association' that 'supported the right, agitating for it, and defraying the expenses of litigation', *Notes and Queries*, 12th series, 9: 113.

This sum would hardly have covered the subscribers' legal expenses, but the judgement was a highly satisfactory one from the farmers' point of view. 'No person', the court announced, 'has, at common law, a right to glean in the harvest field. Neither have the poor of a parish legally settled any such right.'[21] The 1788 case was not simply the result of an individual squabble. It was designed to establish a particular legal precedent that would assist local farmers in their disputes with the gleaners. The local paper carried a paragraph clearly intended to underline this.

Thus three out of the four judges of the Court of Common Pleas being decidedly of the opinion 'that the poor have no right to glean' judgement was given for the plaintiff in this cause – which was not instituted with a view to setting aside that charitable custom, provided the consent of the farmer be first obtained, but only to prevent the poor from improperly trespassing on the farmer's fields and arrogantly assuming as a privilege, what the law of the land has denied – and which is entirely at the option of the farmer either to grant or refuse, at such times as he may think proper.[22]

The Timworth farmers' initial newspaper announcement indicated they were mainly aiming to regulate the gleaning of 'barley and other soft corn'.[23] In a parish such as Timworth, where sheep played a vital part in the local economy, the subscribers may have focused on barley because it was more valuable as livestock feed or because the barley crop had been undersown with grass to provide post-harvest grazing.[24] However, the Timworth farmers had an even more compelling reason for concentrating on barley – wheat was of negligible importance in local crop rotations while barley was the major cash crop. In the mid-1760s, for example, Farmer Worlledge sowed nearly a hundred acres of barley but only fourteen acres of wheat.[25] The 1788 newspaper announcement

---

[21] English Reports (C.P.), 126: 32; *Bury and Norwich Post*, 18 June 1788.

[22] *Bury and Norwich Post*, 17 Sept. 1788. This was the final paragraph of a series of articles in the paper, which had reported in detail each of the judge's arguments. 27 Aug. 1788, 3 Sept. 1788, 10 Sept. 1788.

[23] *Bury and Norwich Post*, 18 June 1788: 'The trial was not instituted by the plaintiff with a view of totally excluding the poor from the exercise of this custom, but to prevent their gleaning barley and other soft corn.'

[24] Arthur Young, in praising the flock masters of the Bury neighbourhood, stressed that in sand districts such as Timworth, 'the discrimination between good and bad farmers depends entirely on this point; good ones consider everything as subservient to sheep', A. Young, *General View of the Agriculture of the County of Suffolk* (London, 1813), 57. On undersowing, see Morgan, 'The Place of Harvesters', 57. It is also possible that barley was considered to be more vulnerable to pilfering by gleaners because, before carting, it had to lie cut in the fields for a longer drying period than wheat.

[25] B. A. Holderness, 'East Anglia and the Fens', in J. Thirsk (ed.), *The Agrarian History of England and Wales, vol. v, 1640–1750: Regional Farming Systems*, 197–239, especially Table 7.1, indicates that in Breckland parishes more than 42 per cent of sown arable land was under barley while only 12 per cent was planted with wheat. Worlledge's pattern was not therefore atypical. SRO Bury St Edmunds FL594/3/26 lists him as ploughing 265 acres.

can therefore be deceptive. It was no great concession to allow the local poor to glean the few acres of wheat they would have found in late eighteenth-century Timworth. Although the subscribers have left no formal records, their two main aims seem clear. First, they were attempting to control the poor's access to the land 'to put a stop to that encroachment which has too long been practised under the assumption of their having a right to enter the fields of a farmer without first acquiring his consent'.[26] Second, they were bent on appropriating the gleanings of the most valuable local crop. They were not necessarily successful. When the farmers of north-east Essex attempted to use the 1788 judgement in a fresh attack on the local gleaners' rights, they achieved very little. However, the local newspaper reports of 1788 suggest that, initially at least, the subscribers were well satisfied with their lawyers' labours, while the gleaners' advocates could only take solace from the fact that one judge had dissented from the final judgement.[27]

II

Why did this fundamental legal attack on the gleaners' rights come to a head between 1786 and 1788? The Timworth subscribers may have been affected by the current acute anxiety about crime. In Suffolk, as in almost every English county, indictment rates rose rapidly after the peace of 1782–3, punishment policies became harsher, and prosecution associations were being formed in increasing numbers.[28] However, there are no indications that a significant proportion of these Suffolk offenders came from the Timworth area, and no Timworth residents seem to have joined the local prosecution associations. Concern about pilfering from the harvest sheaves, which was often associated with gleaning, may have been heightened by the general moral panic in the mid-1780s, but at most this played only a minor part in stimulating the Timworth

---

[26] *Bury and Norwich Post* 18 June 1788.

[27] See Chapter 10. One judge, Henry Gould, supported the gleaners' case, and Lofft tried to argue optimistically that it was 'far from a novelty in our legal history to find the opinion of a single judge acquire at length a decided preponderancy'. *Annals of Agriculture* 10, 218.

[28] Property offenders prosecuted at the Suffolk assizes averaged sixteen per year during the period 1777–82 and thirty-three for 1783–5. PRO Assize 33/6–7 (not-found bills excluded). For rising indictment rates in other counties see P. King, 'Crime, Law and Society in Essex 1740–1820' (PhD thesis, Cambridge, 1984), 35, 62; J. M. Beattie, *Crime and the Courts in England 1660–1800* (Oxford, 1986), 214–35; D. Hay 'War, Dearth and Theft in the Eighteenth Century: The Record of the English Courts', *Past and Present*, 95 (May 1982): 121–6. The proportion of capitally convicted offenders actually hanged on the Norfolk Circuit was 15 per cent during the period 1780–2 and 44 per cent for 1783–5. Prosecution association formations followed the same pattern as in neighbouring Essex. P. King, 'Prosecution Associations and Their Impact in Eighteenth-Century Essex', in D. Hay and F. Snyder (eds.), *Prosecution and Police in Britain* (Oxford, 1989), for Blackburne hundred association formation notice – *Bury and Norwich Post* 27 Apr. 1787.

subscribers.[29] It is also difficult to relate these gleaning cases to rising local concern about poor law administration. The poor law policies of the Timworth vestry, which in 1785 seems to have consisted of John Worlledge and two or three others, were not under any particularly severe pressure in the mid-1780s. In the long term, the poor-rate burden was increasing, but the main rises in Timworth's rates came in the 1770s and the late 1790s.[30]

Did the Timworth gleaning cases coincide with a period of dearth, when disputes about gleaning might become more acute because the gleaned corn would be particularly valuable to both the poor and the farmer? Suffolk bread prices indicate no general connection of this sort. On average, wheat prices were slightly lower in 1785 than they were in the period of 1780–4. Between July 1784 and July 1785 – the year immediately preceding the harvest at which the vital clash between Manning and Worlledge occurred – wheat prices fell by 30 per cent. However, this decline was sharply reversed in the next two months. The genesis of the Timworth gleaning cases coincided with a particularly unpredictable and difficult harvest period. Between mid-July and mid-September 1785 wheat prices rose by 18 per cent and barley prices by 30 per cent as fears grew that the storms and heavy rainfall of these months would destroy part of the crop.[31]

The 1785 harvest was therefore an anxious time for most Suffolk farmers. One recorded that 'much corn laid in the wet two or three weeks' before he could gather it, and barley-growing farmers such as Worlledge seem to have been especially vulnerable.[32] For the gleaners, by contrast, these conditions sometimes proved highly advantageous. Late storms flattened the crops and increased the amount of corn left in the fields after the harvest. This could easily generate conflicts about gleaning before the harvest was cleared between farmers forced to leave crops uncarted in the fields and gleaners anxious to get going before the continued rain caused the grain to deteriorate. Moreover

---

[29] The assize gaol books (PRO Assize 33) contain little information about the place where the offence was committed, but the Bury quarter-sessions records (SRO Ipswich B105/2/47–8) suggest that Worlledge was virtually the only resident of the Timworth area to be indicted there in the later 1780s. On the 'moral panic' see King, 'Prosecution Associations'.

[30] SRO Bury St Edmunds, FL641/7/1. Between 1758 and 1774 the Timworth poor rates never rose above £30 per year, averaging £20, but between 1775 and 1778 they rose rapidly, averaging £80 in 1777–8. By the early 1780s, they had fallen back to between £50 and £60. In 1785–8 the average was £58. In 1796 and 1801 bad harvests led to rates of over £100 and £200 respectively. General Suffolk poor-rate expenditure rose 21 per cent between 1776 and 1783–5 and just over 100 per cent between the early 1780s and 1803. *P.P.*, (1803–4), xiii, 498–9.

[31] *Gentleman's Magazine*, monthly wheat prices: July 1780 to July 1784 averaged 5.46 shillings. From July 1784 to July 1785, the average was 5.0 shillings. On Aug. 25, 1785, the Suffolk farmer William Godwin recorded that 'the last 7 weeks remarkable for heavy storms . . . Bury and several places whole fields of turnips washed up by the roots . . . we have had rain every day the seven weeks'. SRO Ipswich, HD365/1.

[32] *Ibid.*, 27 Aug. 1785. Judging by the larger rise in barley prices that crop seems to have been harder hit.

if, as seems likely, the local turnip crop had also suffered extensively, sheep farmers such as Worlledge would also have been faced with the loss of much of their animals' staple winter feed.[33] The barley stubbles, which provided 'good bite' for the sheep and were often undersown with clover, would have seemed particularly important under these circumstances, and the temptation to ignore or contest the gleaners' rights might have greatly increased. Essex farmers certainly appear to have increased their attacks on gleaners after the 1785 harvest. More Essex petty-sessions depositions relating to gleaning disputes occur in 1785 than in any other year for which records survive apart from 1788 itself.[34]

Thus it seems likely that by disturbing the delicate balance of gleaner–farmer relations in several ways, these weather conditions may have been part of the final impetus that induced the subscribers to take legal action. However, at a deeper level, the timing of the Timworth gleaning cases was bound up with the structure of local landholding and with the fundamental changes that were being introduced in this period by one man, Earl Cornwallis.

III

With the exception of a few small pieces of freehold, Cornwallis owned the entire parish of Timworth by the 1780s, not to mention the neighbouring parishes of Ingham and Culford. His main country residence was at Culford, less than two miles from Timworth.[35] Cornwallis was first and foremost a military man who is best known for his surrender at Yorktown, which effectively put an end to the American War of Independence. He spent more than two thirds of the last quarter of the eighteenth century on military or civil duties abroad – mainly in America, India, and Ireland.[36] These long absences inevitably lessened his

---

[33] *Ibid.*, 2 Sept. 1785 records 'at least one comb per acre of the standing wheat were blown out, beside oats and barley'. Godwin also recorded the local turnip crop had suffered badly. On turnips' importance see Young, *General View*, 57.

[34] The late harvest may also have cut down the period available to the gleaners between crop clearance and the date on which sheep owners were permitted to put their animals onto the stubbles (shack day). J. T. Munday, *An Eriswell Notebook* (typescript SRO Bury St Edmunds E.b.2). In nearby Eriswell, sheep often had precedence over cattle or hogs and in order 'that shack-day should provide really good bite for sheep no one was allowed to use a rake in stubble, neither the cultivator nor a gleaner'. For Essex gleaning conflicts see chapter 10.

[35] 'Survey of the Estates of Culford, Ingham, and Timworth'; W. A. Copinger, *The Manors of Suffolk* (Manchester, 1910), 1, 329; J. Roumieu, *Past and Present: The Three Villages of Culford, Ingham and Timworth* (Bury, 1892). Cornwallis also owned most of the neighbouring parishes of West Stow and Wordwell. *A Concise Description of Bury St Edmunds and Its Environs*, 60, 89–92, 211, 317. (See also Clive Paine's forthcoming volume on the Culford estate.) Cornwallis had three houses but preferred Culford to his other non-metropolitan residence at Brome Hall near Eye. See letterheads in C. Ross, ed., *Correspondence of Charles, First Marquis Cornwallis* (London, 1859), i.

[36] Ross, *Correspondence*, i, 111; *Dictionary of National Biography*, s.v. 'Cornwallis'; W. S. Seton-Karr, *Rulers of India: The Marquess Cornwallis* (Oxford, 1890).

personal impact on the lives of Timworth's inhabitants, but Cornwallis continued to take a great interest in expanding and improving the Culford estate. Although he was governor general in India between 1786 and 1794, the house at Culford was extensively refurbished in the early 1790s to be ready for his return, and despite communication difficulties, he maintained control over decisions relating to his farms whenever possible.[37]

In some ways Cornwallis seems the ideal candidate as prime mover behind the gleaning judgements for he was no run-of-the-mill eighteenth-century landowner. Worlledge and Steel's landlord played an important part in reshaping the nature of customary right and private property in India. The Permanent Settlement he introduced in 1793 made a fundamental change in the nature of Indian land tenure by ignoring the complex and largely unwritten customary laws of many Indian agricultural communities and giving one group, the Zamindars, sole proprietorial rights over the land.[38] The root causes of Cornwallis' determination to introduce private property rights in land maintained by a Western system of law are hard to unravel. The Permanent Settlement was partly a pragmatic response to the revenue-collection problems of the Indian administration, and it had been discussed for decades before his arrival. Although Cornwallis had 'a clear conviction' of its utility, he may have seen it primarily as a means of converting the Zamindars – by the gift of property – into improving aristocratic landlords after the contemporary English model.[39]

While the policies he later pursued in India suggest that Cornwallis would not have felt great sympathy for the poor's right to glean, those policies do not necessarily imply that he was an active opponent of the gleaners' case in the mid-1780s. What was Cornwallis' role? The cases certainly began during one of the few periods when he was actually based in England and making regular visits to his Culford estate,[40] but despite this coincidence, there is no positive evidence that connects Cornwallis to the 1786 and 1788 cases. An extensive

---

[37] It often took a year or more to get a response from Cornwallis about estate matters during his time in India, but his letters to his brother, the Bishop of Lichfield, who oversaw his estates in his absence, showed a passionate interest in Culford, which he referred to as 'that place of which I am so fond'. Kent Archives Office, Mann (Cornwallis), MSS. V.24.c.1.

[38] E. Stokes, *The English Utilitarians and India* (Oxford, 1959), 26, 82–3; V. A. Smith, *The Oxford History of India*, 4th edn (Oxford, 1981), 534–6; R. Guha, *A Rule of Property for Bengal: An Essay on the Idea of Permanent Settlement* (Paris, 1963), 13.

[39] Guha, *A Rule of Property*, 168–93; Stokes, *The English*, 26; G. Dunbar, *A History of India*, 4th edn (1949), 392; Seton-Karr, *Rulers*, 193; P. Griffiths, *The British Impact on India* (London, 1952), 170–1; R. Muir, *The Making of British India 1756–1858* (Manchester, 1915), 184–91; G. Moorhouse, *India Britannica* (London, 1983), 73. The permanent settlement was laid down as policy for Cornwallis by Parliament and by the court of directors.

[40] Cornwallis was 'in the habit of running down frequently for a week to Culford' between 1783 and his departure for India in May 1786, only a week or so before the first gleaning judgement was reached. Much of his time was spent in London although he was abroad on a diplomatic mission during September and October, 1785. Ross, *Correspondence*, i, 14 and chapter 7; KAO, U.24. C.1.

search among the letters he received and wrote while in India between 1786 and 1790 has failed to uncover any reference to either of the cases.[41] Given the patchy nature of the surviving correspondence no firm conclusions can be drawn, but if Cornwallis had been the main instigator of the cases, he would surely have referred to them in these letters or would have received some news of them from his British correspondents. Moreover, unless Cornwallis had anticipated that the 1786 judgement would fail to produce the required result and had left instructions for another case to be initiated in that event, which seems rather unlikely, he could have played no part in the decision to initiate a second case. He left for India before the outcome of the original case was known and he appears to have received no news from England until the early months of 1787,[42] by which time *Steel v. Houghton* would already have been initiated. Although it seems unlikely that his tenants, Worlledge and Steel, would have initiated the gleaning cases if they thought he would oppose them, the failure of any of the contemporary reports to connect Cornwallis with the cases or even to hint at the involvement of an unnamed local magnate suggests that he may have remained largely aloof from the proceedings. However, his policies profoundly influenced the context from which the Timworth gleaning cases arose, for despite the fragmentary nature of the evidence, it is clear that by the early 1780s Cornwallis had decided to enclose.

IV

The Timworth economy, like that of most eighteenth-century Breckland parishes, was based on sheep–corn husbandry. In 1768, for example, Farmer Worlledge owned more than 560 sheep and farmed 470 acres of 'plowed land' growing both grain and fodder crops.[43] In this period, the Breckland parishes were organised under a complex infield–outfield–breck system. Most parishes

---

[41] Many volumes of Cornwallis's official correspondence survive, but little relates to his dealings with his tenants. Neither the accounts sent by his lawyer Vernon nor his extensive correspondence with his brother mention either of the gleaning cases. Nor did the various family members who wrote to him about political events, family gossip, and other legal cases. Ross, *Correspondence*; KAO, V.24.C.1; PRO 30/11/137–9, 142, 147, 154, 156, 212, 270, 275, 277, 280, 288. The case may be mentioned in India-related correspondence, but I have not been through all the files of petitions for patronage, which Cornwallis seems to have kept separate. When the Earl of Iveagh's Elvedon Hall manuscripts become available, further information may come to light although the catalogue at the National Register of Archives (4134) suggests that material for the late 1780s is sparse.

[42] KAO, V.24.C.1, 24 Jan. 1787, 17 Feb. 1787.

[43] J. Thirsk and J. Imray, *Suffolk Farming in the Nineteenth Century* (Suffolk Record Society, 1958), 18; M. R. Postgate, 'Field Systems of East Anglia', in A. Baker and R. Butlin (eds.), *Studies of Field Systems in the British Isles* (Cambridge, 1973), 283; SRO Bury St Edmunds, FL594/3/26; *ibid.*, E3/10/18.5; Raynbird, *The Agriculture of Suffolk*, 4; Roumieu, *Past and Present: The Three Villages*, 61–2; Young, *General View*, 5; SRO Bury St Edmunds T64/1, 2 – the 1840 tithe map schedule.

contained a combination of almost permanently cultivated closes or open fields, of temporary and periodically cultivated brecks, and of sandy heathland or waste seldom if ever under plough, the entire area being overlaid in many cases by a number of foldcourses.[44] Since the dynamic process of enclosing the infield land and of expanding the infield into outfield areas and the outfield into the brecks and heathlands had followed different forms and chronologies in each parish, this pattern was subject to many local variations, but Timworth was probably fairly typical. Much of the parish was farmed under a shift system in the late eighteenth century and despite the presence of several enclosed fields and fairly large areas of heath and grassland, most of it appears to have consisted of arable open fields or brake lands.[45] Although the consolidation of scattered strips into compact, hedged blocks and other forms of informal enclosure continued in the Suffolk Breckland through the eighteenth century, the basic open-field pattern remained. The first two substantial enclosure acts involving open-field land in this part of Suffolk were not passed until the 1770s. The first major wave of such acts did not begin until the 1790s. However, the enclosure process was already gaining momentum by the early 1780s when the Duke of Grafton was informally enclosing parishes to the north of Timworth and a proposed act for the enclosure of Stanton, only six miles away, was being hotly contested.[46]

Since none of the parishes on the Culford estate were ever the subject of parliamentary enclosure acts and since no land-tax returns survive, the chronology of Timworth's informal enclosure has to be reconstructed from more fragmentary evidence. The 1780s and 1790s were clearly the key decades. The Timworth tithe map of 1840 and other nineteenth-century maps indicate that the parish was fully enclosed by this period,[47] but the situation in the mid-eighteenth century was different. A series of loosely connected maps drawn up in the 1760s suggest that most of the parish was still laid out in open fields divided into large numbers of small strips. The only late eighteenth-century evidence available is a

[44] Holderness, 'East Anglia and the Fens', 206. M. R. Postgate, 'The Field Systems of Breckland', *Agricultural History Review*, 10 (1962), 91 provides the best overview of this complex system. A foldcourse was a strictly defined area of open arable lands, heathlands, and closes where grazing was the sole right of a particular flock irrespective of the ownership or occupancy of the soil. See also K. J. Allison, 'The Sheep–Corn Husbandry of Norfolk in the Sixteenth and Seventeenth Centuries', *Agricultural History Review*, 5 (1957), 12–30; A. Simpson, 'The East Anglian Foldcourse: Some Queries', *Agricultural History Review*, 7 (1958), 87–96.

[45] SRO Bury St Edmunds, FL594/3/26 (1760s) and 'Survey of the Estates of Culford, Ingham, and Timworth'; Postgate, 'Field Systems of Breckland', 89 for a reference to farms let in Timworth 'according as the shifts of the fields and enclosures shall then fall in course'.

[46] W. Tate, 'A Handlist of Suffolk Enclosure Acts and Awards', *Proceedings of the Suffolk Institute of Archaeology and Natural History*, 25 (1951), 225–63, especially 240–7; Postgate, 'Field Systems of Breckland', 84–8; D. P. Dymond, 'The Suffolk Landscape', in L. M. Munby (ed.), *East Anglian Studies*, (Cambridge 1968), 17–26; D. Dymond, 'Opposition to Enclosure in a Suffolk Village', *Suffolk Review*, 5 (1980), 13–22; M. Turner, *English Parliamentary Enclosure: Its Historical Geography and Economic History* (Folkstone, 1980), 46–8.

[47] SRO Bury St Edmunds, T 64/1, 2; Timworth Tithe Map 1840.

map of Cornwallis' estates drawn up in 1793, which gives no indication of how the land was divided up between Cornwallis' tenants, but fundamental reorganisation was in motion by 1793.[48] Many of the roads and baulks marked out in the 1760s had disappeared; in several parts of the parish, the closes and fields appear to have been reorganised establishing a new pattern similar to that found in 1840.[49] The schedule attached to the 1793 map described a third of the parish as 'arable inclosed land', a third as 'arable brake land', and just over one fifth as 'grassland' – the remainder being heathland with a small area set aside for roads, cottages, and plantations. The informal enclosure process therefore seems to have been fairly well advanced by 1793, but the precise status of the 'arable brakelands' at this point is problematic. At least two or three small strips of freehold within the 'Home field brakes' did not yet belong to Cornwallis, which could have inhibited his enclosure plans for that area.[50]

The Timworth glebe terriers can be used to date the enclosure more precisely. Those written in the 1760s and 1770s give no indication of any change in field arrangements. Each lists the same five areas as 'enclosed land,' and the same 'arable lands in the open field'. However, the 1784 terrier contains a new proposal that the scattered strips of glebe in the open fields be exchanged for a relatively consolidated area, 'by the desire of Earl Cornwallis, patron'.[51] The beginning of Cornwallis' enclosure initiative therefore predates the first gleaning case by at least one or two years. However, the proposed exchange was not formally completed until more than a decade after 1784. The proposal was appended to the 1791 and the 1794 terriers, but the actual distribution of glebe strips remained unaltered, probably because of local opposition. It was not until the next terrier in 1801 that the exchange was no longer recorded as a proposal but was placed instead in the main body of the document, the formal completion of the enclosure apparently being finalised on 19 December 1796.[52] To what extent was this merely the final legal ratification of alterations that had

---

[48] SRO Bury St Edmunds, FL 594/3/26 and 'Survey of the Estates of Culford, Ingham, and Timworth'. These two sources form the basis of the following analysis.

[49] The area referred to on the 1760s maps as 'the Green' had been divided into three fields by 1793, and, following Cornwallis' instructions, woods had been planted across land previously called 'The Furlongs', KAO V.24.C.1, 16 Sept. 1790.

[50] The closes and isolated enclosures on the 1760s maps represent nowhere near a third of the parish. The hundreds of strips shown on the 1760s maps are almost entirely absent on the 1793 estate plan, but this may reflect the fact that the later map was not designed to provide information on detailed tenancy divisions, rather than indicating a fundamental change in land organisation.

[51] Postgate, *Field Systems of East Anglia*, 288; M. W. Beresford, 'Glebe Terriers and Open Field Leicestershire', in W. Hoskins (ed.), *Studies in Leicestershire History* (Leicester, 1949), 83; SRO Bury St Edmunds, 806/1/156 (series), FL641/2–3. The Timworth terriers are available for 1760, 1763, 1777, 1783, 1791, 1794, 1801, and 1806.

[52] The terriers of all three of Cornwallis' parishes – Timworth, Ingham, and Culford – show the same dramatic change between 1794 and 1801, but the 1801 Culford terrier also records the exact date of the exchange (which seems to have been formally completed on the same date in all three parishes) as December 19, 1796. SRO Bury St Edmunds, 806/1/46.

already taken place? The many changes indicated by a comparison of the 1760s and 1793 maps – including some evidence of glebe consolidation in Timworth by 1793 – suggest that the proposal in the 1784, 1791, and 1794 terriers may have been a description of already planned and at least partly executed arrangements, formal acknowledgement of which was now being sought.[53] Setting aside for the moment the indications that a rearguard action, possibly led by the Houghtons, managed to delay the completion of the enclosure process in Timworth until 1796, there can be no doubt that the gleaning cases arose after Cornwallis' large-scale enclosure plan had been initiated. Indeed, the genesis of the cases in 1785–6 almost certainly coincided with the first and most important stage of the enclosure process.

Whatever the precise chronology of the enclosure, the Timworth gleaning cases obviously arose when the relationships between the main local landowner, the farmers, and the Timworth poor were undergoing a fundamental change. Unfortunately, the attitudes of these groups to the enclosure and to each other remain obscure, but the large tenant farmers almost certainly gained from the enclosure.[54] The Worlledge family clearly prospered. A rearrangement of leases in 1800 gave John Worlledge by far the largest farm on the Culford estate. By the 1820s, John Worlledge, Esq., was renting 1126 acres in Ingham and Timworth and in the 1844 directory 'John Worlledge Esq.' of Ingham is described as a 'banker'.[55] The main burden of the enclosure fell not on the big tenant farmers but on the remaining 25 or so households in Timworth. Even before enclosure, this was a highly differentiated community in which there were no medium-sized landholders. In 1786, 95 per cent of the rate burden was carried by Timworth's 4 large tenant farmers – Worlledge, Steel, Harrison, and Andrews.[56] How reliant were the remainder – the labourers, artisans, and minor

---

[53] In the 1784 Timworth terrier, the words 'proposed to be' were inserted later and in a different hand. The document had originally read simply 'the field glebes exchanged for inclosed lands'. Presumably the original intention had merely been to record an already worked-out, and possibly an already completed, glebe exchange. *Ibid.*, 806/1/186.

[54] *Ibid.*, FL641/7/1. Cornwallis made only minor changes among his Timworth tenancies during the last quarter of the eighteenth century. John Worlledge and James Steel continued to pay around a third and a twelfth respectively of the parish rates until Steel's death in 1799. Cornwallis was keen to avoid any oppressive actions against his tenants that, in his words, might 'hurt my character in a neighbourhood whose esteem I have been so careful to cultivate', and there is no evidence that he put Worlledge and Steel under pressure by raising rents dramatically after the enclosure. KAO V.24.c.1, 20 Aug. 1791.

[55] 'Sale Schedule, Cornwallis estates', 1820s (privately held). SRO Bury St Edmunds, E3/10/18.5 Worlledge's Ingham farm was rented at £780 per annum. His old farm was given to James Walton at £435 per annum. W. White, *History, Gazetteer and Directory of Suffolk* (Sheffield, 1844), 691.

[56] Most breckland parishes were dominated by large estates carved up into sizeable tenancies. Postgate, 'The Field Systems of Breckland', 99. The Timworth overseers' rate books (SRO Bury St Edmunds, FL641/7/1 and 9/1) indicate only four or five other families had sufficient holdings to appear even as minimal ratepayers.

smallholders – on the mesh of local customary rights that was threatened to its foundations by Cornwallis' plans to enclose?

The separate foldcourse rights found in most Breckland parishes almost certainly restricted the common right of pasture enjoyed by Timworth's inhabitants over both open fields and commons.[57] In systematically buying up property in the parish throughout the eighteenth century, the Cornwallis family were particularly careful to ensure they were also acquiring all rights relating to 'feeding grounds, ways . . . commons and rights of commonage'.[58] However, the small area labelled 'the Green' on the 1760s maps may have remained open. In addition, the unrestricted references to 'appurts' in some late eighteenth-century Timworth deeds imply that a few local occupiers enjoyed common rights of pasture over fallow fields, post-harvest stubbles, uncultivated parts of the brakelands, and other commonable areas of the parish.[59] The eagerness of the Cornwallis family to control local grazing rights, which could be leased for large profits to local flockmasters, probably meant that the rights of most Timworth inhabitants were increasingly restricted, but even limited access at certain times of year to pasture, fuel, furze, and wild fruits would have been important to the poor.[60] At enclosure they almost certainly lost whatever vestiges of common right they had been able to retain until that point. Neither the 1840 tithe map nor the Charity Commissioners' reports give any indication that the Timworth poor received compensation for their loss of common rights at the enclosure, and the open area described as 'the Green' in the 1760s was entirely farmed by one of the tenants of the owners of Culford Hall by 1840. If they had ever had any rights of pasture over part of the

[57] The absence of any later seventeenth- or eighteenth-century manorial records or by-laws for Timworth makes it difficult to discuss the nature of common right in the parish. For an excellent discussion of customary right in this period, see J. M. Neeson, 'Common Right and Enclosure in Eighteenth-Century Northamptonshire' (PhD thesis, Warwick University, 1977). The foldcourse system remained important until enclosure in many breckland parishes. Young implies sheepfold reduced the value of common right of pasture in Barningham near Timworth. *General View*, 41–2. On the widespread abuse by sheepcourse owners of rights of commonage on heathland and waste, see Allison, 'Sheepcorn Husbandry', 23–5. On exclusive grazing rights given to the flock by one person in parishes just north of Timworth, see Postgate, 'Field Systems of East Anglia', 322. For references to foldcourses in late eighteenth-century Timworth, see SRO Bury St Edmunds, E3/10/18.5. On the central role of the foldcourse in Ingham and Timworth in earlier centuries, see Postgate, 'Field Systems of Breckland', 88; Simpson, 'The East Anglian Foldcourse', 94; SRO Bury St Edmunds 1674/1–10.

[58] When on two rare occasions they agreed to sell tiny pieces of freehold to a Timworth farmer, they made sure that 'the common pasture and other rights of common in, upon and over the common pasture of Timworth' were not part of the sale and remained 'reserved to Lord Cornwallis and his heirs'. SRO Bury St Edmunds, E3/10/18.1 and 18.3.

[59] R. Butlin, 'Some Terms Used in Agrarian History', *Agricultural History Review*, 9 pt. 2 (1961), 98–101; SRO Bury St Edmunds, E3/10/18.1.

[60] Neeson, 'Common Right', 52–60.

parish, the Timworth poor had almost certainly lost them by the early nineteenth century.[61]

Thus the Timworth gleaning cases arose during a period when the other customary rights of the parish's labouring families were also under serious threat. The conflicts engendered by the enclosure process were almost certainly interwoven with those that created the court cases of 1786 and 1788. Indeed according to local newspaper reports about the trial, the enclosure issue was specifically raised by Worlledge's counsel in 1786. 'The right of enclosing arable land', he contended, 'abolished the right of gleaning because if the poor broke down fences they trespassed.' This was countered by Manning's counsel who asserted that 'if the farmer barred up the passages to the field against the poor, they had a right to break down those fences'. After this initial discussion the enclosure issue played no further part in the legal arguments of 1786 and 1788.[62] It is therefore possible that Worlledge's counsel was simply making a general legal point, but it seems rather more likely that his argument was based on the specific conditions prevalent in Timworth at the time of the alleged trespass.

It would be unwise to assume that Cornwallis's activities as an encloser necessarily imply that he played a positive part in the legal attack on the gleaners. Although he seems to have largely ignored the common rights of the Timworth poor after the enclosure, Cornwallis was not as rapacious a landlord as many of his late-eighteenth-century counterparts. When advised to pull down the village at Culford, because it was too near to his residence, he replied, 'I shall like it (the house at Culford) infinitely better than a more magnificent building and . . . no person shall ever persuade me to demolish the village.'[63] More important, perhaps, gleaning did not affect the larger landowners directly. It was mainly an issue between the farmers and the labouring poor, and the

---

[61] White's *Dictionary* described allotments set aside after enclosure to supply fuel to the poor in several of the parishes around the Culford estate, for example 'Thurston', 317, 'Fornham', 666, 'Bardwell' and 'Barningham', 681–3, 'Stanton' (fifty-four acres), 699, 'Troston', 704, but no such arrangements are recorded in any of the Culford estate parishes. Young, *General View*, 41–4; SRO Bury St Edmunds, T64/1, 2. Reports of the Charity Commissioners, *The Charities of the County of Suffolk* (London, 1840), 344.

[62] *Ipswich Journal* 3 June 1786. The charge in both the 1786 and 1788 cases actually specified 'Trespass for breaking and entering the closes of the plaintiff', *English Reports* (C.P.), 126:32–4, but the implied reference to an enclosed piece of land cannot be taken as evidence in this case, for as Blackstone pointed out, 'Every unwarrantable entry on another's soil the law entitles a trespass by *breaking his close* . . . For every man's land is in the eye of the law inclosed . . . either by a visible and material fence, as one field is divided from another by a hedge; or by an invisible boundary existing only in the contemplation of law, as when one man's land adjoins to another's in the same field.' Blackstone, *Commentaries on the Laws of England*, iii, 209–10. See also Gilbert, *The Law of Evidence* (ed. Lofft), ii, 505.

[63] KAO V.24.C.1; *Ipswich Journal*, 22 Aug. 1792. See also 28 Aug. 1791 for another example of his relative benevolence: his refusal to allow a local malster who was a tenant of his to use manorial privilege to gain a monopoly that would have been detrimental to the local farmers.

approach taken by Capel Lofft and other magistrates suggests that landowners did not automatically take the farmer's side. During the 1780s, some enclosing landlords actually supported the gleaners.[64] It therefore remains an open question whether the 1786 and 1788 cases were initiated by a subscription of local farmers acting independently of the local landowner or whether the cases were partly instigated by Cornwallis or his agents. Whoever instigated the cases, within a decade Cornwallis had become a major beneficiary of the 1788 judgement. It badly damaged the Houghtons' economic position, and their loss was to be Cornwallis' gain, for John Houghton was a major opponent of the enclosure process.

V

Before these connections can be assessed, it is important to establish how deeply the 1786 and 1788 cases affected the lives of the two shoemakers' families against whom these judgements were made. The records are inevitably much more informative about the lives of ratepayers and overseers such as Worlledge and Steel than they are about the poorer inhabitants of Timworth. Even the parish registers are remarkably uninformative about the Houghtons and Mannings. Although the baptisms of two of the Houghton children are recorded, we know from other sources that they had at least four offspring, and the Manning's children have left no trace at all in the local registers.[65] This may reflect the frequent short-distance migrations of these families, but Timworth's inhabitants had a long history of religious dissent, and the paucity of entries probably reflects the deep nonconformist connections of the Houghtons and the Mannings.[66]

---

[64] Capel Lofft for example. Dymond, 'Opposition to Enclosure', 13–22; See also chapter 10.

[65] The overseers' records (SRO Bury St Edmunds, FL641/9/1) indicate that Worlledge took this office every third year in the 1780s and 1790s. The children of the Houghtons I have found records of are Mary (assumed to be John's child, *ibid.*, FL641/4/2) born in 1762; Elizabeth born 1765 (*ibid.*, FL571/4/3); John mentioned as their only son and heir in 1796 (*ibid.*, E3/10/18.1); and possibly Ann Houghton mentioned in 1795 as having a bastard child publicly baptised in Timworth (*ibid.*, FL641/4/2). The Mannings are even more difficult to trace. Although they are known to have had a child called Joseph, neither the registers of Timworth and the surrounding parishes nor the Suffolk section of the International Genealogical Index contain any reference to his birth.

[66] The registers of the Church Gate Street Presbyterian congregation in Bury St Edmunds record the birth of a John Houghton 'son of Houghton' in 1740 (*International Genealogical Index, Suffolk*, s.v. 'John Houghton'; SRO Bury St Edmunds J558/2). John's father's occupation is not recorded, but his older brother Thomas was a shoemaker in Bury and a regular member of the same dissenting congregation throughout the 1770s and 1780s. The eighteenth-century Bury Presbyterian records include two references to Benjamin Mannings and one to William Manning, shoemaker of Chevington. Nonconformist groups were particularly attractive to artisans, and although there is no clear evidence that Timworth had its own dissenting congregation before the early nineteenth century, the Compton census indicates that the parish had a much higher than average proportion of nonconformist families. V. B. Redstone, *Records of Protestant Dissenters in Suffolk* (Woodbridge, 1912), 67, notes a Timworth dissenters' meeting in 1825. The three

The parish registers do, however, indicate the 1780s began inauspiciously for the Mannings of Timworth. In 1780, they record the death of John Manning, cordwainer, who was almost certainly a close relative of Benjamin. John was extremely poor by the late 1770s. The parish gave him a pauper's burial and his widow, Ann, who immediately became dependent on regular parish relief, outlived him by only three years.[67] In the early 1780s, Benjamin Manning was in his mid-fifties, working as a shoemaker and probably also as a casual labourer. He was married and had at least one child still at home. The Manning family had a legal settlement in Timworth, and although they were not regular receivers for most of the 1780s, they were sometimes dependent on the parish for considerable periods. In 1784, Benjamin Manning was given more than £2 10s. in relief, and in March 1786 the parish paid out a larger sum for medicines, financial aid, and finally for a 'shroud, coffin and burial for Joseph, son of Elizabeth and Benjamin Manning'.[68]

His son's death only two months before Benjamin Manning became liable for over £ 26 damages and costs after losing the Common Pleas case brought by Worlledge must have made 1786 a bleak year for him, but he was not easily cowed into submission despite his temporary dependence on relief. In October 1786, he ignored local newspaper reports claiming he had 'deviated from the principles of honesty' by stealing from the harvest sheaves and attempted to prosecute Worlledge for assault at the Suffolk quarter sessions. Benjamin himself did not die until 1804, and his family's fortunes may have revived slightly in the 1790s. He was not given a pauper's burial in 1804, and his widow survived for more than two years before the name 'widow Manning' began to appear among those receiving regular relief from the Timworth parish officers.[69]

Mary Houghton, the other gleaning-case defendant, may also have had a poor reputation. Born in Timworth in 1730 the daughter of a local husbandman, Daniel Clarke, she became the focus of considerable attention from the parish officers in April, 1762, when the Timworth registers record the birth of 'Mary, base child of Mary Clarke'. Two months later she married John Houghton, a shoemaker from Flempton, three miles to the north. The negotiations that preceded the marriage ceremony gave John and Mary a share in Daniel Clarke's tiny freehold property in Timworth, but they do not appear to

major dissenting churches based in Bury St Edmunds were only just over an hour's walk away. *Ibid.*, 85; *The Description of Bury*, 56; D. P. Dymond, 'Suffolk and the Compton Census of 1676', *Suffolk Review*, 111 (Autumn 1966), 103–18.
[67] SRO Bury St Edmunds, FL641/4/2; *ibid.*, 641/7/1.
[68] Benjamin died in 1804 at age 79, *ibid.*, 641/4/2. PRO Ind. 6552 describes him as a shoemaker. He probably did general labouring as well. *Ipswich Journal*, 3 June 1786; SRO Bury St Edmunds, FL641/4/2 and 7/1. These records also include references to the deaths of two other young Mannings during the 1780s, at least one was probably Benjamin's daughter.
[69] PRO Ind. 6552; SRO Ipswich B105/2/48; *Bury and Norwich Post*, 7 June 1786; SRO Bury St Edmunds, FL641/7/1.

have taken up permanent residence there until 1770, when John first appears in the yearly lists of residents liable for highway duties.[70] In many respects the Houghtons were in a similar position to the Mannings. Both household heads were shoemakers. Both Mary Houghton and Benjamin Manning were in their late fifties when a Common Pleas action was brought against them, and both families tended to pass their trade down through the generations. The final stages of the lifecycles of the two families also followed the same path. By 1806 both Mary Houghton and Benjamin Manning's wife were widows reliant on weekly poor relief payments granted by parish officers from the local farming families. By 1813 each of these women was being given more than £6 a year from the parish fund.[71] In the mid-1780s, however, the Houghtons were still in a much stronger position than the Mannings. Although the Houghtons paid the minimum-possible highway duty, as did all but a few of the wealthier inhabitants, they seem to have weathered the storms of the 1770s and 1780s without recourse to the parish. Their relatively secure position was almost certainly due to their access to Mary's father's small freehold. This consisted of two dwellings with gardens and orchards attached and a piece of land containing three roods 'with the appurts' – one of the few Timworth freeholds not yet owned by Cornwallis. Daniel Clarke had agreed to share this property with them during his own and his wife's lifetime and to eventually leave it to them as sole owners. It was a tiny piece of land, rated at the lowest possible level (one pence) and representing less than 0.2 per cent of the parish total, or about an eightieth of Steel's Timworth and Ingham assessments.[72] However, access to common right of pasture was vitally important to the family economies of rural artisans such as the Houghtons. The ability to keep even a minimal number of livestock provided a vital cushion against poverty. In the early 1780s, the Houghtons almost certainly enjoyed the main benefits of the shared freehold. By 1790, Daniel Clarke was dead and his name had been replaced in the Timworth ratebooks by that of John Houghton.[73]

However, John Houghton's apparent increase in status in the early 1790s obscures his family's true position. Around the time of the 1788 case and possibly as a direct result of their involvement in it, the Houghtons began to fall deep into debt. At the beginning of 1789, only a few months after the Court of Common Pleas had required them to find more than £35 damages as well as

[70] SRO Bury St Edmunds, FL641/4/2; E3/10/18.1; FL571/4/3; FL641/8/1; the Houghton's second child, Elizabeth, was baptised at Flempton in 1765.

[71] SRO Bury St Edmunds FL641/4/2. By the 1790s, John Houghton junior was also a shoemaker. E3/10/18.1.

[72] SRO Bury St Edmunds FL641/9/1; E3/10/18.1; 'Survey of the Estates of Culford, Ingham, and Timworth.'

[73] Snell, *Annals of the Labouring Poor*, 166–79; SRO Bury St Edmunds, E3/10/18.1; *ibid.*, FL641/7/1. Daniel Clark was described 'as an old man' in the burial register as he certainly must have been, for he had been married sixty years at his death in 1790, FL641/4/2.

their own costs, they partly mortgaged their small freehold inheritance for just under £15. By 1794, they found it necessary to raise further funds and were given a £50 mortgage by a local tanner. However, they soon found it impossible to pay the interest and in November, 1796, they were forced to put the property up for auction.[74] The 1788 judgement may not have been the only cause of their financial decline. The enclosure process and the Houghtons' attempts to oppose it may have undermined the basis of their makeshift economy in several ways. Moreover, John Houghton was almost certainly in poor health in the last few years before his death in 1797. However, the gleaning judgement of 1788 clearly played an important part in the process by which the Houghtons were turned into landless proletarians. Their Timworth freehold fetched only £78 in the 1796 auction. Within a year John Houghton was dead. Within three years Mary Houghton's meagre capital had gone, and she had become a weekly recipient of parish relief.[75] The main beneficiary of the Houghton's misfortune was, inevitably, Cornwallis whose purchase of the Houghton's freehold enabled him to add a vital piece of the Timworth jigsaw to his vast collection.

VI

The Houghton's freehold was not just any piece of the jigsaw, however. Complete ownership of every tiny piece of freehold or copyhold land in the parish apart from the glebe and townlands was not achieved by the owners of Culford Hall until the second quarter of the nineteenth century,[76] but this did not prevent the enclosure from being completed and ratified in December, 1796, just after this sale was forced on the Houghtons by their creditors. Three factors suggest that the Houghton's property was of particular strategic importance to Cornwallis at this point. First, unlike almost any of the other half a dozen or so tiny freehold properties not yet owned by Cornwallis, the Houghton's freehold consisted of open-field strips in the large area known as the 'Home field brakes', Since it is clear from the 1793 map that the enclosure of the Home field brakes had not been completed in 1793,[77] Cornwallis may well have had to wait until he had purchased the Houghton's freehold before he could obtain the complete agreement necessary to enclose this final part of the parish. Second, while the deeds of other local freeholders, such as the hosier Thomas Cage, record that the Cornwallis family had long since reserved to their heirs 'all commons and rights of commonage' relating to these properties, the

---

[74] SRO Bury St Edmunds, E3/10/18.1; PRO Ind. 6554.

[75] SRO Bury St Edmunds, FL641/7/1; FL641/4/2; E3/10/18.1.

[76] SRO Bury St Edmunds E3/10/18.2. The cottage and two roods owned by John Cage, shopkeeper, did not come into the Culford estate until Richard Benyon de Beauvoir bought them in 1828, but this was not in an open-field area.

[77] SRO Bury St Edmunds T64/1, 2; 'Survey of the Estates of Culford, Ingham, and Timworth'.

Houghtons' deeds contain no such reservations or limitations. They were one of the last families in Timworth to retain a strong legal claim to rights of commonage.[78] Finally, the terriers indicate that the Houghtons had set their faces solidly against the enclosure and were one of its foremost opponents. The glebe terriers were of considerable legal importance not only in the ecclesiastical courts but also, as Burn pointed out in the 1780s, in the temporal courts. It was therefore important to Cornwallis and to his nominee, the rector of Timworth, who was the joint instigator of the exchange proposal of 1784, that the terriers should legally recognise the enclosure that had just been set in motion. Thus the signatures on the contested terriers of the period between 1784 and 1796 may offer indirect evidence about the nature of local opposition to the enclosure process.

Glebe terriers had to be signed by the incumbent and by a church warden, but if the terrier was not countersigned by one or more of the 'substantial inhabitants' of the parish, its value as evidence might be greatly reduced or even nullified.[79] Most of the Timworth terriers of this period were also signed by one of the larger farmers. The 1760s terriers, for example, were signed both by Robert Worlledge, the church warden, and by the parish's next largest farmer. This was not a uniform pattern, but it is surely no coincidence that between the late insertion of the controversial proposal clause in 1784 and the final ratification of the enclosure in 1796, none of the substantial farmers in Timworth were prepared to sign the terriers as an inhabitant. The 1791 and 1794 terriers, which continued to record the enclosure exchange only as a proposal, despite the fact that it had already been partly completed and was the agreed policy of both the incumbent and his patron Cornwallis, were effectively preventing the final legal registration of the enclosure. As such, Cornwallis' large tenant farmers were not likely to put their names to these documents voluntarily and none of them did so. However, two small freeholders did come forward and signed the 1791 and 1794 terriers – the shoemaker John Houghton and the hosier, Thomas Cage.[80] By doing so they were almost certainly declaring their open opposition to the enclosure.

[78] SRO Bury St Edmunds, 43/10/18.1, 3.

[79] James Andrews, Timworth's third-largest farmer, signed every terrier 1776–1806 as church-warden. R. Burn, *The Ecclesiastical Law*, 4th edn (1781), 365–66. 'These terriers are of some weight . . . especially if they be signed not only by the parson and churchwardens, but also by the substantial inhabitants; but if they be signed by the parson only, they can be no evidence for him; so neither (as it seemeth) if they be signed only by the parson and churchwardens, if the churchwardens are of his nomination.' By 1824, imperfect terriers signed by church wardens but not by other inhabitants were recorded in evidence. *Ibid.*, 8th edn (1824), 400.

[80] No 'inhabitants' signed the 1784 terrier. Houghton and Cage were the only inhabitants signing in 1791 and 1794. Thomas Cage's father, who died in 1791 before the terrier was made, had signed one previous terrier in 1777. He is the only other smallholder to have done so.

The opponents of the Timworth enclosure would not have had to look far to gain encouragement. In 1784 and 1785 the smallholders of Stanton just north of Timworth had been faced by a similar alliance of the parson and the largest local landowner, but by concerted action they had undermined the enclosure bill and postponed the enclosure for more than a decade. Overt opposition to enclosure was not as exceptional as some historians have suggested. Muskett's work on East Anglia 1740–1820 concludes that 'opposition to enclosure has probably been underestimated', echoing Neeson's views that enclosure protest of various kinds was neither unusual nor atypical.[81] Cornwallis' ownership of almost all of Timworth made its lesser inhabitants' position much weaker than it was at Stanton, where land ownership was more diffuse,[82] but Timworth still contained a few freeholders whose refusal to acquiesce without a contest almost certainly made them the chief obstacle to Cornwallis' enclosure plans for the Culford estate.

How was this opposition overcome in Timworth? The precise tactics used are unclear, but the final effect was the same for both the Cages and the Houghtons. Both families were completely ruined. Thomas Cage died in 1791 at the age of forty seven leaving his house and freehold to his widow and his son, but within a year the property had to be mortgaged. By 1794 the Cages had to sell it to Mary Siggoe, Worlledge's granddaughter, from whom Cornwallis obtained it a few years later. From 1794 onward, Widow Cage became dependent on poor relief. Like Mary Houghton and Widow Manning she cost the parish more than £5 a year to support, and she remained dependent on relief until her death in 1806.[83] John and Mary Houghton's opposition to the enclosure probably continued until the enforced sale of their property in mid-November, 1796. Is it mere coincidence that the final ratification of the glebe exchange followed less than a month after the Houghtons' opposition was effectively silenced by this sale, or that Cornwallis' plans to block off the old road through the 'Home field brakes' finally moved toward completion just after the Houghton's property came into his hands?[84] All the evidence therefore suggests that the 1788 judgement helped to undermine the financial position of one of the last remaining freeholders who was actively opposing Cornwallis' enclosure plans.

---

[81] Dymond, 'Opposition to Enclosure', 13–22; P. Muskett, *Riotous Assemblies, Popular Disturbances in East Anglia 1740–1822* (Ely, 1984), 41–2; J. M. Neeson, 'The Opponents of Enclosure in Eighteenth-Century Northamptonshire', *Past and Present*, 105 (1984), 135.

[82] Neeson points out that resisting villages were often diffuse rather than consolidated in their land ownership patterns. Neeson, 'Opponents of Enclosure', 131.

[83] SRO Bury St Edmunds, FL641/4/2; FL641/7/1; E3/10/18.3.

[84] SRO Bury St Edmunds Q/SH 102. Cornwallis' plan to block up the old Ampton to Fornham road, which ran through the middle of the 'Home field brakes,' was finally fulfilled by building a new road to the north of the 'Home field brakes' in 1797 and by obtaining a formal highway division order in April, 1798. Once again, the timing of these moves suggests that this was a problem area for Cornwallis until 1796.

Was *Steel v. Houghton* part of a deliberate strategy by Cornwallis' agents? It is possible that when a gleaner needed to be selected as the target of a second prosecution in 1786, Mary Houghton was chosen precisely because her family was holding out against the enclosure but, given Cornwallis' absence and our inability to link him or his agents with the case, we cannot assume automatically that this was the reason.[85] It is equally likely that Benjamin Manning and Mary Houghton were chosen by a farmer-dominated group of subscribers because the economic positions their families held made it difficult for the local farmers and parish officers to influence their behaviour by threatening informal sanctions. Artisans such as the Houghtons or the Mannings were not usually reliant on the farmers for employment, and both they and their wives therefore had more scope for independent action than the local labourers, who were increasingly dependent on the wages paid by Worlledge, Steel, and the other two large farmers. The Houghtons were in a particularly strong position, because their small freehold gave them an alternative source of income to fall back on. Was it coincidence that both the defendants' families followed the specific trade of shoemaker? Unlike most village artisans, who were reliant on the larger farmers and local gentry for their orders, the shoemakers' main customers were the poor themselves, and they were therefore in a much less vulnerable position. As Eric Hobsbawm has pointed out, shoemakers had a reputation as spokesmen and organisers of the country poor in the early nineteenth century.[86] Literacy may also have been important. Unlike the vast majority of Timworth labourers and husbandmen both John Houghton and Thomas Cage were literate, as were their sons.[87] The leaders of Timworth's anti-enclosure group would have had direct access to the local newspaper reports recording similar activities by the Stanton freeholders at almost exactly the same moment as the Timworth opposition was gaining momentum. It remains possible, of course, that the subscribers chose Manning and Houghton at random or because their families had generally bad reputations in the village. However, it seems more likely that they were selected because, like the hosier Thomas Cage, they were relatively immune to the other forms of informal sanctions available to overseers and farming employers. As relatively independent men and women with nonconformist connections and

---

[85] It is even more difficult to link Cornwallis to the first case. There is no evidence that Benjamin Manning had any effective means of opposing the enclosure.

[86] E. Hobsbawm and J. Scott, 'Political Shoemakers', in E. Hobsbawm (ed.), *Worlds of Labour*, (London, 1984), 106–19. E. Hobsbawm and G. Rude, *Captain Swing* (Harmondsworth, 1969), 150–1, note a close correlation in 1830 between the number of shoemakers in a parish and the level of disturbances in 1830.

[87] I have no precise figures for late eighteenth-century Suffolk, but only 13 per cent of Essex labourers and 36 per cent of husbandmen signed rather than put a mark in 1748–1800. King, 'Crime, Law, and Society', 189. The equivalent figures for the diocese of Norwich 1580–1700 were 15 per cent and 21 per cent (shoemakers 35 per cent); D. Cressy, *Literacy and Social Order: Reading and Writing in Tudor and Stuart England* (Cambridge, 1980), 119.

traditions of greater literacy, they were the natural leaders of the poorer part of the Timworth community.

VII

The gleaning judgements of 1786 and 1788 can be viewed from many angles. To the lawyers of later generations the 1788 judgement was 'the great case of gleaning', a useful addition to case law that provided a convenient and relatively clear legal precedent. To Lord Loughborough, the chief justice of the Court of Common Pleas in the later 1780s, it was a cut-and-dried case from the start. For all his detailed arguments and rationalisations, his attitude was clear. 'When the claim of a right to glean was first brought before the court', he explained in 1788, 'I was then of opinion against the claim. First I thought it inconsistent with the nature of property which imports exclusive enjoyment. Secondly, destructive of the peace and good order of society.'[88]

The attitude of Cornwallis remains obscure. He may have been a major, if discrete, force behind both cases. More likely, perhaps, once the campaign had been started by the farmers, his agents may have suggested to them in 1786 that the Houghtons would be particularly deserving targets for their legal attentions. From the point of view of the prosperous tenant farmers Worlledge and Steel, the Timworth gleaning cases seem to have been largely a pragmatic attempt both to control the poor's access to the land in pursuance of their customary rights and to appropriate the gleanings of the most important local crop. However, if this was their main aim they were clearly not very successful in the long term. The mid-nineteenth-century Suffolk writers Raynbird and Glyde indicate that gleaning remained an extremely important source of food for the Suffolk poor, and both the 1834 and 1843 parliamentary reports confirm that gleaning continued to be practised in every part of Suffolk.[89]

To the Suffolk poor in general, the 1788 judgement may not have been particularly important. In many places, they continued to assert their traditional right to glean and resorted to collective action if it was threatened. In 1796, for example, a farmer at Exning in West Suffolk found he had a major riot on his hands when he attempted not to prevent the poor from gleaning, but simply to postpone gleaning operations until the harvest was cleared. As I have shown elsewhere, the detailed north Essex evidence indicates that the gleaning activities of most of the East Anglia poor were not substantially affected by the

[88] *English Reports* (C.P.), 126, 33. For a discussion of the implications of this statement and of the broad attack on customary right it implies, see chapter 10.
[89] Raynbird, *The Agriculture of Suffolk*, 282; J. Glyde, *Suffolk in the Nineteenth Century* (London, 1856), 350; 'Reports of the Assistant Poor Law Commissioners on the Employment of Women and Children in Agriculture', *P.P.*, xii (1843), 227–33; 'Reports from Commissioners, Poor Laws', *P.P.*, xxx (1834).

1788 judgement.[90] Among the Timworth gleaners, the large penalties imposed by the Court of Common Pleas may have acted as a warning, making them more cautious than their counterparts elsewhere, but Mary Houghton was probably the leader of a substantial group of gleaners in 1786. She was clearly willing to glean in defiance of the farmers despite the large fine Manning had already suffered. Ultimately, however, whether she continued gleaning every year or not, the 1788 case proved disastrous for Mary Houghton herself. By the early nineteenth century, she was reliant on the parish officers not only for her weekly dole but also for rent, clothes, and blankets. The 1788 case was a crucial and cruel turning point in her life. By putting the family in debt, it almost certainly deprived Mary and her children of their tiny freehold and of their last tenuous grip on the mesh of customary rights to which it had given them access. In the harvest crisis of 1800, John Houghton, junior, who had been given just ten shillings in 1796 in compensation for his lost birthright, also had to ask the Timworth authorities for relief. The last vestiges of the Houghtons' independence had disappeared.[91] Like the Cages a few years before them, they had joined the ranks of the landless labouring poor.

The late eighteenth century was not a good time to become dependent on wages alone. Most Suffolk labouring families suffered increasing deprivation in the first half of the nineteenth century as underemployment increased, wages remained low, and poor law policies became harsher. The Timworth population declined immediately after the enclosure, a fall that may well have been linked to the destruction of local cottages, for the Houghtons' dwelling was demolished fairly soon after Cornwallis bought it in 1796.[92] Relations between labourers and farmers in Timworth appear to have deteriorated in this period. The farms of both the Worlledges and the Waltons – the biggest occupiers in Timworth after Worlledge moved to Ingham in 1800 – were subjected to damaging arson attacks during the 1840s, and another Timworth farmer suffered a similar fate in 1861.[93] The tradition of local protest that the Houghtons had been part of continued for more than half a century after Mary's death.

Behind the dry legal arguments recorded in the *English Reports*, the story of the 1788 judgement turns out to be one of complex economic changes and social conflicts. The individual life stories of the defendants exemplify a phe-

---

[90] *Cambridge Chronicle* 13 Aug. 1796. See also chapter 10; For an exceptional parish where the authorities did try to control gleaning after 1788, see SRO Bury St Edmunds, FL/506/1/13.

[91] SRO Bury St Edmunds, FL641/7/1.

[92] Timworth's population was 149 in 1801, but was estimated at 169 in the mid-1790s; Young, *General View*, 308; *ibid.*, 283 (1797 ed.). The population of Timworth rose again in the early nineteenth century. By 1821 it had increased to 210. *Victoria County History: Suffolk* 1:683–94. SRO Bury St Edmunds, T64/1, 2 shows that the three cottages marked in the Home field brakes in 1793 had all disappeared by 1846.

[93] J. E. Archer, 'Rural Protest in Norfolk and Suffolk 1830–1870' (PhD thesis, University of East Anglia, 1981).

nomenon often discussed only at a general level by English social historians – the proletarianisation of the rural poor in the late eighteenth and early nineteenth centuries. *Steel v. Houghton et Uxor* resulted from a conjunction of specific conflicts of interest. A small group of rich tenant farmers were probably the prime movers, but it would be unwise to assume that their desire to control the gleaners' access to their holdings was necessarily the only or even the main reason why the case was fought. In 1788, the Houghtons' smallholding was one of the few remaining parts of the Culford estate parishes not yet under Cornwallis' control. Its purchase almost certainly enabled him to complete the enclosure process and to bring to fruition his family's long-term plans to make this a closed parish – a classic estate village. The Houghtons and the Mannings found themselves under intense pressure from two major, if not always unified, forces in eighteenth-century rural society – the united power of a small group of increasingly wealthy, profit-oriented farmers on the one hand, and the immense wealth and prestige of the traditional landed aristocracy on the other. In the long term, their chances of maintaining their independence were extremely small. The 1786 and 1788 cases merely accelerated their decline.

10. Gleaners, farmers and the failure of legal sanctions in England 1750–1850

Through an analysis of the conflicts that arose when the propertied attempted to undermine the gleaning rights of the poor in the century after 1750, this article reassesses both the degree to which the courts could be used by the propertied against the poor and the specific model of a 'transition from custom to crime'[1] used by some historians of law and social relations in this period. Gleaning was an important source of income for labouring families. The uncut or fallen grain left in the fields after the harvest sometimes accounted for more than a tenth of their annual income.[2] Gleaning was particularly important in the predominantly grain-growing region of East Anglia, the area which forms the primary focus of this study. In this region the loss of spinning and other by-employments and the decline of female wage-earning opportunities in agriculture meant that gleaning played an increasingly central part in early nineteenth-century descriptions of women's work.[3] When the farmers began to use legal sanctions to attack the gleaners' rights in the late eighteenth century, one of the few ways by which women could safeguard their households against the privations of winter was severely threatened, and although the resulting disturbances

Acknowledgements: Earlier versions of this chapter were given at a 1986 conference on 'Crime, Perquisites and the Customary Economy' at the University of Birmingham, and at the Institute of Historical Research. I am grateful to participants who offered comments or further references and to John Styles, Joanna Innes, Donald Coleman, Edward Thompson, Bob Bushaway, Keith Snell, David Sugarman, Deborah Valenze, Clive Emsley, Alan Harding and John Archer for more detailed criticisms. The errors remain my own. This research was funded by a University of Liverpool research fellowship.

[1] See B. Bushaway, *By Rite: Custom, Ceremony and Community in England, 1700–1880* (London, 1982), 209.

[2] *P.P.*, 1834, xxx. For detailed discussion see P. King, 'Customary Rights and Women's Earnings. The Importance of Gleaning to the Rural Labouring Poor 1750–1850', *Economic History Review*, 44(3) (Aug. 1991), 461–76. I. Pinchbeck, *Women Workers and the Industrial Revolution* (London, 1969), 56.

[3] *P.P.*, 1834, xxx; W. Armstrong, 'Labour, i: Rural Population Growth, Systems of Employment and Incomes', in G. Mingay (ed.), *Agrarian History of England and Wales, vi, 1750–1850* (Cambridge, 1988), 685, 716–19.

have received scant attention from historians of women's protest, the gleaners were not slow to act collectively in defence of their customary rights.[4]

The farmers' attempts to use legal sanctions to undermine the gleaners' activities have been seen by several historians as part of a broader movement to redefine many customary practices as crimes,[5] as one strand of a 'custom to crime transition' which was itself linked to the growth of absolute conceptions of property ownership. Malcolmson, for example, has portrayed gleaning as one of the customary practices that were 'discovered to be incompatible with the absolute private possession of land'. Gleaning was 'among those rights increasingly denied in the slow transformation of rural society that accompanied the growth of commercial farming. And though the country people clung tenaciously to those rights . . . the law came to redefine them as crimes against property'.[6]

Unlike wood-gathering or the killing of game, many forms of which were specifically named in criminal statutes, gleaning was never formally redefined by parliament as a criminal offence. In order to fit gleaning into this custom-to-crime model, historians have therefore found it necessary to use a civil case and the precedent it established. That case is *Steel v. Houghton* which was decided by the Court of Common Pleas in June 1788.[7] The genesis of the 1788 judgement is a complex story which has been dealt with fully in chapter 9, but the court's decision on whether or not a poor inhabitant had the right to enter a farmer's fields in order to glean was clear and well publicised. 'No person has at Common Law a right to glean in the harvest field', the court

---

[4] Sir F. Eden, *The State of the Poor*, 3 vols. (London, 1797), ii, 546–7. M. Thomis and J. Grimmett, *Women in Protest, 1800–1850* (London, 1982) make no mention of gleaning disputes; nor does J. Bohstedt, 'Gender, Household and Community Politics: Women in English Riots, 1790–1810', *Past and Present*, 120 (1988), 88–122, an important article not yet published when this article was written.

[5] Bushaway, *By Rite*, 25–6; R. Malcolmson, *Life and Labour in England, 1700–1780* (London, 1981), 143–4; E. P. Thompson, *Whigs and Hunters* (London, 1975), 241; J. Beattie, 'The Criminality of Women in Eighteenth-Century England', *Journal of Social History*, 9 (1975), 88; D. Sugarman, J. Palmer and G. Rubin, 'Crime, Law and Authority in Nineteenth-Century Britain', *Middlesex Polytechnic History Journal*, 1 (1982), 48–54; P. Corrigan and D. Sayer, *The Great Arch* (Oxford, 1985), 98; H. Newby, *Country Life: A Social History of Rural England* (London, 1987), 14–15. C. Emsley, *Crime and Society in England, 1750–1900* (London, 1987), 104–7, offers a more qualified version.

[6] Bushaway, *By Rite*, 26; E. P. Thompson, 'The Grid of Inheritance: A Comment', in J. Goody, J. Thirsk and E. P. Thompson (eds.), *Family and Inheritance: Rural Society in Western Europe, 1200–1800* (Cambridge, 1976), 340–1; Malcolmson, *Life and Labour*, 144, explicitly quotes C. B. Macpherson.

[7] Every edition of R. Burn, *The Justice of the Peace and Parish Officer* (London, 1755) in the following century contains long game and wood sections but nothing on gleaning. Nor does T. Williams's equivalent work, *The Whole Law Relative to the Duty and Office of a Justice of the Peace*, 4 vols. (London, 1797). For the 1788 case, *English Reports*, 126, Common Pleas, iv, 32–9; Bushaway, *By Rite*, 141; Thompson, 'Grid of Inheritance', 340.

announced.[8] Henceforward the gleaners would be trespassing if they did not obtain the farmer's permission before entering his fields to glean.

This decision was interpreted by the Hammonds as enabling the farmers to gain control of the gleaning practices of the poor through the threat of a civil action. From 1788 onwards, they suggested, gleaning was 'a privilege given by the farmer at his own discretion'. Although Keith Snell's important book on the labouring poor has briefly reasserted certain aspects of the Hammonds' position, neither he nor the Hammonds undertook any detailed research on local court records or on contemporary discourse about gleaning.[9] Through an analysis of these sources this chapter suggests that, with a few exceptions, the legal attacks mounted against the gleaners in the late eighteenth and early nineteenth centuries were not successful. Overall the 1788 judgement did not allow the farmers to gain control of the poor's gleaning activities and it is dangerous to conflate the existence of this legal ruling with the separate question of its enforcement and usefulness in practice.[10] The article then explores the reasons for the relative failure of legal sanctions in this context and the contribution of the gleaners' collective resistance, before re-examining the custom-to-crime transition in the light of the gleaners' success.

I

The 1788 judgement did not, of course, put an end to gleaning. The autobiographies of the labouring poor and many other nineteenth-century sources make this clear.[11] But was gleaning now under the farmers' control? The judgement was certainly well publicised. It was reported at length, if not always favourably, in both the London and provincial newspapers, which devoted long columns to the 1788 decision and to the 1786 case of *Worlledge v. Manning* on which

[8] Chapter 9; *English Reports*, 126, 32.
[9] B. and J. L. Hammond, *The Village Labourer*, 2 vols. (London, 1948 edn), i, 105; K. Snell, *Annals of the Labouring Poor: Social Change and Agrarian England, 1660–1900* (Cambridge, 1985), 179–80.
[10] This work builds on Bushaway's brief analysis in *By Rite*, 138–48; and on the post-1850 research in D. Morgan, *Harvesters and Harvesting, 1840–1900: A Study of the Rural Proletariat* (London, 1982), 151–61; D. Morgan, 'The Place of Harvesters in Nineteenth-Century Village Life', in R. Samuel (ed.), *Village Life and Labour* (Cambridge, 1975), 53–61. The legal side of this analysis owes much to the introduction in G. Rubin and D. Sugarman (eds.), *Law, Economy and Society, 1750–1914: Essays in the History of English Law* (Abingdon, 1984), 1–123.
[11] *P.P.*, 1834, xxx: 150 parish replies refer to gleaning; *P.P.*, 1843, xii, 227–33. On gleaning practices and bells, see *Notes and Queries*, 2nd series, 10 (1860), 285–8, 356, 476, 519–20; 4th ser., 4 (1869), 216–86; 12th series, 9 (1921), 70, 112–15, 136, 157–8, 216, 256; or *Essex Review*, 34 (1925), 106–11, 162–3, 210–11. Several East Anglian autobiographies referring to gleaning are quoted below; see also C. Smith, 'In Harvest Time', *Essex Review*, 12 (1903); N. E. Coleman (ed.), *People, Poverty and Protest in the Hoxne Hundred, 1780–1880* (n.p., 1982), 60; B. Harvey, 'Youthful Memories of my Life in a Suffolk Village', *Suffolk Review*, 2 (1960), 74.

it was partly based.[12] The legal profession was also well aware of the 1788 judgement. It became the standard case law reference in legal dictionaries and civil law handbooks from 1788 onwards and was referred to in the *Law Reports* more than a century later as 'the great case of gleaning'.[13]

Evidence about the impact of the judgement on the attitudes of farmers and gleaners respectively is extremely scattered, thus turning the historian himself into a gleaner. In East Anglia, where the 1834 parish returns indicate that gleaning was particularly important to the poor,[14] the attitudes of these two groups were often diametrically opposed. In Suffolk and Essex some groups of farmers deliberately publicised the judgement, stressing its message 'that the poor have no right to glean without the consent of the occupiers of the land', and the judgement also reinforced the anti-gleaner stance of other farmers in the region. One farmer's diary noted with obvious satisfaction that 'The gleaning case was given against the gleaners . . . because *all the crop* is of right his who sowest'.[15]

The gleaners' attitude was very different. Eleven years after the judgement one of the largest farmers in Easthorpe, north Essex, challenged a woman gleaning in his fields and 'desired her not to glean any longer'. She refused to comply, answering simply that 'it was not his property but belonged to her'. When he returned next morning he found 'she had brought upwards of thirty other persons with her' who were quietly asserting that the gleanings were their property too. Essex gleaners challenged the local farmers in much the same way both before and after 1788. In 1785 an Epping widow pointed out that 'she had as much right to glean as he [the farmer] had'. In 1796 the Stanway gleaners told Farmer Pratt 'they had a right to glean there and would do it for all him'.[16]

Given this obvious conflict of views, do the surviving court records indicate that the farmers succeeded in using the 1788 judgement to alter the balance of gleaning disputes in their favour? Unfortunately the better-documented major

[12] *The Times*, 22 May, 26 June 1786, 13 June 1788; *Public Advertiser*, 13 June 1788; the *Bury and Norwich Post* carried articles in nine issues: 17 May–7 June 1786, 18 June–17 Sept. 1788; *Ipswich Journal*, 20 May, 3 June 1786, 14 June 1788.

[13] For example, R. Burn, *A New Law Dictionary*, 2 vols. (London, 1792); G. Clark, *Memoranda Legalia: or, An Alphabetical Digest of the Laws of England* (London, 1800), 217; T. Williams, *Everyman his Own Lawyer* (London, 1812), 553; T. Tomlins, *The Law Dictionary*, 3rd edn, 2 vols. (London, 1820); H. Dixon, *A Treatise on the Law of Farm* (London, 1858), 244; J. Wharton, *The Law Lexicon: or, Dictionary of Jurisprudence*, 4th edn (London, 1867), 426; 8th edn (London, 1889), 328.

[14] The proportion of parish replies in Essex, Suffolk and Cambridgeshire that mentioned gleaning was three times the national average: *P.P.*, 1834, xxx. See also King, 'Customary Rights'.

[15] *Chelmsford Chronicle*, 25 July 1788; see also *Bury and Norwich Post*, 17 Sept. 1788. Others used handbills or informal vestry announcements: Suffolk Record Office (hereafter SRO), Bury, FL 506/1/13, Diary of Godwin; SRO, Ipswich, HD 365/1.

[16] Essex Record Office, Chelmsford (hereafter ERO), P/LwR11, 10 Oct. 1799; Epping Petty Sessions Book, 17 Sept. 1785; P/LwR 10, 17 Sept. 1796.

criminal courts heard relatively few gleaning-related cases.[17] The key courts were the petty sessions and, less frequently, the civil side at the assizes. The records of the latter rarely survive and are so cryptic that they reveal very little about the disputes heard or the backgrounds of those involved. The petty-sessions records are sometimes more informative but few good series remain, and in eastern England it seems that only two sets of examinations books are available for the later 1780s.[18] One covers the long-enclosed and predominantly arable north-east Essex division of Lexden and Winstree, the other the neighbouring borough of Colchester, which included a few rural parishes.[19] Over twenty examinations centring on disputes about the gleaning of either barley or wheat can be found in these two petty sessions series.[20] They involve nearly forty gleaners from over a dozen separate parishes and are mainly dated between 1785 and 1808. However, it cannot be assumed that this was a period of more intense conflicts over gleaning, since these are the only years for which good-quality records survive.[21]

Despite a few gaps, the Lexden and Winstree series covers twenty harvest periods between 1785 and 1808 and gleaning disputes can be found at regular intervals throughout these years.[22] The 1788 judgement did have an impact on both the nature and frequency of gleaning disputes. In this division 1788 was the only year which produced more than two gleaning-related examinations. Four of the fifteen gleaning cases heard in those twenty years were brought in 1788. Moreover, while two thirds of the gleaning-related cases found in these two series were brought by gleaners not farmers (the charge usually being assault),

---

[17] Usually only prosecutions involving stealing from the sheaves reached the quarter sessions or the crown side at the assizes.

[18] The *nisi prius* side records on the Home Circuit give only plaintiffs' names and outcome. They are not available before 1792. Public Record Office, London (hereafter PRO), Assi 32/2–4. Petty sessions minute books survive more frequently than examinations books, but lack detail, so gleaning disputes cannot usually be identified.

[19] ERO, P/LwR 1–18; P/CoR 1–25. The Lexden and Winstree division lies on either side of Colchester.

[20] Although the Timworth farmers who brought the Common Pleas' case announced afterwards they wanted it to apply only to soft corn (see chapter 9), the Essex farmers accused both barley and wheat gleaners in 1788. It should not be assumed that wheat gleaning was uncontested: Morgan, *Harvesters and Harvesting*, 155; Emsley, *Crime and Society*, 106.

[21] The twenty examinations represent only a fraction of the gleaning disputes that actually occurred. Many were never taken to a court or were resolved by individual JPs whose records do not survive. The examinations books deteriorate in quality in Colchester after the mid-1780s and in Lexden and Winstree by the 1810s. Assaults by farmers on women in the fields at harvest time continued (for example, ERO, P/LwR17, 28 Aug. 1809), but declining detail makes it impossible to discern whether these were gleaning-related. The main series, P/LwR, covers 1758–60, 1783–5 and 1788 onwards with one or two gaps, but when examinations books are available for pre-1785 years, gleaning cases can be found in them: P/LwR 4, 26 Aug. 1758; P/CoR 7, 22 Aug. 1777. Local newspaper reports about gleaning disputes occur both before and after the years 1785–1808.

[22] In 1785, 1788, 1790, 1794, 1796, 1799, 1800, 1802, 1806, 1808. Harvest periods not covered because of gaps are 1786–7, 1793, 1798. The Colchester series begins in 1770. Its deterioration in the late 1780s may explain the earlier dates of its gleaning disputes: 1777, 1785 (two), 1786.

in 1788 this balance was temporarily reversed. Three of the accusations recorded during the first harvest after the 1788 judgement were brought by farmers.

The central issue in all these cases was not stealing from the sheaves but the act of gleaning itself or the timing of that act within the harvesting process – the farmers stressing that gleaning had continued against their expressed wishes. The gleaners' behaviour also changed after the judgement. Although most of the depositions made by farmers between 1785 and 1808 mentioned that other gleaners were present in the fields with the specific person accused, the depositions of 1788 suggest that the gleaners were in a particularly militant and assertive mood that year. In August 1788 'A great number of people amounting to a hundred or thereabouts' gathered on Farmer Francis' Aldham farm and 'in a tumultuous manner insisted on gleaning wheat', two local women being named as the 'ringleaders of the said gang'. A few days later two different women assaulted Francis when he attempted to remove another group of gleaners from his fields. The Fordham farmer, John Kingsbury, suffered similar difficulties. In accusing five women of illegal gleaning he reported that 'a great number of people had come into his field to glean barley contrary to his will and order, and had insisted on gleaning and taking away a considerable quantity'.[23] Although there were other occasions when gleaners turned out in large numbers to assert their customary rights, in north Essex at least, the gleaners were exceptionally well co-ordinated and belligerent in 1788.

These 1788 cases were not followed by a rush of further attempts to prosecute gleaners at the Lexden and Winstree petty sessions. That the gleaners continued to glean without permission is evidenced by the fact that the farmers continued to assault them. Farmers were brought to the court by gleaners for this offence in 1788, 1790 and 1794, but it was not until 1796 that another farmer brought a charge against a gleaner in these courts.[24] Unfortunately the petty-sessions books rarely record the magistrates' decisions in these cases but they do make it possible to analyse the social backgrounds of the protagonists and the resulting contrasts are stark. All the farmers involved in the gleaning disputes recorded in these two series were male. 93 per cent of the gleaners were female. All the farmers were literate. Only 6 per cent of the gleaners could sign their names. The farmers were not usually mere smallholders. If the Land Tax returns are any guide, most were among the four largest farmers in their parish.[25] By contrast, only two of the gleaners can be definitely linked to households with

---

[23] ERO, P/LwR 6, 21 Aug., 1, 15 Sept. 1788.

[24] ERO, P/LwR 6, 1 Sept. 1788; P/LwR 7, 18 Sept. 1790; P/LwR 9, 1 Aug. 1794; P/LwR 10, 17 Sept. 1796. The farmer was particularly angry because they continued to glean 'in defiance of all he could say to them'.

[25] One out of seventeen gleaners signed rather than marked their petty-sessions or quarter-sessions examinations. Parish poor-law records and Land Tax schedules were searched in each case. Some of the farmers were their parish's largest landholders; about half owned land as well as renting it; nearly 50 per cent were eligible for jury service: ERO, Q/RJ 1/8, 12.

sufficient landholdings to appear in the Land Tax, and both of these had very small holdings and were inhabitants of Dedham, a highly exceptional township which had a relatively diffuse pattern of landholding.[26]

Although the local parish records are extremely patchy, it appears that almost all the farmers were holding, or had held, parish offices. Not surprisingly, given their lack of landholdings and their families' low occupational status, none of the gleaners came from families containing parish office-holders. The vast majority were described as the wives of husbandmen or labourers,[27] although some of the Colchester gleaners came from weaving or shoemaking families and a small number were widows or single women.[28]

II

Since so much recent writing has focused primarily on the way the law was used by the propertied against the poor, it may seem surprising that in the majority of gleaning-related cases it was the substantial farmer rather than the illiterate landless gleaner who was the accused, but this was clearly the pattern in north-east Essex.[29] Moreover in the only gleaning-related case that went on to the major courts from these two petty sessions it was the farmer not the gleaner who was indicted. John Ward was a substantial farmer in the parish of St Giles, Colchester, and was overseer there in 1782–3. Although he had already been accused in 1785 of assaulting a gleaner, in 1786 he went a step

[26] ERO, Q/RPL 582. Dedham had been a weaving centre and was virtually the only parish in the division not yet fully enclosed: C. Vancouver, *The General View of the Agriculture of Essex* (London, 1794), 37–9.

[27] Most of the farmers served in several offices during their lifetime. The petty-sessions records usually described women by their marital status rather than by the kinds of work they did. See also M. Roberts, 'Words They Are Women, and Deeds They Are Men: Images of Work and Gender in Early Modern England', in L. Charles and L. Duffin (eds.), *Women and Work in Pre-Industrial England* (London, 1985), 138–9.

[28] Nearly 85 per cent were married. It is not therefore surprising that only one can be definitely identified as a regular receiver of relief, for most Essex labouring families were not yet dependent on such help except in times of sickness or extreme dearth. Married women were not necessarily as dominant among the gleaners as these figures suggest. The gleaning workforce contained many children, but they were largely excluded from these legal proceedings. Moreover widows and single women with children were often dependent on relief and therefore more vulnerable to the informal sanctions imposed by farmer-dominated vestries and this may have made them more cautious. By the later eighteenth century the medieval practice of restricting gleaning to those too old or too young to reap had long been superseded. See W. Ault, *Open-Field Farming in Medieval England* (London, 1972), 30; King, 'Customary Right'; W. Ellis, *The Modern Husbandman* (London, 1750), 35; A. Young, *A General View of the Agriculture of Essex*, 1 (London, 1807), 310–11.

[29] D. Hay, 'Property, Authority and the Criminal Law', in D. Hay *et al.* (eds.), *Albion's Fatal Tree* (London, 1975). For the relatively high plebeian usage of the major courts, see P. King, 'Decision-Makers and Decision-Making in the English Criminal Law, 1750–1800', *Historical Journal*, 27 (1984), 25–58; J. Beattie, *Crime and the Courts in England, 1660–1800* (Oxford, 1986), 193–6.

further and took away the gleaners' half-filled sacks.[30] As a result, Mary Pepper accused him of theft, claiming that her gleaning sack had also contained personal valuables. Despite Ward's protests that he had been framed and that he would return the property if given an opportunity, the committing magistrate sent the case on to the Colchester borough sessions and the grand jury returned Pepper's indictment as a 'true bill'. Ward therefore found himself on trial for petty larceny and the local bench being less than sympathetic, he might have spent several months in gaol if he had not used complicated legal manoeuvres to extricate himself from confinement. Although the indictment was eventually dismissed at the assizes, these procedures cost Ward dearly.[31] The gleaners, assisted by the local magistrates and jurors, had won a well-publicised victory.

What happened to the other accusations brought by gleaners, all of which involved charges of assault? Like almost all the accusations brought to Essex petty-sessions courts in these years, they were dealt with informally – the magistrates either arranging a settlement between the parties or awarding costs and/or damages. Unfortunately only two examinations recording assaults on gleaners indicate the cases' final outcome, but on both occasions the gleaners obtained at least a limited victory, forcing the farmer to pay costs, damages or fines.[32] This does not mean that the gleaners won every case. Some accusations may have been dismissed. Others probably ended with a compromise not particularly favourable to the gleaners. In one Shropshire case the two sides were told to share the 5 shillings costs between them. But the fact that the Essex gleaners continued to bring cases to the magistrates suggests that the poor often did obtain some redress, as they clearly did in cases involving farmers' refusal to pay wages or overseers' denial of relief.[33]

---

[30] ERO, Q/RPL 1112; P/CoR 10; P/CoR 11, 9 Sept. 1785; P/CoR 11A, 8 Sept. 1786 – this action was in retaliation for the gleaners' failure to stop at his request.

[31] ERO, P/CoR 11A, 8 Sept. 1786; and Essex Record Office, Colchester, Colchester Borough Sessions Book, 1777–87, for the recognisances and Ward's indictment. In October 1786 Ward was 'committed till the next sessions', but in fact the case went to the King's Bench (PRO, KB 20/4) and then to the following assizes: *Chelmsford Chronicle*, 6 Oct. 1786, 16 Mar. 1787, 17 July 1789.

[32] P. King, 'Crime, Law and Society in Essex, 1740–1820' (PhD thesis, University of Cambridge, 1984), 280–1, for informal settlement procedures. ERO, P/LwR 7, 18 Sept. 1790, records that expenses were to be paid by the assaulting farmer. Since he clearly lost the case, he may also have had to pay compensation. Stanway's third-largest farmer had to pay up after assaulting a gleaner: P/LwR 3, 10 Sept. 1800. He was fined for swearing profane oaths at the gleaners – an informal means of exacting justice often used by magistrates: N. Landau, *The Justices of the Peace, 1679–1760* (Berkeley, 1984), 198–9.

[33] Shropshire Record Office, Shrewsbury, 1060/171, Justicing Book of T. N. Parker, 23 Aug. 1815. Whitbread advised the poor 'they had no right' to glean without permission. When they continued to do so and 'complained of abuse' he 'dismissed' the case. A. Cirket (ed.), *Samuel Whitbread's Notebooks, 1810–11, 1813–14*, (Bedfordshire Record Society, 1971), 36, 44; King, 'Crime, Law and Society', 273–4.

How did the farmers fare when they brought accusations of gleaning without permission to the north-east Essex petty sessions? The examinations offer no information on outcomes, but it seems that an immediate informal settlement was always made. None of these gleaners was ever indicted for theft in the major courts and the prison calendars indicate that the magistrates did not use their summary powers to imprison any of them as idle and disorderly persons. In 1788 the magistrates seem to have simply advised the farmers to take the gleaners firmly by the arm and lead them out of their fields,[34] and there is no indication that the magistrates enabled the farmers to extract substantial fines or public apologies from the women concerned. If the nineteenth-century newspapers are any guide, the gleaners were probably let off with a strong reprimand. In 1847 six Essex women who had gleaned without permission were told 'they had all behaved exceedingly ill', but the case against them was dismissed.[35] If the poor disobeyed customary regulations by gleaning before the field was cleared they were more likely to be fined, but even then the amount involved was often very small. Morgan has suggested that even a 2 shilling fine was unusual and in 1799 the Mildenhall magistrates ordered a gleaner to pay precisely that amount to cover the cost of the warrant. They did not award the farmer damages, however. Instead they directed him towards the civil courts, announcing that in such cases 'the farmer has his action of trespass'.[36]

Although the north-east Essex and Mildenhall magistrates did not allow any gleaners to be indicted for theft, some contemporaries clearly believed that this was a possibility after the 1788 judgement, despite the fact that it referred only to trespass. 'The right of gleaning has been proved nugatory', the *Cambridge Chronicle* noted, 'and any abuse thereof . . . is equally indictable with any other offence against the Statute Law'.[37] This view was by no means illogical. At common law the taking of uncut grain could only be prosecuted summarily, but once the farmer had cut the grain it became his property and theft from the sheaves was therefore regularly prosecuted as felony.[38] Gleanings consisted mainly, although not entirely, of cut grain accidentally left behind and

---

[34] No gleaners named in these two petty sessions series appeared in the quarter sessions or assize rolls: ERO, Q/SR, Q/SPb; P.R.O., Assi. 35. Magistrates frequently used summary powers relating to vagrants or the idle and disorderly to imprison 'pilferers' and other offenders: King, 'Crime, Law and Society', 256–8. None of the gleaners appears in the Colchester House of Correction calendars (ERO, Q/SBb) which are calendars of the full turnover. ERO, P/LwR 6, 1 Sept. 1788.

[35] *Cambridge Chronicle*, 25 Sept. 1847. Before the 1830s few newspapers carried detailed petty sessions reports. For fifty years after 1788 information is therefore scarce.

[36] Morgan, *Harvesters and Harvesting*, 157; SRO, Bury, 996/7/1, Mildenhall Petty Sessions Minute Book, 5 Sept. 1799. The charge was 'gleaning by force and without permission'.

[37] *Cambridge Chronicle*, 13 Aug. 1796.

[38] The taking of uncut corn was not felony: Blackstone, *Commentaries on the Laws of England*, iv, 232–3; but the offender could be tried summarily: Williams, *Whole Law*, 920; Burn, *Justice of the Peace* 10th edn (London, 1766), i, 371. For prosecutions for stealing from the sheaves, see n. 41; Emsley, *Crime and Society*, 105.

since property rights were not judged to be lost by temporary abandonment,[39] gleaning without permission could have been reinterpreted as theft once the protection of the previously accepted common law right to enter and glean had been removed in 1788.

This interpretation might have offered the farmers two new avenues through which to prosecute gleaners for theft. First, gleaners stealing from the sheaves may not have found it so easy to use gleaning as a cover after 1788. Even commentators sympathetic to the gleaners admitted that some stole from the sheaves and therefore welcomed the possibility that the judgement might create a situation in which sheaf-stealing 'may be punished as a theft . . . since the pretended justification in the name of gleaning is taken away'.[40] However, the judgement's usefulness in this context remains doubtful. Long after 1788, gleaning continued to be used successfully as a defence by those accused of stealing grain. In 1791 and 1806, for example, Essex juries found in favour of gleaners on this basis.[41]

More important in many farmers' minds was the related question: could gleaning before the crop was cleared be prosecuted as theft? This practice was prohibited in many manorial by-laws because it gave gleaners manifold opportunities to steal from the sheaves and a few gleaners may have been indicted for it before 1788.[42] Did the judgement make this easier to do? The post-1788 editions of the JPs' criminal law manuals continued to make no reference to gleaning, thus leaving their readers in little doubt that it remained a non-indictable act, and the vast majority of magistrates clearly followed this line. The fragmentary evidence available from Suffolk, Oxfordshire and elsewhere suggests that the north-east Essex magistrates' steadfast refusal to allow the gleaners to be indicted was the usual, although not the universal, pattern.[43]

---

[39] Some gleaned corn, however, was flattened before harvesting and therefore never cut. The temporary-abandonment ruling was reiterated by a Common Pleas judge in 1788: *English Reports*, 126, 37.

[40] *Cambridge Chronicle*, 21 June 1788.

[41] ERO, Q/SBb 345/3, a grand jury favouring a Finchingfield gleaner; Q/SBb 405/49, Q/SR 926, a landless White Colne gleaner acquitted by the petty jury of stealing from the sheaves of the parish's largest farmer (Q/RPL 658). Sometimes gleaners were convicted: *The Times*, 19 Sept. 1795.

[42] A. Young, *The Farmer's Calendar* (London, 1805), 431; Bushaway, *By Rite*, 144. For a Berkshire JP who mistakenly committed gleaners for trial as felons in 1766, see *English Reports*, 97, King's Bench, xxvii, 1–21.

[43] SRO, Bury, 996/7/1, 5 Sept. 1799; Morgan, 'Place of Harvesters', 57; and cases quoted below confirm this, but there were a few exceptions. Given the wide variety of attitudes found among eighteenth-century JPs, it is not surprising perhaps that one Essex accusation of gleaning without permission before the crop was cleared did go further than the committal stage. The magistrate in this case was the infamous and highly untypical 'Reverend Bruiser', Henry Bate-Dudley, a litigious, violent former newspaper proprietor, who led a bloody affray against the Littleport rioters in 1816. Although the gleaner was eventually convicted in 1795 after refusing to avoid prosecution by making a public apology, and telling the farmer 'she'd be d—d, if she would not glean as

When parliament gave the summary courts the right to try minor felony charges in the mid-nineteenth century, the farmers may have renewed their attempts to prosecute gleaners for theft, but the newspaper reports suggest that few magistrates proved amenable. In 1856, for example, a Cambridgeshire farmer charged a Fulbourn gleaner with felony for gleaning before the crop was cleared, but the local petty sessions decided that 'a felonious intent was absent'.[44] The 1788 judgement may have made it technically possible for gleaners to be indicted for felony, whether they were operating before or after the harvest was cleared, but with one or two exceptions this did not prove to be a practical possibility.

Did the farmers use other types of indictment? Trespass on to another's land unaccompanied by any breach of the peace was not indictable and the types of trespass that could be prosecuted as misdemeanours in the major courts were limited and difficult to define.[45] It is not therefore surprising that none of the north-east Essex farmers used this approach and that only one gleaning-related accusation of this sort has come to light in the Essex records of this period. This involved Mary Halls of Ashdon who was indicted after the 1806 harvest for entering William Spiller's close, causing a noisy affray and taking away a quantity of barley. Although Halls appears to have led a large crowd of gleaners,[46] the petty jury acquitted her, but her counter-indictment, accusing Spiller's wife of assault, was treated very differently. Sarah Spiller was convicted and fined £15. One of the largest grain producers in Ashdon had been publicly humiliated by a petty jury returning two separate verdicts supporting the landless Halls.[47]

she liked', the quarter-sessions bench took a very different line from Bate-Dudley and released her as soon as the sessions was over: ERO, Q/SR 882. P. Muskett, *Riotous Assemblies: Popular Disturbances in East Anglia, 1740–1822* (Ely, 1984), 57; L. Werkmeister, *The London Daily Press, 1772–92* (Lincoln, 1963), 19–60; A. Barnes, *Essex Eccentrics* (Ipswich, 1975), 32; A. Brown, *Essex People, 1750–1900* (Chelmsford, 1972), 200; *Dictionary of National Biography*; *Essex Review*, 26 (1917), 192; *The Times*, 15 Oct. 1795.

[44] *Bury and Norwich Post*, 16 Aug. 1859; D. Crane, *Fulbourn Chronicle, 1750–1850* (Fulbourn, 1982), 54 (extract from *Cambridge Chronicle*, 27 Sept. 1856), for two cases that went against the farmers.

[45] One judge suggested prosecuting the gleaners for 'a trespass': *The Times*, 19 Sept. 1795; he may have meant either civil or criminal proceedings: B. Lenman and G. Parker, 'The State, the Community and the Criminal Law in Early Modern Europe', in V. Gatrell, B. Lenman and G. Parker (eds.), *Crime and the Law: The Social History of Crime in Western Europe since 1500* (London, 1980), 18; Blackstone, *Commentaries*, iii, 208–9; Tomlins, *Law Dictionary*, ii. Although after 1820 new statutes made certain categories of trespass triable summarily, J. Maule's 1869 edition of Burns's *Justice of the Peace*, 5, 1031, still noted, 'No indictment lies for a mere civil trespass . . . unaccompanied with circumstances constituting a breach of the peace'. Indictments for affray, riot or forcible entry might still be used, however.

[46] ERO, Q/SR 926. Halls was accused, on three occasions, of making 'a great noise, disturbance and affray . . . against the peace' and of taking 'barley in the straw'. Unfortunately no depositions survive, so a fuller analysis is impossible.

[47] ERO, D/P 18/3/102: Ashdon crop returns show the Spillers were the parish's fourth-largest wheat producers. The Halls were not listed among the thirty-three producers. Mary's husband was a landless labourer.

The reasons why both magistrates and jurors often leaned towards the glean-ers will be assessed later, but clearly neither the petty sessions nor the major criminal courts offered the farmers much support. Their only remaining option was therefore the civil courts. Since neither the nearly moribund Colchester Monday and Thursday courts nor the Essex county courts could hear cases of trespass *vi et armis*,[48] an expensive action in the assizes *nisi prius* court would usually have been necessary. Lacking any systematic record, it is impossible to ascertain whether any Essex farmers took this course, but none of the Essex civil cases reported in the *Chelmsford Chronicle* in the 1780s and 1790s involved gleaning and, when cross-checking is possible after 1792, no north-east Essex gleaning cases ever went on to the *nisi prius* court.[49]

The technical obscurity of the law and the protracted, uncertain and expen-sive nature of many civil-court actions made them extremely unattractive to the farmers. The rapacity of the eighteenth-century legal profession was well publicised and the financial costs could be high. The outcome of litigation was also very uncertain and even if a favourable verdict was obtained the bulk of the costs might still have to be met by the farmer. Contemporary writers frequently quoted examples of litigants financially crippled by lawsuits in which they had been technically successful and that was certainly Farmer Ward's experience. In 1789 he stressed that in his dispute with the gleaners he

> had endeavoured to recover damages for his illegal imprisonment; but although he obtained a verdict, the payment of the fine and costs has been evaded, and he is obliged to submit to the loss of at least 400 pounds . . . incurred by the different proceedings in the law.[50]

This does not, of course, mean that civil actions were never undertaken or threatened in gleaning cases. The Wiltshire farmer Edward Perry, goaded by a gleaner's repeated defiance, did commence an action at the Wiltshire assizes in 1792 and, 'notwithstanding the great trouble and expense of the same', he eventually obtained a favourable verdict. Given the poverty of most gleaning families, the farmer rarely regained his costs in this situation, but it did allow

---

[48] The Colchester Monday and Thursday court books do survive (ERO, Colchester), but few cases were brought by 1780 and these courts do not appear to have heard any involving trespass *vi et armis*. Usually only names are recorded, but none of the petty sessions gleaning disputes went into these courts. The county court was still active (ERO, S/C 1–2). Records do not survive for 1784–98. Names and brief descriptions are available post-1798, but none of the petty sessions gleaning disputes came to the court. County courts did not cover trespass *vi et armis*: G. Jacob, *A New Law Dictionary*, 9th edn (London, 1772); but only trespass on the case: Tomlins, *Law Dictionary*, ii.

[49] J. Cockburn, *A History of the English Assizes, 1558–1714* (Cambridge, 1971), 139. Many Essex *nisi prius* cases were reported in the *Chelmsford Chronicle* in the 1790s. PRO, Assi 32/2–4.

[50] Cockburn, *History of the English Assizes*, 145–50; J. A. Sharpe, 'The People and the Law', in B. Reay (ed.), *Popular Culture in Seventeenth-Century England* (London, 1985), 259; J. Sharpe, *Crime and the Law in English Satirical Prints, 1600–1832* (London, 1986), 27–8; *Chelmsford Chronicle*, 17 July 1789. Many Essex farmers would have been well aware of Ward's well-publicised case.

Perry to threaten the gleaner's husband with imprisonment for debt and thus to extract a public apology from her.[51]

It is impossible to know how frequently other farmers used the same tactics, but this case – the only one cited by the Hammonds – was clearly exceptional. No such cases were publicised in the *Chelmsford Chronicle* in the years immediately following 1788 and the threat of imprisonment for debt following a civil action clearly did not deter the north-east Essex gleaners. Despite a fairly extensive newspaper search, only one eighteenth-century East Anglian gleaning dispute involving a successful civil action and a public apology has been found – the defendant being a Hadleigh gleaner whose husband was actually imprisoned for a time in 1790. Two Fulbourn families also printed an apology in 1796 in order to avoid a threatened 'prosecution',[52] but the impact of this kind of publicity can easily be exaggerated. The Fulbourn farmers gained little long-term advantage, it seems, for the local gleaners continued to defy them and refused to alter what the *Cambridge Chronicle* called 'the mistaken notion prevalent in villages that parishioners have a right to glean'. Indeed the gleaners won the 1856 case already quoted after pleading that their gleaning activities were sanctioned by custom.[53] Judging by their continued defiance of the farmers at Exning, Fulbourn, Mildenhall and elsewhere, many Cambridgeshire and Suffolk gleaners seem to have remained as impervious to the threat of civil proceedings as their northern Essex counterparts. No Suffolk summary-court records are available for 1788–98, but when the Mildenhall series begins in 1799 a case of gleaning against the farmer's wishes immediately comes to light.[54]

Many farmers clearly felt the threat of civil proceedings did not offer an effective means of coercing the gleaners. They continued to complain bitterly about the gleaners' uncontrollable behaviour and to look for an alternative legal solution. Writing in 1807, the author of *The General View of the Agriculture of Cambridgeshire* complained about 'the undefined right which the poor claimed of gleaning' before the crops were cleared. 'Gleaning is a general evil in this county, and is unlimited, extending to every grain and without any regulation', he wrote; 'The gleaners going ... in so disorderly a manner as to cause perpetual dispute and complaint'. He then recommended 'a short act' giving magistrates summary powers to punish those found gleaning before the harvest was cleared

---

[51] *Annals of Agriculture*, 17 (1792), 293–5; Hammond, *Village Labourer*, 105. Damages and costs were awarded, but Perry forswore them.

[52] *Ipswich Journal*, 24 Apr. 1790; a complete survey was not attempted. A few more cases may have been reported. *Cambridge Chronicle*, Oct. 1796, from Crane, *Fulbourn Chronicle*, 8. The issue was gleaning before the corn was carried.

[53] Crane, *Fulbourn Chronicle*, 45: 'it was customary', they argued, 'on wet days to glean before the crop was off'.

[54] *Cambridge Chronicle*, 13 Aug. 1796; *Cambridge Intelligencer*, 13 Aug. 1796; *Chelmsford Chronicle*, 25 Sept. 1789; SRO, Bury, 996/7/1, 5 Sept. 1799.

and to fine farmers who turned stock on to the stubbles too early.[55] No such bill was ever presented to parliament, perhaps because, as the writer noted, 'such an act must be local because custom varies'.[56] However, these comments confirm that after 1788 the farmers were not usually able to use the threat of a civil action to gain control over the gleaners' activities. The most they now hoped for, it seems, was a new legal strategy aimed not at controlling gleaning completely, but merely at re-establishing the rule, found in manorial by-laws since the middle ages, that gleaning should not begin until the crop was cleared.[57]

The Hammonds' contention that the 1788 judgement enabled the farmers to 'warn off obnoxious and saucy persons from their fields' is clearly untenable. In Essex, Suffolk and Cambridgeshire such persons continued to glean in open defiance of the farmers and this was also the pattern elsewhere.[58] Successful opposition was certainly not confined to long-enclosed areas such as northern Essex. Gooch's Cambridgeshire *General View* linked the uncontrollable activities of the local gleaners to the fact that 'throughout the open fields of this county, the custom of gleaning all grains is uniform'. Enclosure undoubtedly affected the balance of gleaner–farmer relations in some parishes, but gleaning rights were not generally extinguished at enclosure.[59] In parishes such as Exning and Fulbourn gleaning disputes can be found both before and after it and, as Homer noted in 1766, 'The privilege of leasing [gleaning] . . . remains after the inclosure the same as before'.[60]

III

What lay behind the farmers' failure to use the 1788 judgement to erode the gleaners' rights? If the Hammonds overestimated the usefulness of the threat of civil proceedings they clearly underestimated the gleaners' ability to act collectively in defence of their rights. The large crowds of women who gathered

---

[55] W. Gooch, *General View of the Agriculture of the County of Cambridge* (London, 1813), 132–3. The poor might be fined up to 10 shillings or imprisoned for a month. The farmer faced a £5 fine.

[56] Based on a search of the General Index to *Journals, House of Lords and Journals House of Commons* from the 1770s to the mid-nineteenth century; Gooch, *General View*, 132–3.

[57] Ault, *Open-Field Farming*, 32; W. Ault, 'By-Laws of Gleaning and the Problems of Harvest', *Economic History Review*, 2nd series, 14 (1961), 216.

[58] Hammond, *Village Labourer*, 105; Morgan, *Harvesters and Harvesting*, 154–7; Bushaway, *By Rite*, 144.

[59] Gooch, *General View*, 132–3. The original 1786 and 1788 cases were tied up with the informal enclosure of Timworth in Suffolk – Chapter 9; J. Neeson, 'Common Right and Enclosure in Eighteenth-Century Northamptonshire' (PhD thesis, University of Warwick, 1977), 74, 405.

[60] Exning witnessed gleaning disputes in 1796: *Cambridge Chronicle*, 13 Aug. 1796; and 1859: *Bury and Norwich Post*, 16 Aug. 1859. It was enclosed in 1811–12: P. May and R. Tricker, *The Exning Story* (no place of publication, 1986), 40–1. Fulbourn was enclosed in 1806. Conflicts are recorded in 1796 and 1856. Crane, *Fulbourn Chronicle*, 8 Oct. 54; H. Homer, *An Essay on . . . the Inclosure of Open Fields* (Oxford, 1766), 25.

in the Essex gleaning fields in 1788 were part of a long-standing tradition of collective defiance which, like other forms of protest such as workhouse and enclosure riots, continued deep into the nineteenth century.[61] Although the gleaners' activities can be linked to other forms of protest, including the bread riots of the eighteenth century, they took their own distinctive form.[62]

The gleaners' traditions of protest were partly shaped by their own processes of self-regulation. Those who failed to obey local gleaning times and ignored the gleaning bells or other signals organised by the poor were frequently subjected to collective sanctions. At Shelford any gleaner bold enough to start before the gleaners' 'queen' gave the signal 'had her gleanings . . . scattered on the ground by her angry fellow workers'.[63] Other offenders were simply forced out of the gleaning fields and if they refused to leave quietly other collective sanctions were applied. In the 1780s one Essex widow, who became very abusive after

---

[61] For a debate on the relative importance of overt or covert protest, see R. Wells, 'The Development of the English Rural Proletariat and Social Protest, 1700–1850', *Journal of Peasant Studies*, 6 (1978–9), 115–39; R. Wells, 'Social Conflict and Protest in the English Countryside in the Early Nineteenth Century: A Rejoinder', *ibid.*, 8 (1980–1), 514–30; A. Charlesworth, 'The Development of the English Rural Proletariat and Social Protest, 1700–1850: A Comment', *ibid.*, 8 (1980–1), 101–11. Charlesworth does not mention the gleaners' overt protests in, for example, A. Charlesworth (ed.), *An Atlas of Rural Protest in Britain, 1548–1900* (London, 1983), although they support his case. However, they are briefly discussed in A. J. Peacock, 'Village Radicalism in East Anglia, 1800–50', in J. Dunbabin (ed.), *Rural Discontent in Nineteenth-Century Britain* (London, 1974), 46; and by John Archer who stresses that overt protest – poor-law disturbances, enclosure riots, strikes, charity disputes, etc. – continued to be important in East Anglia in the period 1830–70, despite the emergence of incendiarism and other more covert forms of protest: J. Archer, 'The Wells-Charlesworth Debate: A Personal Comment on Arson in Norfolk and Suffolk', *Journal of Peasant Studies*, 9 (1982), 277–84; J. Archer, 'Rural Protest in Norfolk and Suffolk, 1830–1870' (PhD thesis, University of East Anglia, 1981), esp. 406–74.

[62] Gleaning disputes can be seen as part of a wider tradition of food riot, not only because grain was the main focus but also because a similar triangle of relationships between labouring poor, paternalistic magistrates and farmers/traders was involved. The same notions about the legitimacy of popular actions in defence of traditional rights also formed the basis of both types of activity: for this 'moral economy' of the poor, see E. P. Thompson, 'The Moral Economy of the English Crowd in the Eighteenth Century', *Past and Present*, 50 (Feb. 1971). However, there were important differences. Apart from 1795–6, gleaning disputes were not especially concentrated in years of dearth and continued well after food riots declined, partly because the pre-conditions for successful riot identified by Bohstedt continued to hold. Thus the gleaners' food suppliers were not removed beyond the reach of localised riots; magistrates and farmers continued to recognise certain harvest-time protocols; and communal solidarities among the gleaners remained strong – three contrasts with the food rioters' nineteenth-century situation: J. Bohstedt, *Riots and Community Politics in England and Wales, 1790–1810* (Cambridge, Mass., 1983), 202–3.

[63] Gleaning bells were sometimes parish-organised, but the poor often paid for them: Neeson, 'Common Right and Enclosure', 73; C. Warren, *Happy Countryman* (London, 1939), 50. Gleaning 'queens' were common: E. Porter, *Cambridgeshire Customs and Folklore* (London, 1969), 124; Morgan, 'Place of Harvesters', 60; C. Ketteridge and S. Mays, *Five Miles from Bunkum* (London, 1972), 81; M. Baker, *Folklore and Customs in Rural England* (London, 1974), 162. Elsewhere gleaners recognised less formal leaders: E. Gray, *Cottage Life in a Hertfordshire Village* (St. Albans, n.d.), 120.

being found gleaning before the customary starting time, was taken to Totham pond and swum briefly as if she were a witch, 'in the presence of a great number of the villagers'. Collective action was also taken when the gleaners of a particular parish were threatened by interlopers. In Essex intruders were often 'stubbled' out of the fields and in parts of Suffolk 'feuds and skirmishes' between the gleaners of rival parishes were reported to be 'usual'.[64]

Conflicts between gleaners and farmers also had a long history. Although the gleaners' main tactic in the eighteenth century was simply to ignore the farmers' opposition and enter the fields in substantial numbers, quietly exercising their right to glean, violent conflicts were not unknown. In the 1760s it was reported that the Yorkshire gleaners 'will stone the owners of the lands off their own premises'[65] and although the pre-1788 sources are poor, East Anglian farmers were also threatened with assault or arson if they sent their families or animals into the fields before the poor had a chance to glean. In 1772 a Suffolk farmer was pulled off his horse, dragged through a river and then 'hung up to dry' for this offence.[66] This tradition of collective action against the farmers, which involved violence or threats of violence only when the gleaners' quiet invasion of the fields was opposed, continued for much of the nineteenth century.[67] In the 1830s and 1840s several East Anglian arson attacks were linked to conflicts about gleaning and although it was usually the farmers who resorted to physical violence, newspaper reports indicate that gleaners did occasionally assault particularly obstreperous farmers, as the Essex women did in 1788.[68]

In taking collective action the gleaners were primarily concerned to maintain either access to the gleaning fields or control over the timing of their gleaning activities within the harvesting process. In 1796 large-scale riots at Exning, which eventually forced the local magistrate to send for the dragoons, began when the farmers refused to allow gleaning until the corn had been

---

[64] C. Clark's appendix to Anon., *A Trial of Witches at the Assizes: Bury St Edmunds, 1664* (Bury St Edmunds, 1838), 26–7. My thanks to S. Jarvis for this reference. *Essex Review*, 34 (1925), 162–3, 210–11; Muskett, *Riotous Assemblies*, 99; *Cambridge Chronicle*, 31 Aug. 1844, for a Cambridgeshire feud.

[65] ERO, P/LwR 4, 26 Aug. 1758; P/CoR 7, 22 Aug. 1777; *Museum Rusticum et Commerciale*, 3 (1762), 30.

[66] Muskett, *Riotous Assemblies*, 28: the farmer would not allow the poor to glean, but turned in his cows and hogs to eat the corn. A year later an Essex farmer was threatened with arson for gleaning what the poor should have: *London Gazette*, no. 11383 (28–31 Aug. 1773), quoted in E. P. Thompson, 'The Crime of Anonymity', in Hay *et al.*, *Albion's Fatal Tree*, 311.

[67] Charlesworth suggests the agricultural labourers moved from relative quiescence to open demonstrations between 1790 and 1830: Charlesworth (ed.), *Atlas of Rural Protest*, 145; but the gleaners' tradition seems to have had more continuity. Overt gleaning protests were fairly common before 1790. Their increasing visibility after 1790 may reflect the growth of local reporting in provincial newspapers rather than changing levels of protest.

[68] D. Jones, *Crime, Protest, Community and Police in Nineteenth-Century Britain* (London, 1982), 56; ERO, P/LwR 6, 1 Sept. 1788; *Cambridge Chronicle*, 27 Aug. 1842.

carried.[69] A similar issue sparked off rioting in central Essex in 1842 when more than a hundred women confronted the farmer concerned, stoned him from all sides and nearly inflicted a 'summary punishment on his person . . . shocking to ears polite'. When the farmer retreated 'a shout of exultation was raised . . . and . . . victory was claimed for the gleaners'.[70] Five years later another well-publicised victory occurred after more than forty 'turbulent gleaners' had insisted on gleaning in a Chesterford farmer's fields despite his orders to keep out. In dismissing his later accusation the magistrates instructed the gleaners not to 'make a triumph of it', but about fifty women immediately 'commenced a general shout' outside the court and taunted him by 'flaunting their ribbons as a manifestation of their victory'.[71]

Like the 1788 gleaning riots, all these disturbances, apart from that at Exning, were completely dominated by women, and all those prosecuted or identified as ringleaders were females. The farmers were obviously aware that women gleaners could be formidable opponents. In 1820 the *Farmer's Magazine* spoke of occasions when 'a number of stout women forced their way into a field . . . in defiance of the farmer and will even dare to contend the right with him'. It then suggested that 'the perseverance' of the gleaners 'when they collect together in great numbers' meant 'it was often out of the farmer's power to keep them within reasonable bounds'.[72]

Since provincial newspapers only reported a small fraction of disturbances, it is difficult to assess how frequently the gleaners actually rioted, but the tactical advantages they enjoyed meant that they rarely needed to create large-scale disturbances. If they 'persevered' by moving into the gleaning fields together, the farmers, whose resources were severely stretched at harvest time, would find it extremely difficult to prevent them.[73] Nor were the new county police

[69] *Cambridge Chronicle*, 13 Aug. 1796; *Bury and Norwich Post*, 10, 17 Aug. 1796; *Cambridge Intelligencer*, 13 Aug. 1796; SRO, Ipswich, B 105/2/50. At Exning the men joined the gleaners, marched to Newmarket under a flag of defiance and roused a large riotous crowd. Five were eventually indicted and briefly imprisoned for riot.

[70] *Cambridge Chronicle*, 27 Aug. 1842. Annoyed by the gleaners' refusal to wait until the harvest was cleared, the farmer had retaliated by raking the field.

[71] *Ibid.*, 25 Sept. 1847.

[72] *Farmer's Magazine*, 21 (1820), 413–15. Since this particular form of food riot was dominated by women throughout this period, John Bohstedt's argument that 'the feminine food riot is a myth' may need some reassessment. 'The revolt of the housewives' may be a more useful description of gleaning riots than of bread riots. However, gleaning riots were gradually made obsolete by mechanisation and other changes, and the general structure of Bohstedt's argument is not therefore greatly affected: Bohstedt, 'Gender, Household and Community Politics', 88–122.

[73] Most gleaning disturbances occurred away from market towns where newspapers gathered much of their information and would therefore not have been reported. Other disturbances may have been left unreported for fear of encouraging further outbreaks: see P. King, 'Newspaper Reporting, Prosecuting Practice and Perceptions of Urban Crime: The Colchester Crime Wave of 1765', *Continuity and Change*, 2 (1987). It was imperative to get the harvest in quickly: *Farmer's Magazine*, 3 (1802), 342, noted, 'the attention requisite to keep the gleaners within some tolerable bounds, prevents the possibility of giving that marked superintendence, which is indispensably necessary for keeping the reapers in . . . order'.

forces set up after 1839 necessarily able to alter the situation. In the 1850s the Suffolk police admitted that they simply did not have the manpower to watch the gleaning fields and suggested that the farmers' only remedy was to deal with the gleaners as trespassers.[74]

Given the legal problems the farmers had encountered and the tactical advantages operating in the gleaners' favour, the farmers were often left with only one solution – physical violence. The north-east Essex examinations frequently record 'acts of violence' against gleaners. Many of the women were bruised or had their arms twisted. Others were thrown to the ground, partly stripped, beaten with pitchforks or sticks, horsewhipped or threatened with being 'cut to pieces'.[75] Occasionally the farmers attempted wider manoeuvres against the gleaners. At Colchester in 1777 several were caught in a cart rope deliberately pulled around them 'to give the gleaners a fall' and a young girl was dragged along the ground and badly injured. In 1844 a Lavenham farmer who used similar tactics fractured one gleaner's leg and lamed several others.[76]

The gleaners needed to be stout women indeed to withstand these attacks, but the farmers had to tread carefully. They risked widespread censure and legal proceedings if severe injuries occurred. When a Suffolk farmer rode over and badly hurt a local gleaner in 1789, the *Chelmsford Chronicle* expressed the hope that 'this . . . inhumanity will not pass with impunity but that recourse will be had to law for redress and for curbing the farmer . . . in future'. This was precisely what the gleaners did when they accused farmers of assault at the northern Essex petty sessions in 1790, 1794, 1800 and 1806 and at similar hearings in central Essex.[77] While these courts never fully protected the gleaners, the farmers were clearly aware that assault proceedings might be brought against them. In 1820 the *Farmer's Magazine* pointed out that although the farmer might be justified 'in using . . . moderate force' against 'obstinate or violent' gleaners, he would also be 'amenable to law for all undue force or violence which he may have rashly had recourse to'. East Anglian farmers were occasionally ordered by the courts to pay the gleaners' costs, maintenance or medical

---

[74] Essex took up the option made available by the 1839 Country Police Act immediately, but Cambridgeshire and parts of Suffolk did not: *Bury and Norwich Post*, 30 Aug. 1854; Archer, 'Rural Protest in Norfolk and Suffolk', 477.

[75] *Farmer's Magazine*, 31 (1820), 413–15, noted that gleaning disputes not infrequently occasioned 'acts of violence'. ERO, P/LwR 6, 1 Sept. 1788; P/LwR 4, 26 Aug. 1758; Epping Petty Sessions Book, 17 Sept. 1785; P/CoR 11, 7 Sept. 1785; P/LwR 7, 18 Sept. 1790; P/LwR, 1 Aug. 1794; P/LwR 3, 10 Sept. 1800; P/LwR 16, 27 Aug. 1808.

[76] ERO, P/CoR 7, 22 Aug. 1777; *The Times*, 30 Aug. 1844. Arthur Brown tells me there was lengthy debate about this case: *Suffolk Chronicle*, 24 Aug. 1844; and in the *Northern Star*. The *Times* letter is the farmer's attempt to minimise the bad publicity. However, he does admit the gleaners were injured by his men.

[77] *Chelmsford Chronicle*, 25 Sept. 1789. The gleaners of Nazing, south-west Essex, presented the bailiff of the largest farmer in the parish for an assault on a gleaner in 1806. He was later indicted but not convicted: ERO, Q/SBb 405/46; Q/SR 926.

expenses in this situation, while other farmers paid up in order to avoid a court hearing.[78]

IV

The gleaners' willingness collectively to defend their customary rights does not, in itself, account for the farmers' failure. The gleaners' strong traditions of resistance were reinforced by, and partly dependent on, the attitudes of magistrates, judges and jurors and their tendency to lean towards the gleaners in many cases. Why did courts manned by propertied, locally powerful males prove so sympathetic to these poor and relatively powerless female gleaners? Attitudes varied according to the individual JP or jury involved and the type of prosecution attempted, but three elements of legal tradition operated broadly in the gleaners' favour. Some may have received favourable treatment simply because they were women. John Beattie has suggested that offences committed by women were more readily overlooked and in 1809 Southey observed that in 'all public tumults' women were 'foremost in violence' because they stood 'in less fear of the law', believing they could claim 'the privilege of their sex'. Since female property offenders achieved slightly higher acquittal and pardoning rates than males between 1660 and 1800, some indirect evidence supports this view. Yet women were by no means immune from arrest and prosecution. A substantial number were indicted for the theft of food and grain in the Essex courts and many were convicted.[79]

Nor did the Essex courts' general approach to assault cases involving women offer the gleaners much assistance. The law was notoriously unhelpful to women who had been raped, and committing magistrates rarely allowed men who assaulted women to be indicted at the Essex quarter sessions.[80] Although females accused of assaulting males were slightly more likely to be acquitted than males who had assaulted females, a quarter of both groups were given prison sentences and acquittal rates for males who had assaulted females were higher than those for males who had assaulted males.[81] The gleaners may have

[78] *Farmer's Magazine*, 21 (1820), 413–15; *Norfolk and Norwich Monitor and Police Gazette*, 3 Nov. 1841 (I am grateful to John Archer for this reference); *The Times*, 30 Aug. 1844.

[79] Beattie, *Crime and the Courts*, 436–8; Thompson, 'Moral Economy', 116. Surrey property crimes: acquittal rates were 33.4 per cent for males, 38.1 for females; percentages pardoned were 57.4 and 75.2 respectively. In Essex there was virtually no difference in acquittal rates: King, 'Crime, Law and Society', 308; but women were much more likely to be pardoned (336).

[80] A. Clark, *Women's Silence, Men's Violence: Sexual Assault in England, 1770–1845* (London, 1987), 46–58; Beattie, *Crime and the Courts*, 124–32. None of the twelve women who brought accusations of assault against men to the Lexden and Winstree petty sessions in the period 1788–92 went on to get their attacker indicted at either the quarter sessions or the assizes; nor did any of the three who accused men of attempted rape: ERO, P/LwR 6–8.

[81] ERO, Q/SPb 16–17, 1790–1800, excluding cases removed to other courts and not found bills (not recorded): 38 per cent of females, 29 per cent of males acquitted (n = 16 and 28);

been encouraged by a generalised belief in women's relative immunity from arrest for riot, but the courts' treatment of females was not sufficiently different to justify any overall expectation of leniency after arrest.[82]

The farmers' failure to use the major criminal courts against the gleaners after 1788 was mainly linked by contemporaries to two legal issues not directly related to gender. The first involved the nature of the evidence required in larceny cases. When discussing 'whether an indictment for larceny would lie for simply gleaning' in 1797, a Suffolk magistrate concluded 'the evidence would not support the indictment. For larceny must be the taking of the property of another without apprehension of any legal right to it . . . taking under an apprehended, though erroneously apprehended, legal right, would not be larceny and could only amount to trespass'.[83] This was also the approach taken by the Oxfordshire bench,[84] and a similar logic probably helped to persuade the vast majority of nineteenth-century magistrates, including those at Mildenhall and north-east Essex, to continue treating gleaning disputes as essentially civil matters.

The magistrates did not evolve this approach in isolation. The well-publicised reflections of Justice Rooke in 1795 suggest that juries also played an important role in preventing the criminalisation of gleaning after 1788. 'The poor could not . . . insist on gleaning', he suggested,

> but . . . as they felt they had the right to do so . . . the better way would be to prosecute them for a trespass . . . to charge them with a felony for mere gleaning, was of such a harshness that a jury would lean in favour of the prisoners and say they did not steal and this would, he believed, always be the conduct of juries, until the poor should become more enlightened.[85]

This illustrates Thomas Green's recent conclusion that the judicial authorities' power to determine the content of substantive justice and the development of the law was sometimes severely limited by the attitudes of criminal trial juries. It also indicates that many jurors were expected to side with the gleaners – as the Essex sessions petty jurors did in all three gleaning-related cases

---

25 per cent (four females and seven males) imprisoned (plus one female who attacked a constable). Male acquittal rates were: for males on males, 19 per cent; for males on females, 28 per cent (n = 111 and 28 respectively).

[82] Thomis and Grimmett, *Women in Protest*, 15, 32, 41–2, 45. Riot may have been exceptional. Bohstedt, 'Gender, Household and Community Politics', 119–20, argues persuasively that magistrates in riot cases were no respecters of gender and that men and women were treated nearly equally.

[83] *Monthly Magazine and British Register*, 4 (July–Dec. 1797), 434. The notion that any claim of right would prevent a conviction for larceny was increasingly important in this period: G. P. Fletcher, 'The Metamorphosis of Larceny', *Harvard Law Rev.* (Jan. 1976), 510–11. Gleaners were also protected by the principle of 'manifest criminality' (*ibid.*, 473).

[84] They made it clear in the early nineteenth century that they were not in favour of convictions against gleaners because 'the parties concerned were not aware they were committing a felonious act': Morgan, 'Place of Harvesters', 57.

[85] *The Times*, 19 Sept. 1795; *Northampton Mercury*, 26 Sept. 1795; *Bury and Norwich Post*, 23 Sept. 1795. Defendants were convicted of stealing from sheaves but not of gleaning.

tried before them in 1806.[86] Since nearly half the Essex jurors were farmers, this is somewhat surprising. However, apart from the possibility, discussed in detail elsewhere, that the unanimity clause gave important advantages to jurors holding out for merciful verdicts,[87] these decisions appear to reflect both the ambivalence many farmers felt about attacking the gleaners' rights and the technical legal difficulties encountered in gleaning-related prosecutions.

For the poor the implications of Justice Rooke's remarks were clear – there was much to be gained by refusing to 'become more enlightened'. However, the strength of the gleaners' case and their sympathetic treatment by the courts were not primarily based on the evidential problems and legal inertia that prevented the farmers from redefining gleaning as theft. They depended more crucially on the continued power of local customary law. In civil as well as in criminal cases the gleaners of many localities were able to claim that the 1788 judgement did not undermine the force of local gleaning customs. The Court of Common Pleas had passed judgement solely on a particular issue – whether the resident poor had *at common law* a right to glean. Its conclusion that 'there was no positive law or usage' by which such a universal right 'can be claimed as part of the general common law' won the 1788 case for the farmers. However, it did not necessarily override the power of local custom which 'took the place of the general common law' and 'had the force of law', being in fact 'the local common law' within the particular locality where it obtained.[88]

The farmers' optimistic post-judgement announcements that gleaning without permission was now illegal conveniently glossed over the problems posed by these competing forms of law, but this did not alter the fact that the local customs enshrined in by-laws, manorial regulations or simply in the older inhabitants' memories of what had been practised 'time out of mind' remained unaffected unless a particular local judgement was obtained.[89] This meant that where local customs favouring the gleaners were well established they often enjoyed virtual immunity from the effects of the 1788 judgement. In 1819 *The Farmer's*

---

[86] T. Green, *Verdict According to Conscience: Perspectives on the English Criminal Trial Jury, 1200–1800* (Chicago, 1986), 375. The 1806 pro-gleaner verdicts related to Ashdon and Earls Colne: ERO, Q/SBb, 405/49; Q/SR 926. However, the grand jury that sessions did dismiss a gleaner's accusation of assault: Q/SBb 405/46. Gleaning-related indictments are rare; 1806 was highly exceptional. Overall the majority of Essex verdicts favoured the gleaners (for example, two out of three in the 1786, 1791 and 1795 cases already discussed).

[87] P. King, '"Illiterate Plebeians, Easily Misled": Jury Composition, Experience and Behaviour in Essex, 1735–1815', in T. Green and J. S. Cockburn (eds.), *The Criminal Trial Jury, 1216–1800* (Princeton, 1988), 297–8.

[88] Case report in *Chelmsford Chronicle*, 13 June 1788; *The Times*, 13 June 1788. I found E. P. Thompson's comments at the 1986 conference particularly helpful in writing this section: see *Bulletin of the Society for Labour History*, 3 (1986); Burn, *New Law Dictionary*, 405. *Halsbury's Laws of England*, 4th edn, 56 vols. (London, 1987), 12 para 401.

[89] This would have involved a civil case in a court of record. For a solitary example, see *Ipswich Journal*, 24 Apr. 1790.

Lawyer reluctantly admitted this. After stressing that the poor's idea 'that they have a right, at common law, to glean' was ill founded, it had to acknowledge that they would indeed have a right to glean if there was 'an immemorial custom or usage in the parish' to that effect – provided they waited until the customary time 'after the corn had been carried off'.[90]

Customary law also affected the farmers' approach to physical confrontations with the gleaners. In 1820 the *Farmer's Magazine* advised them that they could only use force to regulate the gleaners before the crop was cleared, since after clearance 'the custom of the country, although not strictly supported in law, would protect the intruders . . . and would preclude the justifying of force in restraining the intrusion'. In noting that the farmer 'might lawfully do before his field is cleared what he could not safely do afterwards', this article implicitly recognised that the 1788 judgement was of little practical assistance to the farmers and that customary law continued to constrain them in their conflicts with the gleaners.[91]

V

The continuing strength of customary law was only one of several strands within contemporary discourse which undermined the impact of the 1788 judgement, for the gleaners' case was also founded on broader humanitarian, scriptural and pragmatic arguments. Many propertied men, including several writers of farmers' manuals, had grave doubts about the legitimacy of attacking gleaning. Attitudes to the farmers who brought the Common Pleas cases were often hostile. One Suffolk writer called their behaviour disgraceful and depraved and told them to remember the generous approach to gleaning advocated by 'the immortal Thomson'. Even the *New Farmer's Calendar*, which saw the 1788 case as 'an act of patriotism in the farmer who tried the cause', largely nullified the judgement's potential impact by stressing that, while it was useful in preventing the gleaning fields from becoming 'a school for juvenile thieves', it would still be 'cruel and illiberal' not to allow the poor their customary gleaning period after the harvest was carted.[92] This 'fair and reasonable settlement' was

[90] T. W. Williams, *The Farmer's Lawyer* (London, 1819), 207. Williams was a JP who also wrote a criminal law manual for magistrates which ignores gleaning and *An Abridgement of Cases Argued and Determined in the Courts of Law during the Reign of George the Third*, 5 vols. (London, 1798–1803), which covers the case in detail (i, 205–9).

[91] *Farmer's Magazine*, 21 (1820), 414. Before the harvest was cleared 'he had both law and custom in his favour'. Arthur Young also paid tribute to the continuing purchase of custom: 'The custom of gleaning . . . is so old and common it is scarcely ever broken through': Young, *Farmer's Calendar*, 431; *ibid.* (1771 edn), 246–7.

[92] *Bury and Norwich Post*, 7 June 1786; *The Times*, 26 June 1786; Thomson's poem 'The Seasons', written in the 1720s, is quoted at length. [J. Lawrence], *The New Farmer's Calendar*, 3rd edn (London, 1801), 89–90.

'adopted by many eminent cultivators', including Arthur Young who made no reference to the judgement in post-1788 editions of the *Farmer's Calendar*, his even-handed entry on gleaning remaining unchanged. Young's denunciation of farmers who tried to appropriate the gleanings as mean and unpardonable double-dealers was supported by a good number of nineteenth-century Suffolk farmers who argued that 'as gleaning has been allowed since time immemorial it ought not to be done away with'.[93]

In 1788 the judgement received little direct support from the provincial newspapers. The local newspaper of the 1788 plaintiff did publish some farmers' announcements, but it also carried long letters from two implacable opponents of the judgement.[94] Several provincial papers published long articles supporting the gleaners. A *Cambridge Chronicle* correspondent praised the one Common Pleas judge who, 'not confining himself to the . . . stubborn rights and rules of landed property', had listened to 'the voice of reason, scripture, humanity and sound policy' and had therefore upheld the gleaners' case. This was 'the Lex populi and Lex Dei', he argued, and since the poor rates would also increase if gleaning declined, he told the farmers to allow it 'without any new necessity or mention of leave or indulgence'.[95]

The specific backing that scripture gave to the gleaners was clearly important. The *Northampton Mercury's* arguments against the judgement were purely biblical. The farmers 'whose intention it is to stop, or at least try to prevent the sacred right of gleaning' were shown the relevant passages in Leviticus and Deuteronomy, which were also widely quoted in the debates about gleaning in the *Annals of Agriculture* and on the Common Pleas bench.[96] Since scripture was frequently used by the propertied to underpin and legitimate their rule, it was not easy to dismiss specific Old Testament injunctions such as 'Thou shalt

---

[93] Young, *Farmer's Calendar*, 431; *ibid.* (1771 edn), 246–7; *ibid.*, (ed.) J. Morton (1862), 419–20, all contain the same entry. Young also pointed out that gleaning, before the crop was cleared must be stopped to prevent widespread abuse. When the Suffolk farmers' clubs debated the issue this pro-gleaner lobby emerged: N. Smedley, *Life and Tradition in Suffolk and North-East Essex* (London, 1976), 83.

[94] Reporting the case at all might be construed as support. *The Northampton Mercury*, a declared opponent, refused to do so. Many papers made neutral comments, claiming to be 'equally a friend to the farmer and an advocate for the poor': *Ipswich Journal*, 3 June 1786; *Chelmsford Chronicle*, 9 June 1786. The *Bury and Norwich Post* was printed three miles from Timworth where the 1786 and 1788 cases originated. It reprinted full details of both, and the victorious farmers' declarations about their aims and intentions, but the longest articles were reserved for opponents of the judgement: 17 May–7 June 1786; 18 June–17 Sept. 1788. See chapter 9.

[95] The writer, a Suffolk man, suggested that Judge Gould, the gleaners' defender, should be lauded when he next came to the local assizes, for founding his judgement on 'reason, justice, religion and charity': *Cambridge Chronicle*, 21 June 1788.

[96] *Northampton Mercury*, 2 Aug. 1788, quoted Leviticus xxiii, 22 and Deuteronomy xxxiv.19; Leviticus xxix.9–10 was also quoted – 'neither shalt thou gather the gleanings of thy harvest' – in the *Annals of Agriculture* debate: 9 (1784), 13–15, 164–7, 636–46; 10 (1785), 218–27; by Gould to the Common Pleas judges: *English Reports*, 126, 34; and by Blackstone, *Commentaries on the Laws of England*, iii, 213.

not ... gather any gleaning of thy harvest, thou shalt leave them unto the poor'.[97] Clergy and clerical magistrates would have been particularly sensitive to the argument advanced in *The Times* that the 'sacred' custom of gleaning 'was no less firmly established [in scripture] than the divine institution of tythes . . . if we doubt the one, we must dispute the other'.[98]

Despite wide individual differences, most clergy seem to have taken an unfavourable view of attacks on gleaning. In 1844 a Cambridgeshire clergyman thought the Bourn farmers were 'very wrong' to prevent the poor from gleaning and persuaded them to change their policy. Some Essex clergy preached harvest-time sermons reminding the farmers that gleaning had 'the sanction of divine command' and that 'preferring the feeding of your cattle to the feeding of your fellow creatures' was a 'wicked practice'.[99]

How did the farmers respond to such arguments? Few would have been unhappy that the tithing system was being questioned, but while some may have responded to these scriptural injunctions through personal Christian conviction[100] or on the more pragmatic basis that poor rates would rise or that it was unwise to upset the local clergyman or magistrate, others may simply have been playing safe. In 1750 a Hertfordshire farmer observed that those who through 'horrible ingratitude and avarice' appropriated the poor's gleanings often suffered 'dire and visible consequences'. Lightning had burned one culprit's stacks, he noted, while disease had struck the flock of another. This notion that ill luck or divine disapproval would strike the gleaners' oppressors was also mentioned by several late eighteenth-century writers and was reinforced in a new, less mystical way by the links observed after 1800 between gleaning-related grievances and incendiarism or animal maiming.[101] The ambivalent attitudes of many farmers and the failure of most clergymen and magistrates to support attacks on gleaning were therefore based not only on legal traditions favourable to the gleaners, but also on various pragmatic and religious considerations.

---

[97] R. McGowen, '"He Beareth not the Sword in Vain": Religion and the Criminal Law in Eighteenth-Century England', *Eighteenth-Century Studies*, 21 (1987), 192–211. For a recent restatement of the centrality of religion to arguments about social order, see J. C. D. Clark, *English Society, 1688–1832* (Cambridge, 1985), esp. 80–7. Leviticus xxiii.22.

[98] *The Times*, 26 June 1786.

[99] The Bourn poor had clearly spread various rumours about the evil intent of the farmers and landlords: *The Times*, 19 Sept. 1844; sermons of the rector of Tilbury, Essex, reviewed in *British Critic*, 7 (1796), 401–2.

[100] At least a small minority of farmers would have been affected by the growth of nonconformist and evangelical movements stressing, among other things, commitment to the poor. For a good discussion using gleaning, see R. Forster, *Freedom of Simplicity* (London, 1981).

[101] Ellis, *Modern Husbandman*, 35–6; *Brit. Critic*, 8 (1797), 402, told the 'cruel and wicked' farmers who 'turned cattle into the fields too soon' to beware 'lest you should draw down the judgement of heaven upon you for such unfeeling conduct'. See also *Bury and Norwich Post*, 7 June 1786, for Thomson on 'the turns of fortune' and the ungenerous farmer. Farmers who stood up to the gleaners may have been afraid of arson attacks in revenge: *London Gazette*, no. 11383 (Aug. 1773); Jones, *Crime, Protest, Community and Police*, 43, 56.

VI

The subgroup of farmers who chose to contest the gleaners' rights despite these arguments were by no means powerless. By the later nineteenth century less wasteful harvesting techniques were becoming available and although the poor themselves sometimes abandoned gleaning as rising real wages undermined their incentives, technical changes played an important part in the long-term decline of the practice.[102] However, the main breakthroughs – the reaping machine and the horse-rake – were not widely adopted before 1850 and the farmers' two principal lines of attack in the period 1750–1850 were not therefore based on technical innovations.[103]

As employers, the farmers could refuse to hire members of a gleaner's family if she offended them. More important, if the majority of the vestry agreed, they could use the local relief and settlement policies to impose informal sanctions, as they did against the Essex gleaner Margaret Laysell. As the wife of an army substitute, Laysell received regular payments via the Wormingford parish officers; in 1806 she continued gleaning when told to stop by the parish's churchwarden and largest farmer, George Nottidge. Within a few months the vestry, which had let her remain in Wormingford for many years, brought the settlement laws into action, spending a considerable sum 'for taking Margaret Laysell home to the parish where she belongs'.[104]

Propertied men like George Nottidge used allotment schemes and charity trusteeships as well as poor law bodies not only to impose informal sanctions but also to make local laws. Many East Anglian vestries passed by-laws regulating various aspects of popular culture, laws backed by informal sanctions

---

[102] *Notes and Queries*, 12th ser., 9 (1921): 'The causes which led to the decline of gleaning seem mechanical and economical rather than anything in the way of legal obstruction'. The horse-rake, the reaper and, by the 1880s, the binder were all discussed in this connection: see *Essex Review*, 34 (1925), 107, 109, 162–3, 210–11. In 1860 it was noted that 'a little while ago leasing was threatened . . . by . . . the horse-rake; however it proved not to pay the expense of working': *Notes and Queries*, 2nd ser., 10 (1860), 476. Gleaning remained important after 1900 and revived in wartime: *Cambridge Chronicle*, 8 Oct. 1942; Baker, *Folklore and Customs*, 162; R. E. Moreau, *The Departed Village* (Oxford, 1968), 122. On the poor's choice to give up gleaning rights, see T. Hennell, 'Gleaning', in *Village Life and Labour: An Anthology*, (ed.) C. Hutchinson and F. Chapman (Cambridge, 1939), 94; *Notes and Queries*, 12th series, 9 (1921), 115.

[103] The reaping machine was not widely adopted till the 1870s: *Essex Review*, 34 (1925); Morgan, 'Place of Harvesters', 61; J. R. Walton, 'Agriculture, 1730–1900', in R. Dodgshon and R. Butlin, *An Historical Geography of England and Wales* (Cambridge, 1978), 248; and the horse-rake also appears to have been little used till 1850 (*ibid.*). Did the changeover from sickle to scythe in wheat harvesting reduce the gleanings, as some Suffolk and Northamptonshire farmers believed? Hennell thought not: 'Reaping with fagging hooks or scythes left more for the gleaners than sickles': Hennell, 'Gleaning', 94; Smedley, *Life and Tradition*, 23; *Museum Rusticum et Commerciale*, 1 (1764), 159; 'Scythes . . . increased the quantity of corn lost', according to M. Roberts, 'Sickles to Scythes: Women's Work and Men's Work at Harvest Time', *History Workshop Journal*, 7 (1979), 16.

[104] ERO, D/P 185/11/1, 12/2, 18/5; P/LwR 15, 8 Sept. 1806.

such as the withdrawal of charitable doles.[105] Roger Wells has argued that this
'social control through poor relief' increased between the 1780s and 1830s and
it certainly continued in new forms after 1834. To the labourer John Clare,
writing in the 1820s, the farmers who dominated many vestries were the local
equivalents of parliamentary lawmakers, running their own 'Parish State'.[106]
The 1788 judgement certainly stimulated this semi-legislative activity in a few
Essex parishes. The Halstead farmers used the occasion to announce that henceforward the poor could only glean after the corn was carried and that anyone
who got drunk, behaved abusively or violently, damaged gates or stole under-
wood or turnips would not be allowed to glean at all. In 1795 the Terling vestry
also attempted to confine gleaning to widows and those with families to support,
by threatening the disobedient with the loss of their flour allowance.[107]

These by-laws were not necessarily successful. The intentions recorded in
vestry minutes are a very poor guide to what actually proved possible. Gleaning was particularly hard to control in heavily populated areas such as Halstead
and it often proved very difficult to ensure that only the deserving went gleaning.[108] However, the power and naked cunning of some vestries should not be
underestimated. The farmers may have felt unable to appropriate the gleanings
directly by sending their animals on to the stubbles or by allowing their families
privileged access to the fields, but they could still use the gleanings to keep poor
rates down if they could ensure that they went only to the deserving resident
poor.

VII

As vestrymen and employers, the farmers therefore had several tactical options.
But the strong tradition of collective protest that developed among the gleaners
between 1750 and 1850, supported as it was by a complex combination of legal

[105] Archer, 'Rural Protest in Norfolk and Suffolk', 475–532; N. Agar, *The Bedfordshire Farm-worker in the Nineteenth Century* (Bedfordshire Historical Record Society, ix, 1981), 22, 151–8. For a discussion of vestry power, see P. King, *Crime,*. For an Ashdon example of vestry law-making, see ERO, D/P 18/8/3.
[106] Wells, 'Development of the English Rural Proletariat', 125; Wells, 'Social Conflict and Protest', 514–30. Although the 1834 act introduced larger poor law units, in East Anglia the new boards were 'chiefly an association of farmers' to whom the ticket system gave new forms of local power: A. Digby, 'The Labour Market and Continuity of Social Policy after 1834: The Case of the Eastern Counties', *Economic History Review*, 2nd ser., 37 (1975); J. Clare, *The Parish: A Satire* (Harmondsworth, 1985), esp. 62.
[107] *Chelmsford Chronicle*, 27 July 1788: an advertisement citing the 1788 judgement. Such notices have rarely survived, but Hatfield Peverell parish certainly considered copying Terling's policy: ERO, D/P 299/8/2; D/P 42/18. At least one Suffolk parish issued a notice in 1788 quoting the judgement and warning they would prosecute those who disobeyed gleaning regulations: SRO, Bury, FL 506/1/13. Others may have followed, but these notices were rarely kept.
[108] M. Reed, 'The Peasantry of Nineteenth-Century England: A Neglected Class', *History Workshop Journal*, 18 (1984), 65; *Farmer's Magazine*, 21 (1820), 413.

and non-legal arguments, proved very difficult to control through the limited legal sanctions available to the farmers either before or after the 1788 judgement. The gleaners' resistance modified the property rights of the farmers and, like the bread rioters, 'their exertion of force at the margin of legitimacy and illegality was a real if limited exercise of political power'.[109] The gleaners' strength arose partly from the weak hold of 'the law' of the Court of Common Pleas compared to that of local customary law, but this local – central dichotomy, important though it is, inadequately expresses the pluralistic nature of the legal frameworks within which both gleaners and farmers operated. Their relationships were constrained not by 'the law' but by several often contradictory systems of normative ordering[110] – by customary law based in part on manorial regulations; by the body of common and statute law-based principles administered through a hierarchy of formal courts of record both civil and criminal; by the ad hoc civil adjudication procedures of provincial magistrates; by the gleaners' own customary communal sanctions; and by the farmers' parish-based rule-making powers. The 1788 judgement may have been of some value to the farmers in undermining the ideological foundations of customary practice but, since both jurors and magistrates remained deeply ambivalent about the legitimacy of eroding the gleaners' rights, the farmers were rarely able to extend the logic of the 1788 judgement into courts that were easily accessible to them.

During the eighteenth century a series of high-court cases indicated that formal legal decisions were now being based on notions of absolute property ownership, and gleaning was no exception. In 1788 Lord Loughborough, chief justice of the Court of Common Pleas, found against the gleaners primarily because 'he thought their claim inconsistent with the nature of property which imports exclusive enjoyment'.[111] However, the continued strength of the gleaners' rights in practice largely prevented the actualisation of Lord Loughborough's absolute conception of property rights. Nineteenth-century labouring autobiographies suggest that his definitions gained little purchase. 'I was fascinated by the occupation [of gleaning]', one Lincolnshire autobiography recalled; 'It was recognised that you could trespass on the farmer's property and gather everything that was left on the ground'. To those brought up on the Essex/Suffolk border in the 1870s, 'harvest gleanings were the cottager's right by immemorial tradition'.[112]

---

[109] Bohstedt, *Riots and Community Politics*, 222. The gleaners' riots, like Bohstedt's bread riots, 'were a dynamic constituent moment in the system of property and power'.

[110] Sugarman and Rubin, *Law, Economy and Society*, 47–52, 72, 113; H. Arthurs, *'Without the Law': Administrative Justice and Legal Pluralism in Nineteenth-Century England* (Toronto, 1985); for the broader definition of 'law' being used here, see page 2 in the above volume. For an American study often very similar to this, stressing 'conflicting socially constituted visions of legal order', see H. Hartog, 'Pigs and Positivism', *Wisconsin Law Review* (1985), 899–935.

[111] Thompson, *Whigs and Hunters*, 241; *English Reports*, 126, Common Pleas, iv, 33.

[112] F. Cresswell, *Bright Boots* (London, 1956), 47; Warren, *Happy Countryman*, 54.

Does this have broader implications for the ways historians have used the custom-to-crime model? That paradigm has obvious relevance in parishes where enclosure completely reshaped the physical and organisational structure of rural communities, destroying much of the poor's grid of customary rights and particularly their access to pasture.[113] Yet by 1788 much of south-eastern England and East Anglia had been enclosed for centuries.[114] To what extent did the important fringe benefits of the communal grid – the rights to glean, cut turves and furze, collect dead wood, gather nuts and wild fruits – survive in these counties? Was 'the extinction by law of indefinite agrarian use-rights'[115] achieved by the propertied in relation to these benefits in the long-enclosed areas or indeed in those more recently enclosed?

In 'The Grid of Inheritance' Edward Thompson comes close to arguing that they were, citing both the gleaning judgement and other court decisions against turf-cutting and the taking of dead wood. However, he also notes Eversley's warning 'not to confuse a legal decision of general significance with the general adoption of it in practice'.[116] If local custom and collective action could protect the gleaners so successfully, was gleaning the only part of the grid of use-rights that the poor managed to keep as of right, rather than only by permission, between 1750 and 1850? Some aspects of gleaning were exceptional. Unlike the breaking of hedges or growing trees, it involved no long-term damage to property or to game-preservers' interests. Moreover it was protected by scripture and perhaps by conventions about the prosecution of women; it was a concentrated activity that encouraged solidarities among its practitioners; and it took place at a time of year when the farmers particularly needed the immediate cooperation of the poor. However, in many areas the gleanings were more vulnerable to attack because they were of much greater value than other use-rights. To many East Anglian farmers, 'the corn obtained by gleaning off a large farm, was of very serious consequence' – as the strenuous attacks made on both barley and wheat gleaners in 1788 and the frequent contemporary references to the stubbles' usefulness for the farmer's livestock indicate.[117]

---

[113] Neeson, 'Common Right and Enclosure'; Malcolmson, *Life and Labour*, 142–3. For a corrective stressing that heaths and commons did not disappear with the advent of enclosure, see Reed, 'Peasantry of Nineteenth-Century England', 57–8.

[114] M. Turner, *Enclosures in Britain, 1750–1830* (London, 1984), 25.

[115] Thompson, 'Grid of Inheritance', 341; Thompson, *Whigs and Hunters*, 264.

[116] Thompson, 'Grid of Inheritance', 339–40.

[117] Smedley, *Life and Tradition*, 83; this quotation refers to wheat. Morgan has suggested wheat-gleanings were less useful to the farmers and that gleaners performed a useful service by clearing the ground: Morgan, *Harvesters and Harvesting*, 161; Emsley, *Crime and Society*, 106. However, Essex farmers specifically attacked wheat-gleaners in 1788: ERO, P/LwR 6, 21 Aug., 1 Sept. 1788; for farmers' general eagerness to turn their livestock on to the stubbles, see *British Critic*, 8 (1796), 401; Young, *Farmer's Calendar*, 431; [Lawrence], *New Farmer's Calendar*, 89–99; the couch that grew in the stubbles was also useful food: T. Batchelor, *General View . . . Bedford* (London, 1808), 13.

Apart from Neeson's important work on Northamptonshire enclosure and common right before 1800, little research is available on the specific constellations of communal solidarities and legal traditions that may have protected other use-rights between 1750 and 1850. Bob Bushaway has established that in the late eighteenth century various forms of wood-taking were attacked using an array of new statutes and legal sanctions. But large-scale attacks on wood-taking had taken place in previous periods without successfully extinguishing the poor's access to wood, and although some of those who broke hedges or timber trees were harshly punished, many remained immune from prosecution.[118] Bushaway has produced no systematic evidence that long-established customs such as the right to collect dead or offal wood were effectively eroded, but he has found parishes where the nineteenth-century poor, like their counterparts in Epping Forest, clearly preserved their wood-gathering rights through communal action.[119]

Many nineteenth-century autobiographies indicate that rural working people continued to have access to a variety of common rights apart from gleaning. Over a century after 1788 the Ashdon poor not only 'invaded the golden stubbles without let, or hindrance', but also cut faggots freely 'from woods and hedgerows' – a pattern also observed in many Suffolk parishes. In Hertfordshire the poor enjoyed relatively free access to furze, fallen wood, nuts, wild fruits and acorns as well as to the valuable gleanings.[120] Contemporaries sometimes spoke of their being 'allowed' access, but often the poor seem to have assumed, as the gleaners did, that provided they followed customary procedures they needed no permission.

Attitudes differed widely between areas according to the strength of local customs, the parish's physical layout and enclosure history, the amount of heath and commons that remained, the approaches taken by landowners and farmers, and the openness of the parish involved. In the 1870s, while admitting that cottagers were 'most tenacious' in preserving footpath and other rights, Richard

---

[118] Bushaway, *By Rite*, 207, 217; Bushaway notes a seventeenth-century wave (214–15). Since the two main quantitative sources – newspaper reports and summary conviction certificates – only became abundant in the late eighteenth century this can create a false impression that prosecutions for wood-stealing increased. Early JPs' notebooks record large numbers: E. Crittall (ed.), *The Justicing Notebook of William Hunt, 1744–1749*, (Wiltshire Rec. Soc., 1982). Batchelor, *General View . . . Bedford*, 609, noted that every parish contained many poor families 'whose firing consists entirely of broken hedges' and who 'carry on the trade with impunity' because farmers feared that prosecution would add burdens to the rates. For the same argument from a magistrate sympathetic to wood-takers, see *P.P.*, 1843, xii, 75–6.

[119] Bushaway, *By Rite*, 230, 232; G. Shaw Lefevre, *English Commons and Forests* (London, 1894), 126–9.

[120] Ketteridge and Mays, *Five Miles*, 80, 125; G. E. Evans, *Ask the Fellows who Cut the Hay* (London, 1965), 56, 99; Warren, *Happy Countryman*, 48, 52–9; E. A. Goodwyn and J. C. Baxter, *East Anglian Reminiscences* (Ipswich, 1976), 53; Gray, *Cottage Life*, 53–4, 93, 97, 116, 118–26.

Jefferies described successful attacks on the poor's customary rights to dead wood and nuts.[121] Since fishing rights were also under increasing pressure[122] it can therefore be argued that a closing up of the countryside occurred after 1850, particularly in the game-preserving areas Jefferies knew well. Yet Jefferies recalled that before the railways came 'the wood in a measure was free and open and . . . provided a man was not suspected of poaching, he might roam pretty much at large',[123] and it is more difficult to argue for such a closure before mid-century. It may have taken place where large-scale enclosure was completed in the century before 1850, but in order to include the long-enclosed counties in such an argument it is necessary to treat gleaning as highly untypical. On balance it seems more likely that the factors that prevented the farmers from using legal sanctions against the gleaners also offered protection to those who followed other customary practices before 1850.[124]

Thus the notion of a custom-to-crime transition, based as it is in part on Macpherson's rather problematic account of the rise of absolute property ownership,[125] may well have done more to obscure than to clarify our understanding of rural social relations in many areas of East Anglia and south-eastern England between 1750 and 1850. The wide disjunction between formal law and social practice meant that the judgements laid down by men like Lord Loughborough played a relatively peripheral role in the process of immiseration and exploitation to which the rural labouring poor were subjected in these years. Through formal enclosure the propertied were often able drastically to curtail the poor's customary access to certain use-rights. In some places the physical division and fencing-off of common lands destroyed the poor's access to pasture, although in others, as Reid has recently pointed out, some commons often remained available.[126] But it should not be assumed that the farmers' attempts to use legal

---

[121] R. Jefferies, *The Gamekeeper at Home* (London, 1878), 133; and 135, on those who continued to gather mushrooms, watercress, dogwood, ferns and saleable flowers. The propertied erected posters in the 1840s forbidding these practices, but they were widely ignored: Jones, *Crime, Protest, Community and Police*, 71; Jefferies, *Gamekeeper at Home*, 105–7, for the erosion of use-rights.

[122] Jones, *Crime, Protest, Community and Police*, 63; Sugarman, Palmer and Rubin, 'Crime, Law and Authority', 52–4, on the erosion of customary fishing rights. Lack of space precludes a fuller discussion of the impact of changes in game laws and game preservation, but on their 'constant evasion' in the period 1840–80, see A. Howkins, 'Economic Crime and Class Law: Poaching and the Game Laws, 1840–1880', in S. Burman and B. Harrell-Bond (eds.), *The Imposition of Law* (New York, 1979), 273–87.

[123] Jefferies, *Gamekeeper at Home*, 108.

[124] But not protection from vestry-based law: for example, ERO, D/P 21/8/1, Steeple Bumstead vestry, order stopping relief to those keeping dogs, 6 Aug. 1791.

[125] Sugarman and Rubin, *Law, Economy and Society*, 27–36; A. Ryan, *Property and Political Theory* (Oxford, 1984), 18–20; J. Tully, *A Discourse on Property: John Locke and his Adversaries* (Cambridge, 1980), 170, 172; J. Innes and J. Styles, 'The Crime Wave: Recent Writing on Crime and Criminal Justice in Eighteenth-Century England', *Journal of British Studies*, 25 (1986), 433.

[126] Reed, 'Peasantry of Nineteenth-Century England', 57–8.

processes other than enclosure acts were equally successful. The gleaners' victories suggest that, enclosure and game laws apart, formal legal sanctions could rarely be mobilised in this period by those who wanted to reshape rural social relations through the imposition of new definitions of property on the poor.[127]

---

[127] Innes and Styles, 'Crime Wave', 432; Sugarman and Rubin, *Law, Economy and Society*, 31. For a rather different example of the ways in which resistance to the erosion of the customary economy was often 'remarkably successful', see C. E. Searle, 'Custom, Class Conflict and Agrarian Capitalism: The Cumbrian Customary Economy in the Eighteenth Century', *Past and Present*, 110 (Feb. 1986), 106–33.

Index

Past and Present Publications

General Editors: LYNDAL ROPER, *University of Oxford*, and
CHRIS WICKHAM, *University of Birmingham*

Family and Inheritance: Rural Society in Western Europe 1200–1800, edited by Jack Goody, Joan
   Thirsk and E. P. Thompson*
French Society and the Revolution, edited by Douglas Johnson
Peasants, Knights and Heretics: Studies in Medieval English Social History, edited by R. H.
   Hilton*
Town in Societies: Essays in Economic History and Historical Sociology, edited by Philip
   Abrams and E. A. Wrigley*
Desolation of a City: Coventry and the Urban Crisis of the Late Middle Ages, Charles
   Phythian-Adams*
Puritanism and Theatre: Thomas Middleton and Opposition Drama under the Early Stuarts,
   Margot Heinemann*
Lords and Peasants in a Changing Society: The Estates of the Bishopric of Worcester 680–1450,
   Christopher Dyer
*Life, Marriage and Death in a Medieval Parish: Economy, Society and Demography in
   Halesowen 1270–1400*, Ziv Razi
Biology, Medicine and Society 1740–1940, edited by Charles Webster*
The Invention of Tradition, edited by Eric Hobsbawm and Terence Ranger*
Industrialization before Industrialization: Rural Industry and the Genesis of Capitalism, Peter
   Kriedte, Hans Medick and Jürgen Schlumbohm*
*The Republic in the Village: The People of the Var from the French Revolution to the Second
   Republic*, Maurice Agulhon[†]
Social Relations and Ideas: Essays in Honour of R. H. Hilton, edited by T. H. Aston, P. R. Coss,
   Christopher Dyer and Joan Thirsk
A Medieval Society: The West Midlands at the End of the Thirteenth Century, R. H. Hilton
Winstanley: 'The Law of Freedom' and Other Writings, edited by Christopher Hill
Crime in Seventeenth-Century England: A County Study, J. A. Sharpe[†]
The Crisis of Feudalism: Economy and Society in Eastern Normandy c. 1300–1500, Guy Bois[†]
The Development of the Family and Marriage in Europe, Jack Goody*
Disputes and Settlements: Law and Human Relations in the West, edited by John Bossy*
Rebellion, Popular Protest and the Social Order in Early Modern England, edited by Paul Slack
Studies on Byzantine Literature of the Eleventh and Twelfth Centuries, Alexander Kazhdan in
   collaboration with Simon Franklin[†]
The English Rising of 1381, edited by R. H. Hilton and T. H. Aston*
Praise and Paradox: Merchants and Craftsmen in Elizabethan Popular Literature, Laura Caroline
   Stevenson*
*The Brenner Debate: Agrarian Class Structure and Economic Development in Pre-Industrial
   Europe*, edited by T. H. Aston and C. H. E. Philpin*
*Eternal Victory: Triumphant Rulership in Late Antiquity, Byzantium, and the Early Medieval
   West*, Michael McCormick[†][*]

[*] Also published in paperback
[†] Co-published with the Maison des Sciences de l'Homme, Paris

East-Central Europe in Transition: From the Fourteenth to the Seventeenth Century, edited by
Antoni Mączak, Henryk Samsonowicz and Peter Burke*
*Small Books and Pleasant Histories: Popular Fiction and Its Readership in Seventeenth-Century
England*, Margaret Spufford*
Society Politics and Culture: Studies in Early Modern England, Mervyn James*
*Horses, Oxen and Technological Innovation: The Use of Draught Animals in English Farming
1066–1500*, John Langdon*
Nationalism and Popular Protest in Ireland, edited by C. H. E. Philpin*
Rituals of Royalty: Power and Ceremonial in Traditional Societies, edited by David Cannadine
and Simon Price*
The Margins of Society in Late Medieval Paris, Bronislaw Geremek[†]
Landlords, Peasants and Politics in Medieval England, edited by T. H. Aston
*Geography, Technology, and War: Studies in the Maritime History of the Mediterranean,
649–1571*, John H. Pryor*
Church Courts, Sex and Marriage in England, 1570–1640, Martin Ingram*
Searches for an Imaginary Kingdom: The Legend of the Kingdom of Prester John, L. N. Gumilev
Crowds and History: Mass Phenomena in English Towns, 1790–1835, Mark Harrison*
Concepts of Cleanliness: Changing Attitudes in France since the Middle Ages, Georges Vigarello[†]
The First Modern Society: Essays in English History in Honour of Lawrence Stone, edited by
A. L. Beier, David Cannadine and James M. Rosenheim*
The Europe of the Devout: The Catholic Reformation and the Formation of a New Society, Louis
Châtellier[†]
English Rural Society, 1500–1800: Essays in Honour of Joan Thirsk, edited by John Chartres and
David Hey
From Slavery to feudalism in South-Western Europe, Pierre Bonnassie[†]
Lordship, Knighthood and Locality: A Study in English Society c. 1180–c. 1280, P. R. Coss*
English and French Towns in Feudal Society: A Comparative Study, R. H. Hilton*
An Island for Itself: Economic Development and Social Change in Late Medieval Sicily, Stephan
R. Epstein*
Epidemics and Ideas: Essays on the Historical Perception of Pestilence, edited by Terence Ranger
and Paul Slack*
The Political Economy of Shopkeeping in Milan, 1886–1922, Jonathan Morris*
After Chartism: Class and Nation in English Radical Politics, 1848–1874, Margot C. Finn*
Commoners: Common Right, Enclosure and Social Change in England, 1700–1820, J. M.
Neeson*
Land and Popular Politics in Ireland: County Mayo from the Plantation to the Land War, Donald
E. Jordan Jr.*
*The Castilian Crisis of the Seventeeth Century: New Perspective on the Economic and Social
History of Seventeenth-Century Spain*, I. A. A. Thompson and Bartolomé Yun Casalilla
The Culture of Clothing: Dress and Fashion in the Ancien Régime, Daniel Roche[†*]
The Sense of the People: Politics, Culture and Imperialism in England, 1715–1785, Kathleen
Wilson*
Witchcraft in Early Modern Europe: Studies in Culture and Belief, edited by Jonathan Barry,
Marianne Hester and Gareth Roberts*
Fair Shares for All: Jacobin Egalitarianism in Practice, Jean-Pierre Gross*
The Wild and the Sown: Botany and Agriculture in Western Europe, 1350–1850, Mauro Ambrosoli
*Witchcraft Persecution in Bavaria: Popular Magic, Religious Zealotry and Reason of State in
Early Modern Europe*, Wolfgang Behringer*
Understanding Popular Violence in the English Revolution: The Colchester Plunderers, John
Walter*

Lightning Source UK Ltd.
Milton Keynes UK
13 March 2010

151331UK00002BA/8/P